GOVERNING OREGON

Governing Oregon

CONTINUITY AND CHANGE

Edited by
Richard A. Clucas
Mark Henkels
Priscilla L. Southwell
Edward P. Weber

Oregon State University Press   Corvallis

Library of Congress Cataloging-in-Publication Data

Names: Clucas, Richard A., editor.
Title: Governing Oregon : continuity and change / edited by Richard Clucas, Mark Henkels,
    Priscilla L. Southwell, and Edward P. Weber.
Description: Corvallis : Oregon State University Press, 2018. | Includes bibliographical
    references and index.
Identifiers: LCCN 2018037793 | ISBN 9780870719530 (original trade paperback :
    alk. paper)
Subjects: LCSH: Oregon—Politics and government.
Classification: LCC JK9016 .G68 2018 | DDC 320.9795—dc23
LC record available at https://lccn.loc.gov/2018037793

♾This paper meets the requirements of ANSI/NISO Z39.48-1992
(Permanence of Paper).

Oregon State University
OSU Press

Oregon State University Press
121 The Valley Library
Corvallis OR 97331-4501
541-737-3166 • fax 541-737-3170
www.osupress.oregonstate.edu

Contents

The U. G. Dubach Chair in Political Science at Oregon State University

This volume would not have been possible without the financial support provided by the U. G. Dubach Chair endowment at Oregon State University. We, the editors of this book, are grateful for the support and for the opportunity to extend Dubach's legacy. As part of this, we wish to take this opportunity to familiarize readers with U. G. Dubach, an OSU and Oregon State legend.

Ulysses Grant Dubach has been hailed as one of Oregon's greatest educators, having devoted thirty-three years to OSU as a professor and administrator. Although he died in 1972 at the age of ninety-one, his Oregon State legacy continues to grow. Gifts from his estate as well as from his widow, Ida, and her estate have endowed the U. G. Dubach Chair of Political Science.

A Kansas native, Dubach earned his doctorate from the University of Wisconsin, then moved west and started his Oregon State career as a political science professor in 1913. In 1924 he was named head of the department and also appointed OSU's first dean of men, positions he held until he turned sixty-five, the state-mandated age for retirement. Dubach moved to Portland and served as head of the political science department at Lewis & Clark College for thirteen years. He retired a second and final time in 1960.

Despite his move to Lewis & Clark, part of Dubach remained at OSU. "My heart is in Corvallis, Oregon State, . . . an institution without any question that hasn't a peer in its field," he wrote in 1948.

In 1951 the *Oregonian* honored Dubach as one of the hundred people who had made the greatest contributions to the state in its first one hundred years. In 1967 Dubach received OSU's Distinguished Service Award in recognition of his career and his impact on countless people both in and out of the classroom. An inspiring lecturer, Dubach spoke frequently to civic, church, and youth groups on active participation in civic affairs. He gave seventy-five off-campus speeches in one year alone. His obituary notes that "a generation of Oregon State students remember that his office door was always open for what he called 'a gentlemanly meeting of the minds.'"

Abbreviations

AAUP	American Association of University Professors
ADA	Americans with Disabilities Act
ADAAA	ADA Amendments Act of 1998
ADEA	Age Discrimination and Employment Act
AFT	American Federation of Teachers
AIM	American Indian Movement
BEF	Bonneville Environmental Foundation
BETC	Business Energy Tax Credit
BLM	Black Lives Matter
BLM	Bureau of Land Management
BOLI	Bureau of Labor and Industries
BPA	Bonneville Power Administration
CAFOs	confined animal feeding operations
CAO	chief administrative officer
CAPA	College Athletes Players' Association
CCAAs	Candidate Conservation Agreements with Assurances
CCDF	Child Care Development Fund
CCOs	coordinated care organizations
CCP	Comprehensive Conservation Plan
CDBG	Community Development Block Grants
CEO	chief executive officer
CMS	Centers for Medicare and Medicaid Services
COGs	councils of government
COHO	Coalition for a Healthy Oregon
COLA	cost-of-living adjustment
CRAG	Columbia Regional Association of Governments
CRITFC	Columbia River Inter-Tribal Fish Commission
CSA	Controlled Substances Act
CTE	career technical education
CTGR	Confederated Tribes of the Grand Ronde
CTUIR	Confederated Tribes of the Umatilla Indian Reservation
CWA	Clean Water Act
CZARA	Coastal Zone Act Reauthorization Amendments
DACA	Deferred Action on Childhood Arrivals
DEQ	Department of Environmental Quality

DHS	Department of Human Services
DISP	DUI Intensive Supervision Program
DLT	Deschutes Land Trust
DMA	designated market area
DMV	Division of Motor Vehicles
DOJ	Department of Justice
DP	Deschutes Partnership
DRC	Deschutes River Conservancy
EBT	electronic benefits transfer
EITC	Earned Income Tax Credit
ELT	Enterprise Leadership Team
EOARC	Eastern Oregon Agricultural Research Center
EQC	Environmental Quality Commission
ERDC	Employment-Related Day Care
ESA	Endangered Species Act
ESD	educational service district
ESF	Education Stability Fund
FERC	Federal Energy Regulatory Commission
FIP	Focused Investment Partnership *or* Federal Implementation Plan
FMLA	Family and Medical Leave Act
FPA	Forest Practices Act
FPL	federal poverty line
FTE	full-time-equivalent
FWS	US Fish and Wildlife Service
GDP	gross domestic product
GMO	genetically modified organism
GPS	Global Positioning Satellite
GPV	greatest permanent value
HB	House Bill
HCP	Habitat Conservation Plan
HECC	Higher Education Coordinating Commission
HHI	Herfindahl-Hirschman Index
HIPAA	Health Insurance Portability and Accountability Act
HUD	US Department of Housing and Urban Development
ICWA	Indian Child Welfare Act
IGRA	Indian Gaming Regulatory Act
IPO	Independent Party of Oregon
IT	information technology
ITC	investment tax credit
LCDC	Land Conservation and Development Commission
LGBTQ	lesbian, gay, bisexual, transgender, and queer
LIHEAP	Low-Income Home Energy Assistance Program
LNG	liquefied natural gas

LTSS	Long Term Services and Supports
LUA	land-use allocation
MCO	managed care organization
MPO	metropolitan planning organization
MSD	Metropolitan Service District
NCSL	National Conference of State Legislatures
NEPA	National Environmental Policy Act
NFF	National Forest Foundation
NGO	nongovernmental organization
NOAA	National Oceanic and Atmospheric Administration
NPG	New Public Governance
NPM	New Public Management
NPR	National Public Radio
NRCS	Natural Resource Conservation Service
NSLP	National School Lunch Program
NWFP	Northwest Forest Plan
OAFP	Oregon Academy of Family Physicians
OARs	Oregon Administrative Rules
ODA	Oregon Department of Agriculture
ODFW	Oregon Department of Fish and Wildlife
ODOE	Oregon Department of Energy
OFB	Oregon Food Bank
OFPA	Organic Foods Production Act
OFS	Oregon Farm to School
OHA	Oregon Health Authority
OHP	Oregon Health Plan
OHSU	Oregon Health Sciences University
OHTF	Oregon Hunger Task Force
OMA	Oregon Medical Association
OPB	Oregon Public Broadcasting
OPERF	Oregon Public Employees Retirement Fund
ORDF	Oregon Rainy Day Fund
ORESTAR	Oregon Elections System for Tracking and Reporting
ORS	Oregon Revised Statutes
OSU	Oregon State University
OTC	Oregon Transportation Commission
OUS	Oregon University System
OWEB	Oregon Watershed Enhancement Board
PAC	political action committee
PERS	Public Employee Retirement System
PGE	Portland General Electric
PSU	Portland State University
PUC	Public Utilities Commission

RFS	renewable fuels standard
RLIS	Regional Land Information System
RMA	riparian management area
RPS	Renewable Portfolio Standard
SAFE	Stop Addiction Forever
SALT	state and local tax
SB	Senate Bill
SBP	School Breakfast Program
SDVCJ	Special Domestic Violence Criminal Jurisdiction
SG	School Garden
SIP	State Implementation Plan
SMR	small modular reactor
SNAP	Supplemental Nutrition Assistance Program
SSBT	salmon, steelhead, bulltrout
SSDI	Social Security Disability Income
SSI	Supplemental Security Income
START	Success Through Accountability, Restitution, and Treatment
STEM	science, technology, engineering, and mathematics
STOP	Sanctions Treatment Opportunity Progress
SWCD	Soil and Water Conservation District
SYMA	Sustained Yield Management Act
TANF	Temporary Assistance to Needy Families
TEFAP	The Emergency Food Assistance Program
TSID	Three Sisters Irrigation District
UDWC	Upper Deschutes Watershed Council
UO	University of Oregon
USDA	US Department of Agriculture
VLTs	video lottery terminals
WAC	Wolf Advisory Committee
WIC	Women, Infants, and Children
WC	watershed council
WOU	Western Oregon University
WW	*Willamette Week*

I

Inputs and Context

1

Change and Continuity in Oregon Politics

RICHARD A. CLUCAS and MARK HENKELS

On March 3, 2016, the Oregon state legislature ended its 2016 legislative session with the traditional choreographed closing gavel by the Speaker of the House, Tina Kotek (D-Portland), and the senate president, Peter Courtney (D-Salem-Keizer). The 2016 short session will stand out historically for creating major policy change and for the unsuccessful efforts of the minority Republican legislators to slow down the majority Democratic Party agenda. Writing on the session, Salem *Statesman Journal* reporter Gordon Friedman noted that at least two laws would likely distinguish Oregon nationally. The first was the passage of a bill that created the highest minimum wage target in the nation but allowed for variable rates in different parts of the state. The second was the decision to establish a schedule for eliminating the use of coal to generate electricity by 2030.[1]

The legislature's success in passing two major policy bills, in a session that ran just over thirty days, was a far cry from a decade earlier. The 2003 legislative session set a record for the number of days in session, and perhaps a record for futility as well. With the state house controlled by Republicans, the senate divided equally between the parties, and the governor's office held by a Democrat, the legislature remained in session for 227 days, as the different sides battled over how to overcome a staggering $800 million gap in the state's $10.4 billion budget. The conflict was so intense that Oregon was among the last three states in the nation to finally pass a budget for that fiscal year.[2] The gridlock in 2003 may have been record-setting, but it was not unusual. Throughout the 1990s and into the first part of the new millennium, a strong ideological split in the state, along with a divided government, led to continuous conflict in the state government.

The political battles went well beyond the walls of the capitol. The ideological conflict played out in the initiative process, as well. Beginning in the mid-1980s and running into the early 2000s, state voters were asked to weigh in on the most initiatives since the early 1900s. The parade of initiatives peaked in 2000, when eighteen proposals appeared on the November ballot. Leading the charge in the initiative drive was Bill Sizemore, the head of Oregon Taxpayers United and an unsuccessful Republican candidate for governor in 1998. Beginning in the mid-1990s, Sizemore championed a long string of initiatives, including proposals for cutting property taxes, restricting the power of labor unions, and setting limits on government. There were several other leading political activists who used the initiative to champion conservative goals, including Lon Mabon, the founder of the Christian Oregon Citizens Alliance, and Don McIntire, the leader of the Oregon property tax revolt in the 1990s. Some liberal activists also sponsored initiatives to rewrite state law, including many major environmental groups, but the conservative proposals were at the front and center of the state's increased use of the initiative.

The legislature's successes in the short 2016 session reveal an important lesson: Oregon and its politics have changed. To be sure, not all aspects of the state changed; the deep-seated political polarization, in particular, remains a significant, though less consequential, part of the state's politics. But the character of the state's politics has evolved significantly over the past decade, and will likely lead it down a different path in the years to come.

Beyond the Democratic legislative dominance in 2016, there have been other indicators of political change. State voters are no longer being inundated every election year with a long roster of initiative proposals. Bill Sizemore and other conservative initiative activists have all but disappeared from the scene. There has been a significant increase in the number of voters who are registered as Democrats, unaffiliated, or under a third party, while Republican Party voter registration has remained stagnant. This change in party registration has, in turn, helped the Democrats gain unified control over the state government. The office of the governor was jolted in 2015 with the resignation of John Kitzhaber, a moderate Democrat originally elected from rural Oregon and the longest-serving governor in the state's history. He was replaced by Governor Kate Brown from Portland, a more liberal, urban-oriented Democrat. In addition, the media's coverage of state politics has been altered, especially with the decline of the state's flagship newspaper, the *Oregonian,* and the rapid rise and consumption of information from various online media sources. With respect to the state bureaucracy, the most important change has been in education, with the restructuring of both the K–12 and university systems.

Broader aspects of Oregon life have gone through significant transformation, and appear to be on the cusp of more changes. Oregon's economy has twice sustained severe blows since the early 2000s—the economic downturn of 2002 and the Great Recession of 2008—but it bounced back, and by 2014, Oregon had one of the fastest-growing economies in the nation. Some of the state's most significant changes have been in its demographics. As its economy expanded, Oregon became one of the most rapidly growing states in the nation, passing more than four million residents in 2015. Along with the growth has come increased diversity. In 1980, minorities represented only 6 percent of Oregon's population. By 2015, Oregonians with some Latino or other minority heritage comprised 23 percent of the state's residents, and this group is expected to continue to grow substantially.[3]

Despite these changes, some aspects of Oregon's politics have remained constant. The Democratic Party may now hold a much larger electoral advantage, but the political divisions that have long troubled the state remain. There are still profound differences in the political ideologies and concerns of urban and rural voters, and between liberals and conservatives. These differences continue to shape the character of political debate in the state. Even though it is being used less often, the initiative-referendum process remains an important fixture in Oregon politics. And despite the reduced level of gridlock in the 2016 session, the legislature still operates within, and seems unable or reluctant to change, a revenue and budgeting system created by the conservative activism of the 1990s, which locks in levels and patterns of revenues that constrain the state's often ambitious educational and health policy goals. Further, the state's economic and population growth occurs disproportionately in the more urban counties in and around Portland as well as in the Bend, Eugene, and Springfield areas. In contrast, and as they have for at least three decades, Oregon's rural areas continue to face profound economic challenges and static or declining populations, with the exception of Deschutes County and the city of Bend.

Oregon's political culture has also provided continuity. Political scientists define political culture as the attitudes that state residents have toward the role of government in society based on the residents' historical experiences and their deep-seated social, ethnic, and religious values.[4] Political cultures develop in response to immigration patterns and historical events, and are sustained by the socialization of each generation into established political expectations and values. Since the Progressive Movement at the end of the nineteenth century, the state's political culture has developed a reputation for being especially supportive of an open political system, maverick politicians, and innovation in public policy. That reputation is captured in the state's official motto, "She Flies with Her Own Wings," but this is not entirely accurate. At times, the state has tried to close the political system to outsiders, especially ethnic and racial minorities. Oregon has also lagged behind the rest of the nation in some policy areas; for example, the state was recently criticized for its low high school graduation rates and its poor handling of mental health issues.[5] Yet, regarding elections, Oregon's high turnout, its practice of voting through the US mail, and its adoption of an automatic voter registration process in 2017 are reminders that the state's political culture tends to support an open political system. Similarly, its support for physician-assisted suicide and the legalization of marijuana reflect its willingness to adopt innovative policies.

The purpose of this book is to give a broad and comprehensive snapshot of Oregon government and politics as we approach the start of the third decade of the twenty-first century, and to shed light on the profound changes that have remade Oregon politics in recent years. Yet it also seeks to make it clear that while Oregon has changed, much has also remained the same.

In this chapter, we begin our exploration of the changes and continuities in Oregon politics by describing the major political eras in Oregon's history. While many of the forces reshaping Oregon politics today are new, it is valuable to begin with a consideration of the state's past.

THE OREGON POLITICAL STORY

The history of Oregon's political development is filled with numerous pivotal events and multiyear trends that have shaped the character of the state's politics for significant periods of time. Oregon's history can be divided into five broad eras. Certainly, different developments played out simultaneously in each of these periods, not all of which fit into our characterization of the era. Nor does every story finish neatly when one era ends and the next era begins. Therefore some developments continue to shape Oregon politics, creating the legacies that are associated with the state today. Despite these caveats, dividing the state's history into these five major periods makes sense because each features distinctive political patterns and practices: (1) the Party Period (1859-1902), (2) a Republican State (1902-54), (3) the Golden Era (1954-78), (4) a State Divided (1978-2012), and (5) an Emerging Liberal Dominance? (2012 to present).

THE PARTY PERIOD, 1859–1902

Two preeminent characteristics defined the political landscape in Oregon's early history: partisanship and populism. Oregon's first immigrants were primarily farmers who had migrated west over the Oregon Trail, attracted by the fertile land in the Willamette Valley and the promise of a more prosperous life.[6] Most came from the Midwest, especially from around the Ohio and Mississippi River Valleys. They brought with them their families, deep religious values, and a moderate conservative ideology, one based on a strong belief in self-government.[7] Yet immigrants were also attracted to Oregon from elsewhere in the nation. One study of Oregon's prestatehood population found that one-third of state residents came from the South. While sharing many agrarian values of the Midwest immigrants, the Southerners brought with them a more sympathetic view toward slavery and Southern interests. A much smaller percentage came from New England and New York, though they had fewer children among them, making their impact larger than their population suggests. This group played a central role in establishing many of the towns dotting the territory and in creating many of the earliest businesses and stores.[8]

These immigration patterns had an important influence on Oregon's early political history. Among other consequences, the divide between the moderate antislavery midwesterners and the Southern settlers led to the compromise in Oregon's constitution banning both slavery and the immigration of blacks to the states. Within the white population there were strong racial prejudices that underlay the ban of blacks to the state. In the decades that followed, these widespread prejudices created broad opposition to Reconstruction, led to the enactment of numerous restrictions on the rights of racial and ethnic minorities, and helped generate support for the Ku Klux Klan in the 1920s.[9] In the immediate aftermath of the Civil War, a large influx of immigrants from the South further strengthened this streak of racism.[10]

While there were differences among these immigrant communities, there was one characteristic that all these groups held in common: a strong devotion to political parties. The mid to late 1800s marked an era in American history in which political parties played a central role at all levels of politics. During the Party Period, as scholars call this era, no other political actors were as dominant. Among other powers, the party organizations hand-selected the names that appeared on the ballot, commanded loyal troops of followers who would support them at the polls, and determined the direction of government policy. But the position of parties went beyond simply dominating government. They also played a central role in America generally, serving as a hub for social life; helping to assimilate the continuing stream of new immigrants into society; and providing jobs, welfare, and other tangible benefits to supporters.[11]

Given the national importance of political parties when Oregon was initially settled, it is not surprising that the parties quickly began to dominate Oregon politics. Both the Republican and Democratic Parties were established in the state before the state joined the Union on Valentine's Day in 1859. From that early start, the parties quickly began to play a preeminent role in Oregon politics.[12] Yet it was not just politics that drove the public to support political parties. During the mid-1800s, most Oregonians simply believed that political parties were an essential part of democracy. It was a strong emotional and social attachment.[13] Within a few years of their founding, Oregon's party organizations quickly transformed into well-oiled machines that dominated almost all aspects of the state's government.[14] Like those in other states, the parties in Oregon were directed by powerful political bosses who were able to control government by commanding a network of loyal supporters throughout the state.[15]

The "Salem Clique" was the first party machine to emerge in Oregon. Led by Asahel Bush, the publisher of the *Oregon Statesman,* the Democratic machine was established soon after the legislature had voted to make Salem the state capital.[16] The clique played a leading role in championing statehood and in forging the state's constitution.[17] The clique was so powerful that, in his detailed history of Oregon parties, Walter Woodward described it as a "junta" that "held Oregon in the palm of its hand."[18] By the early 1860s, the Salem Clique had dissolved, replaced by a Republican machine led by John Mitchell and Joseph Dolph, two prominent Portland-based attorneys and US senators.[19]

Although Oregonians were initially supportive of political parties, their attitudes began to change only a few decades after statehood was established. Disillusionment toward the parties and concern about possible corruption in the political system emerged first among farmers who felt the government was doing nothing to address the financial problems they confronted in the 1880s.[20] With prices for agricultural products falling, the farmers appealed to the transportation companies to drop their rates and take other steps to help the farmers. But their pleas fell on deaf ears.[21] The farmers found the legislature equally unhelpful.

The problem confronting farmers was the close tie between the Mitchell-Dolph machine and the business communities, especially the Northern Pacific Railroad and the Oregon Railway and Navigation Company.[22] The Republican Party used its control over government to channel economic benefits to supportive businesses. The businesses, in turn, used their influence to keep the machine in power.[23] The farmers were among those who were left out of this corrupt equation.

The farmers were the first to join in a populist movement to try to destroy the power of the party machine and upend the power of the state's governing elite.[24] The most prominent of the farm groups seeking change was the Patrons of Husbandry, more commonly known as the Grange. While these reformers were able to get a populist candidate—Sylvester Pennoyer—elected governor as a member of the Democratic People's Party in 1886, their direct impact on Oregon politics and policies was minimal. But the farmers were soon joined by other groups in the state who had grown disillusioned with the corruption in Oregon politics and the power held by the businesses associated with the party machines. The broader populist coalition included labor, as well as many middle-class Oregonians who opposed the corrupt character of Oregon politics.[25] These diverse groups provided the base of support for the Progressive Movement in Oregon.[26]

The Progressive Movement weakened the existing political parties and ended the first era in Oregon politics. One event that marked this transition concerned whom the state would send to the US Senate in 1898. Until the adoption of the Seventeenth Amendment to the US Constitution in 1913, the state legislatures selected US senators. As the 1897 legislative session approached, Republican John Mitchell was up for reelection to the Senate. Leading the opposition to Mitchell was fellow Republican Jonathan Bourne. Bourne cut a deal with William U'Ren, a member of the populist People's Party, in which the Republican promised to support placing a constitutional amendment on the ballot creating the initiative and referendum process if U'Ren and his allies would help stop the session from being called to order. The deal kept the 1897 session from convening and led to a successful vote in the 1899 session that placed the constitutional amendment on the ballot.[27] With the passage of the constitutional amendment, U'Ren became known as the father of the initiative and referendum process in Oregon.

We identify this first era as ending in June 1902 when Oregon voters approved the constitutional amendment allowing for the use of the initiative, since it was the introduction of this form of direct democracy that effectively destroyed the party machines. Over the next several years, the Progressives used statewide initiatives to target the power of the political machines. Among other reforms, the initiative was used to provide for the direct election of US senators, introduce the use of nonpartisan elections for many elective offices, require direct primary elections in partisan races, and permit the use of initiatives and referenda in local government. Of these reforms, the most important in changing the character of Oregon politics was the introduction in 1904 of direct primary elections, enabling voters to directly choose their party's nominees. Denied control over the nomination process, the party machines could no longer dominate Oregon politics.[28]

A REPUBLICAN STATE, 1902–1954

In the early to middle 1800s, migration to Oregon required an arduous trek by wagon for more than two thousand miles along the Oregon Trail, or sailing around Cape Horn at the tip of South America. The isolation ended, however, when the final spike was driven into the Northern Pacific Railroad in Independence Creek, Montana, in 1883, connecting Oregon by train to the rest of the country.[29]

This connection to the transcontinental railroad transformed Oregon. The change was not so much in the social and cultural fabric of the state; like the earlier settlers, most of the new arrivals were from the Midwest and were conservative, family-oriented farmers with strong religious beliefs.[30] Instead, the change was political. The opening of the railroad led to a significant population boom, which shifted the distribution of power in the state. From 1880 to 1890, the population of the state nearly doubled, rising to over 313,000 residents.[31] While many of the newcomers continued to come out of midwestern states, there were relatively fewer from the South and more from the upper Midwest and other northern states, areas in which Republicans dominated. This change in the flow of immigrants benefitted the Republican Party in Oregon. While the Democratic Party had played a major political role in the early years of the state's history, the influx of new residents turned Oregon into a solidly Republican state, a position that defined the state's politics until the 1950s.[32]

The dominance of the Republican Party can be seen both in voter registration and election outcomes. From the turn of the century into the 1930s, the number of registered Republicans remained more than twice the number registered as Democrats, and was often considerably higher. Republican Party registration dropped slightly in the 1930s, though the party retained an advantage until the 1950s.[33] As for election outcomes, the Republicans held almost complete control of the legislature and statewide executive offices throughout this same period. In some legislative sessions, the Democrats held fewer than five of the ninety seats in the legislative assembly. As for statewide office, the Democrats won fewer than ten races for governor and other statewide executive offices from the late 1800s to the mid-1950s.

Yet political parties operated differently during the first half of the twentieth century than they had during the state's early history. Progressive reforms destroyed the old party machines. The new party system featured more battles between narrow interests and candidates whose power came from personal campaign organizations and not the party itself.[34] The decline of the party organizations meant an increase in the power of interest groups.

Many of the most important political battles during this era took place within the Republican Party, especially between the Progressive and conservative wings of the party. Progressive Republicans helped usher in the first period of innovative legislation in the state's history, much of it through the initiative process. The Progressives not only pursued changes in the political process, but they also championed women's rights, economic reform, business regulation, social welfare programs, and labor protection.[35] The Progressive Movement also advocated clean, professionalized government. This "good government" strain sought to remove politics from public administration and municipal government, placing decision-making into the hands of experts rather than politicians.[36] It was this Progressive strain of the Oregon Republican Party that led to the use of nonpartisan elections for local political offices, bureaucratic reform, and the adoption of the commission form of government in Portland.[37] The more conservative wing of the Republican Party, however, opposed many of these reforms, often forcing the Republican Progressives to work with Democratic Party allies to attain their goals. The split was so severe within the Republican Party in the early part of the twentieth century that it enabled a bipartisan coalition to place two Progressive Democrats in the governor's office: George Chamberlain (1903-9) and Oswald West (1911-15).[38]

Although the Progressive Movement died out by the end of the First World War, many Progressive ideals continue to shape Oregon politics, including support for innovative and pragmatic government. The end of the Progressive Movement did not mean a return to unified parties, however. In the early 1920s, the Ku Klux Klan became actively involved in Oregon politics, seeking to control the Republican Party.[39] The Klan's efforts drove a new wedge into the Republican Party, splitting Klan support-ers from the more moderate establishment. The Klan's most prominent battle was its effort to unseat the incumbent Republican Governor Ben Olcott in 1922 by backing Olcott's primary challenger, Charles Hall. When Olcott narrowly defeated Hall, the Klan threw its support behind Democrat Walter Pierce, who went on to win the gen-eral election.[40] Although the Klan's active involvement in politics ended by 1925, the ideas it advocated continued to influence public opinion in the state after that year, while many Klan-supported officials remained in elective office into the 1930s.[41]

During the latter part of the 1920s and through the 1930s, the Republican Party took on a more moderate tone, though divisions remained between the Progressive and more conservative wings.[42] The preeminent political debate throughout the 1930s was whether private interests or the public should control the development and ownership of hydroelectric power generated in the state. State voters approved an initiative in 1930 allowing local communities to create public utility districts, but the supporters of pub-lic power found themselves in continuous battle with business and utility companies seeking to keep ownership and distribution in private hands. Within the two major parties, there were supporters for both sides, keeping the parties from becoming unified.[43]

World War II opened the door to more change, slowly ending this second era. Among the most important changes was the development of the shipyards along the Columbia and Willamette Rivers as part of the war effort. Within several months after the bombing of Pearl Harbor, as workers flocked to the state, the population of Portland grew from 340,000 to 600,000. The shipyards expanded Oregon's economic base beyond its historical reliance on natural resources, greatly increased the state's small African American population, and brought in a large wave of Democratic voters.[44] Although the flooding of the Columbia River destroyed the African American community in Vanport in 1948, Democratic Party registration grew in the next decade. The expansion of the Democratic Party was not just in Portland. Throughout the state, the Democratic Party's numbers surged, and by 1954, the Democrats had become the majority party in Oregon, ending the Republican Party's long control of state politics.[45]

THE GOLDEN ERA, 1954–1978

Calling a political period a "golden era" requires some justification. This label was chosen because, both within Oregon and across the nation, references to Oregon's policy leadership or progressivism are generally grounded in the actions and accomplishments of Oregon's political leaders during this period. Oregon's Golden Era started in 1954 when Senator Wayne Morse set the US Senate's record for the longest filibuster, speaking without interruption for more than twenty-two hours in opposition to the transfer of control over offshore mineral resources to the states, where Morse feared they could more easily be controlled by large corporations. Ultimately that bill passed, but for the next two decades, Oregon was recognized for the independent character of its political leaders.[46] The era can be seen as ending in 1978 when pro-business Republican Vic Atiyeh defeated Tom McCall in the Republican primary and sitting Governor Bob Straub in the general election. Although he was personally nonideological, Atiyeh's governorship coincided with the rise of a broadly acrimonious policy and ideological environment in Oregon.

The Golden Era in Oregon politics was built upon the rise of the Democratic Party, strong independent political leaders, and an unusual pattern of bipartisanship. Demographic changes that began in the state during the World War II enabled the Democrats to regain majority status in party registration and to enjoy profound success in winning elected office in 1954 after decades in the wilderness. That year saw Richard Neuberger become the first Oregon Democrat elected to the US Senate since 1914. In the same election, Democrat Edith Green became only the second Oregon female US representative and the first Democrat in a decade to serve in Congress. Democratic representation in the state legislature went from nine to twenty-five in the house, and from four to six in the senate.

Oregon's politics in the Golden Era stand out because of the willingness of the state's political leaders to take strong stands, frequently against national party positions, and for their ability to work across party lines. Key formative events of this era include US Senator Wayne Morse's decisions to leave the Republican Party in 1952 to become an independent, and then to join the Democratic Party in 1955; the 1958 election of progressive Republican Mark Hatfield as governor; and the relaunching of Republican Tom McCall's political career through the 1962 televised documentary on Oregon's pollution problems, "Pollution in Paradise." Morse epitomized Oregon's independent streak when he was one of only two US senators to oppose the legitimization of the invasion of Vietnam by voting "no" on the 1964 Gulf of Tonkin Resolution. Then-governor Republican Mark O. Hatfield soon joined him in the controversial antiwar position in 1965.[47] Another event was the 1968 election of Republican Robert Packwood to the US Senate, ending Wayne Morse's political career. Packwood soon became a leading supporter in the Senate of women's causes, including introducing legislation in 1970 to legalize abortion.[48] Yet, within and outside of Oregon, the most noted Oregon politician of the era was Governor Tom McCall. The environmental policies that he and his Democratic rival and successor Bob Straub promoted eventually cemented Oregon's reputation as a leading "green state."

The Golden Era featured intense two-party competition within the state, though one based on far greater cooperation than seen in the nation today. Floyd McKay, one of the state's leading journalist during this period, notes that a convergence of factors made the 1960s and early 1970s a good time for policy innovation: a strong economy, an effective state government bureaucracy cultivated by Governor Mark O. Hatfield, vigorous competition between political leaders, and changes within the state, both social and economic, which demanded responses.[49]

This period's most famous policy innovations center on environmental protection. Four policies are particularly noteworthy: (1) statewide comprehensive land-use planning intended to preserve prime farmland and promote coordination of development and services; (2) the preservation of access and public use of beaches along the entire Oregon coast; (3) programs to clean up and promote recreational use of the Willamette River; and (4) the "bottle bill," which created the deposit on beverage containers, dramatically reducing litter and increasing recycling. Innovations in other areas include the creation of an investment program for reserve state funds that generated new revenue; the continued development of the Metropolitan Service District, which would eventually lead to the creation of the nation's only elected regional government (Portland Metro); and the introduction of Project Independence, a program enabling qualified disabled seniors to remain in their homes longer. Governor McCall was responsible for perhaps the most colorful action, a state-sponsored rock festival, "The Vortex," which sought to draw potential antiwar demonstrators away from the 1970 Veterans of Foreign Wars national convention in Portland.[50]

Bipartisan collaboration within the state capitol was critical to creating these poli-cies. Although Democrats controlled the senate from the 1957 session until 1995, the Republicans controlled the house from 1965 to 1972, while Hatfield and McCall kept the governorship in Republican hands from 1959 to 1975. McCall's progressive poli-cies required Democratic votes because conservative Republican legislators dissented. As Richard Chambers, the originator of the bottle bill, has noted, McCall freely bor-rowed good ideas, fashioned them into his own, and built novel coalitions.[51] The rivalry between McCall and Democrat Bob Straub in the 1966 and 1970 campaigns was built on competing progressive agendas, and McCall referred to it as the "Tom and Bob Show."[52]

A STATE DIVIDED, 1978–2012

In the mid-1970s, the political environment in Oregon again began to change. A deep economic recession eroded the state's finances, constraining innovation. Many Oregonians believed the state should rein in progressive regulations and programs in favor of policies promoting private-sector growth. In the 1977 legislative ses-sion, house Republicans aligned with fourteen of their Democratic peers to strip Democratic Speaker Phil Lang of most of his leadership powers, reflecting a new political environment.[53] Although Democrats kept control of both houses of the state legislature in 1978, Governor Atiyeh won while campaigning as a pro-business fiscal conservative.[54] The policy preferences and constituencies of the major parties became more rigid and distinct.

The 1978 election also broke from the past in the number and nature of initiatives on the ballot. From 1954 to 1976, state elections featured only twenty-three initia-tives, less than two per biennial cycle. In November 1978, Oregon voters faced nine initiatives, including one that sought to severely restrict property taxes and another forbidding state funding of abortion. A new era of Oregon politics had dawned, one in which the initiative process would become a central battleground in many of the state's most important policy disputes.

Viewed two decades later, Atiyeh's governorship seems to have preserved many of the policy legacies of the 1960s and 1970s, but Oregon's political landscape was then defined by an uncertain struggling economy, the rise of partisanship, and a polit-ical agenda often controlled by initiatives and their campaigns. After treading water during the political splits and economic travails of the late 1970s and early 1980s, Oregon seemed to get in gear when Democrat Neil Goldschmidt took office in 1986. Goldschmidt left after one term, however, and was replaced by Barbara Roberts, Oregon's first woman governor in 1990. Despite biting debates over taxes and social issues, Democrats dominated the legislature in the late 1980s and early 1990s and had strong leadership under House Speaker Vera Katz and Senate President John Kitzhaber.

Katz and Kitzhaber delivered some notable legislation, but often the state failed to successfully implement key policy innovations of the 1980s and 1990s. John Kitzhaber's most striking new policy was the Oregon Health Plan, adopted in 1989. Built upon the notion that medical dollars should go first to care that yields the highest benefit, Kitzhaber's idea became a fixture in national health-care reform discussions. Vera Katz's signature legislation was the Oregon Education Act for the Twenty-First Century, passed in 1991. This expansive law sought to ensure that all graduating high school seniors would have clear employment pathways and featured systematic testing to ensure that students progressed successfully.

Neither program fully achieved the dreams of their creators, primarily because of the declining economy and the passage of tax limitation ballot measures. By the mid-1980s Oregon's timber-based economy was struggling as stagnant markets, declining timber availability, technological efficiency, and environmental restrictions reduced timber employment. Ultimately, wood-product jobs fell from over eighty thousand in the late 1970s to just over thirty thousand in 2010, as the industry declined from approximately 13 percent of the Oregon economy in 1979 to less than 5 percent in the late 1990s.[55]

Any hopes for significant new government commitments ended in 1990 when voters passed Measure 5, which capped property tax rates, and in 1996 when they passed Measure 47 (rewritten by the legislature and passed by voters as Measure 50 in 1997), which rolled back and capped property tax assessment values. The property tax losses forced large sums of state funds to be directed toward local school districts. To cover the new expenses, the legislature had to freeze or cut funding for other state programs. Oregon abandoned Katz's educational reform, rejecting its demanding regulations on local schools as well as its costs. The Oregon Health Plan would never be fully implemented, although several of its main provisions still exist.

Measures 5 and 47/50 were major victories for anti-tax conservatives and continue to shape fiscal policies today, but socially conservative measures that sought to restrict the rights of homosexuals or access to abortion generally lost, and helped divide the Republican Party. Republicans took the house from the Democrats in 1991 and the senate in 1995, but the split between socially moderate members of the party and the more extreme conservatives complicated their governing, especially when facing Democratic Governor Kitzhaber. The budgeting problems and moral debates were compounded by the growing urban-rural divide in the state, which began to play a central role in Oregon politics after the spotted owl was listed as a threatened species on June 26, 1990, under the Endangered Species Act of 1973.[56] As these battles played out, Oregon seemed to drift, a situation symbolized by Governor John Kitzhaber being called "Dr. No" for making a record number of vetoes during his two first terms.[57] This lack of consensus, which helped define this era, led to the futile 2003 legislative session.

AN EMERGING LIBERAL DOMINANCE? 2012 TO PRESENT

The divide that stymied the state from the late 1970s gradually came to an end in 2012. Changes in the initiative system, making it more complicated and expensive to use, helped inaugurate a new political era. First, the Oregon Supreme Court in the 1998 *Armatta v. Kitzhaber* case began enforcing the state law restricting constitutional amendments to one subject, and, second, in 2007, the state legislature passed House Bill 2082, which forbids the per signature payment of petition signature gatherers. These two actions helped reduce the average number of initiatives from roughly nine per major election in 1978-2008 to just under five between 2010 and 2016.

Changes in the fortunes of the major political parties also altered the character of the state's politics. As the more liberal party, Democrats benefitted in recent decades as Oregon's rural-urban balance strongly shifted in favor of the more liberal urban areas. According to the Oregon Office of Economic Analysis, the great decline in the wood-products sector since the mid-1970s has been matched by increases in the technology field, shifting jobs and wealth from smaller towns in western Oregon to northern parts of the Willamette Valley.[58] The five counties in the broader Portland metropolitan area (Clackamas, Hood River, Multnomah, Washington, and Yamhill) accounted for 53 percent of state jobs and income in 2013.[59] The economic growth has been matched with growth in population, which has helped expand the Democratic Party's base. Those five counties alone accounted for 47 percent of the state's population in that same year. These trends have enabled the Democrats to lead the state in voter registration and in controlling elections. As of October 2016, more than 38 percent of state voters were registered as Democrats, compared with fewer than 28 percent registered as Republicans and 27 percent unaffiliated.[60] Since 2012, Democrats have held continuous unified control over the legislature and the governor's office, reducing the gridlock that defined state politics in the preceding decade.

But the present dominance of the Democratic Party guarantees nothing about the future. The political divide in the state still exists; it is just that the Democratic Party's unified hold on government has stifled conservative activism. Not all trends uniformly bode well for the Democrats. In 2016, Dennis Richardson won the secretary of state position and became the first Republican to win a statewide election since 2002. Oregon's reputation as a "blue state" is also a bit misleading in that only eight counties supported presidential candidate Hillary Clinton in 2016 in her 50 percent victory in the state, and Governor Kate Brown won only seven counties in a similar 50 percent win, with her roughly 195,000-vote margin in Multnomah County being critical to her success. The rural-urban divide yawns still. So, while Democrats and liberalism are ascendant now, demographic and economic change, in addition to the unknown impacts of national policies, will push the state to evolve.

The question we address in this book, however, is not where Oregon is headed, but where it has recently been. The decline of initiative use, the strengthening of the

Democratic Party, and the efficiency of the 2016 legislative session are among the most visible changes that have transformed Oregon politics over the past decade. Yet there have been other political, social, and economic changes—many that are equally as important as these more visible ones. The chapters that follow provide perspective on these changes, as well as on parts of the state's politics that have remained constant, in this new era in the Oregon political story.

Notes

1   Gordon Friedman, "2016 Oregon Legislature Wrap Up: Successes and Failures," *Statesman Journal*, March 7, 2016.

2   Sarah Kershaw, "Oregon, in Crisis, Finally Balances Budget," *New York Times*, August 21, 2003, 18.

3   "Oregon Quick Facts", US Census, accessed April 25, 2018, https://www.census.gov/quickfacts/table/PST045215/41.

4   Daniel J. Elazar, *American Mosaic: The Impact of Space, Time, and Culture on American Politics* (Boulder, CO: Westview Press, 1994).

5   Betsy Hammond, "Oregon Graduation Rate Falls to Third Worst in Country," *Oregonian*, October 17, 2016; Kale Williams, "Oregon Ranked Near Dead Last for People with Mental Health Concerns, Report Finds," *Oregonian*, October 28, 2016.

6   Gordon B. Dodds, *Oregon: A Bicentennial History* (New York: W. W. Norton. 1977), 67-68; Walter Carleton Woodward, *The Rise and Early History of Political Parties in Oregon: 1843-1868* (Portland, OR: J. K. Gill, 1913), 4-5.

7   Dodds, *Oregon*, 68; Robert E. Burton, *Democrats of Oregon: The Pattern of Minority Politics, 1900-1956* (Eugene: University of Oregon, 1970); Robert W. Johannsen, "Spectators of Disunion: The Pacific Northwest and the Civil War," *Pacific Northwest Quarterly* 44 (1953): 107-9.

8   Woodward, *Rise and Early History*, 8; Jesse S. Douglas, "Origins of the Population of Oregon in 1850," *Pacific Northwest Quarterly* 41 (1950): 95-108; Stacey L. Smith, "Oregon's Civil War: The Troubled Legacy of Emancipation in the Pacific Northwest," *Oregon Historical Quarterly* 115 (2014): 154-73; Lancaster Pollard, "The Pacific Northwest: A Regional Study," *Oregon Historical Quarterly* 52 (1951): 211-34.

9   Smith, "Oregon's Civil War."

10 Woodward, *Rise and Early History*, 263-65.

11 Joel H. Silbey, *The American Political Nation, 1838-1893* (Stanford, CA: Stanford University Press, 1991; Ronald P. Formisano, "The 'Party Period' Revisited," *Journal of American History* 86 (1999): 93-120.

12 Dodds, *Oregon*, 102.

13 Woodward, Rise, 40; David Alan Johnson, Founding the Far West: California, Oregon, and Nevada, 1840-1890(Berkeley: University of California Press, 1992):53-54.

14 Dodds, *Oregon*, 153.

15 Dodds, Oregon, 153; David Alan Johnson, *Founding the Far West: California, Oregon, and Nevada, 1840-1890* (Berkeley: University of California Press, 1992), 302; Woodward, *Rise and Early History,* 84; Barbara Mahoney, "Oregon Democracy: Asahel Bush, Slavery, and the Statehood Debate," *Oregon Historical Quarterly* 110 (2009): 202-27.

16 Johnson, *Founding,* 53-55; Woodward, *Rise and Early History,* 80-85. For a detailed overview of the Salem Clique, see Barbara S. Mahoney, *The Salem Clique: Oregon's Founding Brothers* (Corvallis: Oregon State University Press, 2017).

17 Woodward, *Rise and Early History,* 78-79; Johnson, *Founding,* 69.

18 Woodward, *Rise and Early History,* 80.

19 Dodds, *Oregon,* 153; Johnson, *Founding,* 299-302.

20 Dodds, *Oregon,* 157-58; William G. Robbins, *Oregon: This Storied Land* (Portland: Oregon Historical Society Press, 2005), 76.

21 Dodds, *Oregon,* 157-58; Robbins, *Oregon,*76.

22 Dodds, *Oregon,* 153.

23 Dodds, *Oregon,* 157.

24 Dodds, *Oregon,* 156-61; Robbins, *Oregon,* 76-78.

25 Dodds, *Oregon,* 157-58.

26 Dodds, *Oregon,* 161-66.

27 Dodds, *Oregon,* 163-66; Douglas Heider and David Dietz, *Legislative Perspectives: A 150-Year History of the Oregon Legislature from 1843 to 1993* (Portland: Oregon Historical Society Press, 1995), 81-87.

28 L. Sandy Maisel, *American Political Parties and Elections: A Very Short Introduction* (New York: Oxford University Press, 2007), 43.

29 Jan Taylor, "Marketing the Northwest: The Northern Pacific Railroad's Last Spike Excursion," *Montana: The Magazine of Western History* 60 (Winter 2010): 16- 35, 93-94.

30 Dodds, *Oregon,* 116-17.

31 Pollard, "Pacific Northwest," 211-34.

32 Burton, *Democrats of Oregon,* 3.

33 Burton, *Democrats of Oregon,* 6.

34 Burton, *Democrats of Oregon,* 10

35 Dodds, *Oregon,* 168-69.

36 Patricia M. Shields, "Rediscovering the Taproot: Is Classical Pragmatism the Route to Renew Public Administration?," *Public Administration Review* 68 (2008): 205-21; James A. Stever, "The Dual Image of the Administrator in Progressive Administrative Theory," *Administration and Society* 22 (1990): 39-57.

37 E. Kimbark MacColl, *The Shaping of a City: Business and Politics in Portland, Oregon 1885 to 1915* (Portland, OR: Georgian Press, 1976), 445.

38 Burton, *Democrats of Oregon,* 30-32.

39 Burton, *Democrats of Oregon,* 47.

40 Burton, *Democrats of Oregon,* 47; Dodds, *Oregon,* 197; Eckard V. Toy Jr., "The Ku Klux Klan in Tillamook, Oregon," *Pacific Northwest Quarterly* 53 (1962): 61.

41 Dodds, *Oregon,* 197-99; Toy, "Ku Klux Klan," 63-64.

42 Burton, *Democrats of Oregon,* 64; Dodds, *Oregon,* 199; Earl Pomeroy, *The Pacific Slope: A History of California, Oregon, Washington, Idaho, Utah, and Nevada* (Reno: University of Nevada Press, 2003), 249-50.

43 Burton, *Democrats of Oregon,* 71-89.

44 Dodds, *Oregon,* 208-9; Rudy Pearson, "'A Menace to the Neighborhood': Housing and African Americans in Portland, 1941-1945," *Oregon Historical Quarterly* 102 (2001): 161-62; Burton, *Democrats of Oregon,* 96-97.

45 John M. Swarthout, "The 1960 Election in Oregon," *Western Political Quarterly* 14 (1961): 355-64

46 Tom Marsh, *To the Promised Land* (Corvallis: Oregon State University Press, 2012), 228.

47   Floyd McKay, *Reporting the Oregon Story* (Corvallis: Oregon State University Press, 2016), 62-63.

48   Gabriel Trip, "The Trials of Bob Packwood," *New York Times,* August 29, 1993.

49   McKay, *Reporting the Oregon Story,* 2-7.

50   Charles K. Johnson, *Standing on the Water's Edge* (Corvallis: Oregon State University Press, 2012), 161-66.

51   Brent Walth, *Fire at Eden's Gate* (Portland: Oregon Historical Society Press, 1998), 253-62.

52   Walth, *Fire at Eden's Gate,* 173.

53   Marsh, *Promised Land,* 331-34.

54   Walth, *Fire at Eden's Gate,* 428.

55   Josh Lehner, "Historical Look at Oregon's Wood Product Industry," Oregon Office of Economic Analysis, January 23, 2012, https://oregoneconomicanalysis. com/2012/01/23/historical-look-at-oregons-wood-product-industry/.

56   Richard A. Clucas, Mark Henkels, and Brent S. Steel, "The Politics of One Oregon: Causes and Consequences of the Rural-Urban Divide and Prospects for Overcoming It," in *Toward One Oregon: Rural-Urban Interdependence and the Evolution of a State,* ed. Michael Hibbard, Ethan Seltzer, Bruce Weber, and Beth Emshoff (Corvallis: Oregon State University Press, 2011).

57   Michelle Cole, "No More 'Dr. No,' as Gov. John Kitzhaber Vetoes but a Single Bill," *Oregonian,* August 4, 2011.

58   Josh Lehner, "Changing of the Guard," Oregon Office of Economic Analysis, September 4, 2014, https://oregoneconomicanalysis.com/2014/09/04/changing-of-the-guard/.

59   Josh Lehner, "Portland MSA Counties," Oregon Office of Economic Analysis, December 23, 2013, https://oregoneconomicanalysis.com/2013/12/23/portland-metro/.

60   "Voter Registration by County," Elections Division, Oregon Secretary of State, accessed November 28, 2016, http://sos.oregon.gov/elections/Documents/registration/Oct16. pdf.

2
The Oregon Context

ALEXANDRA BUYLOVA, REBECCA L. WARNER, and BRENT S. STEEL

State and local governments in Oregon today confront a need for continuous learning and innovation to adapt to new dynamics brought about by structural changes
in the economy, urbanization, increasing demographic diversity, globalization, and
changes in technology and public values. How public officials address these social
and economic changes will affect the long-term effectiveness of state and local
governments.

Structural economic change has long been an important force confronting state
and local governments. Oregon has been evolving from an agricultural and natural
resource extraction–based economy in the nineteenth century to an industrial-based
economy in the twentieth century and a "postindustrial society" of service sector
and knowledge-based industry dominance in the twenty-first century. Typically,
postindustrial societies have the following characteristics: an economy where the
service sector dominates over manufacturing and agriculture; an educated workforce that employs scientific knowledge and technology in their work; public mobi-
lization over new issues, including the rise of civil rights, anti-globalization, and the
environment; and an increasingly urban population with the subsequent decline in
rural areas.[1] A postindustrial societal shift is often accompanied by growth in postmaterialist social values; higher-value needs, which include a greater concern for
quality of life and environmental protection; more tolerance for diverse lifestyles;
and stronger support for freedom on moral issues.

Other historic changes closely associated with the advent of postindustrial
society include demographic shifts (aging populations, racial and ethnic diversification, and the influx of immigrants), continued urbanization, economic globalization, rapid technological change, evolving social norms, and growing environmental
awareness.[2] These historic changes are discussed below and provide a suitable backdrop to our exploration of state and local government in contemporary Oregon.
These broader forces have reshaped Oregon's politics and have contributed to the
rural and urban political identities that became highly polarized over the course of
state history.

DEMOGRAPHIC CHANGE

Demographic changes are highly important to understanding the shift from an industrial to a postindustrial society. Population and its characteristics can be the driving
force of change and its most telling manifestation. By looking at age, gender, ethnicity, migration, and urbanization, one can see the complexity of the process. Oregon's
population reached four million in 2015, doubling its 1967 population of two million,
owing to both in-migration and natural increase (births minus deaths).[3] Oregon's in-
migration has varied over the years and fluctuated with economic opportunities in
the state. During the economic boom in the 1940s, 1970s, and 1990s, employment
growth was the main driver of in-state migration. In the 1950s, the post–World War II
decade, natural increase in population peaked (this is known as the baby boom generation), while accompanied by the lowest net migration numbers. The severe recession
of the 1980s also signified a major decrease in net migration numbers, when the state
experienced a significant lack of employment opportunities. Today, natural increase in
population is at its lowest since the 1930s owing to aging of the large proportion of the
state population and birth rates being below population replacement levels.[4]

The distribution of age and sex in Oregon in 1900, displayed in figure 2.1, reflects
the state's frontier times, when age distribution was skewed toward greater numbers of
young and middle-aged males and fewer females and elderly. The picture changed dramatically in the 1960s as the baby boomers (aged 0-15 years at that time) became the

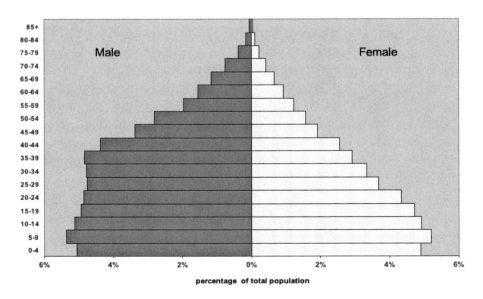

Figure 2.1. **Age and gender, 1900.** *Source: "Oregon's Road to 4 Million," Population Research Center,
accessed April 3, 2018, http://roadto4million.research.pdx.edu/home*

largest age group, while those 20-30 years of age became the smallest group because of the lower birth rates during the Great Depression of the 1930s. In 2010, the age distribution was almost even across all age groups until the age of 65, except that baby boomers (now 50-60 years old) remained the largest age group in the distribution (see fig. 2.2).

Ethnic minority groups constituted about 12.1 percent of Oregon's total population in 2014.[5] The US Census Bureau added a new question to their survey in 1980 that allowed people to identify themselves as belonging to one or more races, such as white and Hispanic or black and Hispanic. Partially as a result of this question, new dynamics in the racial composition of the state can be observed, as displayed in figures 2.3 through 2.7. The black population in Oregon grew from 2,565 in 1940 to 11,529 in 1950, when African Americans moved to Oregon for job opportunities that supported the war effort. By 2010, the US Census counted 98,479 Oregonians who identified themselves as black or African American alone or in combination with other races, representing 2.6 percent of Oregon's population. Oregon's history is entrenched with racism against African Americans, today manifested in increasing gentrification processes, discriminatory employment and housing practices, and political ignorance of the institutionalization of white class dominance.[6] Popular media suggests that African Americans are leaving "West Coast liberal hubs" as a result of persistent, continuous ethnic discrimination despite efforts across the United States to combat historic and institutional discrimination.[7]

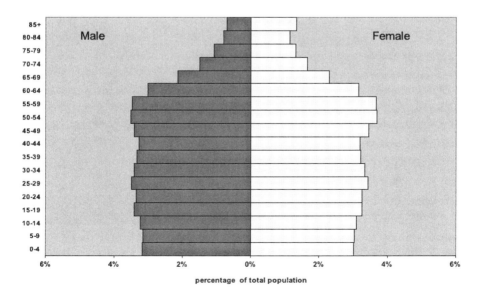

Figure 2.2. **Age and gender, 2010.** *Source: "Oregon's Road to 4 Million," Population Research Center, accessed April 3, 2018, http://roadto4million.research.pdx.edu/home*

The number of Oregonians identifying as Native American has also increased in the last thirty years (fig. 2.4). Interestingly, as of 2000, the number of Oregonians who claim American Indian or Alaska Native identity in combination with other races exceeds the number of those who claim American Indian or Alaska Native status alone.

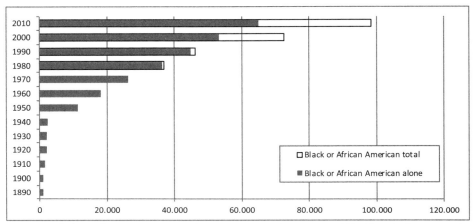

Figure 2.3. **Black or African American population, 1890–2010.** Beginning in 1980, "alone" refers to people who identified only as the specified race, and not Hispanic, while the larger category includes people who also identified as Hispanic or, beginning in 2000, another race. *Source: "Oregon's Road to 4 Million," Population Research Center, accessed April 3, 2018, http://roadto4million.research.pdx.edu/home*

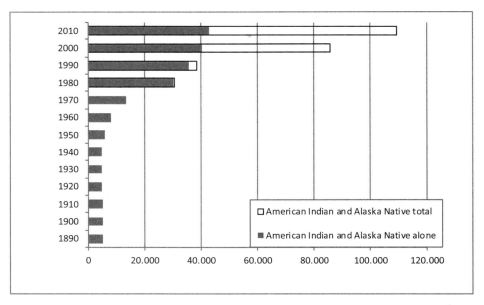

Figure 2.4. **American Indian or Alaskan Native population, 1890–2010.** Beginning in 1980, "alone" refers to people who identified only as the specified race, and not Hispanic, while the larger category includes people who also identified as Hispanic or, beginning in 2000, another race. *Source: "Oregon's Road to 4 Million," Population Research Center, accessed April 3, 2018, http://roadto4million.research.pdx.edu/home*

The population of Asian and Pacific Islanders showed a large increase in 1980 compared to previous years, and continued with a steady growth until 2010. In 2010, the Asian and Pacific Islanders population alone or in combination with other races comprised 5.3 percent of Oregon residents (see fig. 2.5).

A total of 11.7 percent of Oregonians identified themselves as being of Hispanic origin in 2010. The number of people of Hispanic origin grew significantly, from 65,000 to 450,000, between 1980 and 2010 (see fig. 2.6).[8]

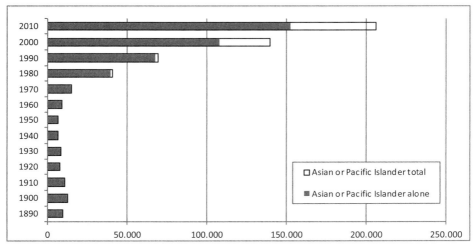

Figure 2.5. **Asian or Pacific Islander population, 1890–2010**. Beginning in 1980, "alone" refers to people who identified only as the specified race, and not Hispanic, while the larger category includes people who also identified as Hispanic or, beginning in 2000, another race. *Source: "Oregon's Road to 4 Million," Population Research Center, accessed April 3, 2018, http://roadto4million.research.pdx.edu/home*

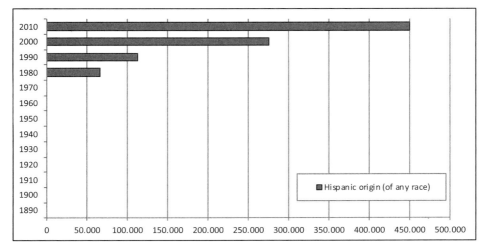

Figure 2.6. **Hispanic origin (of any race) population, 1980–2010**. *Source: "Oregon's Road to 4 Million," Population Research Center, accessed April 3, 2018, http://roadto4million.research.pdx.edu/home*

Although growth of ethnic minority populations is evident, most Oregonians still identify as white (78.5% of the total state population). Even so, the number of white people who identify themselves with more than one race has been continuously growing since 1980 (fig. 2.7).

At the turn of the twentieth century, most of the Oregon population lived in rural areas (68%). By 1940, the state was split evenly between those in rural and urban areas but has since become increasingly urban, and in 2010 only 17 percent of Oregonians

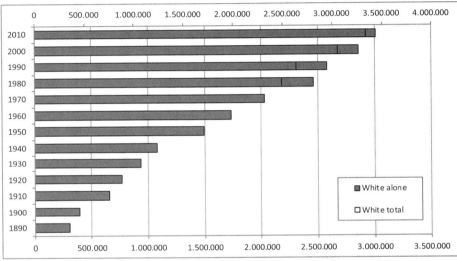

Figure 2.7. **White population, 1890–2010.** Beginning in 1980, "alone" refers to people who identified only as the specified race, and not Hispanic, while the larger category includes people who also identified as Hispanic or, beginning in 2000, another race. *Source: "Oregon's Road to 4 Million," Population Research Center, accessed April 3, 2018, http://roadto4million.research.pdx.edu/home*

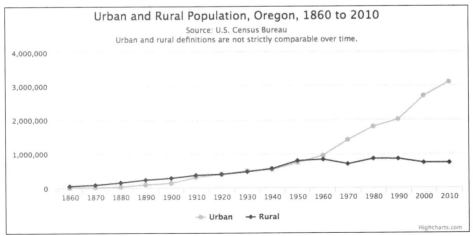

Figure 2.8. **Urban and rural population, Oregon, 1890–2010.** Urban and rural definitions are not strictly comparable over time. *Source: "Oregon's Road to 4 Million," Population Research Center, accessed April 3, 2018, http://roadto4million.research.pdx.edu/home*

resided in rural areas. During the 1960s, 86 percent of state population's growth took place in the Willamette Valley. While some of this growth can be attributed to in-migration into Oregon, considerable population shifts were also occurring within the state. In the 1960s, Oregon started to experience within-state rural-to-urban migration, with younger residents moving to cities in search for jobs and education while retirees moved to larger population centers to be closer to good health-care services. Downturns in timber industry employment in the second half of the twentieth century, mostly situated in rural areas, also contributed to the increase in the urban share of state's population. Figure 2.8 displays Oregon rural and urban population change from 1860 to 2010.

In 2010, 78 percent of Oregon's population resided in one of Oregon's six metropolitan statistical areas. The three most populous regions at that time were the Portland metropolitan area (43.5% of the state total), Willamette Valley (27%), and the South Coast combined with the inland valleys of southwest Oregon (12%). But central Oregon's population share has increased from 2.3 percent in 1970 to 5.3 percent in 2015, the biggest growth rate among state regions. Portland is the largest population center in Oregon, with 632,309 residents as of July 2015.[9] Portland's population is characterized by a high percentage of young, college-educated individuals moving to the area, attracted to its lifestyle as well as political and cultural values. This trend redefines the understanding of migration, which traditionally has been driven by employment opportunities. Portland residents, mainly young and educated, are fostering the city's reputation as a place where "young people migrate to retire."[10] Table 2.1 shows that net migration of young, college-educated people in Portland more than doubled since 1980.[11] These numbers are highly representative of the state's shift to postmodernist values and a postindustrial economy that attracts a more educated labor force.

Table 2.1. Portland, Oregon, migration streams by age and education attainment

	1980	1990	2000	2005-7	2008-10
Bachelor's Degree or Higher					
Gross in-migration, 25-39	6,460	30,156	40,534	15,603	16,650
Gross out-migration, 25-39	3,240	17,947	23,135	9,227	9,120
Net in-migration, 25-39	3,220	12,209	17,399	6,376	7,530
Less than a Bachelor's Degree					
Gross in-migration, 25-39	26,920	50,542	61,803	18,150	15,751
Gross out-migration, 25-39	16,620	32,846	42,427	13,972	13,161
Net in-migration, 25-39	10,300	17,696	19,376	4,178	2,590

Source: J. R. Jurjevich and G. Shrock, Is Portland Really the Place Where Young People Go to Retire? Migration Patterns of Portland's Young and College-Educated, 1980-2010 (Portland, OR: Population Research Center, 2012), http://pdxscholar.library.pdx.edu/cgi/viewcontent.cgi?article=1004&context=prc_pub

The influx of a demographic group that is economically well-off, in search of a healthy lifestyle and sustainable living, contributes to the process of gentrification (the replacement of low-income residents living in inexpensive housing with high-income residents living in high-cost housing), especially in metropolitan Portland. For instance, in only two decades (1990-2010), the black population in the Portland neighborhood of Boise declined from 70 to 25 percent.[12] One of the drivers of gentrification is the rise of expensive grocery stores in neighborhoods with low-income residents. So-called food mirages (expensive grocery stores) force low-income families to travel longer distances to lower-cost grocery stores, contributing to the migration of low-income households out of "food mirages" and into "food hinterlands."[13] Oregon's cycling culture may also be contributing to the gentrification process, as investments in cycling infrastructure close to downtown are attracting privileged populations and marginalizing low-income residents.[14] Reinforcing gentrification are the city's commitment to sustainable growth, investment in the greening of its core, and maintenance of urban growth boundary—a process known as eco-gentrification.[15]

ECONOMIC CHANGE: THE GROWTH OF THE POSTINDUSTRIAL ECONOMY

The greatest postindustrial change is reflected in Oregon's economy, where the service and high-tech sectors dominate the economic base and technological innovations are reshaping traditional industries, while postmaterialist social values are driving government policies that affect the economy. As the data in table 2.2 demonstrate, in 2016, services and the government sector accounted for more than 80 percent of the state employment, a shift from a 72 percent share in 1969 and more than doubling the number of jobs in these sectors. In agriculture and the natural resource extraction sector, even though total employment more than doubled between 1990 and 2016, its representation in the economy still accounts for a small share of just 3.4 percent. Taken together, the manufacturing and construction sectors have seen the largest decline in the share of state employment, from 26.7 percent in 1969 to 15 percent in 2016, adding only a minimal number of jobs from 1969 to 2016, and losing jobs between 1990 and 2016.[16] Technological advances in machinery and automation of production help push the decline of employment in construction and manufacturing. These sectors have not kept pace with employment growth in key postindustrial sectors such as high-tech industries, health care, education, professional and business services, and government, which added about 360,000 jobs over the past sixteen years. In fact, the advanced technology company Intel is now the state's largest private employer in Oregon, with 19,500 employees alone.[17]

Despite, or perhaps because of, this major shift in the composition of Oregon's workforce, the state's twenty-first-century economy has done well, even when taking into account the Great Recession of 2009. In fact, Oregon's unemployment rate in

Table 2.2. Economic change: Employment in Oregon

Employment Sector	1969	1990	2016
Agriculture, forestry, fishing, hunting, and mining	10,221 (1.2%)	30,571 (2.0%)	65,404 (3.4%)
Manufacturing and construction*	231,527 (26.7%)	310,901 (20%)	289,872 (15.0%)
Services and government	626,495 (72.1%)	1,220,869 (78%)	1,582,146 (81.6%)
Trade, transportation, utilities	142,765	264,300	357,346
Information	–	27,700	34,100
Financial activities	67,712	72,700	97,200
Professional and business services	–	103,000	244,000
Education and health services	–	129,800	274,800
Leisure and hospitality	–	109,200	194,100
Other services	–	46,300	65,200
Government	151,789	232,100	315,400

*Includes millworkers.

Source: State of Oregon Employment Department, Oregon's Minimum Wage Jobs: Facts, Figures, and Context (Salem: State of Oregon Employment Department, 2016), https://www.qualityinfo.org/documents/10182/13336/Oregon%E2%80%99s+Minimum+Wage+Jobs+Facts%2C+Figures%2C+and+Conte xt?version=1.2

May 2017 had dropped to 3.6 percent, one of the lowest levels ever recorded, which was lower than the national rate of 4.3 percent. Moreover, the 2017 numbers had declined from 4.5 percent in March 2016, 5.7 percent in March 2015, and 7.1 percent in March 2014.[18] These strong employment numbers have been boosted by the decline in Oregon's labor force participation since 2000 owing to aging of the state population and fewer teenagers joining the labor force.

Oregon's economy has also experienced rising average hourly wages in the aftermath of the Great Recession, and in 2015 had finally reached the pre-recession level of $23.50 per hour in 2008.[19] As of January 2016, the minimum wage in Oregon was $9.25 per hour, compared to $7.25 at the national level, making the minimum wage's purchasing power similar to that of the 1970s.[20] In addition, Oregon's legislature in 2016 enacted Senate Bill 1532, which increases the standard minimum wage to $13.50, in the Portland Metro to $14.75, and in nonurban counties to $12.50 by the year 2023.[21]

At the same time, many of the state's rural areas have experienced sustained continuous economic challenges since the early 1980s. In 2017, for example, Benton and Washington Counties in western Oregon had the lowest unemployment rates in the state, 2.5 and 2.9 percent, respectively, and the OR-WA Metropolitan Statistical Area (Portland-Vancouver-Hillsboro) had an unemployment rate of 3.4 percent. Southern and eastern Oregon had the highest unemployment rates, ranging from 4.7 percent in Douglas and Coos Counties to 6.5 percent in Wallowa County and 7.7 percent in Grant County.[22] In 2005, the only counties outside of the Willamette Valley and the northwest coastal region not identified by the state as being economically "distressed" or "severely distressed" were Jackson County in the south and Deschutes County in central Oregon, both of which are major recreational destinations and popular retirement centers.

Part of the economic struggle in many rural regions of Oregon stems from the significant declines since the post–World War II boom in the agricultural and timber industries, which have long been central to the rural economy and arguably defined Oregon as a "natural resource" state. The long downturn in Oregon's timber economy occurred for several reasons: technological innovations in timber harvesting and milling, the concentration of production, globalization, structural changes in the timber industry, and the rise of competing values regarding public lands that favored environmental protections.

Timber production in Oregon expanded significantly, beginning during the Great Depression and arising from demands by the impending World War II that incentivized the federal government to pass the Oregon and California Act (also known as the O and C Act) in 1937. The O and C Act solidified the principle of sustained yield as central to forest management, and when modified by the Sustained Yield Management Act (SYMA) in 1944, it resulted in expanded timber production on federal lands. Between 1942 and 1952, Oregon production of timber increased by 24 percent, while the harvest from public lands rose by almost 300 percent, representing half of state timber production by 1962.[23] Lumber production in Oregon peaked in 1950s, partially owing to new technological innovations in harvesting and milling, specialized division of labor, and automation of the work process. At the same time, these innovations reduced the number of sawmills in western Oregon from thirteen hundred to three hundred between 1947 and 1964, while increasing annual average lumber mill production from six to seventeen million board feet per year.

Concentration of production and increased productivity and efficiency reduced the demand for employment and transformed the job market of rural Oregon, changing the social composition of rural communities and forcing many to move to urban areas in search of new opportunities.[24] In the 1980s, economic recession, industry restructuring, increased competition from the southeastern United States and Canada, the decline in the power of organized labor in timber industry, continuous technological progress, and changes in the resource base contributed to a further reduction in the number of workers employed at sawmills (who count in "Manufacturing and construction," not "Agricultural, forestry etc." in table 2.2) from 25,500 to 18,500 between 1969 and 1989.[25] In fact, the severe recession of the 1980s contributed not only to a great number of jobs being lost in timber industry, but also to the overall population decline in Oregon.

Over the years, the total employment in the wood industry per volume harvested changed little, because the decrease in primary wood-processing jobs was followed by a rise in secondary wood-manufacturing jobs (e.g., industries such as mobile-home construction and millwork, windows and doors, etc.), which made structural changes in the industry less devastating for the job market. But a different type of employment altered social dynamics within rural communities more than the raw job numbers suggest. Secondary wood manufacturing jobs pay significantly less than primary wood processing jobs and are concentrated closer to markets, forcing people to migrate to cities.[26]

The impacts of technological innovations and market dynamics of globalization on the timber industry that started in 1950s were accompanied by a gradual shift to postmaterialist public values on the global and national levels, largely reflected in environmental movements in the industrialized countries. The by-products of rapid economic growth during the post–World War II era and the intensive use of natural resources put a significant stress on the physical environment—ozone depletion, water and air pollution, deforestation, land degradation, and the like—threatening human health and the sustainability of the economic resource base. Driven by these threats and emergent public environmental consciousness, the United States passed a series of pioneering pieces of legislation: the 1969 National Environmental Policy Act (NEPA), the 1970 Clean Air Act, the 1972 Clean Water Act, and the 1973 Endangered Species Conservation Act.[27] A shift of values took place in Oregon as well and had an impact on natural resource and manufacturing sectors while reinforcing the growth of service, high-tech, education, health-care, finance, and leisure industries.

Starting in the 1980s, the federal government began to adopt a forest management approach that placed a greater emphasis on wildlife habitat protection and ecosystem-based services. The Northwest Forest Plan (NWFP), a new forest management policy for federal forest lands in California, Oregon, and Washington, passed in 1994, transferring eleven million acres of public lands from timber production to old-growth forest protection jurisdiction. Adoption and implementation of NWFP were partially driven by efforts to protect the habitat of northern spotted owls, listed under the Endangered Species Act (ESA). The process resulted in a decade of court cases between environmental groups and forest management agencies (e.g., *Babbitt v. Sweet Home*, 1995), as the passage of the new legislation occurred when Oregon was still strongly timber-dependent. Timber production on public lands declined from five billion board feet in 1989 to less than two hundred million board feet in 2001. Timber production on private land between the 1980s and 2000s still averaged about eight billion board feet per year. Out of 405 lumber mills that operated in Oregon in 1980, 282 closed in the following decades.[28]

Implementation of the NWFP has been a controversial issue. Some members of rural communities lost income and wealth owing to the decline in timber harvest on public lands, while there has been an observed overall increase in wealth creation (measured in real property value per capita) partly as a result of amenity-migration effects in communities adjacent to NWFP territory.[29] The new forest management plan appears to have redistributed economic benefits of natural forest capital from timber-dependent communities to a broader range of towns in the proximity of protected lands, reflecting growing environmental and postmaterialist values that were revealed in disputes over the value of public lands. Overall, the timber industry's output, measured by gross domestic product (GDP), maintained approximately the same level since the mid-1970s in nominal terms, but its share of the state's GDP and share of employment declined over the years, mostly owing to the rise of other industries in the state, especially high technology.[30] "Currently, Oregon's high-tech industry accounts for the same number of workers and nearly the same share of state wages as the forest sector did in the 1970s," according to the Oregon Office of Economic Analysis.[31]

The change to a postindustrial economy is also reflected in the state's agricultural sector. Ranching and farming have always been the center of livelihoods for many Oregonian families who continue to farm on homesteads established by their ancestors to this day. At the same time, innovations in production—including continuous development of more resistant and high-yield crops, growth of alternative agricultural sectors such as wine and fruit, and immigration of farm workers—are reshaping the face of the traditional agricultural sector.[32] Table 2.3 shows the change within the farming sector in Oregon over the last two decades. Between 1997 and 2012, the total number of farms went down by 11.3 percent, total farming lands in the state decreased by 7.7 percent, while an average size of a farm increased by 4.1 percent, indicating a higher concentration of farming industry over time.[33] According to the Oregon Department of Agriculture (not included in table 2.3), the number of farms was even lower in 2015 than in 2012, while the average size of a farm grew from 460 to 474 acres.[34]

The marine and ocean economy is restructuring as well, displaying postmodernist values and responding to challenges caused by the changing environment. Oregon's culture and identity have long been tied to salmon subsistence as well as recreational

Table 2.3. Change within farming sector in Oregon over the last two decades

	1997	2002	2007	2012
Number of farms	39,975	40,033	38,553	35,439
Farming lands (acres)	17,658,213	17,080,422	16,399,647	16,301,578
Average size of farm (acres)	442	427	426	460
Number of cropland farms	31,194	30,305	26,650	23,829
Cropland (acres)	5,479,479	5,417,387	5,010,408	4,690,420
Number of beef cattle farms	15,462	13,063	12,876	11,557
Number of milk cattle farms	1,194	1,133	596	686

Source: US Department of Agriculture (USDA), "Historical Highlights: 2012 and Earlier Census Years," in 2012 Census of Agriculture—State Data (Washington, DC: USDA, 2012)

and commercial fishing. Salmon remains an important source of tangible and intangible benefits for the people of Oregon. In 2014, commercial salmon fisheries contributed $20 million in personal income to the economy, while recreational salmon fishing contributed around $6 million in personal income. While on the rise compared to the recession years of late 2000s, salmon fisheries contributions in 2014 are lower than during the 1970s and 1980s.[35] At the same time, other marine economy sectors are on the rise, including, among others, marine science research and education, tourism, and the seafood industry.

Major changes have occurred in Oregon's natural resource–based industries—timber, agriculture, and fishing—affecting the composition, distribution, and well-being of the state population. But the shift in social values that is driving the rise of new industries is also happening independently, as well as crowding out traditional natural resource sectors and heavy manufacturing jobs from the market. The shift to knowledge-based high-tech jobs affects state and local governance, altering how the public engages with the political process, reshaping ideas of democracy, and in the end redefining the future of the state economy and society.

GOVERNMENT IN A KNOWLEDGE-BASED POSTINDUSTRIAL SOCIETY

Oregon state and local governments face seemingly ceaseless change in information technology as the state becomes a contemporary knowledge-based postindustrial society. Technological infrastructure plays an essential role in attracting the knowledge-based businesses that are characteristic of postindustrial societies. Modern information technology (IT) is becoming an important component of state and local governance to access government information, to pay taxes, to file government forms, to renew drivers' licenses, to register to vote, to reserve state park camp grounds, and to communicate with administrative and elected public officials. In fact, technology is so important to state and local government operation that a new Strategic Technology Office was set up in the Department of Administrative Services to "facilitate efficient decision making, policy and statutory adherence and provides tools and training to assist agencies in achieving project success."[36]

Oregon state local and governments rely heavily on electronic communication networks and computers to conduct their work. The development of government technology capacity has been called "online government" and "e-government."[37] And while there have been a few major problems in the implementation (e.g., the failed Oregon Health Plan website in 2013 and 2014), local and state governments are increasingly providing services and exchanging information with the public, businesses, nongovernmental organizations (NGOs), and other governments in an effort to promote efficiency and increased accountability. For example, Oregon's E-Government Program in the Department of Administrative services claims: "The Oregon CIO's Electronic Government Program helps Oregon government provide online services to Oregon residents and businesses over the internet. Our most well known service is Oregon.gov and we manage over 250 different services and are growing at a rate of about 15-20 new government services per year."[38] Oregonians in many communities can now pay local property and state income taxes online as well as access updates concerning weather, construction projects, or traffic congestion on the Oregon Department of Transportation's "Trip Check" government website.

State and local governments are also using the Internet to engage citizens in the policymaking process. Termed "e-democracy," this innovation includes websites—including Oregon's Oregon.Gov—with extensive information about all branches of government, various departments and agencies, and how and where citizens may contact their elected and career service officials. An excellent example of the improved accessibility of government information is the online availability of the *Oregon Blue Book*, a compendium of important information and addresses regarding Oregon's state and local governments, featuring an extensive account of the state's historical and current elected officials and electoral system.[39] The Office of the Secretary of State produces the *Oregon Blue Book* biennially.

The rapid technological innovation in Oregon and the United States has generated what some scholars call the "democracy versus technocracy quandary."[40] Postindustrial entities, and state and local governments, face many policy problems that are highly technical in nature and require scientific knowledge to manage effectively. At the same time, Oregon is a democratic society where citizens and elected officials make important policy decisions. Frank Fischer, a renowned expert in public policy from Rutgers University, has described this quandary as follows: "The tension between professional expertise and democratic governance is an important political dimension of our time. Democracy's emphasis on equality of citizenship, public opinion, and freedom of choice exists in an uneasy relationship with the scientific expert's rational, calculating spirit."[41] Democratic citizen participation and the need for scientific expertise (technocracy) to frame issues and develop appropriate policy options in complex areas of public policy may therefore come into conflict.[42] On one hand, placing too much emphasis on science and technical expertise in policy risks the erosion of democracy.[43] On the other hand, the direct involvement of ill-informed citizens in policymaking may relegate technical and scientific information to a peripheral role whereby the adoption of "political" solutions will not adequately address complex problems.[44]

VALUE CHANGE

Changes in a state's economy and its governance are important to consider because they affect the attitudes that residents have toward society and the demands that they place on their government. Many social scientists argue that the shift from an agricultural to an industrial society, and then to a postindustrial one, has led to profound changes in American values, producing a fundamental cultural realignment.

The advent of the postindustrial society is seen as reshaping citizens' value structures, causing many to become more concerned with what psychologist Abraham Maslow has termed "higher-order" needs, such as social affiliation, quality-of-life concerns, and connection to transcendent values.[45] These are referred to in the literature as "postmaterialist" values. As these higher-order needs have become more important to individuals, they have supplanted more fundamental subsistence needs (such as concern for health and safety, referred to as "materialist" values) in motivating individual and societal behavior. The growing importance of these higher-value needs is, in turn, thought to have brought about changes in attitudes toward society and government. These include a greater concern for quality-of-life issues and environmental protection; more tolerance for diverse lifestyles; and stronger support for freedom on moral issues, such as abortion, gay rights, and the position of women in society.

The challenge confronting the state, however, is that the development of the postindustrial society and the rise of these new values have not developed uniformly across the state. Rather, the emergence of the postindustrial society has affected the rural and urban areas of the state quite differently.

The continual decline in the traditional rural agricultural/industrial economy and changes in migration patterns reinforce the rural-urban split and synergistically feed a division along social values. It is in the urban areas, where the postindustrial economy and postindustrial values are the most evident, that we find the greatest support for these new issues. In the more rural areas, where the economy has not developed as fully into a postindustrial one, the voters are not as supportive of these new issues. One result of this different development is the state's political divide.

A 2012 survey of Oregonians by Oregon State University (OSU) sheds some light on these value changes in Oregon's rural and urban areas. Table 2.4 displays results from a statewide survey of rural and urban Oregonians. Drawing from the research by Ronald Inglehart on postindustrial societies, the table shows three types of values: materialist, postmaterialist, and mixed (a combination of both types of values).[46] The table indicates that postmaterialist values, those that are associated with the postindustrial society, are more prevalent in metropolitan Portland areas and other urban areas. Materialist values, however, are more prevalent in rural areas.

Table 2.4. Postmaterialist values in rural and urban Oregon counties

Value Type	Portland Metro, %	All Urban, %	Rural, %
Materialist	16	17	38
Mixed	25	37	45
Postmaterialist	59	46	17

Oregon State University Policy Analysis Laboratory website, accessed May 29, 2018, http://liberalarts.oregonstate.edu/spp/opal

Table 2.5. Postmaterialist values and political ideology

	Materialist, %	Mixed, %	Postmaterialist, %
Liberal	12	21	49
Moderate	48	50	33
Conservative	40	29	18

Oregon State University Policy Analysis Laboratory website, accessed May 28, 2018, http://liberalarts.oregonstate.edu/spp/opal

Table 2.6. Postmaterialist values and support for gender equity policies

	Materialist, %	Mixed, %	Postmaterialist, %
Comparable worth	37	53	66
Affirmative Action (employment)	8	18	34
Affirmative Action (higher education)	11	23	41
Title IX	33	48	69
Parental leave (publicly funded)	20	36	65
Daycare (publicly funded)	13	26	42

Oregon State University Policy Analysis Laboratory website, accessed May 29, 2018, http://liberalarts.oregonstate.edu/spp/opal

The data presented in tables 2.5 and 2.6, also from the 2012 OSU Policy Survey, provide some insight into the relationship of postmaterialist values to political orientations and attitudes in the state. Table 2.5 compares the relationship between the respondents' value system and their self-identified ideology. The table shows that postmaterialists tend to be more politically liberal than materialists. Table 2.6 compares the respondents' value system with their support for a variety of prominent policies related to gender equity. When examining the relationship between value systems and support for these policies, one finds that postmaterialists are much more willing to express "strong support" for gender equity when compared to those respondents with materialist and mixed value orientations. Combined, these two tables reveal that postmaterialists hold distinct political preferences when compared with materialists.

The development of new values and potentially new social movements among Oregonians can result in the questioning of many traditional state and local government institutions and long-established policies. Indeed, issues dealing with environmental protection versus economic growth tradeoffs or with the rights and needs of historically disadvantaged groups (e.g., women, minorities, gays, disabled, aboriginal people, etc.) are typical of the new and often elite-challenging politics of value change found in postindustrial society.

CONCLUSION

Oregon state and local governments currently face many ongoing social, economic, and political changes, while at the same time, governmental institutions are largely continuous from a previous era. How current institutions and public officials adapt or do not adapt to these changes will affect the long-term viability of state and local governments. Oregon has developed from a rural, agricultural, and forest-based economy into an industrial economy, and now, as it becomes increasingly a postindustrial society with a knowledge-based economy, state and local governments must cope with a wide array of changes brought on by urbanization, demographics, technology, the economy, and values.

The resiliency and success of Oregon state and local governments will be affected by how our governmental institutions adapt and respond to these major changes. The presence of established and effective governmental and community-based institutions increases the ability of these institutions to facilitate management and help community stakeholders deal with various potential risks (e.g., economic transformation, value change, etc.). Also, such institutions can help communities to adapt to change to the extent they are participatory, proactive, and representative of the population.[47] Proactive institutions increase community capacity by planning ahead through such measures as mitigation of the problem, strategic planning, and the formulation of emergency management plans.[48]

Notes

1   Robert Inglehart, *Culture Shift in Advanced Industrial Society* (Princeton, NJ: Princeton University Press, 1990); Robert Inglehart, *Modernization and Postmodernization: Cultural, Economic, and Political Change in 43 Societies* (Princeton, NJ: Princeton University Press, 1997); Daniel Bell, "The Coming of the Post-Industrial Society," *Educational Forum* 40, no. 4 (1976): 574-79, doi: http://dx.doi. org/10.1080/00131727609336501.

2   Roger L. Kemp, "Cities in the 21st Century: The Forces of Change," *Economic Development Review* 17, no. 3 (2001): 56-62.

3   "Oregon's Road to 4 Million," Population Research Center, accessed April 3, 2018, http://roadto4million.research.pdx.edu/home.

4   "Oregon's Road to 4 Million."

5   Felicia Bechtoldt, "Population Growth Faster among Minority Groups," Oregon Workforce and Economic Information, State of Oregon Employment Department, March 16, 2015, https://oregonemployment.blogspot.com/2015/03/population-growth-faster-among-minority.html.

6   Alana Semuels, "The Racist History of Portland, the Whitest City in America," *The Atlantic*, July 22, 2016, https://www.theatlantic.com/business/archive/2016/07/racist-history-portland/492035/.

7   Daniel M. Sullivan and Samuel C. Shaw, "Retail Gentrification and Race: The Case of Alberta Street in Portland, Oregon," *Urban Affairs Review* 47 (2011): 413-32.

8   "Oregon's Road to 4 Million."

9   "Oregon's Road to 4 Million."

10 Josh Lehner, "Who Moves to Oregon?," Oregon Office of Economic Analysis, January 11, 2016, https://oregoneconomicanalysis.com/2016/01/11/who-moves-to-oregon-graph-of-the-week/.

11 J. R. Jurjevich and G. Shrock, *Is Portland Really the Place Where Young People Go to Retire? Migration Patterns of Portland's Young and College-Educated, 1980-2010* (Portland, OR: Population Research Center, 2012), http://pdxscholar.library.pdx.edu/cgi/viewcontent.cgi?article=1004&context=prc_pub.

12 Jordan Jordan, "An Examination of Gentrification and Related Displacement of Black Residents in Portland's Boise Neighborhood, 1990-2010" (PhD thesis, Portland State University, 2013), doi:10.15760/honors.23.

13 Betsy Breyer and Adriana Voss-Andreae, "Food Mirages: Geographic and Economic Barriers to Healthful Food Access in Portland, Oregon," *Health and Place 24* (2013): 131-39, doi:http://dx.doi.org/10.1016/j.healthplace.2013.07.008.

14 Elizabeth Flanagan, Ugo Lachapelle, and Ahmed El-Geneidy, "Riding Tandem: Does Cycling Infrastructure Investment Mirror Gentrification and Privilege in Portland, OR, and Chicago, IL?," *Research in Transportation Economics* 60 (2016): 14-24, doi:http://dx.doi.org/10.1016/j.retrec.2016.07.027.

15 Erin Goodling, Jamaal Green, and Nathan McClintock, "Uneven Development of the Sustainable City: Shifting Capital in Portland, Oregon," *Urban Geography* 36, no. 4 (2015): 504-27, doi:10.1080/02723638.2015.1010791.

16 "SA25 Total Full-Time and Part-Time Employment by SIC Industry," Bureau of Economic Analysis, US Department of Commerce, accessed May 22, 2018, https://www.bea.gov/iTable/iTable.cfm?reqid=70&step=30&isuri=1&7022=5&7023=0&7033=-1&7024=naics&7025=0&7026=12000&7001=45&7027=2011,2010,2009,2008,2007,2006,2005,2004,2003,2002,2001,2000&7028=1004&7031=0&7040=-1&7083=levels&7029=31&7090=70#reqid=70&step=30&isuri=1&7022=5&7023=0&7033=-1&7024=naics&7025=0&7026=41000&7027=-1&7001=45&7028=-1&7031=0&7040=-1&7083=levels&7029=31&7090=70.

17 "Intel in Oregon," Intel website, accessed April 4, 2018, https://www.intel.com/content/www/us/en/corporate-responsibility/intel-in-oregon.html.

18 "Labor Force Statistics from the Current Population Survey," Bureau of Labor Statistics, accessed March 12, 2017, http://data.bls.gov/timeseries/LNS14000000.

19 "Labor Force Statistics."

20 State of Oregon Employment Department, *Oregon's Minimum Wage Jobs: Facts, Figures, and Context* (Salem: State of Oregon Employment Department, February 2016), https://www.qualityinfo.org/documents/10182/13336/Oregon%E2%80%99s+Minimum+Wage+Jobs+Facts%2C+Figures%2C+and+Context?version=1.2 .

21 "Oregon Minimum Wage Rate Summary," Oregon.gov, accessed April 4, 2018, http://www.oregon.gov/boli/WHD/OMW/Pages/Minimum-Wage-Rate-Summary.aspx.

22 "Labor Force Statistics."

23 William S. Prudham, "Timber and Town: Post-War Federal Forest Policy, Industrial Organization, and Rural Change in Oregon's Illinois Valley," *Antipode* 30, no. 2 (1998): 177–96, doi:10.1111/1467-8330.00073.

24 Prudham, "Timber and Town."

25 Prudham, "Timber and Town."

26 Prudham, "Timber and Town."

27 Pamela S. Chasek, D. L. Downie, and J. W. Brown, *Global Environmental Politics* (Boulder, CO: Westview Press, 2014).

28 Bruce Weber and Yong Chen, "Federal Forest Policy and Community Prosperity in the Pacific Northwest," *Choices* 27, no. 1 (2012): http://www.choicesmagazine.org/choices-magazine/theme-articles/rural-wealth-creation/federal-forest-policy-and-community-prosperity-in-the-pacific-northwest-.

29 Hunt H. Eichman, G. L. Kerkvliet, and A. J. Plantinga, "Local Employment Growth, Migration, and Public Land Policy: Evidence from the Northwest Forest Plan," *Journal of Agricultural and Resource Economics* 35, no. 2 (2010): 316-33; Fabian Waltert and Felix Schlapfer, "Landscape Amenities and Local Development: A Review of Migration, Regional Economic and Hedonic Pricing Studies," *Ecological Economics* 70, no. 2 (2010): 14152; Yong Chen and Bruce Weber, "Federal Forest Policy, Amenity Migration and Rural Community Income: Did the Northwest Forest Plan Raise Incomes in Oregon's Rural Communities?" (presented at the annual meeting of the North American Regional Science Council, Miami, FL, 2011); Yong Chen and Bruce Weber, "Federal Policy, Rural Community Growth, and Wealth Creation: The Impact of Federal Forest Policy and Rural Development Spending in the Pacific Northwest," *American Journal of Agricultural Economics* 94 (2012): 542-54.

30 John Lehner, "Historical Look at Oregon's Wood Product Industry," Oregon Office of Economic Analysis, January 23, 2012, https://oregoneconomicanalysis.com/2012/01/23/historical-look-at-oregons-wood-product-industry/.

31 John Lehner, "Changing of the Guard," Oregon Office of Economic Analysis, September 4, 2014, https://oregoneconomicanalysis.com/2014/09/04/changing-of-the-guard/.

32 US Department of Agriculture (USDA), "Historical Highlights: 2012 and Earlier Census Years," in *2012 Census of Agriculture—State Data* (Washington, DC: USDA, 2012), https://www.agcensus.usda.gov/Publications/2012/Full_Report/Volume_1,_Chapter_1_State_Level/Oregon/st41_1_001_001.pdf.

33 USDA, "Historical Highlights."

34 USDA, "Historical Highlights."

35 National Oceanic and Atmospheric Administration (NOAA), *National Overview* (Silver Spring, MD: NOAA, 2012), http://www.st.nmfs.noaa.gov/Assets/economics/documents/feus/2012/FEUS2012_NationalOverview.pdf.

36 "Learn About STO," Strategic Technology Office, accessed April 4, 2018, https://www.oregon.gov/das/OSCIO/Pages/Strategy.aspx.

37 M. Jae Moon, "The Evolution of e-Government among Municipalities: Rhetoric or Reality?," *Public Administration Review* 62 (2002): 4-24.

38 "E-Government Program," Oregon.Gov, accessed May 22, 2018, http://www.oregon.gov/DAS/OSCIO/Pages/EGov.aspx.

39 Oregon Secretary of State, *Oregon Blue Book* (Salem: State of Oregon, 2017), bluebook.state.or.us.

40 John C. Pierce and Nicholas P. Lovrich, "Democracy and Technocracy," in *Science and Politics: An A to Z Guide to Issues and Controversies*, ed. Brent S. Steel (Los Angeles: CQ Press, 2015), 134-37.

41 Frank Fischer, *Citizens, Experts, and the Environment: The Politics of Local Knowledge* (Durham, NC: Duke University Press, 2000).

42 Gregory E. McAvoy, *Controlling Technocracy: Citizen Rationality and the NIMBY Syndrome* (Washington, DC: Georgetown University Press, 1999).

43 Peter DeLeon, *Democracy and the Policy Sciences* (Albany: State University of New York Press, 1997).

44 Richard Nathan, *Social Science in Government: The Role of Policy Researchers* (Albany, NY: Rockefeller Institute Press, 2000).

45 Abraham Maslow, *New Knowledge in Human Values* (New York: Harper and Row, 1959).

46 Inglehart, *Culture Shift*; idem, *Modernization and Postmodernization.*

47 Ellen Wall and Katia Marzall, "Adaptive Capacity for Climate Change in Canadian Rural Communities," *Local Environment* 11 (2006): 373-97.

48 Ronald D. Brunner et al., *Adaptive Governance: Integrating Science, Policy and Decision Making* (New York: Columbia University Press, 2005).

3
Political Parties and Elections
PRISCILLA L. SOUTHWELL

Oregon distinguished itself from other US states in March 2015 when Governor Kate Brown signed a bill into law providing for the automatic registration of voters using the state's Department of Motor Vehicle records. Many Western democracies provide for automatic voter registration, but Oregon became the first state to use its powers to ensure that all eligible voters are automatically registered to vote. This landmark piece of legislation follows the state's heritage of innovative politics, including becoming in 1998 the first state to adopt an all vote-by-mail election rule, yet Oregon's overall record for innovation and change in rewriting electoral rules has been mixed in recent years. While the state has been at the cutting edge of reform in some aspects of how elections are conducted, in others it has remained traditional. This lack of change is especially visible in the state's redistricting process and campaign financing laws.

The rules of the game are just one element useful for understanding how Oregon politics has evolved in recent years. Not only have the state's election rules seen both innovations and continuities—so has the character of state elections themselves. The most important recent transformation has been a significant relative decline in Republican registrants. This shift has not meant a proportional growth in Democratic Party registration, however. Although the absolute number and proportion of registered voters affiliated with the Democratic Party rose strongly during the Obama presidential election years, overall, the absolute increase in Democratic registration has paralleled the general increase in registered voters, being about 38 percent in 2001 and 2017. Figure 3.1 shows how the Republican share dropped from 36.2 to 29.6 percent. The decline in Republican registration has primarily benefitted the category of nonaffiliated voters and, to a lesser degree, the newly emerged Independent Party of Oregon (IPO). As for election outcomes, however, the Democratic Party has steadily gained a firmer hold on the state legislature and continues to control the governorship and most other statewide offices. The use of the initiative and referendum process—a type of direct democracy found in Oregon and many other states—has seen significant changes but remains an important political feature of Oregon's electoral landscape. This chapter analyzes these various changes, and continuity, in the state's political parties and elections.

INNOVATION IN REGISTRATION AND ELECTIONS

Since the adoption of the initiative and referendum process by voters in 1902, Oregon has frequently pursued reforms in how it conducts elections. In part, many of these reform efforts have reflected the state's populist heritage, which has sought to open up the political system to ensure broad public participation. The adoption of vote-by-mail and the enactment of the motor voter registration law represent the most recent efforts to follow this tradition.

VOTE-BY-MAIL

Oregon voters have long voted at relatively high levels, but the introduction of vote-by-mail enhanced this record. Vote-by-mail elections, also referred to as all-mail elections, have been held in Oregon over the past two decades, and since 1998 have been the sole method by which all elections are conducted in the state. Under vote-by-mail, all registered voters are sent a ballot approximately three weeks before Election Day. Ballots are not forwarded if the voter no longer lives at an address. After marking their votes, voters put their ballots in a secrecy envelope, which contains no identifying information. The secrecy envelope is then placed into a second envelope for mailing. Voters are required to sign the outside of this second envelope, which they can then place in the mail or take to one of the numerous drop-off sites in the community if they want to save a stamp. When the ballots arrive at the local elections office, the outside signature is compared to the original registration signature on record to protect against fraud.

The lengthy voting period of the vote-by-mail system contributes to increased voter participation. In essence, the potential voter is not rushed, as there is ample time to review the official voter's pamphlet, consult with others, or simply deliberate about the electoral options. Vote-by-mail eases the burden of voting by reducing the impact of unanticipated difficulties, such as illness or inclement weather, which often prevent individuals from voting on Election Day. A potential voter also does not have to worry about long lines at the polling place, transportation to the polling place, or making special work arrangements. As such, vote-by-mail makes it easier to vote, and it is popular among Oregonians in general. Even so, vote-by-mail remains controversial, as discussed below.

The introduction of all-mail elections in Oregon, similar to its neighboring state of Washington, has been incremental. The pivotal turning point came in September 1995 when Bob Packwood resigned from the US Senate. The special Senate election to replace him was the first time in US history that a vote-by-mail election was used to decide a federal election. Prior to this 1996 election, vote-by-mail had been used only for local elections or statewide ballot measures, primarily because of lower administrative costs. In 1987, the legislature made vote-by-mail an option for local and special elections, and a majority of counties then adopted vote-by-mail for local elections. In 1993, vote-by-mail was used for the first time in a statewide ballot measures.

In 1995, the Republican-controlled state legislature passed a bill that would have adopted vote-by-mail for all types of elections. The impetus for this bill was the high level of absentee voting (22%) in the 1994 general election, which delayed the certification of certain races for many weeks, including a US House seat. However, John Kitzhaber, Oregon's Democratic governor, vetoed the bill. He argued that it was too early for Oregon to adopt such a drastic electoral reform without further study or experimentation.[1]

The special nature of both the December 1995 primary and the January 1996 general election to fill Senator Packwood's seat allowed Secretary of State Phil Keisling to adopt the vote-by-mail format for these two elections. Secretary Keisling chose the vote-by-mail format because he was a strong supporter of the reform, and, given the governor's explanation for his veto of the vote-by-mail bill, this election would provide an opportunity for the type of experimentation that the governor felt was needed. As secretary of state, Keisling was the state's chief elections officer, empowering him with the right to determine the format of any "special" election (an election not held on one of the four designated election dates in the year). In both elections, turnout was high. Nearly 58 percent of eligible voters participated in the December 1995 primary, and approximately 66 percent of Oregon's registered voters cast a ballot in the January 1996 general election.

Controversy soon arose within both political parties after the election as to whether vote-by-mail was advantageous to one party over another. As a result, the push for making it a permanent feature of Oregon election rules lost support among most party leaders.[2] However, the Oregon League of Women Voters led a successful petition drive to put a vote-by-mail measure on the 1998 general election ballot. This ballot measure passed, winning 67 percent of the vote. Since that time, all elections in Oregon have been conducted by mail.

While generally popular, not everyone in Oregon has supported vote-by-mail. Some critics have voiced concern about the possibility of undue influence on the voter, as there is no guarantee of a secret ballot. Others have focused on the potential of voter fraud, a concern raised in other states with liberalized absentee voting laws. Finally, some observers have lamented the loss of the ritual of going to the polls, as voting is now a solitary experience for most Oregonians. Despite these concerns, there has been no evidence that vote-by-mail has led to pernicious undue influence or any voter fraud.[3]

Previous research has generally supported the argument that the vote-by-mail format increases turnout, although not for every type of election.[4] Looking at the overall turnout in sixty-one Oregon elections from 1980 to 2016 in table 3.1 below, vote-by-mail appears to boost turnout modestly, particularly in special and presidential elections. The results are not surprising, given that special elections are usually low-stimulus elections, often centering on one replacement seat or ballot measure. In such a situation, even politically aware voters might find it less important to go to the polling place for a single issue, but the vote-by-mail format makes it easier for them to vote on even one ballot measure or race. The positive effect of vote-by-mail for the high-stimulus presidential election is also expected, as these elections typically motivate first-time voters, who may have had difficulty locating their polling place in traditional elections but faced no such problems under vote-by-mail. Despite this general increase in turnout in presidential elections, turnout declined in the 2016 presidential election, falling to 77.2 percent from 82.8 percent in 2012. The decline was most likely a result of the increase in the number of registered voters through the automatic voter registration system adopted in January 2016. Whatever the benefits of this new automatic registration system, it did add fewer politically motivated registrants to the rolls.

Residents of Oregon have always voted at higher rates than residents of most other states, so the effect of an electoral reform such as vote-by-mail is marginal in primary and off-year general elections, but significant in presidential and special elections. Concerns about unintended and unforeseen consequences of any proposed electoral reform are inevitable and understandable, but there is no evidence that Oregon has experienced any significant problems from the introduction of this innovation, which has helped dispel most of these concerns.

MOTOR VOTER REGISTRATION

The second major innovation in Oregon election rules in recent years has been motor voter registration. On January 1, 2016, Oregon began its automatic voter registration process—the first state in the nation to do so. Automatic voter registration is a two-step process: when a person applies for a license, permit, or identification card through the Oregon Division of Motor Vehicles (DMV), the person's name and address are sent to the secretary of state's office. If the person is eligible to vote, a voter card is issued through the mail, which then allows the person to opt out of the registration process or to choose a party affiliation. If the voter takes neither of those steps, he or she will remain registered as nonaffiliated.

By September 2017, twenty months after the program's inception, the state had sent out 438,268 of these registration cards. A few of these cards were undeliverable

Table 3.1. Comparison of turnout of registered voters across electoral format and election type, 1980-2016

	Polling Place, %	Vote-by-Mail, %
Presidential elections (10)	78.1	82.3
Off-year general elections (9)	69.6	70.7
Primary elections (19)	46.5	47.5
Special elections (23)	43.9	50.5
N	(28)	(33)

Source: State of Oregon. 2016. Calculations by author.

(2.6%) and some residents chose to opt out (7.5%), but the result was that 390,014 new voters were added to voting registration lists across the state during this period.[5] Of course, these new voters might have registered to vote through the traditional process, but this reform clearly has increased the size of the potential electorate.

Approximately 87 percent of these new voters did not choose to register with a party and were listed as "nonaffiliated." Under the closed primary system used by both the Democratic and Republican Parties, such nonaffiliated voters could not vote in the May 2016 primary elections, although the Independent Party of Oregon and a few other minor parties did allow nonaffiliated voters to participate. As such, one might have expected the turnout in the May 2016 primary to have declined, but it did not. The turnout increased to 54 percent, nearly matching the high watermark of 2008.

Studies on election participation have long found that one of the main reasons the United States has low election participation rates is because the burden for registering to vote in the United States falls entirely on voters. In most Western democracies, the government ensures that citizens are registered to vote. The introduction of motor voter registration means that Oregon is following a path similar to that used in other democracies. While Oregon has long had better participation rates than most other states, the introduction of motor voter is likely to increase that rate even further. The initial evidence from this change is that the law is indeed opening up the election process to all eligible voters in the state.

PARTIES, DIRECT DEMOCRACY, CAMPAIGN FINANCE, AND REDISTRICTING
Party Competition in Oregon

For most of the previous half century, Oregon has been a competitive party state, often with divided control of the state legislature or divided control between the legislative and executive branches. However, the last decade has shown a decisive shift toward the Democratic Party as well as the rise of the Independent Party of Oregon. The state's electoral vote was cast for the Republican presidential candidate from 1972 to 1984, but since then, Democratic presidential candidates have carried the state. In the 2016 presidential election, 50.1 percent voted for Hillary Clinton; 39.1 percent for Donald Trump; 4.7 percent for the Libertarian candidate, Gary Johnson; 2.5 percent for the Pacific Green candidate, Jill Stein; and 3.6 percent for other independent or third-party candidates.

Similarly, Oregon's governors were Republican for most of the post–World War II period until 1986, when Democrats began to hold this office, although the election contest has often been close. Oregon's two US Senate seats were held by Republicans Mark Hatfield and Robert Packwood for a quarter century. These two Republican senators, along with the popular governor Tom McCall (1967-75), earned reputations as moderates and were thus able to attract the support of Oregon voters, although most registrants were independents or Democrats at the time. Mark Hatfield was an outspoken opponent of the Vietnam War, and Bob Packwood was the influential chair of the US Senate Finance Committee, which successfully negotiated tax reform in 1986. He was also one of the few Republicans in the Senate who was pro-choice. Governor McCall promoted environmental reforms, including the Oregon Bottle Bill and the public ownership of beaches on the Oregon coast. Similarly, Republican Attorney General Dave Frohnmayer was reelected in 1984 and 1988 with the support of both major parties. Frohnmayer went on to become the Republican nominee for governor in 1990 but lost because of an independent candidate, Al Mobley, who captured 13 percent of the vote. In recent years, the Republican Party has had more difficulty attracting, or been less willing to nominate, moderate candidates. The Republican candidate for governor in 1998, anti-tax advocate Bill Sizemore, won only 30 percent of the vote, and he was later charged with racketeering. In 2010, a former Portland Trailblazers basketball player narrowly lost to his Democratic opponent, John Kitzhaber, and he has since moved out of state. Since the mid-1990s, the two major parties each held a Senate seat until the defeat of Republican Gordon Smith in 2008. Since that time, Oregon has had two Democratic senators, Ron Wyden and Jeff Merkley. The state has had a Democratic governor since 1987.

Although Democrats currently dominate its federal and statewide offices, Oregon remains a politically competitive state because its partisan divisions are geographic in nature. The Republican Party always secures a sizeable number of rural state house and senate seats, as is true elsewhere in the nation. However, most of Oregon's population is concentrated west of the Cascade Mountains and has tended to favor the Democratic Party. This western portion of the state, particularly the Portland metropolitan area and several university communities to the south (Ashland, Corvallis, Eugene), has grown in population over the past decades as its communities have been attracting younger professionals. In contrast, the eastern portion of the state is characterized by high-plains farming and ranching. As discussed in chapter 2, Oregon has experienced a proportional drop in its rural population (and an absolute decline a few counties), mainly owing to the decline in extractive natural resource industries, such as timber and mining. These population trends help explain the growing advantage of the Democratic Party and the challenges confronting the Republican Party.

These trends are reflected in the state's voter registration, as shown in figure 3.1. Although the Democratic Party enjoyed a surge during the 2008 presidential election, its overall proportion of registered voters has remained similar to that in 2001, despite the increase in its absolute number. The losses in the Republican Party's share have primarily benefitted the nonaffiliated category and Oregon's minor parties. Many new registrants in the "Other" category have affiliated with the newly emerged Independent Party of Oregon. This trend is consistent with patterns seen in other states nationwide.[6] Oregon's electoral law allows multiple parties to list the same person as a candidate for a particular office in the same election. This process, called "fusion voting," is a way

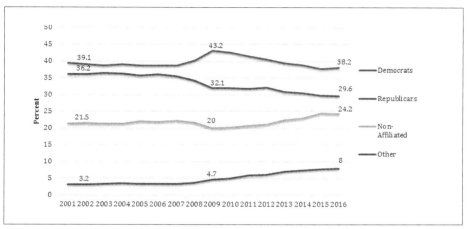

Figure 3.1. **Change in party registration, 2001-16.** *Source: Oregon Secretary of State, "Oregon Motor Voter: Cumulative Program Statistics through July 31, 2016," accessed September 6, 2016, http://sos.oregon. gov/elections/Documents/OMV/OMV_MonthlyReport_All_JULY percent202016.pdf*

for smaller parties to raise their visibility and to influence major party candidates to consider their concerns in exchange for their nomination.

Emergence of the Independent Party of Oregon

The Independent Party of Oregon (IPO) began as an independent voter movement. The events that triggered its emergence were the decisions of the state legislature to double the number of petition signatures needed for nonaffiliated candidates to qualify for the ballot and to replace the word "independent" with "nonaffiliated" as a descriptor on the ballot for such candidates. After failing to stop this legislation from passing, the movement leaders collected more than thirty thousand signatures in 2006 to form the Independent Party of Oregon, which was first recognized as a ballot-qualified minor party by the secretary of state in January 2007. In 2015, the Independent Party of Oregon achieved major party status when more than 5 percent of the state's registered voters listed their party affiliation as IPO. One of the innovative aspects of the party is that it conducts its primaries through the Internet, and often cross-nominates candidates from other political parties. Supporters of the IPO have applauded the rise of the party for giving voters alternative to the other two major parties. Some opponents have criticized the IPO for being misleading, arguing that the use of the term "independent" attracts voters who wish to be independent from a formal party organization. As of January 2017, according to the Secretary of State's Office, 119,399 voters were registered as members of the IOP, or 4.6 percent of the electorate.[7]

In addition to the three major parties, the minor parties in Oregon include: Americans Elect, Constitution, Libertarian, Pacific Green, Progressive, and Working

Families. The registration numbers for these alternative parties is low, and their preferred candidates are usually a member of another party as well.

Direct Democracy: The Initiative and Referendum Process

As described in the introduction to this book, the use of the initiative and the referendum is a major part of Oregon's story. Oregon adopted this process in 1902. It is now a regular feature of most primary and general elections as well as some single-issue special elections, such as Measure 101, the health insurance tax of January 2018 discussed in chapter 19.

Three types of ballot measures are possible under this process. First, the legislature may refer a proposed bill to voters rather than adopting the bill through the regular legislative process. An example of this type of "legislative referral" is Measure 94 from 2016, which called for abolishing the state's constitutionally mandated retirement age of 75 for state judges.

After legislative referrals, the second most common type of ballot measure is the "citizen initiative," in which private citizens can gather a required number of signatures to place a proposed law on the ballot. The number of signatures needed to place a *statutory* initiative on the ballot is 6 percent of the total number of voters in the previous gubernatorial election. An example is the 2014 ballot measure that legalized the recreational use of marijuana. The number of signatures required to place a *constitutional* initiative on the ballot is 8 percent of the number of voters in the previous gubernatorial election. Petitioners often favor a constitutional initiative, as it avoids the prospect of amendment during the subsequent legislative session. An example is the unsuccessful Measure 82 from 2012, which would have authorized private casinos.

The third type of ballot measure, the "citizen referendum," is less frequently used. The referendum provides a means for Oregonians to force a public vote on a recently enacted law if they can gather sufficient signatures within ninety days of when the relevant legislative session ends. The process for gathering signatures for referenda is identical to that of the citizen initiative, but the signature threshold is lower. The number of signatures needed to place a referendum on the ballot is only 4 percent of the number of voters in the previous gubernatorial election. An example is 2014's Measure 88, which was placed on the ballot to overturn a recently passed state law allowing undocumented residents to obtain a driver's license. The voters overwhelmingly voted against Measure 88, overturning the law. A more recent example is Measure 101, on health insurance taxes, on the January 2018 ballot.

Many ballot measures have been controversial, and the success rate is quite low. Usually less than 50 percent of all ballot measures are passed. In 2016, five measures (71%) were adopted, but in 2014 and 2012, only 43 percent and 44 percent were successful, respectively.[8] Ballot measures that have attempted to enact a sales tax in Oregon have failed nine times. Moreover, getting voter approval is not usually the final word on ballot measures. Many go on to face legal challenges or are altered by the legislature or future ballot measures. Most noteworthy was the battle over permitting assisted suicide in Oregon. In 1994, Oregon voters approved the Death with Dignity Act by a vote of 51.3 to 48.7 percent. After a federal court injunction delayed its implementation, a repeal of the measure was referred to the voters by the state legislature in the 1997 election. Voters affirmed their support for assisted suicide with a 60 percent rejection of the repeal effort. The act was then challenged by US Attorney General John Ashcroft on the basis of the Controlled Substances Act (CSA). Finally, the US Supreme Court upheld Oregon's law in the case of *Gonzales v. State of Oregon* (2006). In contrast, other successful ballot measures have not survived a court challenge. For example, in 1996, the Oregon Supreme Court ruled that a ballot measure approved in 1994 that attempted to reform the Public Employee Retirement System (PERS) was a violation of contract law. Similar court challenges have doomed campaign financing reform measures.

The entire initiative and referendum process has also evoked controversy. Although supporters of this process can point to women's suffrage or the adoption of vote-by-mail as success stories, some observers view this process as a repudiation of the republican form of government whereby elected representatives propose and enact legislation. Critics of this process also point out the vast sums of money that are spent each year trying to pass or defeat ballot measures, much of it from out of the state. In 2016, Measure 97 set a new record when over $42 million was spent on the business tax reform, far exceeding the previous total spending record of roughly $29 million spent on an initiative requiring the labeling of genetically modified foods in 2014.[9] In both cases, business interests that opposed the measures far outspent the supporters. Recently, the initiative process has shifted toward a "gun behind the door" type of action, one in which initiative sponsors threaten to place a measure on the ballot unless the legislature takes action on a particular policy. Some political observers viewed the $15 minimum wage petition initiative, which was eventually withdrawn, as a way to get the state legislature to raise the state's minimum wage, as they did in 2016. Chapter 5 describes in more detail the use of ballot measures to try to force legislative action.

There have been some significant changes in the use of direct democracy in recent years, reducing its relevance in the state's politics. In particular, the Oregon Supreme Court has begun to enforce the state constitutional clause restricting constitutional amendments to one subject. The court's role became much more prominent when it considered the legality of Measure 40, a proposed constitutional amendment passed by voters in the 1996 general election that would have established stronger victims' rights protections. Opponents argued that the measure changed more than one part of the constitution; thus voters had to adopt each part of the proposal separately. Supporters argued that the measure only affected one subject—victims' rights—and thus was constitutional. In the landmark case of *Armatta v. Kitzhaber* (1998), the court sided with the opponents, ruling that the measure affected five different sections of the constitution, each of which required a separate vote. The court action has subsequently led the secretary of state's office and the courts to reject a larger number of constitutional amendments.[10] The initiative process was further hampered by the legislature's adoption of House Bill 2082 in 2007, which forbids the payment of petition signature gatherers on a per signature basis. Combined, these two events have reduced the number of initiatives from roughly nine per major election in 1978-2008 to just under five between 2010 and 2016.

Despite the controversial nature of initiatives, and these recent changes, the initiative and referendum process is ingrained in the political culture of the state, and voters have come to expect to vote on ballot measures in each general election. It is unlikely that voters, the legislature, or the courts will curtail their use.

Redistricting

While the state has gone through some important changes in how voting is conducted and in voter registration, some aspects of its election system have seen little change in recent years. Redistricting is a good example.

Under the state constitution, the Oregon Legislative Assembly is assigned the primary duty of redrawing the state's sixty house and thirty senate district lines, as well as the state's congressional districts. As the population shifts within a state, the constitution requires these boundaries to be redrawn following each national census to equalize the population of each district. The redrawing of legislative boundaries is one of the most contentious issues in state legislatures because it affects the reelection chances of individual candidates and the control of the legislature by the political parties.

The Oregon legislature did not redraw district lines in the first half of the twentieth century. With the Republican Party in firm control of the legislature and the governor's office through most of this period, the party apparently had little motivation to change the election maps.[11] By the early 1950s, Oregon voters had become so dissatisfied with the inability or unwillingness of the legislature to complete this task that they approved a ballot measure amending the state constitution to give the secretary of state the power to devise a redistricting plan for the legislature if the legislature failed to so. In 1961, the state legislative district lines were redrawn for the first time since 1911. The involvement of the secretary of state in the redistricting process has proven necessary, as the legislature has often been unsuccessful in completing this redistricting process, including in the 1991 and 2001 legislative sessions.

Recent redistricting battles have arisen primarily because of the strong regional divide between the parties and the shifts in the state's population described above. The population of eastern Oregon has declined relative to the rest of the state, although many out-of-state retirees have recently moved to Deschutes (Bend) and Jackson (Ashland) Counties and therefore have slowed this trend. Although state law says that the legislature cannot draw lines for partisan advantage, redistricting is routinely driven by partisanship. With the parties battling to protect or even expand their seats while trying to address the population shifts, redistricting has become a difficult and controversial process. In addition, the secretary of state's powerful role has fueled the fires of the debate over redistricting.

The redistricting process starts in the state legislature early in the year following the national census, which is conducted at the beginning of each decade. The legislature has until July 1 to adopt new district boundaries. If the legislature is successful at this task, the proposal for the new districts goes to the governor, who has until August 1 to sign or veto the proposal. If the governor concurs, the plan goes into effect for the upcoming elections, unless legal challenges are filed.

If the legislature fails to meet the July 1 deadline, or if the governor vetoes the redistricting bill, then the next step in the process differs between state legislative and congressional district plans. When the legislature is unable to agree on a legislative districting plan, or if the governor vetoes the legislature's plan, then the secretary of state becomes responsible for drawing the new legislative boundaries. When the legislature is unable to pass a bill redrawing congressional district lines, or if the governor vetoes the legislature's proposal, then the federal courts have responsibility for drawing the new district lines. The final redistricting plan for state legislative seats must be completed by December 15 of the year following the national census. No deadline exists for congressional redistricting, although noncompliance by the next primary season would invite court challenges.

While the legislature is assigned the primary duty of redistricting under current law, the state supreme court has the authority to review the redistricting plan at each stage of the process. When legal challenges are filed against redistricting plans, they are sent directly to the supreme court for judicial review. If the supreme court determines that a plan does not comply with constitutional requirements, the plan is declared void, with specific references to the areas of noncompliance. The plan is then usually referred to the secretary of state for revision. If the legislature's plan is voided, the secretary of state must draft a redistricting of the state legislative districts, conduct a public hearing, file a transcript of the hearing, and file a corrected redistricting plan with the supreme court by November 1 of this same year. The court may order additional corrections; otherwise, the new plan becomes operative on November 15.

The role of the Oregon Supreme Court in redistricting is not only defined by the Oregon Constitution, but it is also constrained by the Fourteenth Amendment to the US Constitution, which requires state legislative districts be equal in population when drawn. The Oregon Supreme Court also evaluates redistricting plans according to the criteria described in Oregon Revised Statutes as well as the secretary of state's administrative rules. The supreme court must provide written opinions. In addition, the plan approved by the court must maintain the ratio of population to senators and representatives.[12]

Because of the political and legal battles that have characterized the redistricting process in recent decades, there have been attempts to reform it. Anticipating that Oregon might gain a US House seat after the 2010 census, and perhaps frustrated with the stagnated reform efforts in the 2007 and 2009 legislative sessions, proponents of redistricting reform used the petition initiative to attempt put a measure on the 2010 ballot. This proposal would have created a nonpartisan redistricting commission made up of five retired judges, one from each congressional district. The effort was unsuccessful after about 10 percent of the signatures gathered by the chief sponsor, Common Sense for Oregon, were deemed invalid by the secretary of state's office.[13] Similarly, in 2011, a joint resolution was introduced in the state legislature to amend the Oregon Constitution and establish a panel of twenty-four retired judges, or what were called "special masters," to create state legislative and congressional redistricting plan after each census—an extension and elaboration of the proposed ballot measure of 2010. This resolution died in a legislative committee. Thus, despite the controversies surrounding redistricting, the process has remained generally unchanged since 1952.

CAMPAIGN FINANCING

Oregon is one of the six states in the country that allow unlimited contributions to its nonfederal candidates or ballot measure campaign committees.[14] There have been numerous efforts to establish contribution limits, but none of the proposals that have been enacted into law have withstood court challenges, leaving the state's current campaign finance structure unchanged.

The most extensive effort to control contributions was the passage of ballot Measure 9 in 1994. This measure set strict campaign contribution limits on individuals and political action committees (PACs) in both legislative and statewide races. Individuals and PACs were limited to contributing a maximum of $100 to legislative candidates and $500 to statewide candidates during each election. However, the Oregon Supreme Court threw out the restrictions in *VanNatta v. Keisling* (1997), finding that campaign contributions are a form of speech protected by the Oregon Constitution. Measure 6, which was also approved by voters in 1994, would have limited out-of-district contributions to 10 percent of a candidate's total funds. However, the federal court found that this limit violated the First Amendment to the US Constitution. In making its ruling, the court argued that the state had no evidence that out-of-district or out-of-state contributions posed special dangers of corruption.[15]

In 2006, voters considered two additional campaign finance reform measures. One of them, Measure 46, provided for a change in the state constitution specifically allowing the legislature or voters to create contribution and spending limits in election campaigns. The second proposal, Measure 47, then established specific restrictions on contributions to candidates, PACs, and political parties, while also limiting what candidates could spend on their own candidacy. The latter measure was enacted into law, but Measure 46 was defeated. The attorney general and the secretary of state linked the two measures, however, arguing that the limits established in Measure 47 could not be put into force without the changes in the constitution established under Measure 46. The Oregon Supreme Court upheld this decision, ruling that Measure 47 would be held in "abeyance," pending an appropriate constitutional amendment or judicial decision in *Hazell v. Brown* (2012).[16]

In 2015, Secretary of State Kate Brown introduced two bills in the Oregon State Senate that would have set restrictions on campaign contributions. Despite Brown's appointment as governor in the middle of the session and her continued support for campaign finance reform, both bills died in committee.[17]

The result is that a great deal of money flows into the coffers of Oregon candidates, even given its relatively small population of nearly four million. Table 3.2 shows that average contribution per registered voter in 2014 was higher in Oregon for state house, state senate, and gubernatorial races than either Washington or California.[18] This figure represents the total dollar amount of contributions made to house, senate, and gubernatorial candidates, as three distinct sets of contributions, divided by the total number of statewide registered voters. The figure is higher for the state house in all states, because there are obviously a greater number of lower house seats for all three states, and therefore total contributions to candidates. These figures suggest that campaign contributions, and therefore expenditures, remain relatively high in Oregon.

Who are these contributors? Table 3.3 lists the largest contributors in 2014 from Oregon, including to federal candidates and those committees in support or opposition to ballot measures. This list includes the Democratic and Republican state campaign committees, as well as one union, several professional associations, and one corporation.

The largest individual contributor in Oregon in 2014 was Phil Knight, the founder and CEO of Nike Corporation. He donated $270,000, primarily to the

Table 3.2. A Comparison of total campaign contributions per registered voter by elected office in three states, 2014

	State House	State Senate	Governor
Oregon	$11.88 (149)	$6.37 (35)	$5.24 (12)
Washington	$6.34 (213)	$4.49 (56)	no race
California	$10.69 (246)	$4.43 (76)	$3.71 (26)

Note: Values in parentheses indicate number of candidates.
Source: "Election Overview," National Institute on Money in State Politics, accessed September 13, 2016, http://www.followthemoney.org/election-overview?s=OR&y=2014

Table 3.3. Top fifteen non-individual contributors in Oregon, 2014

Donor	Total Contributions
Oregon House Democratic Campaign Committee	$1,800,095
Oregon Democratic Party	$1,329,757
Oregon Public Employees Local 503	$1,012,173
Promote Oregon Leadership*	$791,169
Oregon Senate Republican Leadership Fund	$773,431
Oregon Education Association	$604,990
Oregon Health Care Association	$565,233
Oregon Senate Democratic Campaign Committee	$534,404
Nike	$422,788
Oregon Nurses Association	$407,260
Associated Oregon Industries	$406,112
Coalition for a Healthy Oregon	$400,613
Oregon Trial Lawyers Association	$397,961
Oregon League of Conservation Voters	$372,027
ACTBLUE**	$342,376

Source: "Election Overview," National Institute on Money in State Politics, accessed September 13, 2016, http://www.followthemoney.org/election-overview?s=OR&y=2014

incumbent governor John Kitzhaber. This contribution, just three weeks before the 2014 general election, became a subject of much controversy. Phil Knight had previously given primarily to Republican candidates, including John Kitzhaber's opponent in 2010. Previously, however, in December 2012, Governor Kitzhaber had called the legislature into a special session to consider a special long-term tax break for Nike.[19] The governor also relaxed his initial concerns about using state funds to support a 2021 track event in Eugene, a project supported by Phil Knight.[20] The unsuccessful Republican candidate for governor in 2014, Dennis Richardson, also received large contributions from several individuals, including $150,000 from Robert Freres, owner of Freres Lumber Company, and $122,000 from James Young, a retired CEO of Entek Manufacturing.[21] The level of these contributions to the gubernatorial candidates in Oregon would not have been possible under either Washington's or California's existing contribution limits.

In addition, 2014 data from the National Institute on Money in State Politics indicate that the bulk of contributions to all types of candidates in Oregon, both federal and state, went to incumbents (65.2%), followed by challengers (21%) and candidates in open seats (12.9%), with the remaining amount going to uncontested races. These amounts are not surprising. Yet a relatively high percentage (59.2%) went to Democratic candidates, who are more likely to be incumbents. Republican candidates received 39.5 percent of all contributions, while minor party or nonpartisan candidates each received less than 1 percent of all campaign contributions.[22]

The silver lining is that Oregon's campaign finance and ethics law make such campaign contributions quite transparent. In 2005, the Oregon legislature passed legislation that requires all campaign contributions and expenditures to be electronically reported to the secretary of state's office within thirty days through the Oregon Elections System for Tracking and Reporting (ORESTAR). This system now allows the public to access all campaign contributions and candidate spending for state and local candidates through the secretary of state's website. Despite this transparency in the reporting of campaign contributions and expenditures, the absence of contribution limits has caught the attention of watchdog organizations such as Common Cause, and seems to defy Oregon's other more innovative and progressive election laws.[23]

CONCLUSION

Over the past two decades, Oregon has experienced significant changes throughout its political system. Elections, political campaigns, and party politics have not been immune from this trend. Among the most important changes have been the efforts to open up the election process through the introduction of vote-by-mail and motor voter registration. Oregon has long had a reputation for supporting an open political system, and these changes are consistent with that reputation. There has been significant change, however, not just in the election process but in electoral politics itself. Here, among the most important changes have been the strengthening of the Democratic Party's success in election campaigns, the increase in the number of voters registered as nonaffiliated as well as of third-party candidates, and the decline in the use of the initiative/referendum process.

These changes have significantly changed the character and importance of elections in Oregon, which, as is discussed in later chapters, has affected politics and policy in the state. While much has changed, some key parts of the election system remain the same. Oregon still lags other states in the area of campaign financing reform, and its redistricting process remains traditional and partisan. In other words, while the last few decades have brought considerable change in the election system, it was also a period marked by continuity.

Notes

1   Harry Esteve, "Mail Vote Experiment to be Watched Closely," *Register-Guard*, October 17, 1995.

2   Brad Cain, "Senate Election Prompts Vote-by-Mail Worries," *Register-Guard*, October 8, 1995.

3   Phil Keisling, "Vote from Home, Save Your Country," *Washington Monthly* (January 2017); Priscilla L. Southwell and Justin Burchett, "The Effect of All-Mail Elections on Voter Turnout," *American Politics Quarterly* 29 (2000): 72-79.

4   Sean Richey, "Voting by Mail: Turnout and Institutional Reform in Oregon," *Social Science Quarterly* 89 (2008): 902-15; Priscilla L. Southwell, "Analysis of the Turnout Effects of Vote-by-mail Elections, 1980– 2007," *Social Science Journal* 46 (2009): 211-17.

5   "Oregon Motor Voter: Cumulative Program Statistics through July 31, 2016," Oregon Secretary of State, accessed September 6, 2016, http://sos.oregon.gov/elections/Documents/OMV/OMV_MonthlyReport_All_JULY percent202016.pdf.

6   Renata Sago, Ben Markus, and Jude Joffe-Block, "Sick of Political Parties, Unaffiliated Voters Are Changing Politics," *National Public Radio*, February 28, 2016, https://www.npr.org/2016/02/28/467961962/sick-of-political-parties-unaffiliated-voters-are-changing-politics.

7   "Voter Registration Comparison by County," Oregon Secretary of State, accessed April 5, 2018, http://sos.oregon.gov/elections/Documents/registration/Jan17.pdf.

8   Calculated by the author using "Oregon Election History," in Oregon Secretary of State, *Oregon Blue Book* (Salem: State of Oregon, 2017), http://bluebook.state.or.us/state/elections/elections06.htm.

9   Hillary Borrud, "Spending by Measure 97 Campaigns Surpasses $97 Million," *Oregonian*, November 6, 2016.

10   Richard J. Ellis, "Direct Democracy," in *Oregon Politics and Government: Progressives versus Conservative Populists*, ed. Richard A. Clucas, Mark Henkels, and Brent S. Steel (Lincoln: University of Nebraska Press, 2005), 77.

11   Common Cause, *Oregon's 2011 Redistricting: Successes, Concerns, and Recommended Improvements* (Portland, OR: Common Cause, 2012).

12   "Background Brief on Redistricting," Oregon State Legislature, Legislative Committee Services, accessed September 2, 2016, https://www.oregonlegislature.gov/citizen_engagement/Reports/Redistricting.pdf.

13   Kimberly Melton, "Restricting Initiative Comes Up Short," *Oregonian*, July 27, 2010.

14   "State Limits on Contributions to Candidates 2015-2016 Election Cycle," National Conference of State Legislatures, accessed September 13, 2016, http://www.ncsl.org/Portals/1/documents/legismgt/elect/ContributionLimitstoCandidates2015-2016.pdf.

15   "Background Brief on Campaign Finance: Contribution and Expenditure Limits," Oregon State Legislature, Legislative Committee Services, accessed September 13, 2016, https://www.oregonlegislature.gov/citizen_engagement/Reports/CampaignFinance.pdf.

16   "*Hazell v. Brown*," Oregon Department of Justice, accessed September 13, 2016, http://www.publications.ojd.state.or.us/docs/S059245.pdf.

17   Denis C. Theriault, "Brown Takes Election Cash Reform Effort to Capitol," *Oregonian*, April 22, 2015.

18   An earlier version of this analysis was published in Priscilla L. Southwell, "Campaign Contribution Limits in California, Oregon & Washington: What a Difference It Makes," *Journal of Politics and Law* 10 (2017): 82-87.

19 Laura Gunderson, "Phil Knight Donates $250,000 to John Kitzhaber Campaign," *Oregonian*, September 24, 2014, http://www.oregonlive.com/politics/index. ssf/2014/09/phil_knight_donates_250000_to.html.

20 Saul Hubbard, "Cash Trail Leads to Track Subsidy," *Register-Guard*, January 6, 2016.

21 "Election Overview," National Institute on Money in State Politics, accessed September 13, 2016, http://www.followthemoney.org/election-overview?s=OR&y=2014.

22 "Election Overview."

23 "Common Cause Oregon Interns Speak Out about the Lack of Oregon's Campaign Contribution Limits," Common Cause, April 6, 2015, http://www.commoncause.org/ democracy-wire/interns-speak-out.html.

4

Media in Oregon
Doing a Lot More with a Lot Less
SANNE A. M. RIJKHOFF

"We're planning on staying here for years, absolutely,"[1] claimed Ammon Bundy on the first day of the occupation of the Malheur National Wildlife Refuge. The Bundy occupation of Malheur National Wildlife Refuge, situated in eastern Oregon, lasted from January 2 until February 11, 2016, and turned out to be the biggest media story of the year in the state. The dramatic politics and standoff surrounding the occupation dominated local, regional, and even national news coverage for weeks. While capturing national attention, the coverage also received much criticism as reporters struggled to find the best language to describe the situation. The descriptive controversy sparked a larger debate about the proper role of the media in such cases, both within Oregon and across the nation. Specifically, the coverage provides an opportunity to better understand the role and importance of local and state media coverage.

In a broad sense, local, state, and national media operate similarly with regard to political matters. The media inform the public on various political developments, election outcomes, and policy decisions, often providing a platform for agendas of politicians and candidates alike. However, subnational politics and media coverage occur on a smaller scale and can be easily ignored. Journalists operate differently, working with limited space, time, and budgets. Over recent decades, state and local media underwent a major transformation, largely driven by large-scale market demands.[2] As a result, newspaper circulation declined, television news became more uniform and lacking in content, and journalists normalized work under the pressure of the 24/7 news cycle—all with fewer resources.

This chapter provides an overview of the unique features of state and local media and what sets them apart from national media. Next, recent changes the media have undergone, and specifically how these affect Oregon's coverage of local and state politics, are discussed. Finally, the Malheur occupation is used as a backdrop to discuss local media coverage and the Oregonian urban-rural divide. The chapter concludes by highlighting the characteristics of local and state media in Oregon.

FEATURES OF STATE AND LOCAL MEDIA

Media are essential links between the people and their government. Without the media, most people would know little if anything about politics, government, and its actors. On the one hand, the media act like a watchdog, keeping governmental power in check. On the other hand, politicians use the media to get their message out, trying to shape public opinion and win electoral support. State and local news is important for state and local politics for the same reasons that make the media important on the national scene. However, local and state media must deal with national structures and influences that affect their coverage and content.

Structural limitations affect local and state television, for instance. This is particularly true for political news, as compared to national news, because local and state coverage lacks quantity, analysis, and depth. In fact, the coverage of local and state politics has been cynically nicknamed "Swiss cheese journalism" because "Swiss cheese has more substance than holes while the reverse is true for the press in their coverage of state government."[3] One feature that works against quality news coverage of state and local politics is the structure of the national news media.[4] Within and across state lines, counties are grouped in so-called designated market areas (DMAs), which form "an exclusive geographic area in which the home market television stations hold a dominance of total hours viewed."[5] DMAs make it particularly difficult to target relevant local news to the appropriate audience. Television stations often reach people in multiple counties, sometimes dozens of them, making comprehensive local coverage impossible. Furthermore, because DMAs and political communities do not necessarily coincide, news coverage is more focused on general topics and soft news (e.g., personal stories and entertainment) and less on important local problems.[6]

Another contributor to the lack of coverage of local and state politics is the "new age" of media.[7] This is a twofold phenomenon, including a national decline of print press and a shift to online resources, combined with the twenty-four-hour, on-demand media. The gap in local coverage due to declining newspaper resources is regularly filled by digital and social media.[8] However, these online sources do not provide different, or even additional information, from what the print and television media already provide. Therefore the focus is typically on crime, traffic, and weather or national politics. In addition, despite the large visitor numbers, one might ask whether these readers receive a lot of information since the average visit to the website lasts only three minutes.[9] It seems that people often merely scan headlines rather than read the entire story.

An additional alternative source for local political news is provided by cable television channels that allow somewhat immediate access to the government. They broadcast or stream, for instance, city council meetings, committee hearings, and court procedures, all without the interference and interpretation of journalists. While this may seem to be a great resource for citizens, the audience for this type of media is usually quite small.

Although the lack of quantity and quality of news differentiates local and state from national media in a negative way, there is another distinction of a more positive nature. According to Gordon Friedman, state politics reporter for the *Oregonian* and formerly for the *Statesman Journal*, relations between journalists and with legislators are relatively good,[10] whereas at the national level there seems to be a more adversarial relationship. Government reporters in Oregon work in the basement of the capitol building, where they are close to unfolding news stories. "Oregon has the spirit of a small state," in which the state capitol is considered to be a public space with relatively easy access to lawmakers.[11] Furthermore, formal communication channels allow the press instant access to the legislature while inside the chambers during sessions. Additional informal channels are also available, as journalists and politicians often exchange private phone numbers and follow each other on social media. Nevertheless, both journalists and public officials remain on their toes, always aware of the potential effects of information on public opinion. As Friedman explains, "When push comes to shove, we need to get good information, as there is a need for accountability and transparency."[12]

THE CHANGING MEDIA MARKET IN OREGON

Over recent decades, media outlets have weathered major changes to their focus, such as a constant demand for news among the public, while resources in time, money, and personnel dwindled. Transitions from traditional media companies to digital-first news were driven by national market demands, pressuring state and local media to follow suit in all aspects—television, newspaper, and radio.[13]

Television

Designated market areas determine a great deal of the content and coverage of local and state television stations. Oregon has four media markets covering Bend, Eugene, Medford-Klamath Falls, and Portland. As shown in table 4.1, some markets include counties in California, Idaho, and Washington, allowing those households to receive news about both Oregon and neighboring states. Additionally, with the state's rural layout, the Portland media market covers the metro area and parts of eastern Oregon. Subsequently, coverage in that market rarely addresses affairs of eastern Oregon (i.e., east of the Cascade Mountain Range).

Furthermore, recent developments have influenced local and state media. Since the 1990s, mass media have been characterized as fragmented—increasing options for people to receive their news that offer more homogenous news coverage but often resulting in more distrust of the media. Deregulation and increased competition of mass media have resulted in an explosion of new television channels, and the power of established media has declined.

Table 4.1. Media markets in Oregon counties

Designated Market Area	Covered Counties (or County Equivalents)	TV Homes, 2016-17	Major Network Affiliates (ABC, CBS, Fox, NBC)
Bend #188 Oregon	Deschutes	67,430	KBNZ-LD (CBS)/KOHD (ABC)[k] KFXO-LD (Fox)/KTVZ (NBC)/KQRE-LP (Telemundo)[f]
Eugene #117 Oregon	Benton, Coos, Douglas, Lane	239,710	KEZI (ABC)[j] KLSR-TV (Fox)/KEVU-CD (MyNetworkTV)[h] KMTR/KMCB/KTCW (NBC)[e] KVAL-TV/KCBY-TV/KPIC (CBS)[a]
Medford– Klamath Falls #139 Oregon	Curry, Jackson, Josephine, Klamath, Lake, Modoc (CA), Siskiyou (CA)	168,710	KDRV/KDKF (ABC)[j] KMVU-DT (Fox)/KFBI-LD (MyNetworkTV)/KMCW-LD (MundoMax)[b] KOBI/KOTI (NBC)[h] KTVL (CBS)[a]
Portland #25 Oregon	Baker, Clackamas, Clark (WA), Clatsop, Columbia, Cowlitz (WA), Crook, Gilliam, Harney, Hood River, Jefferson, Klickitat (WA), Lincoln, Linn, Marion, Multnomah, Polk, Sherman, Skamania (WA), Tillamook, Union, Wahkiakum (WA), Wasco, Washington, Wheeler, Yamhill	1,143,670	KATU (ABC)/KUNP (Univision)[a] KGW (NBC)[d] KOIN (CBS)[h] KPTV (Fox)/KPDX (MyNetworkTV)[i]
Boise #106 Idaho	Ada, Adams, Boise, Camas, Canyon, Elmore, Gem, Grant (OR), Malheur (OR), Owyhee, Payette, Valley, Washington	270,200	KBOI-TV (CBS)/KYUU-LD (CW)[a] KIVI-TV (ABC)[l] KNIN-TV (Fox)[m] KTVB (NBC)[d]
Spokane #73 Washington	Adams, Asotin, Benewah (ID), Bonner (ID), Boundary (ID), Clearwater (ID), Columbia, Ferry, Garfield, Grant, Idaho (ID), Kootenai (ID), Latah (ID), Lewis (ID), Lincoln (MT), Lincoln, Nez Perce (ID), Okanogan, Pend Oreille, Shoshone (ID), Spokane, Stevens, Wallowa (OR), Whitman	422,550	KAYU-TV (Fox)[b] KHQ-TV (NBC)[g] KLEW-TV (CBS)[a] KREM (CBS)/KSKN (CW)[d] KXLY-TV (ABC)/KXMN-LD (MeTV)[c]
Yakima– Pasco– Richland– Kennewick #122 Washington	Benton, Franklin, Kittitas, Morrow (OR), Umatilla (OR), Walla Walla, Yakima	230,950	KAPP (ABC)/KVEW (ABC)[c] KEPR-TV (CBS)/KVVK-CA/ KORX-CA (Univision)/KIMA-TV (CBS)/KUNW-CA (Univision)[a] KCYU-LD (Fox)/KFFX-TV (Fox)[b] KNDO (NBC)/KNDU (NBC)[g]

Note: Superscript letters indicate that television stations share the same owner company: a, Sinclair Broadcast Group; b, Northwest Broadcasting; c, Morgan Murphy Media; d, Tegna Media; e, Roberts Media; f, News-Press and Gazette Company; g, Cowles Company; h, California Oregon Broadcasting, Inc.; i, Meredith Corporation; j, Heartland Media; k, Zolo Media; l, E. W. Scripps Company; m, Raycom Media; n, Nexstar Media.

The designated market area number indicates the nationwide ranking of the markets by size (e.g., #25 Portland is nationally ranked number 25 based on the number of television homes the market includes.

Source: "Nielsen Local Television Market Universe Estimates," Nielsen, effective September 24, 2016, http://www.nielsen.com/content/dam/corporate/us/en/docs/solutions/measurement/television/2016-2017-nielsen-local-dma-ranks.pdf

Table 4.2. Major newspapers in Oregon in order of frequency of publication

	Oregonian	Register-Guard	Statesman Journal	Bend Bulletin	Portland Tribune
Type	Daily newspaper	Daily newspaper	Daily newspaper	Daily newspaper	Semi-weekly newspaper
Format	Tabloid	Broadsheet	Broadsheet	Broadsheet	Broadsheet
Established	1850	1867	1851	1903	2001
Owner	Newhouse Newspaper/Advance Publications	GateHouse Media	Gannett Company, Inc.	Western Communications, Inc.	Pamplin Media Group
Area	Oregon	Eugene	Mid-Willamette Valley	Bend	Portland/Oregon
Circulation	247,833	53,812	36,946	31,796	30,000

	Willamette Week	Salem Weekly	Eugene Weekly	Portland Mercury	Capital Press	Clackamas Review
Type	Alternative Weekly, city guide	Alternative twice a month, city guide	Alternative Weekly, city guide	Alternative weekly, city guide	Weekly agriculture paper	Weekly newspaper
Format	Tabloid	Tabloid	Tabloid	Tabloid	Broadsheet	Broadsheet
Established	1974	2005	1982	2000	1928	1916
Owner	City of Roses Newspapers	A. P. Walther	Anita Johnson	Index Newspapers, LLC	East Oregonian Publishing Company	Pamplin Media Group
Area	Portland Metro	Salem and surrounding Willamette Valley	Eugene	Portland	California, Idaho, Oregon, Washington	Clackamas
Circulation	80,000	80,000	40,000	35,899	35,582	33,300

Note: Circulation numbers are not publicly available. The numbers from the *MondoTimes* are estimates and change frequently. While in general circulation is declining, some papers may show more fluctuation, including increasing circulation. For instance, the estimate for the Oregonian in 2016 is higher than it was in 2012, as reported in William Mackenzie, "The Long, Slow, Agonizing Death of the Oregonian," Thinking Oregon, January 7, 2016, https://thinkingoregon.org/2016/01/07/the-long-slow-agonizing-death-of-the-oregonian/.
Source: "Biggest Oregon Newspapers," MondoTimes, accessed April 24, 2018, http://www.mondotimes.com/newspapers/usa/oregon-newspaper-circulation.html.

The nationalization of news media, and particularly the 1996 Telecommunications Act, made it much easier for cross-ownership of media outlets. Similarly, it removed the limit on how many local television stations any corporation could own, and expanded the limit on reachable audience areas. The act was presented as fostering competition, but it ultimately resulted in the subsequent mergers of several large companies. Nationwide, Sinclair Broadcasting, one of the major companies in Oregon, owns or provides service to 167 stations in 77 media markets, reaching almost 40 percent of the US population.[14] Local television stations are thus increasingly owned by corporations that do not prioritize local news and events.

Oregon is not immune to these trends. In 2013, 290 local television stations changed owners. In comparison, only 95 stations were sold in 2012. Although many of these stations already worked together by sharing resources, such as helicopters, one corporation now wields sole ownership. Table 4.1 includes all Oregon television channels, and shows that the same company owns many of them, even though they are affiliated with different networks. Now stations routinely share news content, so that about a quarter of all stations do not produce any news on their own. In addition, local television stations share news content with other media types, including radio stations and newspapers.[15] News coverage has consequently become more uniform.

Sharing resources, but more so mergers of stations, has led to fewer media employees. For example, in Eugene, local television station KMTR (an NBC affiliate) fired thirty-one people after their station was bought by a new owner and was merged with the local CBS affiliate, KVAL.

Newspapers

The largest newspaper in Oregon, the *Oregonian*, has gone through a similar transformation. At the zenith of its newspaper readership, the *Oregonian* was economically stable, promised its reporters lifetime jobs, and paid them well. Since then, major changes have occurred, with some noting that "It's tough to find a place with more news change than Portland, Oregon."[16] For instance, circulation decreased with the daily edition, from 360,000 readers in the late 1990s to 228,599 in 2012.[17] In addition, the corporate owner of the *Oregonian*, Advance Publications, began a major reorganization in 2009 and pushed for a "digital-first" approach to publication. Instead of focusing on print news, resources and time were put into the paper's website. This is in line with a fragmented media environment, where a constant demand for information fuels a rush for the news and print media to beat the Internet for news scoops. The online version of the paper, *OregonLive*, appears successful, as it receives widespread attention, generating an average of about ten million unique visitors a month.[18]

In 2013, the *Oregonian* announced that it would take additional steps in the digital direction by reducing home delivery to four days per week and issuing newsstand editions only on the days it does not deliver. Therefore, while they still provide a seven-day print edition, subscribers do not receive them daily. These changes are apparent in the content of the paper. Full-day editions are provided on Wednesday, Friday, and Sunday, while Monday, Tuesday, and Thursday prints are much shorter. Furthermore, the Saturday edition is now mainly a bonus issue filled with sports, advertisements, and little political content.

Consequently, there were cuts in staff, including many in the newsrooms, with about a sixth of staffers losing their jobs.[19] Where during the 1990s there were approximately four hundred journalists at the *Oregonian*, it is now down to about one hundred and sixty, who also work for lower pay. The new editor, Mark Katches (former editorial director of the Center of Investigative Reporting), who started in 2014, planned to "be aggressive about breaking news and watchdog reporting . . . we're going to figure out more cool, creative ways to engage with readers on topics they care most about."[20] Responding, some reporters noted his approach as meaningful. For example, Jeff Mapes, a well-established journalist in Oregon, states that "In a way they [Oregonian Media Group] tried to change the field by doing what others had not tried."[21] Table 4.2 provides background information for the *Oregonian* and the ten other newspapers and alternative print media with the largest current circulation in Oregon.

The declining dominance of the *Oregonian* has influenced the news field in Portland and the rest of Oregon, as they gave way to the growth of other news organizations. For instance, a new group of newspapers, labeled "the alternative press," emerged. These newspapers, such as the *Portland Tribune*, tend to focus narrowly on issues of interest to people representing minority political cultures, or people with distinctive lifestyles and cultural tastes.[22] Despite the lack of resources, they continue to grow, doubling their print frequency in 2014 by adding a Tuesday edition to their lone Thursday one. Moreover, they added new and expanded features for their readers by providing more regional news and expanding their local community editions to a total of twenty-five.[23] According to Mapes, they "perform satisfactorily in their news and political coverage."[24] Likewise, the *Willamette Week* (*WW*), printed weekly, expanded its mobile presence and now provides print and digital city-guide editions. Circulation of the print edition has increased, and content offering has diversified, especially through Internet blogs. The *WW* also regularly publishes report cards of metro-area legislators called the "Good, Bad & Awful Survey," which receives attention among political insiders.[25]

Radio

Oregon radio also underwent changes as a result of the Telecommunications Act of 1996 and the decline of the *Oregonian*. Although the number of commercial radio stations remained relatively stable in the Portland area between 1996 and 2011, variety in ownership declined.[26] This led to a vast reduction of employees per station and a shift in content. News coverage and programming on commercial radio stations declined and focused mainly on national news instead of local events. Instead, Portland-area radio listeners shifted in large numbers to Oregon Public Broadcasting (OPB) a radio and digital news operation, and local affiliate of National Public Radio (NPR).[27]

OPB's audience is particularly strong in Portland, as compared to the rural areas of Oregon. This occurs despite its broader coverage of statewide and local news, as it is the only full-time, all-news AM radio station.[28] Recently, OPB has made some significant changes in their reporting. They cover more topics, including breaking news, and provide coverage on a 24/7 basis. In a sense, "OPB is no longer just a radio or television station, but a complete media organization that just works a bit differently."[29] For instance, the major news story in 2016, the Malheur National Wildlife Refuge occupation, was especially important for OPB and its future. Mapes explains that it was a milestone because "it made OPB think about what kind of coverage they should have."[30] Responding to the reconceptualized coverage, the podcast *Politics Now* was started to provide more in-depth coverage and has seen great success.[31] OPB plans to introduce more political podcasts to attract younger listeners who prefer to consume these combinations of social media and news.[32]

Commercial radio in Oregon is also still popular. The *Lars Larson Show* on KXL Radio, for instance, is a show on a commercial station that receives rather high ratings. Although politically conservative, the host prefers to take calls from listeners who disagree with him in order to spark a debate where both sides can weigh in. This desire for balanced news characterizes much of the Oregon audience, as reflected by comments of Steve Dunn, anchor for KATU in Portland since 1986: "Oregonians want in-depth coverage of politics. People want to see both sides of the story; they want to hear it all."[33]

MEDIA COVERAGE OF POLITICS IN OREGON
Television

Present-day coverage of general and political news is less professional, more partisan, and more tabloid-oriented in comparison to previous decades. As mentioned, the nationalization of news broadcasting brought uniformity and deemphasized politics, especially at the local stations. Most television stations use the same broadcast structure for local news: "mayhem at the top, teasable soft features at the end, and the rest of the day's news in the middle."[34] The news in the middle is therefore often overlooked and overshadowed by crime, accidents, and other more exciting news. Civic news such as politics and government, and other social issues, is broadcast, on average, after the sixth story. In addition, about 73 percent of all stories on government policy last less than a minute, and 39 percent are less than thirty seconds long.[35] Topics involving state and local government are difficult to cover, largely because there are many nuances and technicalities, and these stories cover a wide range of public policies. In addition, most coverage on politics is not visually compelling. With television providing about sixty seconds of coverage of public affairs, these stories do not receive sufficient time to be discussed properly, and politicians often dictate the spin of a story as they provide the "facts" necessary for journalists.[36]

These national trends are also visible in Oregon. A content analysis of late-night local television news broadcasts in the Portland media market in 2005 shows the lack of hard news coverage.[37] The study showed that typical newscasts were dominated by soft news, or "infotainment," as 82 percent of the content entertained rather than informed and educated the viewer. Consequently, the author of the study, Carey Lynne Higgins, claimed that "the Portland late night newscasts do not provide its civic-minded citizens with adequate socially responsible information."[38]

Notwithstanding the shortcomings of local and state media regarding political coverage, journalists argue that their contributions are indispensable, and particularly so in Oregon: "Oregonians stand out from others in their desire for in depth coverage of politics."[37] "People pay more attention than you might think. They read the stories and our work does have an impact, perhaps less than 20 years ago, but it really has an impact."[38] Moreover, interest in local news is growing. Studies by the Pew Research Center showed that throughout the country, 72 percent (in 2012) and 78 percent (in 2016) of adults follow local news closely, making use of newspapers as well as other sources.[39] Yet the top source of local news for most people is still television. Even in this age of the Internet, Americans receive their news from local television news broadcasts more than from any other sources.[40]

Attention for political matters peaks during various local, state, and national elections. Although the actual news broadcast may not spend sufficient time on the elections, candidates running for office primarily target local television news to place their campaign ads. For example, over a third of presidential campaign advertising in the 2008 election appeared during local news commercial breaks. Even during midterm elections, campaigns placed over 40 percent of all their advertisements on local television news broadcasts.[41] Candidates thus view the local news broadcast as their prime mechanism for informing voters. Gubernatorial races rely greatly on paid advertising, while candidates for the state legislature place significant importance on direct contact with the voters, although even in these races campaign advertisements are becoming increasingly important.[42]

Beyond news broadcasts, candidates have other local resources to reach citizens. Oregon television stations, for instance, have their local version of political programming such as *Your Voice Your Vote* on the KATU channel (associated with ABC) and *Straight Talk* on the KGW channel (associated with NBC), which cover local political issues with public officials, members of the community, and local experts. In addition to these weekly programs, candidates for the gubernatorial elections are invited to participate in locally televised debates. These programs are popular in Oregon and exemplify the interest among Oregonians for in-depth coverage of politics. During the election cycle of 2016, ratings increased with more people tuning in than before.[43]

Outside of elections, local- and state-level politicians do not necessarily rely on the news media as much. At the local level, physical proximity makes it easy for public officials to stay in touch with each other about their work, reducing the need for formal press conferences. When politicians do reach out to the media, they often control the story owing to the technical and difficult nature of state and local politics. In a way, political officials become unchallenged agenda-setters through the media.[44]

The status of state and local television coverage of politics is not insignificant, however. Despite a lack of detail, political information is still provided, and, as mentioned, television news attracts the largest audience among media outlets. Many of these viewers are low-information citizens (i.e., they are poorly informed on political issues). Therefore local television news broadcasts are potentially powerful providers of content to citizens who otherwise might not gain any information at all.

Newspapers

Political coverage remains important for print media, but reporters are limited in resources and time, and must decide quickly what is most important, most relevant, and most relatable to their audience. While the *Statesman Journal* used to be the relied-upon paper for Oregon politics, they now split the duties with other papers. With only one government reporter left for the *Statesman Journal*, there are simply too many political topics to cover thoroughly. Many other journalists, including radio and television reporters, share this sentiment. Even so, the press corps in the state capitol of Salem is respectable and diligent in providing in-depth coverage of state and local politics. Reporters are conveniently stationed inside the capitol building and thus have direct access to the government.

During elections, most newspapers—or, more accurately, their editorial boards—publish endorsements for state and local candidates. Newspaper endorsements are more important at the state and local levels, as compared to the national level, because voters are less familiar with most candidates for state and local offices. For many voters, these endorsements provide guidance, mainly through name recognition, so that when voters receive their election pamphlet, they may remember reading the endorsement of the candidate.

For instance, the *Oregonian* endorsed twenty-two candidates in the 2000 elections, and twenty-one of their endorsed candidates ultimately won the race.[45] This does not necessarily indicate that readers base their vote on endorsements, especially since the *Oregonian* typically supports incumbents. While the *Oregonian* is traditionally viewed as a conservative-leaning newspaper, in 2004, the editorial board endorsed, for only the second time since its founding, a Democratic presidential candidate. In recent elections, the *Oregonian* has stopped endorsing presidential candidates altogether. The editorial board argued that the goal of the newspaper is to have an impact in the community and that their endorsement for president would not make a difference in the outcome for Oregon. "We zeroed in on those races and issues where an endorsement could provide a trusted voice through the din and help readers make tough choices on issues that matter most to our state."[46] Other large newspapers in Oregon publish endorsements for national, state, and local elections.

In addition to endorsements for political candidates, some newspapers also provide guidance for ballot measures and initiatives. These are arguably the most impactful of all endorsements, because they involve complex issues and decisions, and voters often cannot rely on clear partisan clues. Yet it is becoming more common to

Table 4.3. Endorsements by newspapers on statewide ballot measures, 2016

Measure Number: Topic	Vote Result	Oregonian	Register-Guard	Statesman Journal	Bend Bulletin	Willamette Week
94: Repeal mandatory retirement age of 75 for state judges	No	Yes	Yes	–	Yes	Yes
95: Allow public universities to invest in equities	Yes	Yes*	Yes*	–	Yes*	Yes*
96: Provide 1.5 percent of lottery funds for veterans' services	Yes	No	Yes*	Yes*	No	Yes*
97: Tax businesses with sales exceeding $25 million	No	No*	No*	No*	No*	No*
98: Require funding to address dropout prevention, career readiness	Yes	Yes*	Yes*	–	Yes*	No
99: Divert lottery money to fund outdoor school	Yes	No	No	–	No	Yes*
100: Prohibit sales of twelve endangered species and related products	Yes	Yes*	Yes*	–	No	Yes*

Note: Endorsements with an asterisk (*) indicate the same judgement as the election result. The endorsements of the *Statesman Journal* are missing owing to limited accessibility for their online archive.

Sources: "The Oregonian/OregonLive Editorial Endorsements 2016," Oregonian/OregonLive, updated November 8, 2016, http://www.oregonlive.com/opinion/index.ssf/2016/10/the_oregonianoregonlive_editor_2.html; "Summary of Recommendations," Register-Guard, October 31, 2016, http://registerguard.com/rg/opinion/34935023-78/election-2016-summary-of-the-register-guard-recommendations.html.csp; "Statesman Journal Endorsements for the 2016 General Election," updated October 22, 2016, http://www.statesmanjournal.com/story/opinion/editorials/2016/10/07/statesman-journal-endorsements-2016-general-election/91734882/; "The Bulletin's Endorsements," October 23, 2016, http://www.bendbulletin.com/opinion/editorials/4732295-151/the-bulletins-endorsements?referrer=fpblob; "WW's Fall 2016 Endorsements: State Measures," Willamette Week, updated November 8, 2016, http://www.wweek.com/news/2016/10/12/wws-november-2016-endorsements-state-measures/

see widespread media campaigns for high-profile measures aiming to influence voters. Accordingly, as shown in table 4.3, voters do not always follow the endorsements from newspapers' editorial boards.

IMPACT OF URBAN-RURAL DIVIDE ON MEDIA COVERAGE IN OREGON

A major factor of change for decades in Oregon is the increasing urban-rural divide. Since the 1980s, the differences between Oregon's urban west and rural east have become more apparent and increasingly important. This resulted in a different media landscape in the "two Oregons."[47] Not only do people in rural communities have fewer news sources (e.g., you cannot get a print copy of the *Oregonian* in eastern Oregon), but there is also a discrepancy in relevant coverage.

Most of the state's population lives along the I-5 corridor, and thus most of the news, especially local television news, is focused on this region. As a result, the news coming from the larger Portland area does not reflect the interests of rural people per se.[48] While a homicide in Gresham, a Portland suburb, for instance, may not affect people in Burns, it is still covered with headlines in the news. The limited resources and staff available for news organizations also affect the divide in news coverage. As a local general assignment reporter for television news in Portland puts it:

> We only have about five to seven reporters throughout the day and perhaps 11 or 13 per 24 hours thus we always have to pick between news stories. It is my job to go in there every day, be as unbiased as I can be and tell people both sides to a story. I want to give local viewers a voice and I enjoy going to the smaller communities so they can tell us their stories. Because we are based in Portland, it is fairly rare that reporters travel about two hours to the east side of the state to cover news, unless it is really important. People always want to know what is happening in their community and I have empathy for people who feel under represented.[49]

Despite these problems, Oregonians across the state stand out in their interest in political news.[50] Oregonians want to see, hear, and read both sides of a story, and they want to receive nonpartisan coverage. The Internet and social media can do a lot to fill any gaps that may exist in this coverage, as "both can be a big transition belt for information, providing a source of information."[51] Consequently, news from rural Oregon is often first published online and shared through platforms such as Facebook.

OREGON'S MAIN NEWS STORY OF 2016

Between January 2 and February 11, 2016,[52] the Malheur National Wildlife Refuge in eastern Oregon experienced mass media attention because of an occupation. Ammon Bundy and his fellow occupiers were initially energized by convictions in federal court of the local Hammond family, who had stood trial for backlighting fires on their ranch in 2006 to protect their cattle's winter feed supplies from a growing lightning-caused wildfire on adjacent Bureau of Land Management (BLM) property. The Hammond case also involved several allegedly illegal fires set on BLM property in 2001 that were designed to cover up hunting violations by one of the Hammonds. However, the occupation quickly shifted focus to the broader cause of the group: the transfer of control over western US public lands to residents. What started with a peaceful protest of more than three hundred people on January 1 in the nearby city of Burns ultimately resulted in a forty-one-day armed occupation, one fatality, twenty-seven federal indictments, and $6 million in damages.

Events like the Bundy occupation are particularly difficult to cover, and reporters try to stay as objective as possible, knowing that their words may influence public opinion and elicit reactions from government officials. This is often a uncoordinated effort, as local reporters in this case do not recall an official meeting or discussion in the newsroom or among colleagues.

> I do not know how or when we came to call them a militia or occupiers, it just kind of happened . . . but we are always very careful.[53]
>
> Personally, my stories went between militants, occupiers and protesters . . . I know that there was a conversation about it on Twitter but I did not talk to other reporters about it.[54]
>
> I recall some discussion among the crew on how the group should be described and I think we settled on armed stand-off . . . we also focused on the group itself and how they would like to be called.[55]

In addition to daily updates, KATU (the local ABC affiliate) broadcast a special edition of *Your Voice, Your Vote* three weeks into the occupation.

Although Oregon's local and state media mostly cover I-5 corridor news, the major story of 2016 arose in the rural east. The occupation received a lot of attention from local, state, and national media alike. Most of the coverage focused on the day-to-day developments of the occupation, but the content was increasingly scrutinized and eventually became its own story. Some complaints from viewers, listeners, and readers appeared in letters to the editor[56] and opinion articles in newspapers, with some critics expressing concerns over a potential racial bias in the media coverage or even a racial double standard. These critics argued that the news coverage would have had a different, more judgmental and aggressive tone if the occupiers were black, Hispanic, or anything other than white. Some international responses mirrored this sentiment and used the case to point out lasting issues of race and terrorism in the United States.[57] Others, including *The Late Show* host Stephen Colbert, mocked the situation,[58] and some users on social media ridiculed the occupation by including tags of #YallQaeda, #VanillaISIS, #YeeHawd, and #Talibundy in their tweets.[59]

This example demonstrates that understanding the communities and context from which news develops is vital for appropriate media coverage. For that reason, people are more likely to talk to local journalists as they write and publish stories based on the needs and preferences of their own audience.[60] This is especially important in times of crisis, such as during the Malheur National Wildlife Refuge occupation.

CONCLUSION

In recent decades, American media has been transformed, altering local and state media as well. In addition to obvious changes and developments in all modes of media, including radio, television, and the Internet, there have been philosophical changes, too.[61] Since the 1830s, low printing costs made newspapers a commercial item. While more people were exposed to the news, the content often included exaggerations and poorly researched information, known as "yellow journalism." A shift to a focus on truth, justice, fairness, and objectivity in news took place around the 1940s, with improved training and professionalization for journalists. During the 1970s and 1980s, the field changed again as journalists began to go beyond reporting by also providing their own interpretation of the news. Stories were contextualized within a set of facts that reporters deemed important. Furthermore, the appearance and inclusion of political pundits became standard in coverage of politics and political events.

Since the 1990s, mass media are characterized as fragmented offerings, with increased options for people to receive their news. Deregulation and increased competition of mass media resulted in an explosion of new television channels, both national and local, but ownership rests in the hands of a few companies that do not prioritize local news and events. Furthermore, declining circulation and financial limitations have forced many newspapers to merge or to cut staff, leaving journalists struggling to cover the same information with fewer resources. Nationalization of news broadcasting brought uniformity and deemphasized politics, particularly at the local stations.

These developments make it more difficult for the media to fulfill the demands of the public, which are now not only instant, but also constant. The coverage of the Malheur National Wildlife Refuge occupation is an example of the challenging conditions that local and state media face. People no longer wait for the news broadcast or the daily newspaper, instead preferring to access news instantly. Breaking news is often published online first, and people browse for the latest headlines. Journalists are thus trying to do a lot more with a lot less time, manpower, and other resources.

As a result, news reports come with a ready-made interpretation, easy-to-remember soundbites, and attractive headlines. Television news often lacks detail and is increasingly homogenous. News organizations focus increasingly on soft news in an attempt to attract the largest audience. There is not only a shift in the way journalists cover the news, but also the characteristics that made events newsworthy have changed as well. Policy issues are no longer the major topics of interest. Increasingly, reporters focus on the personal lives of politicians and candidates.[62]

Despite these shortcomings, there is still a positive picture to present. For decades, local media in Oregon has been characterized by a high demand for in-depth political coverage.[63] Local television stations meet this demand through public affairs programs airing on Sunday mornings. Newspapers, although reduced in circulation, publish investigative stories, and there is a rigorous press corps in Salem with close and quick access to information, politicians, and interest groups. Finally, as a radio and digital news operation, Oregon Public Broadcasting remains popular and offers news on more topics than they used to do, including breaking news and coverage on a 24/7 basis.

It is not clear what the philosophy, role, and influence of the media will be in the coming decades. What is certain is that the media remain a key source of political information and continue to be an important mediator between the people and public officials.

Notes

1   Les Zaitz, "Militia Takes over Malheur National Wildlife Refuge Headquarters," *Oregonian / OregonLive*, January 2, 2016, http://www.oregonlive.com/pacific-northwest-news/index.ssf/2016/01/drama_in_burns_ends_with_quiet.html.

2   Sanne A. M. Rijkhoff and Jim Camden, "The Washington Press and Politics: News Coverage in Changing Times," in *Governing the Evergreen State: Political Life in the Evergreen State*, ed. Cornell W. Clayton, Todd Donovan, and Nicholas P. Lovrich (Pullman: Washington State University Press, 2018).

3   Doris A. Graber, "Swiss Cheese Journalism," *State Government News* 36 (1993): 19-21.

4   Tari Renner and Patrick G. Lynch, "A Little Knowledge Is a Dangerous Thing: What We Know about the Role of the Media in State Politics," in *Media Power Media Politics*, ed. Mark J. Rozell and Jeremy D. Mayer (Lanham, MA: Rowman & Littlefield, 2008), 137-57.

5   "Local Television Market Universe," Nielsen, accessed January 10, 2017, http://www.nielsen.com/content/dam/corporate/us/en/docs/solutions/measurement/television/2016-2017-nielsen-local-dma-ranks.pdf.

6   Doris A. Graber and Johanna L. Dunaway, *Mass Media and American Politics* (Thousand Oaks, CA: CQ Press, 2015).

7   For an excellent overview of the history of media in Oregon, see Russ Dondero, William Lunch, and Jim Moore, "Media," in *Oregon Politics and Government: Progressive versus Conservative Populists*, ed. Richard A. Clucas, Mark Henkels, and Brent Steel (Lincoln: University of Nebraska Press, 2005), 99-114. For a historical overview of media in a national context, I recommend Darrell M. West, *The Rise and Fall of the Media Establishment* (Boston: St. Martin's Press, 2001).

8   Jeffrey Gottfried and Elisa Shearer, "News Use across Social Media Platforms 2016," *Pew Research Center*, May 26, 2016, http://www.journalism.org/2016/05/26/news-use-across-social-media-platforms-2016/.

9   William Mackenzie, "The Long, Slow, Agonizing Death of the Oregonian," *Thinking Oregon*, January 7, 2016, https://thinkingoregon.org/2016/01/07/the-long-slow-agonizing-death-of-the-oregonian/.

10 Gordon Friedman, in discussion with the author, November 29, 2016. Friedman was named 2015 Rookie of the Year by the Oregon Territory Chapter of the Society of Professional Journalists. The quotes are used with permission of Gordon Friedman.

11 Gordon Friedman, November 29, 2016.

12 Gordon Friedman, November 29, 2016.

13 Rijkhoff and Camden, "Washington Press and Politics."

14 Amy Mitchell, "State of the News Media 2014," Pew Research Center, March 26, 2014, http://www.journalism.org/2014/03/26/state-of-the-news-media-2014-overview/.

15 Deborah Potter and Katerina Eva Matsa, "Impact of Shared News Production on Local TV Viewers," Pew Research Center, March 26, 2014, http://www.journalism.org/2014/03/26/impact-of-shared-news-production-on-local-tv-viewers/; Deborah Potter and Katerina Eva Matsa, "Local News Services," Pew Research Center, March 26, 2014, http://www.journalism.org/2014/03/26/local-news-services/.

16 Ken Doctor, "The Newsonomics of Advance's Advancing Strategy and its Achilles' Heel," *NiemanLab*, June 27, 2013, http://www.niemanlab.org/2013/06/the-newsonomics-of-advances-advancing-strategy-and-its-achilles-heel/.

17 Mackenzie, "Long, Slow, Agonizing Death."

18 "John Maher Named President of Oregonian Media Group," *Oregonian / OregonLive*, August 4, 2016, http://www.oregonlive.com/editors/index.ssf/2016/08/john_maher_named_president_of.html.

19 Ken Doctor, "The Newsonomics of the *Oregonian*'s New Editor's Challenge," *NiemanLab*, July 3, 2014, http://www.niemanlab.org/2014/07/the-newsonomics-of-the-oregonians-new-editors-challenge/.

20 Doctor, "Newsonomics of the *Oregonian*'s."

21 Jeff Mapes in discussion with the author, November 30, 2016. Mapes is a senior political reporter at Oregon Public Broadcasting. Previously, he covered state and national politics for the *Oregonian* for nearly thirty-two years. The quotes are used with permission of Jeff Mapes.

22 Doris A. Graber, *Mass Media and American Politics* (Thousand Oaks, CA: CQ Press, 1997), 315.

23 "Look for Your New Tribune on Tuesdays," *Portland Tribune*, February 13, 2014, http://portlandtribune.com/pt/9-news/210594-68351-look-for-your-new-tribune-on-tuesdays.

24 Jeff Mapes, November 30, 2016.

25 Dondero et al., "Media."

26 Rebecca Webb, "Diminished Democracy? Portland Radio News / Public Affairs after the Telecom Act of 1996" (master's thesis, Portland State University, 2011).

27 Webb, "Diminished Democracy?," 68.

28 Doctor, "Newsonomics of the *Oregonian*'s."

29 Jeff Mapes, November 30, 2016.

30 Jeff Mapes, November 30, 2016.

31 The podcast is available on the website of Oregon Public Broadcasting, accessed April 5, 2018, http://www.opb.org/news/series/election-2016/tag/Politics%20Now%20Podcast/.

32 Jeff Mapes, November 30, 2016.

33 Steve Dunn in discussion with the author, December 8, 2016. Dunn is the anchor at
    KATU, an ABC affiliate in Portland since 1986. He won several Associated Press Awards
    and won the Emmy Award for the Top News Anchor in the Northwest in 2004, 2012,
    2014, and 2016. The quotes are used with permission of Steve Dunn.

34 Tom Rosenstiel et al., *We Interrupt This Newscast: How to Improve Local News and Win
    Ratings Too* (New York: Cambridge University Press, 2007).

35 Rosenstiel et al., *We Interrupt This Newscast*, 34-35.

36 Renner and Lynch, "A Little Knowledge Is a Dangerous Thing."

37 Higgins, "Does the 'News' Come First?," 93.

38 Gordon Friedman, November 29, 2016.

39 Carolyn Miller, Kristen Purcell, and Tom Rosenstiel, "72% of Americans Follow Local
    News Closely," Pew Research Center, April 12, 2012, http://www.pewinternet.
    org/2012/04/12/72-of-americans-follow-local-news-closely/; Amy Mitchell, Jeffrey
    Gottfied, Michael Barthel, and Elisa Shearer, "The Modern News Consumer: News
    Attitudes and Practices in the Digital Era," Pew Research Center, July 7, 2016, http://
    www.journalism.org/2016/07/07/the-modern-news-consumer/.

40 Mitchell et al., "Modern News Consumer."

41 Erika, F. Fowler, "Making the News: Is Local Television News Coverage Really that Bad?,"
    In *New Directions in Media and Politics*, ed. Travis N. Ridout (New York: Routledge,
    2013).

42 Renner and Lynch, "A Little Knowledge Is a Dangerous Thing."

43 Steve Dunn, December 8, 2016.

44 Graber, *Mass Media and American Politics*.

45 Dondero et al., "Media."

46 Laura Gunderson, "Editorial Endorsements 2016: A Note from the Editor,"
    Oregonian / OregonLive, September 28, 2016, http://www.oregonlive.com/opinion/
    index.ssf/2016/09/the_oregonianoregonlive_editor_1.html.

47 Jeff Mapes, November 30, 2016..

48 Jeff Mapes, November 30, 2016.

49 A general assignment reporter for a local television station in Portland, Oregon, in
    discussion with the author, December 8, 2016. The reporter gave permission to use
    quotes from the conversation; however, the reporter requested to remain anonymous.

50 Steve Dunn, December 8, 2016.

51 Jeff Mapes, November 30, 2016.

52 For a more complete overview, see reports by Oregon Public Broadcasting (e.g., "An
    Occupation in Rural Oregon," *Oregon Public Broadcasting*, accessed May 23, 2018,
    https://www.opb.org/news/series/burns-oregon-standoff-bundy-militia-news-
    updates/) and by OregonLive (e.g., "Oregon Standoff Timeline: How the Occupation
    Unfolded," *Oregonian / OregonLive*, March 8, 2016, http://www.oregonlive.com/oregon-
    standoff/2016/03/oregon_standoff_timeline_how_t.html).

53 Steve Dunn, December 8, 2016.

54 Gordon Friedman, November 29, 2016.

55 Jeff Mapes, November 30, 2016.

56 "Ranchers' Concerns and the Oregon Refuge Takeover," *Washington Post*, January 20,
    2016, https://www.washingtonpost.com/opinions/ranchers-concerns-and-the-oregon-
    refuge-takeover/2016/01/20/1722d508-be0c-11e5-98c8-7fab78677d51_story.
    html?utm_term=.c2a23fb702ab.

57   Cecily Hilleary, "World Media Frame Oregon Standoff in Terms of Race, Terrorism," *Voa News*, January 5, 2016, http://www.voanews.com/a/world-media-frame-oregon-standoff-in-terms-of-race-terrorism/3132356.html.

58   Ken Meyer, "Colbert Mocks Bundy Militia's Begging for Supplies to Sustain "Revolution," *Mediate*, January 13, 2016, http://www.mediaite.com/tv/colbert-mocks-bundy-militias-begging-for-supplies-to-sustain-revolution/.

59   Harrison Jacobs, "People Are Mocking the Oregon 'Militia' on Social Media by Calling Them 'YallQaeda' and 'VanillaISIS,'" *Business Insider*, January 3, 2016, http://www.businessinsider.com/social-media-mocking-oregon-militia-by-calling-them-yallqaeda-and-vanillaisis-2016-1.

60   Graber, *Mass Media and American Politics*.

61   Darrell M. West, *The Rise and Fall of the Media Establishment* (Boston: St. Martin's Press, 2001).

62   West, *Rise and Fall of the Media Establishment*, 69.

63   Steve Dunn, December 8, 2016.

II

Government Institutions

5

Changing Partisanship, People, and Pressures in the Legislature

RICHARD A. CLUCAS

Budget battles are routine in state politics, but the problem confronting the Oregon Legislative Assembly at the start of the new millennium was especially daunting. When the 2003 session was called to order on January 13, the legislators had to decide how to balance the biennial state budget after struggling through five special sessions in 2002 seeking a solution.

The legislative assembly had adopted a $12 billion budget in July 2001 for the 2001-3 biennium. But the nation's economy had begun to descend into a severe recession before the session had even adjourned. Triggered by the crash of the high-tech industry, the recession caused state revenue to fall precipitously, forcing the governor and the legislature to find ways to fill the gap. In percentage terms, the decline in revenue was the largest the state had experienced since the Great Depression. By September 2002, the projected revenue shortfall had reached $1.7 billion.[1]

By cutting spending, borrowing money, and taking other steps, the legislature came close to balancing its budget by the end of the fifth special session. But it had reached a point where it felt it could cut no more. As part of a package to make ends meet, the legislature agreed to put a referendum before voters in January 2003 to provide for a three-year temporary income tax increase, raising the highest personal income tax bracket to 9.5 percent and slightly increasing the corporate income tax. When voters rejected the legislature's proposal (Measure 28), the legislature once again needed to find a way to fill the gap in the 2001-3 budget. But it now also faced the difficult task of balancing the 2003-5 budget with revenues continuing to stagnate.[2]

The real challenge confronting the legislature was not simply the decline in revenue. The challenge was also in the state's culture, politics, and tax laws. Despite its reputation as a progressive liberal state, Oregon's culture is much more complex than this image suggests. There is a conservative side to the state's culture, one that has especially strong roots in small towns and rural areas. While voters in Portland and other liberal parts of Oregon may support an active government, many Oregonians believe in small government and limited taxes. During the 1990s and early 2000s, the divide between these two ideologies was one of the defining characteristics of the state's politics, making governing difficult.

The challenge created by the state's tax laws was from the lack of a state sales tax, the recent passage of two property tax limitation measures (Measure 5 in 1990 and Measure 50 in 1997), and the existence of Oregon's unique kicker law, which requires the legislature to return taxpayer funds when income tax revenues exceed projections. The lack of a sales tax meant the state was almost solely dependent on volatile income tax revenue to pay its bills and fill the funding gap. The passage of the two tax limitation measures had placed a greater burden on the state's budget, requiring the legislature to channel billions in funds to local schools.[3] The kicker law had made it difficult for the state to build a reserve fund. During the 1990s, a strong economy enabled the legislature to increase state spending, but when the recession hit in 2001, these components of the state's tax law made it especially challenging for the state to raise sufficient revenue to pay for desired programs and to balance the budget.

When voters rejected Measure 28 in 2003 and the legislature was then forced to fill another $800 million gap in the state's budget, battle lines were drawn between the different sides. With the Republican Party in control of the legislature and a Democrat in the governor's office, the government was divided not only by party but also by the ideological split in the state. Finding a resolution when the politics was so divided and the options so restricted was difficult.[4] The result was an acrimonious battle that kept the legislature in session for a record 227 days. In late August, the legislature finally adjourned when a group of moderate Republicans joined with the Democratic minority to pass a tax increase to resolve the budget crisis.[5] The session may have been, as the senate president later described it, "the most grueling in Oregon history."[6]

CHANGES IN THE NEW MILLENNIUM

The Oregon legislature has changed since the 2003 legislative session. In many ways, the 2003 session marked the nadir in the divisiveness that defined the state at the end of the twentieth century and at the start of the new millennium. While the legislature achieved some important successes in the 1980s, it became repeatedly mired in gridlock and conflict throughout the next decade.[7] The conflict did not end after the contentious 2003 session, but it had become substantially more muted by 2016 (see chapter 1), when the legislature met briefly and adopted major legislation on minimum wage, affordable housing, and clean energy without the same stalemate and rancor experienced thirteen years earlier.[8]

The most important change since 2003 has been in the partisan composition of the legislature and the governor's office, with one party gaining control of both branches. It is this change more than any other that has made the legislature less acrimonious. Yet the legislature has also experienced changes in the people who serve, the strength of different interest groups, and the pressures placed on it by the initiative process. Yet not all has changed. There is at least one significant aspect of legislative politics that has remained unaltered and may generate conflict in the future, similar to that experienced in 2003.

PARTISAN POLITICS

Political parties have long played a central role in Oregon's political history, though their relevance has ebbed and flowed. From the mid-1950s to the late 1970s, Oregon developed a national reputation for innovative ideas, progressive legislation, and idiosyncratic politics. This Golden Era of Oregon politics was made possible, in part, by the ability of Republican and Democratic Party lawmakers to work across party lines. One of the factors that enabled the parties to work together was the strong role played by political moderates in leading the Republican Party and the state during this period. Among these Republican leaders was Mark Hatfield, who was elected governor in 1958 and served in that position until 1966, when he was elected to the US Senate. Other moderate Republicans included Governor Tom McCall and US Senator Bob Packwood. At some point in the 1980s or 1990s, however, the moderate leaders began to disappear from the Republican Party and the bipartisanship came to an end, ushering in the era of confrontational politics that followed, as well as opening the door to the liberal dominance the state is witnessing today.

What led to the rise in partisanship? One of the central factors was that Oregon went through a realignment in the 1980s similar to that found across the nation.[9] Even before the Golden Era of Oregon politics, the state had developed a distinct political culture that was supportive of open politics, maverick politicians, and innovative public policy. The realignment in the 1980s, however, made Oregon politics more closely aligned with that of the rest of the nation, with the urban parts of the state becoming more liberal and more supportive of Democratic Party candidates, while the rural regions and small towns became more conservative and Republican. As the parties realigned, the political positions between the regions became more polarized and the moderate politicians began to disappear in the state, a trend that was also playing out in New England and elsewhere across the nation during this period.[10] Economic, social, and demographic changes unfolding in different parts of the state created and reinforced this political realignment between the urban and rural areas. In the decade after the 1981 recession ended, Oregon began to see strong economic growth, but most of it was concentrated in the urban and suburban communities. Many rural parts of the state, which have long depended on natural resources for their economic well-being, never recovered from the recession. In addition, the population of Oregon became more ethnically and racially diverse, further reshaping the character of the state. These and other changes created two politically different Oregons— one urban and one rural—which sent legislators to Salem to represent their divergent perspectives. With the development of this urban-rural divide, Oregon's suburban areas became increasingly important in the state's politics. Populated with a mix of moderate, liberal, and conservative voters, the suburbs helped determine which party would control the legislature and the direction of public policy.

Within the legislature, several factors have been considered important in generating the increased partisanship. One cause cited by some observers is the central role that legislative party caucuses began to play in elections beginning in the 1980s. The legislative party caucuses are the organizations within each chamber that are composed of all the party's members. These are the organizations that consist of the house Democrats, the house Republicans, the senate Democrats, and the senate Republicans. As state politics and election campaigns became more professional in the 1970s and 1980s, legislative party caucuses across the country began to become more involved in election campaigns.[11] The party caucuses in the Oregon legislature were part of this trend. Among other activities, the Oregon caucuses began to raise campaign funds for party members, recruit and train candidates, and provide professional campaign advice.[12] In competitive districts, the support of the caucus started to become particularly important in helping candidates raise sufficient funds to compete and attain office. The efforts of the party caucuses in helping candidates succeed may have encouraged the parties to work more closely together as a team.[13]

The importance of the legislative party caucus committees today can be seen in table 5.1, which shows the amount of money the party caucuses raised through their leadership political action committees (PACs) since the 2000 election cycle.

Table 5.1. Contributions to party caucus political action committees (PACs), 1999-2016

	House Leadership PACs		Senate Leadership PACS	
	FuturePAC (Democrats)	Promote Oregon Leadership PAC (Republicans)	Senate Democratic Leadership Fund (Democrats)	The Leadership Fund (Republicans)
2000	$926,769	$808,375	$824,130	$661,448
2002	$1,190,840	$969,129	$970,871	$734,709
2004	$1,384,535	$1,002,514	$1,576,895	$852,201
2006	$1,752,944	$1,220,159	$749,717	$851,570
2008	$2,745,296	$1,344,687	$625,351	$547,949
2010	$2,677,607	$1,333,062	$2,197,699	$1,614,060
2012	$3,409,980	$1,966,744	$1,089,436	$1,258,712
2014	$3,298,448	$1,700,977	$1,753,969	$1,523,967
2016	$3,687,326	$1,718,432	$1,207,100	$1,524,663

Sources: For 2000-2008, Janice Thompson, Money in Oregon Politics: History, Trends, and Reform (Portland: Democracy Reform Oregon, 2009); for 2010-16, ORESTAR website, accessed May 10, 2018, http://sos.oregon.gov/elections/Pages/orestar.aspx

The biggest success story is that of FuturePAC, the caucus committee that supports house Democratic Party candidates. Since the 2000 election, the amount of money that FuturePAC has raised during each election cycle has quadrupled. Given that the median expenditure for winning house candidates in 2014 was $120,000, FuturePAC and its Republican counterpart (Promote Oregon Leadership PAC) can provide much needed support to legislative candidates.[14] However, most of the money from these caucus committees is channeled to the competitive races, where the funds have the greatest potential to affect results.

There were also several specific events within the legislature to which the rise in partisanship has been tied.[15] One was the changeover in party control in the late 1980s, when the Democrats were able to gain a majority in both chambers. Many Republicans felt that the Democrats mistreated the Republican legislators during this period, spurring the Republicans to work more closely together. Among other complaints was the decision by Democratic House Speaker Vera Katz (D-Portland) to make all committee appointments, including Republican ones.[16] Others point to the 1993 session as the time in which the legislature became overly partisan. In particular, these observers attribute the initial rise in partisanship to Larry Campbell's (R-Eugene) leadership as the Republican House Speaker during the conflict-filled 1993 session.[17] Russell Sadler, a political commentator in southern Oregon, wrote that Campbell spurred on the partisanship by "unilaterally" repealing the legislature's unwritten rule that legislators should not vote against their constituents or conscience. Campbell, Sadler wrote, "declared those rules 'no longer operative' and the bullying began."[18]

Still others point to the introduction of term limits on legislators, arguing that the short terms created by the law encouraged a combative environment, one in which members did not serve long enough to build civil relationships.[19] Enacted through an initiative in the November 1992 general election, the term limits law was one of the most severe in the nation, restricting service in the house to six years and to the senate to eight years, while setting a combined lifetime limit of twelve years. The initiative also modified the term limits on other state executives and established term limits on members of Congress. The Oregon Supreme Court threw out the law in its *Lehman v. Bradbury* decision (2002), arguing that the initiative was unconstitutional because it amended more than one section of the constitution. Under the Oregon constitution, each amendment to the constitution must be voted on separately by the public.[20]

The newfound partisanship in the legislature led to a government that seemed dysfunctional at times. With the Republican Party in control of at least one chamber between 1991 and 2005 (see fig. 5.1), and Democrats holding the governorship throughout this period, it made conflict and gridlock inevitable. Given the small size of both chambers—the house has sixty members, the senate thirty—the conflict turned the legislature's intimate setting into a hostile environment.

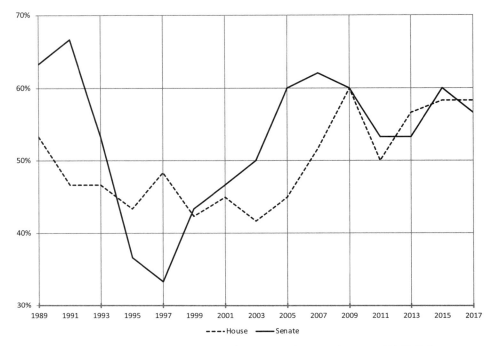

Figure 5.1. **Percentage of Democratic members of the Oregon house and senate, 1989-2017.** *Sources: Oregon State Archives, Oregon Legislators and Staff Guide, and Oregon Senate and House Journals*

The legislature began to change, however, in the middle of the first decade of the new millennium. The 2005 session was not much shorter, at 208 days, or much less combative than the 2003 one, but the 2007 session was different, as the ideological and partisan divide became less disruptive. The change in tone occurred because of a change in partisan control. In the 2004 election, the Democratic Party gained control of the senate for the first time in a decade. In the 2006 election, the Democratic Party then regained a slim majority in the house, giving it unified control of the state government. The result was that the 2007 session was the shortest since 1995, and one that was viewed by many as being the most efficient in decades.[21] The sessions that followed were not stifled by the same ideological and partisan conflicts, either. As with any legislative body, the legislature continued to battle over issues in the latter part of the decade, especially over how to address the decline in revenue after the onset of the 2007 recession, but the legislature was able to avoid the profound partisanship that kept it mired in conflict and unable to adjourn in 2003 session.

Underlying the change in the legislature were changes in Oregon's population. The state was becoming more Democratic. The change can be seen, in part, in voter registration. In the late 1990s, the Democrats held only a slight advantage over the Republicans. The number had expanded by the 2004 election, but then jumped considerably higher in 2008, when Barack Obama's presidential campaign brought an influx of new voters to the Democratic Party.[22] From November 2002 to November 2008, the number of voters registered as Democrats grew from 726,187 to 931,318, while Republican registration remained all but stagnant. Since then, the Democrats have maintained a substantial edge. Along with the growth in Democratic registration, the state also saw a significant increase in the number of voters registered as nonaffiliated or under a third party. This increase was so large that by the 2014 election there were more voters registered in these other categories combined (708,622) than registered as Republican (656,366).[23] More important, these trends have given the Democratic Party a sizeable advantage at the polls. The result has been that the Democrats have since maintained a majority in both chambers, with the exception of the 2011 session, when the parties were evenly divided in the house.

The change in the environment in Salem does not mean that the legislature and the state are no longer split by ideological differences. What it means is that unified control has given the Democratic Party the ability to dominate lawmaking, and to adopt policies without the legislature being mired in gridlock. The one policy matter in which the Republican legislators have been able to retain some influence is in raising revenue. The state constitution requires the approval of 60 percent of the members in both chambers to raise revenue, which gives the Republicans the power to stop tax increases unless the Democrats can attain a supermajority—a difficult challenge for Democrats even with their dominance in both chambers.[24]

CHANGES IN WHO SERVES

Beyond the emergence of the Democrats as the dominant party, several other trends have helped reshaped the Oregon Legislative Assembly over the past decade. Among these trends have been changes in the people who serve in the legislature. In particular, there are many new faces in Salem. The reason for this is that the legislature has relatively high turnover, with an influx of new members every session. As figure 5.2 shows, more than one-quarter of house members routinely turn over each session. The rate was even higher in the 1990s after term limits were adopted in 1992, but it has remained strong even after the term limits law was ruled unconstitutional in 2002. With only half the senate up for reelection every two years, the turnover rate in the upper chamber is usually lower, though it is also high. The high turnover is likely caused in part by low legislative salaries, which scholars have long found influence turnover rates.[25] The members' annual salary as of 2017 was $23,568.[26]

The high turnover means that the people who are serving in the house and senate have changed considerably from just a decade ago. Of the sixty representatives who served in the acrimonious 2003 session, only four remained in the house in 2015. The two most senior members of the house—Phil Barnhart (D-Eugene) and Greg Smith (R-Heppner)—were elected in 2001. There were also only five remaining senators.

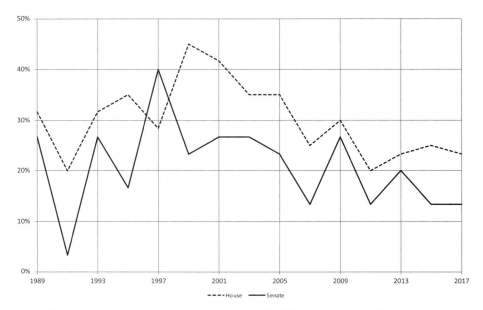

Figure 5.2. **Turnover in the Oregon house and senate, 1989-2017**. *Sources: Oregon State Archives, Oregon Legislators and Staff Guide, and Oregon Senate and House Journals*

The most senior—Ginny Burdick (D-Portland) and Ted Ferrioli (R-John Day)—were elected in 1996. Also remaining in the senate was Peter Courtney (D-Salem), who was first elected to the house in 1981 and the senate in 1998. He had served thirty years in both chambers combined before the 2015 session. Courtney was elected senate president at the opening of the rancorous 2003 session, a position he still held in 2017.

While each session brings in many new faces, some membership changes occur slowly over many sessions. One of the most important long-term trends has been in the occupations that are represented in the legislature.[27] In the 1960s, both chambers were dominated by legislators from legal and business backgrounds (fig. 5.3). This includes many from farming, ranching, timber, fishing, and other natural resource–related occupations, which have historically been central to Oregon's economy. Conversely, the number of legislators who came out of public service, education, and labor tended to be smaller.

Since the 1960s, the number of attorneys in the house has remained fairly constant. In general, there has also been little change in those who identify their career as being in business or a profession. The significant exception is that the number of representatives who say they work in any of those historically important occupations has declined considerably. In 1963, sixteen representatives, or more than 25 percent of the house, identified their occupation as being in one of these traditional Oregon occupations. This number changed little throughout the 1960s before slowly starting to decline.[28] In the 2013 session, none of the representatives listed their jobs as being in any of those fields. Conversely, there has been considerable growth in the number of representatives from nonlegal and business occupations (the "Other" category). Part of this growth reflects the fact that more legislators began to identify their careers as being a "legislator." Until the mid-1970s, no one in either chamber listed legislative service as his or her career.[29]

The trends in senate occupations (not shown) have been slightly different. The most significant change in the senate has been a steady decline in attorneys. In 1963, one-third of the members identified their careers as lawyers. In 2013, only one did. The number of senators from traditional Oregon occupations has remained fairly constant. Those in other businesses have grown a little, though the largest growth has been in the Other category, as it was in the house.

Two important conclusions can be drawn from these trends. One is that the legislature has become more diverse. In 1963, a few occupations dominated in the legislature. Over time, a wider variety started to appear, with legislators no longer identifying their careers as being primarily in law or business. The second is that despite the high turnover that occurs each session, there are far fewer representatives today who come out of the economic interests historically associated with Oregon's rural economy. In fact, it has been more than fifteen years since more than three representatives in any session have listed their careers as being in one of these natural resource–based fields. While there are a few ranchers, foresters, and farmers in the senate, the traditional occupations from the rural areas are just not as well represented as they once were.[30]

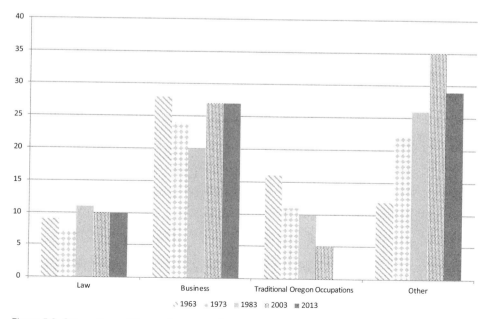

Figure 5.3. Occupations of Oregon house members, 1963-2013. *Source: Oregon Secretary of State, Oregon Blue Book (Salem: State of Oregon, various years)*

As for demographics, the legislature has changed little over time, with one important exception. In general, the legislature has been and continues to be filled primarily by white middle-aged (mid-50s) males.[31] It was not until the 1970s that any racial or ethnic minority was elected to the Oregon legislature. Since then, only a few minorities have served, and the total number in any given session has been low. The legislature was generally the most diverse in 1990s, when several African Americans and Asian Americans served in different sessions, along with one Latina and one Native American. In the sessions that followed, minority representation declined. Since the beginning of the new millennium, the only session in which there were more than four minorities in the legislature was in 2001. The 2017 session brought a major change in this trend, however, with four blacks, four Latinos, and one Native American serving in the legislature. Given that minorities represent almost one-quarter of Oregon's population, the state's minority population remains underrepresented.[32]

One important demographic that has changed significantly is the number of women elected. In the 1960s, no more than nine women served in the legislature in any one session. The number has grown steadily since then. Over the past decade, women have routinely held more than 30 percent of the seats in each session. The gain has been so large that female legislators held a majority of Democratic Party seats in the senate in 2009 and in the house in 2017, giving them a majority of votes in the powerful party caucuses those years.[33] Also important, women began to gain control of many of the top leadership positions in the legislature. During the 2017 session, the Speaker, the house majority leader, and the senate majority leader were all women.[34] A few months after the 2017 session ended, the senate Republicans elected a woman to serve as minority leader. The Republican's selection—Jackie Winters (R-Salem)—was also the first African American to serve in that office.[35] The 2017 session was not the first time that some of these positions were held by women. One of the most important earlier women leaders was Vera Katz, who played an influential role in shaping Oregon politics as the first female house Speaker for three sessions beginning in 1985. Yet there had never been so many top female leaders in the legislature. The increase in the number of women in the legislature, and their rise into leadership position, is important because studies have found that female legislators tend to pursue policies that are different from those pursued by male legislators, and they tend to lead in a different way, too. In particular, women are more likely to introduce legislation that is important to women and families, and to support more liberal social causes. Female legislative leaders generally use more collegial leadership styles.[36] Whether the increase in women in the Oregon legislature has begun to influence the legislature's behavior is beyond the scope of this study, but these past studies suggest that this trend will affect the legislature, if it has not done so already.

CHANGING INTEREST REPRESENTATION

The Oregon legislature met for a one-day special session in December 2012 to consider only a single piece of legislation: a bill promising the Nike Corporation that it would not change the law used to calculate the athletic shoe company's corporate tax bill for thirty years. Nike had threatened to expand outside of Oregon unless the legislature and governor agreed to retain the state's policy of taxing the company only on its sales within the state rather than on its worldwide sales. Within a few hours after the legislature was called into session, both chambers voted overwhelmingly to adopt the proposal, which Governor John Kitzhaber promptly signed into law.[37]

Although Nike's success in getting the legislature to act may have represented a brazen display of power, what transpired is not that unusual for how interest group politics works in state legislatures. Since the early 1980s, scholars who study interest groups have argued that there is an inverse relationship between the complexity of a state's economy and the power of interest groups. States with more complex economies tend to have less powerful interest groups. Conversely, states with less complex economies tend to have more powerful groups.[38] It is not surprising, then, that the Oregon legislature was attentive to Nike's needs given that the company in 2012 was one of only two Fortune 500 companies in Oregon, one of the state's largest employers, and an iconic symbol of the state's infatuation with running and recreation. State Senator Ginny Burdick (D-Portland) captured this dynamic well when she told a reporter in justification of Nike's special treatment, "You can almost say Nike and Oregon share DNA."[39] The legislature's actions in accommodating Nike constituted the most prominent display of interest group lobbying in Oregon in recent years, yet interest groups have continued to play a significant role in Oregon politics, though there have been some important changes in interest group politics in the capitol in the past two decades.

In their analysis of interest groups at the end of the twentieth century, Russ Dondero and Bill Lunch listed anti-tax groups, business organizations, the health industry, law enforcement, environmentalists, the public education lobby, and local governments in the Portland area as being among the most powerful interest groups in Salem.[40] With the Democratic Party gaining control over both the legislature and the governor's office since then, there has been a shift in the power of groups, with those aligned with the Democratic Party gaining greater advantage. Anti-tax groups, as discussed below, no longer have the influence they once did. Business groups, such as the Oregon Business Association and Associated Oregon Industries, are still considered powerful players in Salem.[41] Among the recent beneficiaries in the change in partisan control have been labor unions, public sector employees, environmental groups, and organizations advocating for the disadvantaged, including those supporting the needs of children, women, workers, and immigrant communities. The success of these groups can be seen in the passage of bills in recent sessions raising the minimum wage over time to nearly $15 an hour, defending abortion and reproductive rights, protecting public employee retirement benefits, and expanding the state's health coverage to include undocumented immigrant children.[42]

Along with this shift in power, the legislature has also seen change in the number and type of interests being represented by lobbyists in the legislature. Drawing from Oregon Ethics Commission's lobbying reports, table 5.2 groups all the different organizations with lobbyists in Salem into twenty-one different categories on the basis of type and policy focus of the organization. The table rank orders the categories with the most numerous organizations in 2015 at the top.

The single most prevalent type of group with lobbyists in Salem is the government. Local, state, and tribal governments, along with public school and universities,

Table 5.2. Number of organizations represented by lobbyists in Salem, 2003-15

Type of Interest	2003	2009	2015
Governments	131	131	144
Health care	95	120	139
Other economic interests	59	81	101
Advocacy groups	36	57	64
Insurance	33	39	48
Agriculture and natural resources	37	44	47
Energy	17	32	38
Telecommunications and high-technology	25	37	38
Social services	22	25	34
Transportation	21	29	34
Labor unions	22	30	33
Environment and conservation	17	15	32
Manufacturing	26	29	31
Entertainment, hospitality, and leisure	22	24	30
Education	11	26	24
Financial services	20	30	24
Construction	26	22	22
Real estate	17	12	18
Retail	8	9	13
Unknown	6	6	6
Utilities	4	5	6
Total	**655**	**803**	**926**

Source: Oregon Government Ethics Commission, Client/Employer List (Salem: Oregon Government Ethics Commission, April 2003, April 2009, and March 2015)

routinely hire lobbyists to represent them directly in Salem, or they have lobbyists represent them through umbrella associations. While governments are the most common entities with lobbyists, they have been closely followed by health-care interests.

The status of three other types of groups is worth noting. Even though there are fewer advocacy groups with lobbyists, a sizeable number of civil rights, good government, and single-issue groups are represented in Salem. Moreover, the advocacy category does not include environmental groups, which are listed separately, or groups that advocate on health issues (see table 5.3 below). The number of organizations associated with agriculture and natural resources is in the middle of the pack. This is the same category referred to as "traditional Oregon occupations" above. Thus, although this important segment of Oregon's economy may not be electing farmers and ranchers to the house, it still works to have its voice heard. The number of labor unions with representatives in Salem is lower down the list. This might seem surprising given labor's reputation as being among the strongest actors in the legislature, but the rankings in table 5.2 do not measure power. Instead, they simply reveal what interests are lobbying the legislature.

One of the most striking patterns in table 5.2 is the large growth of interests represented by lobbyists over time, especially in health care. Why is the number of interests being represented by lobbyists increasing? Some of it reflects the rise of new issues, interests, and political battles in the state. For example, the Ethics Commission's lobbying report for 2015 lists eighteen different interests associated with marijuana, from growers to retailers to advocacy groups. Of these groups, only one appeared on the 2009 list. Similarly, the 2015 list includes Uber, Airbnb, and the association representing the manufacturers, retailers, and users of vaping products. These new interests want to be in Salem as the legislature considers how to regulate them.

Yet the rise also reflects nationwide trends. Studies of states nationwide have found an increase in the number of interests represented by lobbyists over the decade, especially in health care.[43] To be sure, health-care interests have been found to be the largest and fastest-growing segment in interest representation in state capitols.[44] Some of the growth in health interests was generated by the passage of the national Affordable Care Act. With the details of the act being hammered out in statehouses, the health-care industry— including health-care providers—wants to be able to influence decisions. The growth also reflects the growing costs of health care, especially prescription drugs. As costs have gone up, there has been greater demand for government to respond. Pharmaceutical companies and other health-care industries want to protect their interests, while some advocacy groups battle to control costs. The growth in advocacy groups with lobbyists also reflects a desire among these organizations to make lawmakers more aware of issues associated with specific health problems. Table 5.3 shows that care providers, pharmaceutical companies, and advocacy groups have all become better represented in the legislature. Health-care professionals is the one category that has seen little change.

Table 5.3. Health interests with representation in Salem, 2003 and 2015

	Organizations with Lobbyists		
Type of Interest	2003	2009	2015
Providers	20	31	43
Professional associations	30	36	36
Pharmaceuticals	19	24	28
Education and advocacy	10	21	21
Other	16	8	11
Total	95	120	139

Source: Oregon Government Ethics Commission, Client/Employer List (Salem: Oregon Government Ethics Commission, April 2003, April 2009, and March 2015)

The changes seen in the Ethics Committee reports are also reflected in the membership of the Capitol Club, the association for professional advocates in Oregon. Membership in the Capitol Club is voluntary, yet a look at its membership directory shows an increase of almost 25 percent in the number of interests represented from 2003 to 2015. Moreover, the Capitol Club's categorization shows the greatest growth as being in health-care interests. Combined, these two sets of records reveal how important state legislatures are to interest groups and how strongly interest groups want to have their voices heard today in Salem.

THE GUN BEHIND THE DOOR

One complaint raised about Oregon politics in the 1990s was regarding the ability of initiative sponsors to set the legislature's agenda despite the fact the sponsors were not elected by voters. The complaint may have reached its crescendo after the 1998 gubernatorial election. Although John Kitzhaber defeated Republican Bill Sizemore by a two-to-one margin in the election, Sizemore was able to dominate the direction of political debate in the state after the election by putting forward an initiative proposal to drastically slash state income taxes. Rather than being able to focus on his legislative agenda, Governor Kitzhaber turned his attention to defeating Sizemore's efforts.[45]

State politics scholars refer to the use, or threatened use, of the initiative to force a legislature to adopt particular policies as being a "gun behind the door," a characterization coined by Woodrow Wilson in 1911. In the 1990s, conservative groups in Oregon repeatedly used the initiative for that purpose. Sizemore, the head of Oregon Taxpayers United, was the most active champion of initiatives, but other conservatives also used initiatives to put pressure on the legislature to act, or just to get the state to vote directly on their ideas. These include Lon Mabon, the founder of the Oregon Citizens Alliance; Don McIntire, the leader of the Oregon property tax revolt in the 1990s; and Loren Parks, the largest campaign contributor in Oregon's history.[46] This tactic had become so prominent that the *Bend Bulletin* observed, "Once, governors and legislators set the agenda in Oregon. Now, they respond to the initiative system, and an anti-tax juggernaut that was spawned by two activists, Don McIntire and Bill Sizemore."[47]

Among the important changes that have transformed legislative politics over the past decade have been the decline in initiatives and the disappearance of most of these conservative actors in Oregon politics. The threat of initiatives has not entirely disappeared as a means to prompt the legislature to act, but it is not as prevalent as it once was, and the pressure has come more recently from activists on the left rather than the right.

The decline in initiatives has been caused by two factors. One was the 1998 Oregon Supreme Court decision in *Armatta v. Kitzhaber.* In this case revolving around a 1996 victims' rights initiative (Measure 40), the court ruled that the measure was unconstitutional because it violated the state's law limiting constitutional amendments to one subject. The court's decision led the state's attorney general office, as well as lower courts, to reject many initiatives for violating this restriction. The second was the passage of House Bill 2082 in 2007, which stiffened regulations and recordkeeping rules placed on initiative sponsors, including ending their ability to pay signature gatherers on a per signature basis. Combined, these two factors have made the initiative more complicated and expensive to use. Figure 5.4 shows the decline in initiatives.

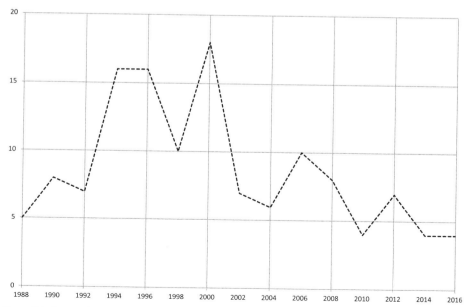

Figure 5.4. **Oregon ballot initiatives, 1988-2016.** *Source: Oregon Secretary of State,* Oregon Blue Book *(Salem: State of Oregon, 2016)*

While these two acts reduced the number of initiatives, and may have weakened their value as a threat, activists continue to try to use it as a gun behind the door. Most recently, the threat of an initiative has put pressure on the legislature to raise the minimum wage, rewrite the state's liquor laws, and to consider alternatives to raising corporate income taxes.[48]

LEGISLATIVE CHANGE IN PERSPECTIVE

These changes in Oregon politics over the past dozen years have altered the legislature's environment. More than anything else, the changes have affected the distribution of political power, the character of representation, and the efficiency of the legislature. With the new restrictions on initiatives and the disappearance of the leading initiative sponsors of the 1990s, the voices of conservative activists have been weakened. More groups are being represented by lobbyists in the legislature, while the number of female legislators has grown. Unified control of Oregon's government has allowed the Democratic Party to dominate policymaking, giving those living in urban areas and liberal groups a greater say in the direction of the state. One-party control has, in turn, made policymaking easier and more efficient.

Not everything has changed. The state is still divided along urban and rural lines. Strong partisan differences remain. Interest groups continue to be prominent actors in Salem politics. Yet perhaps the most significant aspect of Oregon's politics that has remained constant since the 2003 legislative session is the state's tax laws. Today, the state government remains almost solely dependent on income taxes for paying its bills (see chapter 18). Moreover, the property tax measures passed by voters from 1990 to 1997 continue to force the legislature to channel billions in funds to local schools, while the kicker law makes it difficult for the state to build a reserve fund.

Since the Great Recession ended in 2009 and the economic recovery began, the legislature has been able to meet its budgeting needs without the same rancor and delay it faced in 2003. Yet the existence of these laws makes for a less bright future. When revenue stagnates in the future, and the legislature finds itself again trying to find a way to balance the budget, it is possible that a repeat of 2003 may happen. The Democrats' current dominance of the government may help it overcome these problems and find some solutions with less conflict, yet these laws will continue to restrict the legislature's options. Without a supermajority, the Democrats cannot raise revenue without Republican support. With that bit of power in the hands of the minority party and with the state divided ideologically, finding a solution to a budget crisis in this situation may again be daunting.

Notes

1   Ken Rocco, *Background Brief on 2001-03 Biennium Budget* (Salem: Oregon Legislative Fiscal Office, November 2002); Michael Leachman, *How Big an Umbrella Does Oregon Need?* (Portland: Oregon Center for Public Policy, January 8, 2008).

2   Oregon Legislative Budget Office, *Budget Highlights: 2003-05 Legislative Approved Budget* (Salem: Oregon Legislative Budget Office, September 2003).

3   Russ Dondero and Bill Lunch, "Interest Groups," in *Oregon Politics and Government: Progressives versus Conservative Populists*, ed. Richard A. Clucas, Mark Henkels, and Brent S. Steel (Lincoln: University of Nebraska Press, 2005), 82.

4   Harry Esteve and James Mayer, "Headache, Not Handshake, New Norm in Budget Deals," *Oregonian*, August 17, 2003.

5   Charles E. Beggs, "Lawmakers End Longest Session," *Associated Press State and Local Wire*, August 28, 2003.

6   Peter Courtney, Senate President, *Oregon Senate Journal*, January 10, 2005, SJ2.

7   "Lawmakers Buoyed by End to Legislative Gridlock," *Oregonian*, May 5, 1993; Jeff Mapes, "Animal House Session Ending in Division, Turmoil," *Oregonian*, June 10, 1995; Jeff Mapes, "Legislature Conducts Management Session," *Oregonian*, July 6, 1997.

8   Gordon Friedman, "2016 Oregon Legislature Wrap Up," *Statesman Journal*, March 7, 2016.

9   See Thomas E. Mann and Norman J. Ornstein, *It's Even Worse Than It Looks: How the American Constitutional System Collided with the New Politics of Extremism* (New York: Pegasus, 2012); Jeffrey M. Stonecash, *Political Parties Matter: Realignment and the Return of Partisan Voting* (Boulder, CO: Lynne Rienner, 2005); Jeffrey M. Stonecash, Mark D. Brewer, and Mack Mariani, *Diverging Parties: Social Change, Realignment, and Party Polarization* (Boulder, CO: Westview Press, 2006).

10 Richard A. Clucas, Mark Henkels, and Brent S. Steel, "The Politics of One Oregon: Causes and Consequences of the Rural-Urban Divide and Prospects for Overcoming It," in *Toward One Oregon: Rural-Urban Interdependence and the Evolution of a State*, ed. Michael Hibbard et al. (Corvallis: Oregon State University Press, 2011), 113-42.

11 Cindy Simon Rosenthal, "New Party or Campaign Bank Account? Explaining the Rise of State Legislative Campaign Committees," *Legislative Studies Quarterly* 20 (1995): 249-68; Richard A. Clucas, *The Speaker's Electoral Connection: Willie Brown and the California Assembly* (Berkeley: Institute of Governmental Studies, University of California, 1995).

12 See Sarah B. Ames, "Parties Pass Political Action Committees in Spending," *Oregonian*, November 4, 1988; "Influential Citizens," *Bend Bulletin*, September 28, 2006; Jeff Mapes, "Political Machine Hums behind Legislative Races," *Oregonian*, November 1, 1998.

13 City Club of Portland, *Bridging the Partisan Divide: A City Club Report on Reducing Excessive Partisanship in the Oregon Political System* (Portland: City Club of Portland, January 16, 2009).

14 Calculated by the author from ORESTAR reports for 2013 and 2014. ORESTAR website, accessed April 9, 2018, https://secure.sos.state.or.us/orestar.

15 "Influential Citizens," 105; Russell Sadler, "Our Childish Legislature," *BlueOregon.com*, August 7, 2005, http://www.blueoregon.com/2005/08/our_childish_le.html.

16 City Club of Portland, *Bridging the Partisan Divide*; "Influential Citizens."

17 "Influential Citizens."

18 Sadler, "Our Childish Legislature."

19 Mike Kiefer, "The Man behind the Speaker," *Willamette Week*, August 12, 2003; City Club of Portland, *Bridging the Partisan Divide*.

20 Marjorie Taylor, *Background Brief on Term Limits* (Salem: Oregon Legislature, Legislative Committee Services, May 2004); Thad Kousser, *Term Limits and the Dismantling of State Legislative Professionalism* (New York: Cambridge University Press, 2005).

21 Dan Bates, *City of Portland 2007 Legislative Report* (Portland, OR: Portland Office of Government Relations, 2007); "Oregon Lawmakers Adjourn 2007 Session," *Eugene Daily News*, June 29, 2007.

22 Edward Walsh and Michelle Cole, "Democratic Voter Registration Surges in Oregon," *Oregonian*, April 26, 2008.

23 "Election Statistics: Voter Registration by County," Oregon Secretary of State, accessed May 23, 2018, http://sos.oregon.gov/elections/Pages/electionsstatistics.aspx.

24 Ann Ereline, "Oregon's 2009 Session Ends with Trail of Big Taxes," *Oregonian*, June 29, 2009.

25 Gary F. Moncrief, Richard G. Niemi, and Lynda W. Powell, "Time, Term Limits, and Turnover: Trends in Membership Stability in U.S. State Legislatures," *Legislative Studies Quarterly* 29 (2004): 357-81.

26 Office of the Chief Clerk, *Oregon House of Representatives, 79th Legislative Assembly, New Member Guide* (Salem, OR: Office of Chief Clerk, 2017), 3.

27 The categorization is based on the listings in the *Oregon Blue Book*, published by the Oregon Secretary of State. The business category includes all business and professional occupations, with the exception of legislators from occupations related to journalism and the media. Given the distinct role that the fourth estate has traditionally played in politics, I included those legislators in the "Other" category. The Other category also includes legislators with backgrounds in public service, government work, teaching, and labor, or those who identify their jobs as being legislators, students, housewives, or retired. Some representatives listed more than one occupation, so the totals equal more than sixty.

28 See Richard A. Clucas, "The Oregon Legislature and the Professionalism Movement" (presented at the Pacific Northwest Political Science Association Meeting, Eugene, Oregon, October 14-16, 1999).

29 Clucas, "Oregon Legislature."

30 See Clucas, "Oregon Legislature."

31 Oregon Secretary of State, *Oregon Blue Book* (Salem: State of Oregon, various years).

32 Paris Achen, "Diversity Increasing in Oregon Legislature," *Gresham Outlook*, December 26, 2016; "Oregon Quick Facts," US Census, accessed May 23, 2018, https://www.census.gov/quickfacts/OR.

33 Hillary Borrud, "Oregon House Democrats Look Ahead to Female Majority in 2017," *Oregonian*, November 16, 2016.

34 "Oregon House Democrats Elect Leadership Team for 2017 Session," Oregon House Press Release, November 15, 2016.

35 Gordon R. Friedman, "Jackie Winters Named Minority Leader of Oregon Senate, First Black Person to Hold Position," *Oregonian*, November 21, 2017.

36 Anne Marie Cammisa and Beth Reingold, "Women in State Legislatures and State Legislative Research," *State Politics and Policy Quarterly* 4 (2004): 181-210.

37 Christian Gaston, "Nike Eyed Austin, Vancouver until Oregon Special Session," *Oregonian*, January 12, 2013; Harry Esteve, "Oregon Legislature Approves Nike Tax Deal in One-Day Special Session," *Oregonian*, December 14, 2012.

38 L. Harmon Zeigler, "Interest Groups in the States," in *Politics in the American States*, 4th ed., ed. Virginia Gray, Herbert Jacob, and Kenneth Vines (Boston: Little, Brown, 1983), 97-132.

39 Esteve, "Oregon Legislature Approves Nike Tax Deal."

40 Dondero and Lunch, "Interest Groups."

41 Jeff Manning, "Oregon's Powerhouse Business Lobby Groups Vote to Merge," *Oregonian*, November 16, 2016.

42 Manning, "Oregon's Powerhouse"; Lauren Hernandez and Diane Dietz, "Oregon Legislature Reflects Growing Latino Influence, But Will It Last?," *Statesman Journal*, October 21, 2017; Don McIntosh, "A Landmark Session, but Oregon Labor Wanted More," *nwlaborpress.org*, July 14, 2015; Valerie Richardson, "Oregon Becomes the First State to Offer Free Abortions for All, Including Illegal Aliens," *Washington Times*, August 16, 2017; Amber M. Winkler, Janie Scull, and Dara Zeehandelaar, *How Strong Are U.S. Teacher Unions: A State-by-State Comparison* (Washington, DC: Thomas Fordham Institute, October 2012); Hillary Borrud, "With Democrats in Majority, Environmental Lobby Hits Hard," *Portland Tribune*, March 31, 2015; Ian K. Kullgren, "Oregon Governor Signs Landmark Tiered Minimum Wage Increase into Law," *Oregonian*, February 18, 2016.

43 Liz Essley Whyte and Ben Wieder, "Amid Federal Gridlock, Lobbying Rises in the States," Center for Public Integrity, February 11, 2016, https://www.publicintegrity.org/2016/02/11/19279/amid-federal-gridlock-lobbying-rises-states; Matt Grossman, ed., *New Directions in Interest Group Politics* (New York: Routledge, 2014).

44 Whyte and Wieder, "Amid Federal Gridlock"; George Lauer, "Health Care Lobbying in California Tops List in Record Year," *California Healthline*, March 12, 2012; "Massachusetts Healthcare Industry Spent $19m Lobbying State Lawmakers," *Modern Health Care*, May 23, 2015.

45 Richard J. Ellis, "Direct Democracy," in Clucas et al., *Oregon Politics and Government*, 74; B. Drummond Ayers Jr., "Political Briefing: Oregon Initiatives Torment Governor," *New York Times*, April 30, 2000.

46 Janice Thompson and Charles Buttermore, *Loren Parks: Oregon's $13 Million Man* (Washington, DC: Common Cause, October 2009); Nigel Jaquiss, "U.S. Tax Court Rules GOP Funder Loren Parks Owes Taxes for Foundation's Political Spending," *Willamette Week*, November 20, 2015.

47 "Influential Citizens."

48 Gordon Friedman, "Ballot Measure Battle Prompts Legislature to Move on Minimum Wage," *Statesman Journal*, January 21, 2016; Harry Esteve, "Grocers Tell Oregon Lawmakers: Update Liquor Laws or Face Initiative," *Oregonian*, September 13, 2012; Ryan Maness, "Oregon Leaders Seek Tax Compromise to Avoid Election Showdown," *Multistate Insider*, February 7, 2016.

6
The Governor and Oregon's Executive(s) Branch
PHIL KEISLING

It was a moment few could have imagined a month earlier. On February 18, 2015, just thirty-four days after Democrat John Kitzhaber had been sworn in for an unprecedented fourth term as Oregon governor, he resigned, and it was Secretary of State Kate Brown's turn to take the official oath of office as Oregon's thirty-eighth governor. Since Oregon achieved statehood in 1859, four other Oregon governors had resigned, and another four had died in office. Yet the suddenness of Brown's ascension was the first such dramatic transition in the memory of most Oregonians.

Kitzhaber had made his own history in 2010, as Oregon's first chief executive elected to a third term. Within months of his 2014 election to an unprecedented fourth term, however, Kitzhaber earned a more dubious distinction, becoming Oregon's first governor to resign under a cloud of controversy, amid allegations involving ethics law violations, conflicts of interest, and improper e-mail deletions. A brief profile of his unique political career appears at the end of this chapter.

OREGON'S FIVE EXECUTIVES
Kitzhaber's sudden fall from political grace set off a round of political musical chairs affecting almost every corner of Oregon's executive branch or, more precisely, the state's "executive(s) branch." In contrast to the federal government, almost every US state divides its executive branch's power among multiple statewide elected officials. Oregon now has four such offices in addition to the governor, all independently elected to four-year terms. Oregon's 1859 constitution created three executive offices: governor, secretary of state, and state treasurer. The Oregon legislature created the offices of attorney general in 1891 and commissioner of the Bureau of Labor and Industries (BOLI) in 1903. The 2011 legislature abolished a sixth statewide elected office—the superintendent of public instruction—and reassigned its duties to the governor.

The Oregon Constitution provides that any vacancy in the governor's chair is to be filled by the secretary of state, provided that he or she has already been elected, and not appointed. Brown's ascension thus created another vacancy, opening her position as secretary of state. Soon after taking office, Brown appointed Democrat Jeanne Atkins as the new secretary of state. With Atkins having pledged not to run for election to the office in 2016, BOLI Commissioner Brad Avakian announced his candidacy for the job. Meanwhile, Treasurer Ted Wheeler, who had previously been contemplating a 2018 gubernatorial run at the end of Kitzhaber's fourth term, decided instead to seek election as mayor of Portland.

When the electoral dust finally cleared after the November 2016 election, Brown had been easily elected to serve the last two years of Kitzhaber's original term. Democrat Tobias Read, a former state representative, had been elected treasurer. And in an electoral surprise, given Brown's and Democratic presidential nominee Hillary Clinton's wins in Oregon, voters chose Republican Dennis Richardson to be Oregon's secretary of state. This put Richardson next in line of succession should another gubernatorial vacancy occur—the first time that different party members occupied these top two positions since Republican Norma Paulus served during Democratic Governor Bob Straub's last two years of office (1977-78).

So 2016 began with Oregon's top three officials having been elected to office for the first time. Not since 1947, when Oregon's governor, secretary of state, and senate president were all killed in a private plane crash on a goose-hunting trip to Lake County, had so many of Oregon's top executive branch officials had such relatively little combined tenure among their offices.

Prior to this flurry of new faces and new roles, the recent history of Oregon's executive branch had been one of relative stability. For the two previous decades (1995-2015), Oregonians had known just two governors. Kitzhaber, after nearly a decade as senate president, was first elected governor in 1994 and then reelected in 1998. Fellow Democrat and former attorney general Ted Kulongoski then won election in 2002 and was reelected in 2006. Kitzhaber then reclaimed the office in 2010 by narrowly defeating former professional basketball player Chris Dudley, before winning his unprecedented fourth term in 2014 just three months before his abrupt resignation.

As the 2017 legislature convened, Democrats had held the governor's chair for thirty consecutive years, an unprecedented stretch in Oregon history for either political party. During most of the twentieth century, Republicans dominated statewide elected offices. When Democrat Barbara Roberts won her 1984 bid for secretary of state, for example, she broke a seventy-eight-year uninterrupted run of Republicans in that office.

However, Republicans had not been quite so dominant with the governorship, as a smattering of one-term Democrats (and one Independent) had also occupied the chief executive's chair during the twentieth century. One-term Democrats Oswald West (1911-15), Walter Pierce (1921-25), Charles Martin (1935-39), Robert Holmes (1957-59), and Bob Straub (1975-79) were all preceded—and succeeded—by Republicans. From 1931 to 1935, Julius Meier, a lifelong Republican, served as Oregon's only elected independent to the office.[1]

Oregon's Four Other Executives

It is certainly too early to say whether recent events will usher in a new period of instability and change in Oregon politics, or simply prove to be a once-in-a-generation reshuffling of Oregon's upper ranks of statewide officials. Yet it is demonstrably true that these and other changes have brought a good deal more public attention to Oregon's executive branch.

What will these changes mean for Oregon's executive branch, and specifically to the key role the governor will play going forward? What constraints—both institutional and contextual—will affect the ability of Oregon's governor to propose and achieve a policy agenda? How will other key players and institutions—including interest groups, the traditional media, social media, and Oregon's long-standing initiative/referendum process—constrain or empower the ability of current and future governors to affect state politics and government? Before delving into detail about the governor's job, let us first take a brief look at the major powers and duties of Oregon's four other executive branch officials.

Secretary of State

The 1859 constitution created the office of secretary of state as a separately elected position and assigned it two major duties. The first is to "keep a fair record of the official acts of the Legislative Assembly and Executive Department of the State." The second is the designation of the secretary "by his office (to be) Auditor of public accounts"; Oregon's secretary of state is the only one in the nation with this constitutionally assigned duty.

The secretary of state, along with the governor and the treasurer, also serves as one of three members of the State Land Board. State Land Board members serve as trustees with fiduciary duties, overseeing the management and income-generating activities of millions of acres of state-owned property. These include the Elliott State Forest in southwest Oregon, grazing lands in eastern Oregon's high desert, and the beds and banks of Oregon's navigable rivers as well as its territorial seabeds.

Today, most Oregonians familiar with the office know it for the duties that the legislature later added. The most prominent of these is overseeing the state's election system, ensuring the fair and uniform application of state election laws across the state's thirty-six counties. Should the Oregon legislature fail to perform its duty to redraw state legislative boundaries after the decennial census, that job falls to the secretary of state. (This is a situation that occurred in 1981, 1991, and 2001.) Secretaries of state have often advocated for major election law changes. For example, as secretary of state in 1998, this author pushed to make Oregon the first US state to automatically mail ballots to every registered voter through its universal vote-by-mail system. Secretary Kate Brown led another pioneering effort in 2015 to enact an automatic voter registration law, by which new voters are proactively registered based on Department of Motor Vehicle records (see chapter 3).

As Oregonians learned in 2015, the secretary of state is also next in line to fill a gubernatorial vacancy, as Oregon is one of just five states with no lieutenant governor position. The line of succession runs next to the elected state treasurer, followed by the senate president and then the Speaker of the House of Representatives. But this line of succession has not always been followed. Between 1920 and 1973, the senate president was next in line to the governor, and officially became "acting governor" whenever the governor was physically absent from the state. During his tenure, Governor Tom McCall reportedly relinquished his chief executive duties nearly a dozen times during a single day while on a rafting trip down the Snake River along the Oregon-Idaho border.

State Treasurer

The 1859 state constitution described the treasurer's duties as simply "what may be prescribed by law." Those duties have evolved significantly since then. Today, the treasurer serves as the state's chief investment officer and official banker, responsible for managing and investing public trust assets such as the Oregon Public Employees Retirement Fund (OPERF) and the Oregon Short Term Fund. These accounts were valued at more than $90 billion as of December 31, 2017, with OPERF alone accounting for almost $80 billion. Investment returns from OPERF finance the lion's share of obligations to current and future retirees in Oregon's Public Employee Retirement System (PERS).

The treasurer's office also oversees and reports on the debt obligations of state agencies and other units of government. This oversight is a key factor in determining Oregon's credit rating, which in turn affects how much interest the state must pay to borrow money. The treasurer also oversees a tax-incentive college savings plan for citizens. Starting in 2017, the treasurer has had responsibility for "OregonSaves," a new, first-in-the-US state retirement savings option for private sector workers, which operates separate from the state's PERS system.

Attorney General

The attorney general's most important duty is serving as Oregon's official attorney of record in any civil action or legal proceedings in which the state is a party or has an interest. When most state agencies seek legal advice, they are required to get it from the attorney general and the Oregon Department of Justice's (DOJ) legal staff. The attorney general also at times serves as a prosecutor, deciding whether the evidence merits the prosecution of a particular case under certain specific statutes.

Over the years, the DOJ has also been assigned responsibility to manage a number of other program areas. These include administering public records law, enforcing payment of child support, providing assistance to elected district attorneys, overseeing programs to provide compensation to crime victims, registering and enforcing regulations about charitable activities, and protecting consumers from fraudulent activities and scams. In 2016, for example, the Oregon attorney general's office announced a major settlement of $73 million on behalf of Oregon consumers in the wake of a cheating scandal involving the automaker Volkswagen and its auto pollution controls.

Commissioner of the Bureau of Labor and Industries

In 1903, the Oregon legislature created the Bureau of Labor and Industries (BOLI) and decided its occupant should also be a statewide elected official. It was a turbulent time in Oregon's economic and political life, as the rapid rise of labor unions and growing societal concern over working conditions led to a number of Progressive Era reforms, such as prohibitions on child labor, legislation to establish an eight-hour work day, and the creation of Oregon's workers' compensation system.

The BOLI commissioner today is responsible for ensuring compliance with key elements of Oregon employment law, including wage-and-hour provisions and parental and family leave. The commissioner also enforces certain state and federal laws relating to discrimination in employment, housing, and public accommodation. For example, in 2013, after the owners of a Gresham company, Sweet Cakes by Melissa, refused to bake a wedding cake for a lesbian couple's marriage ceremony, BOLI initiated action that resulted in the couple being awarded $135,000 in damages. After paying the amount, the company—now shut down—appealed unsuccessfully to the Oregon Court of Appeals and Oregon's Supreme Court. While the US Supreme Court in 2018 decided for a Colorado baker, in a case with similar facts, the ruling was relatively narrow and likely won't affect the Oregon case.

In 1995, the Oregon legislature decided to make the BOLI commissioner a nonpartisan elected office. All candidates now run in the May primary election. If one candidate wins more than 50 percent of the vote, that candidate is elected; if none of the candidates passes the 50 percent threshold, then a runoff election is held in November among the top two vote recipients. The other four statewide positions are elected on a partisan basis.

A CLOSER LOOK AT THE POWERS OF THE GOVERNOR

While it is certainly important to understand the split nature of Oregon's executive branch, the governor is virtually the only statewide official most Oregonians can name, much less have an opinion about. The vast majority of the state's executive branch employees ultimately report to the governor, whose scope and reach of institutional power vastly exceed those of any other statewide official.

So, what are the key roles that the governor plays within Oregon's system of government? There are many key aspects to the job, but it's worth focusing on seven of them.

Oregon's "Chairman of the Board"

As with President Harry Truman's famous sign on his White House desk that read "The Buck Stops Here," Oregon citizens expect their governor to be ultimately responsible for the legal and effective operations of state government. This is not 100 percent true; for example, the governor cannot override certain decisions made by other statewide officials, such as which executive branch agencies the secretary of state's office decides to audit. But in the clear majority of cases, Oregon's governor and those officials the governor appoints administer almost all of Oregon's diverse and complex laws. Even if the governor personally opposes such laws, it is the governor's constitutional obligation to "faithfully execute the laws" and "uphold the Constitution of the state of Oregon and the United States," as stated in the oath of office.

Those laws are voluminous. In addition to the Oregon Constitution, which contains roughly five times more words than the US Constitution, there are more than eight hundred chapters (and seventeen separate volumes) in the current version of *Oregon Revised Statutes* (ORS). These statutes, though, are only the tip of the legal iceberg. To clarify and add more detail to acts of the legislature, thousands of Oregon Administrative Rules (OARs) have been formally adopted over the decades in response to what often are general legislative directives. (For more on these rules and key administrative functions, see chapter 7, on bureaucracy).

Within this structure there is also discretion. Governors can and do prioritize how they deploy limited state resources and exercise their legal authority. For example, Governor John Kitzhaber was heavily criticized by death penalty supporters, and praised by its opponents, when he announced early in his third term that he would "suspend" any pending executions that might arise under his watch. The Oregon Supreme Court later upheld the governor's decision, citing his broad discretion under the Oregon constitution to issue reprieves and pardons.

Oregon's Chief Executive Officer

In any organization, the power to "hire and fire" is among the most important that a chief executive officer possesses. So, it is important to understand just what powers the Oregon governor has and does not have in this regard when it comes to the more than forty thousand state agency positions that ultimately report to the governor. Governors seldom have, much less exercise, direct authority to hire and fire below the uppermost tip of the employment pyramid. Long gone are the nineteenth- and early twentieth-century days of political patronage, when a new governor might sweep into office, quickly securing the resignation of most state government workers and doling out coveted jobs to campaign workers, other supporters, or even family members.

Like most states, Oregon enacted strong civil service reforms in the first half of the twentieth century, providing for merit-based employment and retention decisions. In 1973, the legislature explicitly required that state employees and their unions be given the right to collectively bargain contracts. In addition to wage and benefits, those contracts typically spell out the processes by which employees can be hired, disciplined, or discharged. Other entities, such as Oregon's Employment Relations Board and the courts, also exist to protect employees from improper treatment.

Oregon's governor still has broad and explicit authority to hire and fire most, though not all, of the hundreds of top managers that run key departments within state government. But key "intermediary organizations" are often part of this "hire, fire, and manage" equation, requiring governors to exercise a higher order of managerial deftness and skill than might be required in states with more direct chains of command.

These intermediary organizations are Oregon's more than two hundred and fifty boards and commissions whose citizen members oversee state government functions from the licensing of certified public accountants through the State Board of Accountancy to the resolution of employee injury issues by the Oregon Workers Compensation Board. Not every major state agency is overseen by a board. Two notable exceptions are the Department of Corrections, which as of 2018 incarcerated more than fourteen thousand inmates, and the more than nine thousand employees of Department of Human Services. More than one thousand Oregon citizens serve on these boards, most appointed by the governor. Of these entities, more than one hundred are considered powerful enough that the Oregon legislature has required that proposed members be subject to senate confirmation.[2]

The legislature has given most of Oregon's boards and commissions certain powers, particularly when it comes to formally adopting administrative rules. The governor alone, for example, cannot set hunting and fishing license fees; that task falls to the Oregon Fish and Wildlife Commission.

For a handful of agencies, board and commission members comprise the appointing authority for the head of the relevant agency. For example, the Environmental Quality Commission (EQC) appoints the director of the Department of Environmental Quality (DEQ), which oversees the enforcement of a wide range of state and federal pollution laws. In March 2017, the EQC's process for picking a new director displeased Governor Kate Brown, who then fired three of the EQC's five board members. Other high-profile agency directors that the governor cannot directly hire or fire include the Oregon state forester (Board of Forestry) and the heads of the Public Employee Retirement System, State Parks and Recreation, and the Department of Land Conservation and Development.

But these cases are now far more the exception than the rule. Either directly or after a required "consultation" with the board, Oregon's governor has the clear authority to appoint or fire, subject to following proper procedures, nearly all the major state agency heads.

Budget Proposer and Negotiator

"The governor proposes; the legislature disposes" is a timeworn axiom of state budget politics. Or, as University of Oregon political scientist Jerry F. Medler has observed in his analysis of Oregon governors, "the dynamic of budgeting is an elaborate *pas de deux* between the executive and the legislative branches of government."[3]

Just how well the governor performs on this political dance floor is determined in no small part by her or his savvy, patience, and negotiating prowess. Oregon's governor must submit a biennial (two-year) budget to the legislature. But it is the legislature that has legal responsibility and power to enact—or ignore—as much of it as it chooses. The only rule that both branches must honor is that the final budget must end up "balanced," since Oregon's constitution (like those of almost all other states) prohibits deficit spending.

Legislative leaders and powerful individual legislators often have different spending priorities than the governor, even when the same party controls both branches. In recent decades, the budget process has often been contentious amid frequent budget crises driven by a combination of factors. These have included periodic recessions exacerbated by Oregon's reliance on highly volatile personal income tax revenues, as well as anti-tax ballot measures (e.g., 1990's Measure 5) and the state's kicker law (see chapter 6), which forces tax refunds even when the economy is in a downturn.

In their 2012 book *The Power of American Governors: Winning on Budgets and Losing on Policy*, Thad Kousser and Justin Phillips point out that governors are generally far more successful in the budget-making arena because of their inherently superior position in the "staring match" of late-session budgetary deliberations. "All governorships are well paid, full-time jobs that allow their occupants to reside in the state capital year-round and engage in protracted negotiations," Kousser and Phillips write. "Many legislatures, however, only meet in short sessions, and their members maintain outside careers."[4]

"Issue Definer" and Policy Advocate

While often referred to as "Oregon's ninety-first legislator," the governor's formal power in this regard is technically only a negative one. Governors can veto bills and specific "line item" budget appropriations they do not like. To accomplish their own policy goals, governors instead must rely on "soft power" and the ability to use persuasion (and, at times, public outreach and the "bully pulpit"). A potential or threatened veto can also be wielded as a form of "affirmative persuasion" to encourage legislators to bend toward a chief executive's wishes lest their own legislative priorities get delayed or even thwarted.

Governors generally use the official opening day of the Oregon Legislative Assembly—the second Monday of January in odd-numbered years—to urge lawmakers to take specific actions. The state's media is out in force, editorial boards are primed to offer their own thoughts on legislative priorities, and the governor has a captive audience, however briefly, to outline top priorities. Perhaps no one used this "bully pulpit" better than Governor Tom McCall, who served from 1967 to 1975. A moderate Republican and former journalist, McCall became widely known for his 1962 television documentary *Pollution in Paradise*, which presaged what he came to define as "the doctrine": the belief that economic growth and environmental protection should be complimentary, not at odds.

As governor, McCall's comfort with reporters—he would often pay impromptu visits to the capitol pressroom to drop a colorful quote or two—and that era's rapid advent of television news combined to give him unprecedented visibility among Oregon citizens. Even though Democrats controlled one or both legislative houses during McCall's entire governorship, his media savvy and political skills (despite never having served in the legislature) found success in the passage of such policies as the bottle bill, protecting Oregon's beaches from development, and creating the Land Conservation and Development Commission (LCDC).

McCall's particular skills, and the far less partisan era in which he could deploy them, obscured a more prosaic political reality. Governors get little done by eloquent speeches; most of any governor's advocacy efforts are exercised far more subtly when they (or, more often, their staff members) weigh in on hundreds of discreet occasions as approximately a thousand bills wend their way to eventual passage. "Does the governor support or oppose this bill? Does she/he dislike it so much a veto will be hinted at—or even promised? What changes in the language might make it acceptable? What support might the governor provide on another front, in exchange for modifying this particular language?" These are just a few of the questions that the governor and her or his staff typically confront during legislative sessions.

The governor's influence on policy is also strongly affected by whether political allies control the legislative process. From the beginning of the Golden Era of Oregon politics in 1955 (see chapter 1) to 2017, Oregon experienced twenty-one instances of "divided" government, with each major party controlling at least one leg of the house-senate-governor triad. In only ten instances—a total of twenty years out of sixty-two—has the same party controlled all three entities.

For example, Governor Kitzhaber faced a solidly Republican legislature during all eight years of his first two terms as governor (1995-2003). So frequently did he end up vetoing bills that this former emergency room physician quickly earned the moniker of "Doctor No." During four regular sessions, and several special sessions, Kitzhaber vetoed more than two hundred bills or appropriation line items, including a record-setting sixty-nine vetoes in 1999 (none of the 1999 vetoes were overridden). Republican leaders also tried to end-run Kitzhaber's veto pen by referring a record twenty-one measures to the voters in 1999 and 2000, many of them dealing with criminal justice and tax issues. Eleven passed, and ten were defeated.

The situation has calmed considerably in the last decade. Since the 2008 election cycle, Democrats have controlled all three bodies outright, except in 2011, when the house was evenly split with thirty members from each party. But Democratic progressive ideas have often taken a backseat to budget-related crises, such as the severe economic recession that dominated the 2009 and 2011 legislative sessions, and the 2013 legislature's efforts to reduce the future costs of the PERS. Even during the 2017 legislation session, when an economic boom increased state general fund revenues by more than 10 percent, the legislature struggled to balance the 2017-19 budget owing to rapidly rising Medicaid, K–12, and PERS costs.

"Court Shaper"

Throughout American history, intense battles have often flared between the respective powers and prerogatives of the executive and legislative branches when it comes to the third branch of government: the judiciary. At first glance, an Oregon governor seems to have relatively little ability to affect the makeup of the judicial branch, as the Oregon Constitution since 1859 has required judges to be elected by direct popular vote. But in recent decades, a distinct pattern has emerged as to how judges hang up their judicial robes. Rather than announce they will not file for reelection—thereby creating a competitive open seat—most judges now retire or resign during their six-year terms. The governor can then choose a new judge to fill the vacancy, who can then run at the next election as an incumbent.

In the half century between 1950 and 2003, twenty-four of the thirty-two Oregon Supreme Court justices first took their seats as the result of a gubernatorial appointment to fill a vacancy. Only eight had initially won their seat by winning a statewide election. Since 2003, the pattern has grown even stronger. With the December 2017 retirement of Judge Jack Landau, all seven members of the Oregon Supreme Court will have initially been appointed by the governor, rather than via an election.

Land Manager

One of the state's more obscure but important entities is the three-person State Land Board, which is chaired by the governor and includes the secretary of state and the treasurer. As part of Oregon's 1859 admission to the union, the US Congress granted to the state approximately 6 percent of Oregon's landmass (over three million acres) to manage as trustees on behalf of the state's common schools. Within a half century, most of this heritage, including some of the world's most productive timber-producing lands, had been given or swindled away by unscrupulous land agents and high-ranking politicians.[5]

Today, the board manages about seven hundred thousand acres. Whereas Washington's extensive holdings of three million acres of primarily of high-producing timber and other land assets generated over $300 million in revenue in 2016, Oregon's state lands generated just $9 million. When management costs were considered, Oregon's portfolio actually lost money, according to the board's annual report.[6]

In 2015, the State Land Board—consisting at the time of three Democrats, Governor Kate Brown, Secretary of State Jeanne Atkins, and Treasurer Ted Wheeler— generated significant controversy when it decided to solicit bids to sell the Elliott State Forest, an 82,500-acre parcel in Oregon's Coos and Douglas Counties that makes up the board's single most valuable asset. In early 2017, two newly elected State Land Board members—Republican Secretary of State Dennis Richardson and Democratic Treasurer Tobias Read—initially outvoted Governor Brown 2-1 to move forward with a $221 million proposal submitted by a private company in partnership with several Native American tribes. In the wake of Brown's change of mind and significant public outcry, the 2017 Oregon legislature voted to borrow $100 million to keep the Elliott State Forest in public hands while compensating the State School Fund for its loss.

Military Leader

Just as the US Constitution designates the president "commander in chief" of the armed forces, Oregon's 1859 constitution granted the governor similar authority over the state's military and naval forces. Over the decades, these loosely organized militia units—whose duties in the nineteenth century mostly involved fighting Native Americans—evolved into today's modern version of the Oregon National Guard, whose adjutant general is directly appointed by and reports to the governor.

During the Iraq and Afghanistan conflicts of the early 2000s, state army and air national guard units (including Oregon's) bore major responsibilities and casualties in direct combat roles. As titular head of the Oregon National Guard, Governor Ted Kulongoski—himself a former Marine who served in Vietnam—attended more than one hundred military funerals for Oregonians killed during his eight years in office. In addition to their combat roles, Oregon's military personnel also have increasingly been called into service, along with other civilian public safety personnel, to respond to natural disasters, such as the 1996 and 2007 floods that wiped out much of Vernonia, and many devastating wildfires in recent decades. In an era of declining press coverage and civic awareness, many Oregonians today might be more familiar with the Oregon governor's "responder in chief" role than with her or his legislative policy agenda.

JUST HOW POWERFUL IS OREGON'S GOVERNOR?

As with any elected chief executive in American politics, Oregon's governor is granted her or his powers through a combination of sources. The most important foundational document is the Oregon Constitution itself. Article V and its eighteen sections spell out most of the governor's duties, though others are sprinkled elsewhere in the document, such as the governor's power to fill judicial vacancies or appoint the head of the state's Military Department.

State constitutions typically define gubernatorial powers in general terms. This can give a governor significant discretion in how to interpret such provisions. For example, in 1973, a combination of a winter drought that reduced hydroelectricity generation and the first Arab oil embargo led Governor Tom McCall to order that energy use be curtailed in all state-owned buildings. After encouraging citizens to do the same, he then ordered private businesses to curtail their electricity use (including outdoor advertising lights), darkening the Portland skyline. The move was viewed favorably by most of the public and was widely complied with; it also left legal experts scratching their heads trying to find the source of the governor's presumed authority to issue such an edict. In his 1975 "farewell speech" to the Portland City Club, McCall himself admitted the order had no real authority in law.

The second major source of an Oregon governor's powers are those responsibilities that have been added—and thus can be amended, or even taken away entirely—by the Oregon legislature. Sometimes a sympathetic legislature simply accedes to a governor's request for more power, such as when the 2011 Oregon legislature embraced Governor Kitzhaber's proposal to abolish the elected position of school superintendent and transfer its duties to the governor. At the other extreme, the legislature sometimes moves to impose certain duties upon, or restrictions on the power of, the executive branch, over the governor's strenuous objections.

For example, it was a Democratic-controlled legislature during the administration of Democratic Governor Bob Straub that in 1978 referred a constitutional amendment to voters requiring senate confirmation of certain gubernatorial appointments. The amendment passed, resulting in what is arguably the single biggest constitutional change relevant to the balance of power between the executive and legislative branches during the past fifty years. Still, it was hardly a radical move, since it merely gave the Oregon Senate the same power to confirm Oregon's top state managers as the US Senate has long exercised for presidential cabinet appointments.

Is Oregon's governor relatively more constrained and hamstrung than most state executives? During the 1990s, Thad Beyle of the University of North Carolina published widely read rankings that put Oregon's governor as the nation's fifteenth weakest in terms of institutional power, owing to such factors as the extent to which the executive power is split and the balance of executive versus legislative powers.

Yet it is difficult to see how Oregon's executive is significantly more enfeebled when so many of these same constraints are the rule elsewhere among the states, rather than the exception. As noted above, the "split executive" is nearly universal among the states, and while Oregon's governor is subject to term limits (no more than two consecutive terms), only fourteen governors lack such constraints. And a closer look suggests that Oregon's governors have roughly the same powers, and in some cases more, than many state counterparts.[7]

With the exception of a few of the oldest states (e.g., Maine, New Hampshire, and New Jersey), almost every state has rejected the US presidential framework of a single elected chief executive. In her 2006 book *The Executive Branch of State Government: People, Process, and Politics*, Margaret Ferguson notes that "the average number of executive branch elected officials across the states is about 8."[8] Oregon is on the low end of the spectrum with just five such offices. Its top four elected posts—governor, secretary of state, treasurer, and attorney general—are also found in most other states.

Oregon's governor has the same constitutional powers of most other states' chief executives to veto laws passed by the legislature, including the ability to "line item veto" specific provisions of a budget bill. Only if both houses of the legislature muster a two-thirds majority can an Oregon governor's veto be overridden—the same ratio as in most states.[9] A dozen states give their governors a more anemic veto authority than Oregon; six allow a veto override with just 60 percent, and another six require just a majority vote.[10] As in thirty-five other states, Oregon's governor can call a special session of the legislature and demand that it consider specific legislation. No state, including Oregon, constitutionally requires the legislature to pass or even vote on such legislation, however. And, alone among the fifty states, Oregon's constitution contains no provision for the impeachment of Oregon's chief executive, or that of any other executive branch official.[11] Like the constitutions of eighteen other states, however, Oregon's allows a recall election to remove a governor from office, though no such petition drive has ever succeeded.[12] Efforts by some legislators in 2015 to refer a constitutional amendment to voters to provide for legislative impeachment powers were unsuccessful.

The "legislative clock" that exists in Oregon's part-time legislature also serves to boost the governor's power. Oregon's constitution limits regular legislative sessions to one hundred and sixty days, and the even-numbered year sessions authorized by a 2010 voter-approved ballot measure is limited to just thirty-five. Although these limits can be suspended, such deadlines inevitably put more pressure on citizen legislators to reach final agreements on budget matters. A governor willing to "wait it out" can often exercise considerable leverage.

In their 2012 study of gubernatorial power, Kousser and Phillips conclude that "Our nation's governors rely on their informal powers to persuade more than on the formal privileges of office. Because of this, it makes less sense to talk about strong governor and weak governor states than it does to speak of individual governors as being potent or feeble."[13] Indeed, Oregon's recent history shows how strong a role personality—and circumstances—can play in determining a governor's powers. For the past half century, McCall's outsize personality and public relations savvy (not to mention Oregon's largely booming economy during his 1967-75 tenure) have arguably made him the yardstick against which all subsequent governors have been measured. Yet all seven of McCall's successors had far more years (even several decades) of experience as elected officials, often in multiple branches of government. Their effectiveness as Oregon's top executive arguably depended far more on how well each individual governor's personal abilities and vision matched the contemporary political pressures, economic conditions, and budget realities of their tenures than on any specific legal or organizational strictures inherent in the office.

CHANGES IN THE GOVERNOR'S ROLE

Oregon's 1859 constitution, which was modeled in large part on Indiana's 1851 version, reflected a common view of executive power at the time. Such powers should be spelled out in considerable detail, but also limited. With its power of crafting budgets and appropriating money, the legislature, not the executive, was intended to be the primary power in Oregon politics.

That said, the governor's role and prominence changed dramatically in the first decades of the twentieth century. Governor Oswald West (1911-15), a Democrat, used the office (along with the state's new "initiative and referendum" system) to advocate for several progressive causes, including women's suffrage, abolition of the death penalty, and prohibition. West also led the successful legislative effort to declare the beaches a "public highway," paving the way for Oregon's later Beach Bill. Democrat Walter Pierce (1923-27) won election in part with support from the Ku Klux Klan and its effort to prohibit Catholic schools. But Pierce also led the fight to enact a progressive income tax, which finally came to fruition in 1929 after seven statewide votes. Another notable governor of this era, Julius Meier (1931-35), was the only Oregon governor elected as an independent. Though a lifelong Republican, he was a strong advocate for public power.

As the Great Depression and World War II brought a huge influx of federal cash and then wartime workers to Oregon, the state's chief executive became more important and powerful. But after popular Governor Earl Snell, along with Oregon's secretary of state and senate president, were all killed in an October 1947 plane crash in eastern Oregon, a decade of instability followed, punctuated by several political defeats, a resignation, and the sudden death in 1956 of Governor Paul Patterson. During a twelve-year stretch between 1947 and 1959, seven different individuals served as Oregon governor.

The election of Mark O. Hatfield as governor in 1958 ushered in a far more stable period in Oregon's executive branch. Beginning with Hatfield's two terms (1959-67), five governors served two full consecutive terms in this period. The others have been Tom McCall (1967-75), Victor Atiyeh (1979-87), John Kitzhaber (1995-2003), and Ted Kulongoski (2003-11). Democrats Bob Straub (1975-79), Neil Goldschmidt (1987-91), and Barbara Roberts (1991-95) each served just a single term during this period. Straub lost his 1978 reelection bid; Goldschmidt and Roberts both declined to seek second terms.[14]

THE GOVERNOR AND THE EXECUTIVE BRANCH: A LOOK AHEAD

For the foreseeable future, Oregonians will continue to look largely to their governor, far more than any other elected officials within the executive or legislative branches, for the qualities of leadership and persuasion that will be key to resolving future budget predicaments as well as the many other challenges on the current landscape, from funding road repair and other critical infrastructure to providing affordable housing and improving Oregon's dismal educational performance in such areas as high school completion rates. Success or failure on these and other fronts likely will not rest on the office's specific institutional powers, but on the governor's skills at those most basic of political tasks—persuasion and influence—in getting various parties to cooperate and compromise around the political bargaining table.

Governor John Kitzhaber: A Most Remarkable Career

John Kitzhaber's fall from political grace was almost as rapid as his rise to political success. Oregon raised, Dartmouth educated, and trained at Oregon Health and Science University as an emergency room physician, Kitzhaber, a Democrat, first won election in 1978 to the Oregon House of Representatives from Roseburg, a timber-dependent community in rural Douglas County, two hundred miles south of Portland. Elected state senator in 1980, in 1985 the 37-year-old was chosen senate president, a post he held for four legislative sessions. Kitzhaber quickly distinguished himself for his legislative acumen and willingness to tackle wrenching problems. In late 1987, he took center stage on the nightly news as a defender of "health care rationing," arguing that far more lives could be saved by spending limited Medicaid funds on prenatal care and the treatment of chronic disease rather than large sums on low-probability treatments that most private insurance plans didn't cover.

In 1992, Kitzhaber decided not to seek reelection from his timber-dependent district. In October 1993, saying he was concerned that Republican legislators would dismantle key elements of the Oregon Health Plan, he met with Governor Barbara Roberts to discuss the upcoming gubernatorial election. Roberts later characterized the session as both painful and abrupt, especially given the imminent death of her husband (and Kitzhaber's former senate colleague), Frank Roberts. Shortly after, Kitzhaber declared that he would run for the 1994 Democratic nomination for governor. In early 1994, Roberts announced that she would not seek a second term. That November, bucking a national tide of massive Democratic defeats, including the loss of the US Congress, Kitzhaber handily defeated Republican Denny Smith.

Oregon's political culture by this time had changed markedly from the one Kitzhaber had encountered as a young legislator. Republican voters increasingly were electing strong conservatives who rejected the McCall-inspired moderation of the previous generation. By the mid-1990s, as Republicans controlled both the Oregon state house and senate,

Kitzhaber had earned the moniker of "Dr. No," vetoing sixty-nine bills passed by the 1997 legislature. This surpassed Governor Oswald West's previous record of fifty-eight vetoes in 1911.

Kitzhaber had some notable successes during this period: protecting and expanding the Oregon Health Plan and creating the Oregon Watershed Enhancement Board (OWEB), a collaboration-based effort to protect and restore endangered salmon runs. However, upon leaving due to term limits in 2003 amidst a struggling economy, Kitzhaber was widely quoted for stating that Oregon had become "ungovernable."

Out of office, Kitzhaber burnished his credentials as one of the nation's most articulate and knowledgeable health policy experts. Following Governor Kulongoski's two terms, in 2010 Kitzhaber won an unprecedented third term by edging Republican Chris Dudley, a former Portland Trailblazer basketball player with no previous political experience, by just 23,000 votes out of 1.4 million cast. Kitzhaber had carried all but one of Oregon's thirty-six counties in his 1998 reelection bid against anti-tax activist Bill Sizemore; twelve years later, he carried just seven.

Kitzhaber found a far friendlier legislative environment when he returned, including a rare 30-30 split in the 2011 house that resulted in Republican and Democratic "co-Speakers." Most notably, Kitzhaber successfully pushed major health-care reform legislation that enabled the state to use President's Obama's Affordable Care Act program to front-load nearly $2 billion of federal money to help launch coordinated care organizations (CCOs) (see chapter 14). Governing magazine that fall named Kitzhaber one of its nine "public officials of the year," noting that "Dr. No" had vetoed just four bills in his third term.

As 2014 began, political planets—among them legislative Democrats' growing margins, Oregon's booming economy, and Kitzhaber's own popularity—were aligning to make a fourth Kitzhaber term a rousing capstone to a long career, despite some bumps in implementing the new health-care program. But that fall, questions about his domestic partner, Cylvia Hayes, began to dominate public discussion. Just before the November 2014 election, Portland's Willamette Week newspaper reported that Hayes had received several consulting contracts from nonprofit advocacy groups, for which she promoted her proximity to the governor and her titular status as Oregon's "First Lady." Subsequent news stories detailed Hayes's admission—before meeting Kitzhaber—of being paid $5,000 to marry an Ethiopian national seeking to immigrate to the United States. She also admitted to working with a former boyfriend to establish an illegal marijuana growing business in Washington State.

Kitzhaber still defeated Republican Dennis Richardson in November 2014 to earn an unprecedented fourth term. But events quickly snowballed. By early February, state ethics and potential criminal investigations had opened, and controversy surrounded allegations about Kitzhaber aides requesting the deletion of private emails from government servers. On February 4, the Oregonian editorial board called for Kitzhaber's *resignation. Just one day after Senate President Peter Courtney and House Speaker Tina Kotek publicly called on him to step down, Kitzhaber announced his resignation, effective on February 18, 2015, while expressing considerable bitterness toward his fellow Democrats and the media. Three years later, state and federal criminal investigations had been closed without any charges filed. While denying any attempt to attain financial gain for himself or Hayes, Kitzhaber in March 2018 agreed to pay $20,000 in civil penalties to settle ten violations of Oregon state ethics laws.*

Kitzhaber's abrupt exit from the public stage capped nearly thirty years of elected public service. Twenty of those years were spent in the most powerful posts in two Oregon branches of government: twelve years (and thirty-seven days) as governor, and eight years as senate president. It's a record unmatched by any other politician in Oregon history, and one that future historians may find of more lasting consequence than the circumstances of his resignation.

Notes

1   Oregon Secretary of State, *Oregon Blue Book: 2017-18 Edition* (Salem: State of Oregon, 2017). Terms of state elected officials can also be found at the Oregon Blue Book website, accessed May 15, 2018, http://bluebook.state.or.us/state/elections/elections23.htm.

2   "Agency Head and Board/Commission Appointment Requirements," State of Oregon Department of Administrative Services, accessed May 15, 2018, http://www.oregon.gov/das/Policies/50-060-01.attachment.pdf.

3   Jerry Medler, "Governor," in *Oregon Politics and Government: Progressives versus Conservative Populists*, ed. Richard A. Clucas, Mark Henkels, and Brent S. Steel (Lincoln: University of Nebraska Press, 2005), 135.

4   Thad Kousser and Justin H. Phillips, *The Power of American Governors: Winning on Budgets and Losing on Policy* (Cambridge: Cambridge University Press, 2012), 3.

5   Stephen A. Douglas Puter, *Looters of the Public Domain* (London: Forgotten Books, 2015).

6   "Annual Report on Common School Fund Real Property for Fiscal Year 2016," Oregon Department of State Lands, May 9, 2017, http://www.oregon.gov/dsl/Land/Documents/slb_apr2016_item6.pdf.

7   "National Governors Association: Governors' Power and Authority," National Governor's Association, accessed May 15, 2018, https://www.nga.org/cms/management/powers-and-authority#overview.

8   Margaret Robertson Ferguson, ed., *The Executive Branch of State Government: People, Process, and Politics* (Santa Barbara, CA: ABC-Clio, 2006), 62.

9   "Book of the States 2017, Chap. 4: State Executive Branch," Council of State Governments, accessed May 15, 2018, http://knowledgecenter.csg.org/kc/system/files/4.4.2017.pdf.

10 "Book of the States 2017, Chap. 4."

11 "Book of the States 2017, Chap. 4.'

12 "Recall of State Officials," National Conference of State Legislatures, accessed May 15, 2018, http://www.ncsl.org/research/elections-and-campaigns/recall-of-state-officials.aspx.

13 Kousser and Phillips, *Power of American Governors*, 25.

14 Oregon Secretary of State, *Oregon Blue Book*. Terms of state elected officials can also be found at the Oregon Blue Book website, accessed May 15, 2018, http://bluebook.state.or.us/state/elections/elections23.htm.

7

The Role of Bureaucracy in Oregon State and Local Government

DOUGLAS MORGAN, JEANINE BEATRICE, and SAJJAD HAIDER

> For most of American history the terms "bureaucrat" and "bureaucracy"
> have been used in popular discourse as epithets . . . The historical origins of
> the American hostility to public organizations are based on the belief that
> something is inherently anti-democratic in the growth of bureaucracy . . .
> The battle between bureaucracy and democracy is written into our history.
> So is the fact that democracy must win. All we have left to debate is the cost.
> —Barry Karl, "The American Bureaucrat"

Oregonians, like most American citizens, have long been ambivalent about the role of bureaucracy (see chapter 9). The signers of the Declaration of Independence viewed bureaucracy as an active agent in the executive abuse of government power. This tradition remains alive and well in Oregon as a result of a populist tradition that measures the success of bureaucracies by the extent to which they are responsive to the citizens they serve. But this dominant populist tradition sits alongside a progressive tradition, which views bureaucracy as the instrument for ensuring efficient, fair, consistent, and effective policy implementation. One of the great challenges facing bureaucratic leaders is that citizens frequently hold both expectations simultaneously, without recognizing how this view affects public policy, public funding, and effective operations. While citizens may at times favor giving career administrators more leeway in taking administrative initiative, most citizens share Barry Karl's observation that bureaucracies should be treated as "sheep in wolves' clothing."

THE ROLE OF THE BUREAUCRACY IN BALANCING CONFLICTING DEMOCRATIC VALUES

The populist and progressive traditions necessarily put state and local bureaucracies in the business of balancing competing democratic values: efficiency, effectiveness, responsiveness, protection of rights, and sensitivity to community values. Street-level bureaucrats, middle managers, and senior administrators have lots of discretionary room to significantly affect these values. While much of this implementation discretion is legally controlled by administrative rulemaking and adjudication processes discussed later in this chapter, much discretion unavoidably remains in the hands of individual administrators at all levels of the bureaucracy. How this discretion is exercised affects our daily well-being: who gets arrested and ticketed; whether our home repairs and remodeling are covered by, and in compliance with, building codes; what constitutes a "pothole" in our streets; what is meant by "excessive noise," "disturbing the peace," "unlawful possession"; and dozens of other examples of vague and ambiguous language in our laws. Every day, our street-level bureaucrats are deciding what values should receive priority at a given point in time. This widespread discretion is one of the reasons bureaucracies operate under a constant cloud of suspicion.

Another important reason our bureaucracies are viewed suspiciously is that organizations can "go off the rails." Sometimes, natural processes of bureaucratic inertia through time create bureaucratic agencies with high levels of independence and autonomy.[1] This is the case with local public safety organizations. Some bureaucracies get too cozy with the interest groups that they are supposed to serve and regulate.[2] This has been a criticism of the Oregon Department of Environmental Quality.[3] At other times, organizations succumb to a phenomena known as groupthink, where everyone has a high level of excitement for "getting the job done" while losing sight of the larger moral purposes of their work (e.g., the Tuskegee Syphilis experiments, the Challenger disaster, the torture of prisoners at Abu Ghraib, and the recent lawsuit by Bullseye Glass against Governor Kate Brown).[4] Most of the participants in these organizations believed they were acting ethically. That is why we don't leave public service ethics to matters of merely personal judgment. First, we tether bureaucrats to an oath of office that commits them to uphold the core values of our democracy.[5] Second, we create organizational, political, and administrative systems of control and accountability. We review these various systems in the sections that follow. We start with the core democratic values that guide the exercise of administrative discretion in Oregon's multiple systems of government.

The Goal of Efficient and Effective Bureaucracy

Despite Oregon's populist leanings, its citizens have long embraced the progressive value of bureaucracy as a mechanism to advance the efficient and effective functioning of democratic institutions. For example, the expertise of professional engineers, planners, and natural resource experts has been at the forefront of timber harvesting, the commercial fishing industry, and developing our waterway systems and ports.[6] Since the early 1900s, Oregonians have relied heavily on professional planners to design our cities, parks and transportation systems.[7] Citizens have embraced the "good government movement" that was part of the progressive reform period at the turn of the twentieth century, which replaced a patronage system of appointment to public service with a merit-based system. This movement established the council-manager form of government, which is the form used by most cities in Oregon with populations over twenty-five hundred.[8] This system relies on professional administrators to maintain organizations that deliver programs and serve with maximum efficiency and effectiveness. But this progressive model has spawned populist reactions that utilize citizen initiatives to check perceived professional and bureaucratic excesses such as excessive land-use planning, overharvest of our natural resources, and restrictions on individual freedom (i.e., right-to-die and marijuana initiatives). When these policy shifts occur, it is the career bureaucrats who bear the brunt of citizen disaffection and criticism, rather than the policies that are responsible for their ire.

Ensuring Responsive Government: The Case for a Representative Bureaucracy

Another democratic value served by bureaucracy is that it mirrors the values of the citizens it serves. This populist idea was first promoted by the Anti-Federalists in opposing the adoption of the newly proposed US Constitution in 1787. They worried that the new government would attract public servants who would be driven by a desire to advance their "grandeur, personal power and splendor" at the expense of self-sacrifice and service to the community.[9] Oregon's populist legacy has prevented these fears from becoming reality. At the state level, the "representative function" of bureaucracy is reflected in extensive use of citizen commissions to provide policy and organizational oversight of state agencies—an issue discussed in the last section of this chapter.

At the local level, the concern for a "representative bureaucracy" has resulted in the creation of multiple elected public offices that give rise to their own independent administrative structures. (See chapter 6 for an explanation of the impact on state government.) For example, citizens of Oregon counties elect their own assessor/tax collector, county clerk, sheriff, treasurer, and chief judge (who serves as commission chair in counties without its own home-rule charter). The need for a "representative bureaucracy" is also reflected in the state requirement that all local budgets be reviewed by citizens,[10] the use of numerous citizen oversight and advisory committees (see fig. 7.1), and ongoing efforts by all public service agencies (particularly police, fire, and social service providers) to create bureaucracies that look more racially and socioeconomically like the citizens they serve.

Protecting Rights

Over the years, appreciation has grown for the role bureaucracies play in protecting the rights of citizens. Oregon's constitution is more protective of free speech rights than the US Constitution. Since 2011, for example, emails of all Oregon public

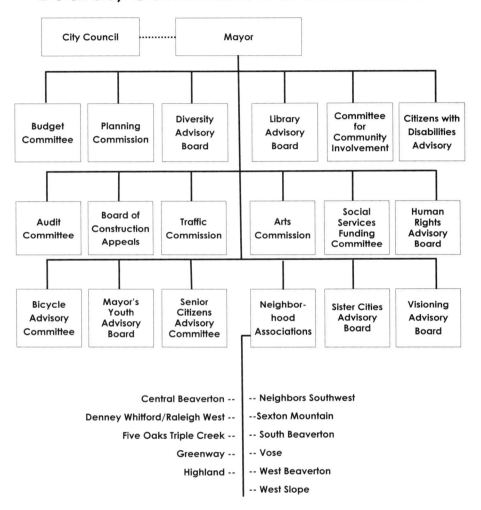

Figure 7.1. City of Beaverton citizen advisory committees.

employees, including legislators, have been declared a part of the public record, sub-ject to access and retrieval by citizens.[11] Since 1987, Oregon citizens "can write, print, read, say, show or sell anything to a consenting adult even though that expression may be generally or universally 'obscene.'"[12] As the *New York Times* observed, "this doc-trine of total freedom of expression differs from Federal standards that have developed on the assumption that suppressive laws may apply to obscenity."[13] This right to total freedom of expression takes on meaning through the daily vigilance of state and local administrative agencies. Oregon citizens can sleep at night knowing that their water, electricity, driver's license, local planning permit, and access to numerous public services cannot be denied for discriminatory purposes or be ended without some kind of "due process" opportunity to be informed and to respond. Bureaucracies and their legal counsels are necessary to ensure compliance with open meeting laws, freedom of information, conflict-of-interest prohibitions, and dozens of other state and federal legal requirements all aimed at creating a transparent and accountable government. In recent decades, the bureaucracy has shifted its role to include the protection of rights, in addition to its traditional role of efficiently and effectively administering public programs. The bureaucracy now stands on an equal footing with the courts in protecting citizen rights from abuses of executive power.[14]

Aligning Public Purposes with Community Expectations

Oregon bureaucracies, as in most states with a mixture of highly urban and rural communities, face the challenge of providing equitable service to all, evidenced in a number of ways: in how state agencies organize their regions and program functions (see particularly the websites of the Departments of Environmental Quality and Transportation); in the work of institutes and foundations (see the websites of the Ford Family Foundation and Oregon Solutions); in strong citizen advisory committees and neighborhood association programs in larger urban jurisdictions (see fig. 7.1); and in the City of Portland's continued support of the commission form of government and a bottom–up array of citizen activist organizations that are an exception to the national norm.[15]

To summarize, citizens are ambivalent about bureaucracy because of their multiple and conflicting expectations and experiences. Citizens fear tyrannous overreach yet want bureaucracies to be responsive as well as efficient and effective in administering programs and services. At the same time, they expect bureaucracies to be vigilant in protecting rights and guarding against government excess. Such ambivalence is not so much a reflection of our views of bureaucracy as it is a reflection of what we want from our democratic systems of government, writ large. In the following section, we explore the ways in which local bureaucracies address these multiple expectations.

OREGON'S LOCAL GOVERNMENT BUREAUCRACIES

Studies consistently show that local systems of government across the nation enjoy a 72 percent level of trust compared to 57 and 28 percent for state-level and national governments, respectively.[16] Furthermore, studies suggest that there is generally more trust for career administrators than there is for elected officials at the local level.[17] While this research has not conclusively documented the differences among states or why greater trust exists for local governments, issues of proximity, nonpartisanship, perceptions of access and control, and consistency and predictability of service delivery have been cited.[18] We review some of these factors in the sections that follow.

Professional Standards and Legal Mandates

While services at the local level may vary because of funding levels, a combination of legal mandates and professional best practices that are memorialized in codes of national professional associations ensure a high level of uniformity of structure and predictability in the delivery of local services, also known as isomorphism.[19] Because all local governments are creatures of state authority, they are required to conform to state and federal legal standards that affect many bureaucratic practices, including budgeting, reporting, and auditing requirements; public meeting protocols; ethical, financial, and conflict-of-interest reporting requirements; employment practices, including hiring, promotion, and termination; workplace safety; discrimination issues related to race, gender, ethnicity, sexual identity, and age; and contracting and purchasing (see note 14 below).

In addition to legal requirements, local citizens experience consistency in service delivery because administrators adhere to myriad "best practice" requirements established by national professional associations (e.g., the Municipal Finance Officers Association, multiple professional accounting organizations, American Society for Testing and Materials, American Society of Civil Engineers, American Library Association). Our public safety, social service delivery, civic infrastructure, and public services in general share a high level of uniformity and consistency across the state because of these professional standards.

Reliance on Professional Administrators

Citizens can take comfort in knowing that local governments are administered by professionally trained administrators. All Oregon cities with populations of more than twenty-five hundred (except Portland and Beaverton) use a council-manager form of government in which a senior career manager oversees the city's administrative operations. Even most special districts and most counties rely on a chief administrative officer (CAO) or chief executive officer (CEO) to oversee daily operations. This kind of oversight is beyond the capacity of part-time and unpaid members of the elected council and helps to ensure high quality and uniformity in local government performance.

Local Citizens Play a Large Role in Shaping the Services They Receive

Local citizens have opportunities to significantly influence local policy and budget priorities that do not exist at the state level. Consider public education. Despite the fact that the state and federal governments have centralized the funding of public education and control of the curriculum through mandated testing, local citizens still elect their school boards and site councils, who together decide how to configure curricula, types of schools, school boundaries, transfer policies, special education programs, extracurricular activities, and numerous other activities about which parents care deeply.

Because of the local property tax limitations described in chapters 9 and 18,[20] service levels vary considerably across the state. To illustrate, let's compare the bureaucracies of the City of Eugene with Burns, Oregon. In 2016, the City of Eugene (160,561 population) had a budget of $306,706,841, with 1,445 public employees working in the following four functional areas: public safety (546), infrastructure planning (561), culture and recreation (174), and central business services (164). By contrast, the City of Burns (2,722 population) had a total budget of $6,512,191, with a workforce of 13 full-time-equivalent administrative employees in the following functional areas: airport, city attorney and engineer, city hall, fire, planning commission, police, and public works. You would find a similar picture if you compared Ashland with Condon or Eugene with Lakeview.

To summarize, local government bureaucracies in Oregon, while administered by highly qualified and trained career professionals, operate in a context established by populist political processes that give citizens a high degree of control over their services. They can choose to add services through special tax levies and the creation of special districts or annexations. In the May 2016 primary election, there were fifty-six local tax measures consisting of a combination of bonds, tax levies, and proposals to increase the local gas tax. These measures passed by a margin of 3 to 1, about the same margin as the margin of trust that citizens have in their local governments in national surveys.[21]

STATE-LEVEL BUREAUCRACY: FRAGMENTED AND SHARED CONTROL

Chapter 6 describes the executive branch of Oregon state government, which is organized into five independent administrative structures that operate under the supervening authority of five separately elected political officials, as illustrated in figure 7.2.

Together, the governor, treasurer, secretary of state, commissioner of labor and industries, and attorney general oversee more than two hundred and fifty separate agencies, boards, commissions, and departments, many of which operate quite autonomously.[22] This complex structure creates a large amount of fragmentation and results in ongoing debate over what kinds of political, organizational, and legal accountability are required to ensure the successful functioning of Oregon state government. While the fragmentation may not be an outlier among state-level bureaucracies (as presented in chapter 6), it does require a strong-willed and skilled governor to bring the state bureaucracy into unified policy alignment. In the absence of this will and skill, the bureaucracy defaults to the diverse and sometimes competing pushes and pulls of organizational and political controls, which we discuss more fully in the sections to follow.

STATE OF OREGON ORGANIZATIONAL CHART

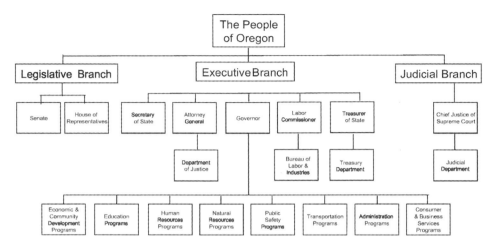

Figure 7.2. State of Oregon organizational chart.

POLITICAL CONTROL

By political control, we mean holding state agencies accountable to citizen oversight bodies and elected officials, especially the governor and the legislature. Measured against this standard, Oregon is like most other states where control is shared. Oregon law permits the governor and other elected executives to appoint many department heads, and have controlling influence over the appointment of the "deputy of each division within a department of state government" and all "principal assistants and deputies." The legislature exercises its political control by making the laws and providing the funding that enables the bureaucracy to function. But this shared control is more extensive in Oregon and includes accountability to independent commissions that oversee agency policies, budgets, and performance. Instead of being appointed by the governor, some state agency directors are appointed by and serve at the pleasure of these independent governing boards and commissions. In an interesting twist, these appointing and reporting relationships are defined by statute. This arrangement creates two structures of authority, one that consists of hierarchical instruments of political control by the governor and the legislature, and another that consists of horizontal and populist-centered independent commissions that tie the bureaucracy to more grassroots constituencies.

The state's reliance on citizen commissions to oversee the bureaucracy was established early in Oregon's history with the creation of Fish and Wildlife (1878); the Board of Forestry, which adopted fire-prevention rules (1907), and the Department of Transportation (1913). The pattern continued as the state took on increasing regulatory and social welfare responsibilities after the turn of the century and into the New Deal (Labor and Industries, 1903; Public Utility Commission, 1915; Public Welfare Commission, 1934). The commission system continued to be the preferred model during the rapid expansion of single-issue interest groups in the 1960s and 1970s, as each significant political constituency sought to have its own commission to provide oversight of its interests (Asian Affairs Commission, 1995; Black Affairs Commission, 1983; Commission on Women, 1964; numerous product promotion commissions, such as the cherry commission, hazelnut commission, fescue seed commission, etc.; and the professional self-regulatory commissions, such as teachers, radiologists, geologists, doctors, dietitians, dentists, etc.).

All states make extensive use of commissions, commonly to deal with issues that fall outside the traditional functional-centered policy domains (i.e., transportation, health and human services, environmental regulation), and focus on crosscutting issues such as ethics, gaming, equity, and the like. In Oregon, commissions go further. They are commonly used to provide policy and administrative oversight of core state functions. This means the governor has to exert especially strong leadership to control agencies for either policy or managerial ends.

Commissions are created by the legislature and are composed of members appointed by the governor. For example, the Department of Transportation has a five-member Oregon Transportation Commission (OTC) appointed by the governor for a four-year term. The governor is required to take into consideration the different geographic regions of the state in making recommendations that must be confirmed by the senate. No more than three members can belong to the same political party (Oregon Revised Statute [ORS] 184.612). The OTC has far-reaching authority to "develop and maintain a state transportation policy" (ORS 184.618). In fact, the statute charges the director with the responsibility of preparing and submitting implementation programs to the commission for approval. The political control over state agencies that is shared by the legislature, the governor, and citizen commissions produces a state bureaucracy that is quite nonpartisan in its approach to policy implementation and is subject to populist reactions when there are administrative missteps.

The Nonpartisan Nature of State Bureaucracy

The history, structure, and function of Oregon's system of executive, legislative, and citizen oversight produce a high level of nonpartisanship in the bureaucracy. Long-time career administrators consistently observe that they have never been asked their party affiliation in more than twenty years of state public service, even when appointed by the governor to serve at the highest and most trusted levels of government (e.g., as directors of the Department of Transportation, the Executive Department, the Department of Administrative Services, or the Oregon Department of Forestry).[23]

This has not always been the case. In the 1930s and 1940s, party affiliation was an important qualification for appointment to many high-level administrative positions.[24]

Bureaucratic Crises and Populist-Centered Remedies

When members of the legislature are surprised by bureaucratic failures, they react swiftly and predictably with populist-centered remedies, as was the case in 2015, when the Department of Human Services (DHS) faced a series of incidents involving child abuse and welfare fraud. In response to these stories, there were public demands for more oversight, demands from the media for more real-time information, demands from stakeholders for more high-quality partnerships and realistic rate-setting, and demands from legislators for a reduction in DHS's discretion in regulating licensed childcare agencies. In short, while the providers of child services were complaining about too much administrative and regulatory burden, the public was demanding even more control over providers to prevent and stop children from being harmed while in the state's care.

The DHS controversy produced three responses. First, Governor Brown appointed a new DHS director with the specific charge to oversee child and youth safety in substitute care and required an independent review of the state system. Second, the governor signed Senate Bill 1515 (2016) into law to address child safety in substitute care by increasing the authority of DHS to regulate providers and increasing the responsibility of all DHS employees to report concerns about children in childcare agencies. The increased authority was packaged as a "mandated rule" that removed discretion from DHS and forced the department to take legislatively prescribed action against providers for different kinds of violations (an administrative form of "mandated sentencing"). Third, House Bill 4080 (2016) was signed by the governor to establish a Governor's Child Foster Care Advisory Commission. This commission, with members appointed by the governor, advises the governor and the DHS director, makes recommendations for legislation, and monitors foster care outcome measures. Moreover, the commission membership was specifically designed by legislation to not include DHS staff as members or conveners of the commission.

The response to the child safety crisis was inherently populist: the public was fed up with relying on the discretionary expertise of professionals. The solution was also inherently populist, as an independent review was called for, a new senate bill was passed that reduced departmental discretion in decision-making, and another citizen commission was established to advise and oversee the foster care activities undertaken by the state.

ORGANIZATIONAL CONTROL

In addition to political control, career managers have the lead responsibility for organizational accountability. In Oregon's local governments, this is the special responsibility of the CEO / city manager / CAO. At the state level, the Department of Administrative Services (DAS) has assumed this role. DAS is one of the few agencies created to explicitly work on behalf of the governor to make the state bureaucracy perform more efficiently, effectively, and responsively. The Oregon Legislative Assembly created DAS in 1993 by combining two large existing agencies, the Department of General Services and the Executive Department. This 1993 consolidation was driven less by the governor's desire for political and policy control over executive agencies and more by a desire to consolidate and centralize administrative activities in the name of greater efficiency, effectiveness, and executive accountability (ORS 184.305).

How much emphasis is placed on organizational forms of bureaucratic control in Oregon waxes and wanes with larger national movements and moods that reflect levels of satisfaction and dissatisfaction with government performance in general. For example, at the end of the nineteenth and early part of the twentieth century, Oregon followed the national trend of implementing a series of populist reform that became known as the Oregon System (see chaps. 1 and 2). These reforms emphasized opening up governmental agencies to more outside access and control by grassroots influences. The national mood changed in the latter part of the twentieth century, and so did Oregon's.

Reinvention of Government and the New Public Management Movement

The Reagan Revolution in the 1980s spawned what came to be known as the "reinvention of government movement," which over the years has become more commonly known as the New Public Management (NPM) movement.[25] There are two impulses that drive NPM, one that is conservative and populist in its orientation, and the other that is more liberal and progressive. The conservative orientation emphasizes reducing the size of government and contracting out some services to the private and nonprofit sectors. The progressive impulse emphasizes a management-centered approach to improve the performance of public programs through the elimination of unnecessary rules and the creation of high-performing organizational systems that raise customer satisfaction and increase effectiveness and efficiency.

Oregon's state bureaucracy has undertaken initiatives that reflect both of these impulses. The conservative impulse is reflected in the legislature's decision (ORS 240.185) in the early stages of the Reagan Revolution in 1984 to limit the number of state employees to 1.5 percent of the state's population in the prior year. Every two years, the DAS updates information applying the limit to the number of budgeted full-time-equivalent (FTE) positions. Analysis of the growth in state FTE by the Legislative Fiscal Office spanning the 2007-9 biennium and the previous six biennia indicated that growth in both the number of positions and total FTE was roughly 20 percent compared to growth of 110 percent in the total funds budgeted for the same period. The General Fund budget grew by 88 percent over the same period.

The progressive impulse of the "reinvention agenda" is reflected in Oregon's decision in 1989 to create a Progress Board with the responsibility of tracking the success of administrative agencies in meeting a set of economic, social, and environmental goals in the state strategic plan, called Oregon Shines. Agencies now had to undertake benchmark-based planning, budgeting, and management of their organizations. This initiative lasted for ten years before it ran out of steam, becoming a victim of attrition and inertia. Some stakeholders actively sought to minimize the importance of benchmarks, and there was turnover in legislative and commission members who no longer had ownership in the benchmark process. After the 2009 report was completed, the state legislature decided to discontinue funding the Progress Board.

The Impact of New Public Governance and the Rise of Collaborative Bureaucracies

The past two decades have seen increasing recognition that many public problems cannot be solved through command-and-control hierarchies that rely on rules and roles. The emergence of "wicked problems" that transcend the capacity of any single organization to solve has given rise to the New Public Governance (NPG) movement.[26] This movement, discussed extensively in chapter 11, emphasizes value-based collaboration among multiple parties with a heavy reliance on building trust horizontally among stakeholders and leveraging fiscal, political, organizational, and human resources among all participating organizations.

Oregon bureaucracies engage in collaborative governance when pressured by the governor or when it is required to meet the success criteria of external stakeholders. For example, in 2011, Governor Kitzhaber invoked a legal provision that enables the governor to "assume the office of director of the department whenever and for whatever time the governor deems advisable" (ORS 184.315). The governor used this provision to appoint Michael Jordan as Director of DAS, which is the governor's chief instrument for controlling all executive agencies. In addition, however, he bestowed on Jordan the title of chief operating officer for the governor. This sent a message that DAS was not only a department providing centralized support services to other state agencies, but also that its director was the governor's personal chief operating officer and policy agent. Governor Kitzhaber hoped to use this arrangement to force collaboration across inward looking state agencies.[27] With support from the governor, Michael Jordan created the Enterprise Leadership Team (ELT), consisting of the directors (or their designees) of about twenty of the largest state agencies. The ELT helped harmonize policy and programs across agencies and also served as Jordan's management team for state government.

After Kitzhaber resigned in 2015, however, state agency agendas drifted back to control by the mix of board/commission direction, ongoing legislative direction and interaction, and stakeholder pressures. The result was a lack of performance coordination across government to deal with outcomes that implicate multiple departments and external partners. For example, getting third graders to reading standards or cleaning up a watershed requires multiple agencies and programs working together through a shared governance model. Overall, the ability of the governor and career administrators to sustain performance improvement through organizational and management innovation is frustrated by Oregon's fragmented bureaucratic structure that is more often than not controlled by its populist roots.

LEGAL CONTROL OVER THE BUREAUCRACY: COURTS, ADMINISTRATIVE RULEMAKING, AND ADMINISTRATIVE ADJUDICATION

In addition to relying on political and organizational controls to ensure accountability of administrative agencies, the state bureaucracy is controlled on a day-to-day basis by a plethora of legal requirements—defined by statutes and administrative rules—that often fall under the general rubric of "due process" protections. Granting licenses, protecting vulnerable populations, taking away benefits, and allowing access to public lands and resources are all bureaucratic activities that are highly constrained by judicial and other legal precedents. Figuring out the implications of this complex body of law for a contemplated agency action requires frequent communication between state agencies and Oregon Department of Justice attorneys, who are specifically assigned to advise government agencies and their administrators on the legal limits of their discretionary authority.

A second important means of legal control is administrative rulemaking, or what one scholar has called "the greatest inventions of modern government."[28] Administrative rulemaking addresses one of the most troublesome questions posed by modern government: How does the legislative branch anticipate all of the myriad circumstances and conditions facing administrators who are charged with implementing the law? This "gap-filling" role is what rulemaking is supposed to do. Legislative bodies have designed the process so that agencies fill in the gaps in a political environment that "mirrors the political forces that gave rise to the agency's legislative mandate long after the coalition behind the legislation has disbanded."[29]

Oregon's rulemaking guidelines are spelled out in the Oregon Administrative Procedures Act (*Oregon Revised Statutes*, chapter 183). The act is similar to rulemaking guidelines at the federal level and in other states. This similarity includes: providing notice to those who wish to participate in the process, a specification of the processes for participation, an agency requirement to respond to all issues raised in the hearing process, and formal public promulgation of the final rule.

But Oregon rulemaking is different in two major respects from the federal system. First, agencies in Oregon can initiate a rule so long as they *perceive a need* (ORS 183.335(2)(b)(C)), which has been defined by Oregon courts as the need "that the rule-proposing agency *perceives*."[30] This "burden of proof" standard is far less than what is required of federal agencies, which must meet the test of "substantial evidence based on the record taken as a whole."[31]

Another difference in Oregon rulemaking from the federal process is the definition of a rule. This is critically important, since administrative agencies undertake numerous actions that provide employees with guidelines on what policy means, how to set priorities, and how to interpret and apply their discretionary authority. For example, if the superintendent of the state police issues a directive that prioritizes drug trafficking over, say, missing persons or the recovery of stolen property, is the superintendent engaged in rulemaking? Or consider, for example, the simple question of whether a state Department of Environmental Quality (DEQ) administrator can allow a solid-waste operator in Burns to cover disposal debris with dirt only once a week, in contrast to a DEQ administrator in the Portland metropolitan area who may require debris to be covered daily. The amount of debris, the density of the population, and the prevailing winds may create quite different health hazards at the two separate sites. Where is the line between administrative rulemaking and routine management oversight and control? At the federal level, this distinction is formally recognized by exempting "interpretive rules" from rulemaking requirements; see 5 U.S.C. § 553(b), 553(d)(2)). In Oregon, there is no obvious distinction. As a result, the Oregon attorney general advises agencies to undertake formal rulemaking whenever any action "acts like a rule."

Imagine what our local hardware stores would be like if this definition were used to define what belonged in the hammer section! Some stores (or state agencies) would find the overly inclusive definition reason enough to avoid promulgating rules and concentrate their energies on other sections of the store. Such is the case with administrative rulemaking across Oregon state agencies.[32] Small and large agencies are tasked daily with managing resources and simply do not have the staff necessary to promulgate rules for everything they do that "acts like a rule." It surely is a calculated risk for agencies to operate with unpromulgated rules in order to save money, preserve managerial discretion, and provide geographic flexibility. And, for some agencies that risk is too high, as is the case for the Department of Corrections, which has a clearly defined and a well-organized constituency whose members will readily sue the department if they deviate from required rulemaking protocols.

CONCLUSION: DO OREGON BUREAUCRACIES HAVE THE CAPACITY TO MEET FUTURE CHALLENGES?

Oregon bureaucracies are progressive outposts that are controlled by populist impulses. These outposts lack the mediating influence of strong political institutions that exist in most other states, which anchor bureaucracies to a larger common and consistent political agenda. At the local level, these agendas are carefully constructed through the initiative of professional managers who work with the part-time elected officials to get agreement on the community's strategic plan. If managers are lucky, they can build agreement on this plan so that it carries forward from one election cycle to another. At the state level, the bureaucracy often lacks a centralized enduring anchor. The governor occasionally serves this function, but it does not last for long because any "good government" reform agenda can be set aside by a new election, a legislative initiative "to take control" of an issue that the bureaucracy is mishandling, or some kind of political emergency that redirects the energy and attention of the governor's office (e.g., the spotted owl controversy of the early 1990s and the resignation of Governor Kitzhaber in 2015).

Looking to the future, we can expect bureaucracies to continue performing their traditional functions at high levels: being responsive to citizens, protecting rights, ensuring efficient and effective policy implementation, and aligning policy with community expectations. However, property tax limitations, pension fund liabilities, and state and federal mandated services will continue to put considerable pressure on our bureaucracies to do even more. And Oregon bureaucracies will need to design new approaches to service delivery that reduce and spread the costs and educate citizens on funding realities. These initiatives will include more jurisdictional mergers, consolidations, and shared service agreements; more collaborative governance approaches to addressing policy challenges; and more reliance on contracting out for services.

Four challenges to watch for in the coming decades include:

1. **New leadership skills and conciliatory practices**. Building service agreements across boundaries requires the acquisition of new leadership and administrative skills by agency managers, what have been described as "boundary-spanning" or "conciliatory practice" skills.[33]

2. **Data access, management, and sharing**. Successful collaboration requires data sharing, but there are considerable barriers in the social service area. For example, the right-to-privacy requirements of the Health Insurance Portability and Accountability Act of 1996 (HIPAA) prevent the free flow of patient information and outdated "legacy" data systems that cannot support new integrated service models.

3. **Millennials and the challenge of long-term commitment**. Collaborative agreements take time to build and manage in ways that create enduring trust and confidence. The millennial generation will become the stewards of these agreements as current managers, subject matter experts, and leaders retire. The challenge for current administrators is to find ways of managing the millennial generation to secure their long-term commitment to the projects they will lead.[34]

4. **Increased contract management capacity and transparency.** Contracting out services to third parties can produce a "shadow

government,"[35] an arrangement where there is little public understanding of the policy goals of the contracts and where accountability requirements of responsiveness, equity, and fairness are sacrificed to the single goal of "getting the biggest bang for the buck."[36] Citizens and elected officials will need to understand the policy consequences of a jurisdiction's contracting practices. Administrators will need to take the lead in changing current practices.[37]

We end this chapter with confidence that Oregon bureaucracies will continue to perform their traditional management roles at a high level. The tools are available for our bureaucracies to perform their growing collaborative governance roles, but administrators will need the support of elected political leaders who make this a priority and create the enabling conditions for it to be successful.[38]

Notes

This chapter has benefited greatly from the wise and insightful comments of longtime career administrator Doug Decker, a retired Oregon State forester who led the Oregon Department of Forestry from 2011 to 2016.

    Epigraph. Barry D. Karl, "The American Bureaucrat: A History of a Sheep in Wolves' Clothing," *Public Administration Review,* 47, no. 1 (January–February, 1987): 26.

1   Daniel Carpenter, *The Forging of Bureaucratic Autonomy: Reputations, Networks, and Policy Innovation in Executive Agencies, 1862-1928* (Princeton, NJ: Princeton University Press, 2001).

2   Theodore Lowi, *The End of Liberalism: The Second Republic of the United States* (New York: W. W. Norton, 2009). Oregon's commission system of government provides a legally defined structure of authority for interest groups to have official representation and control over state agencies. This transparency, coupled with a citizen legislature whose members have limited staff, mitigates the heavy-handed and "backroom" role of interest groups in "calling the shots" in how administrative agencies interpret and implement their missions.

3   David Einolf, "Department of Environmental Quality Suffers Key Weaknesses," *Oregonian,* February 16, 2016; Bob Davis, "Gov. Kate Brown Taps Attorney as Newest Interim Leader at Department of Environmental Quality," *Oregonian,* April 6, 2016.

4   James Jones, *Bad Blood* (New York: Free Press, 1993); National Aeronautics and Space Administration, *Report of Columbia Accident Investigation Board* (Washington, DC: Government Printing Office, 2003); Seymour M. Hersh, *Chain of Command: The Road from 9/11 to Abu Ghraib* (New York: HarperCollins, 2004); *Bullseye Glass v. Kate Brown et al.* 2017, Oregon District Court, 3:17-cv-01970. Bullseye accused DEQ of systematically misrepresenting its test results, leaking incomplete and misleading information to the press to paint Bullseye as the center of industrial pollution in Portland, and generally abusing its authority to drive Bullseye out of business, thus improving DEQ's image in the face of accusations that it was too easy on "polluters."

5   Douglas Morgan et al., *Foundations of Public Service,* 2nd ed. (New York: Routledge, 2013), chap. 6; John Rohr, *Ethics for Bureaucrats: An Essay on Law and Values,* 2nd ed. (New York: Marcel-Dekker, 1989).

6   Jewel Lansing, *Portland: People, Politics and Power; 1851-2001* (Corvallis: Oregon State University Press, 2003).

7   Carl Abbott, *Greater Portland: Urban Life and Landscape in the Pacific Northwest* (Philadephia: University of Pennsylvania Press, 2001).

8   League of Oregon Cities, *City Handbook* (Salem: League of Oregon Cities, 2013), http:// www.orcities.org/Portals/17/CityResources/LOCCityHandbook.pdf. Portland (commission system) and Beaverton (strong mayor) are the major exceptions.

9   Patrick Henry, as quoted in Herbert J. Storing, ed., *The Complete Anti-Federalist*, vol. 5 (Chicago: University of Chicago Press, 1981), 214.

10 Oregon law requires all local governing bodies to create a budget committee consisting of the members of the local governing body and an equal number of citizens at large. The citizens are appointed by the governing body and serve terms of three years. Terms are staggered so that about one-third of the appointed terms end each year (*Oregon Revised Statutes*, chap. 294).

11 Molly Harbarger, "John Ludlow, Tootie Smith Launched Shake-Up without Telling Colleagues," *Oregonian / OregonLive*, March 21, 2013, http://www.oregonlive.com/ clackamascounty/index.ssf/2013/03/john_ludlow_tootie_smith_launc.html. See also *Dumdi v. Handy*, Lane County Circuit Court Case No. 16-10-01760 (2011).

12 *State of Oregon v. Henry*, 302 Ore. 510; 732 P.2d 9; 14 Media L. Rep. 1011 (Ore. 1987)

13 Wallace Turner, "Oregon Court Broadens Free Speech Rights," *New York Times*, April 15, 1987.

14 Bureaucracies are responsible for complying with an increasing array of "rights-centered" requirements, including Titles VI and VII of the Civil Rights Act of 1964, the Family and Medical Leave Act (FMLA), the Age Discrimination and Employment Act (ADEA), the Americans with Disabilities Act (ADA) and the ADA Amendments Act of 1998 (ADAAA), the Rehabilitation Act of 1973, Oregon's Family Medical Leave Act, and the Oregon Equality Act. A growing part of the work of our public bureaucracies involves knowing and educating employees and citizens on their rights.

15 Robert D. Putnam, Lewis M. Feldstein, and Don Cohen, *Better Together: Restoring the American Community* (New York: Simon and Schuster, 2003), chap. 12.

16 Pew Research Center, "State Governments Viewed Favorably as Federal Rating Hits New Low," April 15, 2013, http://www.people-press.org/2013/04/15/state-govermnents-viewed-favorably-as-federal-rating-hits-new-low/. Amy Adkins, "Majority of U.S. Employees Not Engaged Despite Gains in 2014," *Gallup*, January 28, 2015, http://www. gallup.com/poll/181289/majority-employees-not-engaged-despite-gains-2014. aspx?utm_source=alert&utm_medium=email&utm_content=morelink&utm_ campaign=syndication.

17 Eric J. Mundy, "Public Trust in Local Government: An Examination of Citizen Trust Differentials in Public Administration and Other Government Officials at the Federal, State and Local levels" (PhD diss., University of Akron, 2007).

18 Aaron C. Weinschenk and David J. Helpap, "Political Trust in the American States," *State and Local Government Review* 47, no. 1 (2015): 26-34; Mitchel N. Herian, "Trust in Government and Support for Municipal Services," *State and Local Government Review*, 46 (2014): 82-90; Gregg G. Van Ryzin, "Outcomes, Process, and Trust of Civil Servants," *Journal of Public Administration Research and Theory* 21 (2011): 745–60.

19 P. J. DiMaggio and W. Powell, "The Iron Cage Revisited: Institutional Isomorphism and Collective Rationality in Organizational Fields," *American Sociological Review* 48 (1983): 147-60.

20 See also Oregon Department of Revenue, *Local Budgeting in Oregon*, 1.

21 League of Oregon Cities, "Overview of Election Results," May 17, 2016, http://www.
    orcities.org/Portals/17/A-Z/2016%20Unofficial%20Primary%20Results.pdf.

22 The authors found it impossible to identify a comprehensive and definitive list of
    departments, agencies, boards, commissions, and advisory councils. The *Oregon Blue
    Book* for 2016 lists sixty-five boards/councils/commissions and fifty-three departments/
    agencies; see Oregon Secretary of State, *Oregon Blue Book* (Salem: State of Oregon, 2016.
    The governor's website lists 193 boards, commissions, and advisory committees; see
    "Board List," Oregon.gov, accessed April 16, 2018, https://www.oregon.gov/gov/admin/
    Pages/Board-List.aspx. An audit report on boards and commissions identified over 250
    boards/councils/commissions but concluded, "The state lacks a complete list of all
    boards, member contact information and other basic reference items. In addition, the
    information that is available is sometimes outdated. Combining information from various
    sources we identified over 250 state boards, but we cannot provide assurance that the list
    is complete." Secretary of State Kate Brown, *Boards and Commissions: Common Risks,
    Needed Oversight, and Steps to Manage Them* (Salem: State of Oregon, June 2012), http://
    sos.oregon.gov/Documents/audits/full/2012/2012-20.pdf, 15.

23 Fred Miller, former director of the Department of Administrative Services, personal
    interview by Douglas Morgan, 2001; Jon Yunker, former director of the Department of
    Administrative Services, personal interview by Douglas Morgan, 2001; Doug Decker,
    personal e-mail, December 26, 2017.

24 Doug Decker, personal communication, December 26, 2017.

25 David Osborne and Ted Gaebler, *Reinventing Government* (New York: Plume, 1993);
    David Osborne and Peter Hutchinson, *The Price of Government: Getting the Results We
    Need in an Age of Permanent Fiscal Crisis* (New York: Basic Books, 2004); Douglas F.
    Morgan et al., *Foundations of Public Service* (New York: Routledge, 2013), 119-22.

26 Douglas F. Morgan and Brian J. Cook, *New Public Governance: A Regime-Centered
    Perspective* (Armonk, NY: M. E. Sharpe, 2014); Stephen P. Osborne, *The New Public
    Governance? Emerging Perspectives on the Theory and Practice of Public Governance* (New
    York: Routledge, 2010).

27 Governor John A. Kitzhaber, *Governor's Budget* (Salem: State of Oregon, 2015), http://
    www.oregon.gov/gov/admin/Documents/2015-17_gb_ForWeb.pdf.

28 Kenneth Culp Davis, *Discretionary Justice: A Preliminary Inquiry* (Baton Rouge: Louisiana
    State University Press, 1967), 65.

29 Mathew McCubbins, Roger Noll, and Barry Weingast, "Administrative Procedures as
    Instruments of Political Control," *Journal of Law, Economics, and Organization* 3 (1987):
    2, 243-77.

30 *Fremont Lumber Co. v. Energy Facility Siting Council*, 325 OR 256, 262, 936 P2d 968
    (1997).

31 Morgan et al., *Foundations of Public Service*, 431-33.

32 Douglas F. Morgan, interview with a panel of six administrative rules coordinators for
    Oregon state agencies, June 28, 2001.

33 Morgan et al., *Foundations of Public Service*, 364ff.

34 Adkins, "Majority of U.S. Employees Not Engaged."

35 John J. Dilulio Jr., "Facing Up to Big Government," *National Affairs* 35 (Spring 2012):
    http://www.nationalaffairs.com/publications/detail/facing-up-to-big-government.

36 Phillip J. Cooper, *Governing by Contract: Challenges and Opportunities for Public Managers*
    (Washington, DC: CQ Press, 2003).

37 Data on the extent of contracting out across various Oregon state agencies are not
    centrally available, and practices for collecting and maintaining this data vary from one

agency to another. The authors sought this information because of concern for the rise of "shadow government," an arrangement that preserves a large and active government but relies on private, nonprofit, and interjurisdictional providers to deliver these services. This arrangement potentially raises numerous problems of accountability, meeting unique community needs, concerns for equity, and protecting the rights of citizens. Tracking the contracting process of the various state agencies that address these issues is a growing concern for citizens and a source of research for scholars interested in accountability in all of its multiple forms.

38 Edward P. Weber, "Politicians and Collaborative Governance: The New Logic of Support," in *The Challenges of Collaboration in Environmental Governance: Barriers and Responses*, ed. Richard D. Margerum and Cathy Robinson (Northampton, MA: Edward Elgar, 2016), 223-45.

8
The Oregon Judicial Branch

PAUL J. DE MUNIZ

Throughout Oregon's history, Oregon courts have been at the intersection of every major social, political, economic, and legal issue in the state. Many of the hallmark laws, either legislatively enacted or initiated, that have defined Oregon—its public beaches, bottle bill, land-use planning—were challenged in court and upheld by the Oregon Supreme Court. More recently, the court has twice decided the constitutionality of Public Employee Retirement System (PERS) reforms; the constitutionality of campaign finance laws; the constitutionality of laws regulating the financial relationship between legislators, lobbyists, and constituents; the constitutionality of the legislature's funding level for K–12 public education; the constitutionality and administration of the death penalty; and hundreds of other cases affecting human services, public safety, victim's rights, and the enforcement of property and economic rights. In effect, Oregon's courts stand at the pinnacle of Oregon's public institutions because they have the power to overrule the putative laws and acts of Oregon's other branches of government.

HISTORY OF OREGON'S COURTS

In 1841, the men of the Oregon Country gathered at "The Primary Meeting of the people of Oregon [and] . . . elected Dr. I. L. Babcock . . . to act as Supreme Judge, with Probate Powers" to probate the estate of a man named Ewing Young, whom the settlers believed had died intestate.[1] Young had arrived in the Oregon Country in 1834 and became the first settler of European descent west of the Willamette River. At the time of his death in 1841, Young was one of the wealthiest men in the Oregon Country, owning almost all of the Chehalem Valley (most of Yamhill County today).[2] Dr. Babcock was elected to fulfill an immediate need of the inhabitants of the Oregon Country administering Young's estate. But Babcock's term as supreme judge was set to end on the adoption of a code of laws.[3] Establishing a form of judicial government only when confronted by a pressing circumstance lends some credence to the view that the original settlers of the Oregon Country wanted only the government that they needed. And in 1841, they did not need much.

At statehood in 1859, the Oregon Constitution established the Oregon Supreme Court as an appellate court and the circuit courts as general jurisdiction courts for initial trials and hearings and the entry of judgments. The supreme court was initially composed of four justices who were also designated as circuit court judges.[4] Between 1862 and 1913, the composition of the supreme court fluctuated between three and five justices. The supreme court was increased to seven justices in 1913 and remains at that number today.

The 1913 legislative session produced Oregon's first district court, exercising its authority under Article VII (Amended) of the Oregon Constitution, "vesting the judicial power in one Supreme Court and in such other courts as may from time to time be created by law."[5] Before 1913, most civil and criminal cases were heard in "justice courts" created and administered by local governments and overseen by local justices of the peace. The 1913 reform allowed for the creation of a state system of district courts that were, in large part, a substitute for justice courts in urban areas, having (like justice courts) limited civil and criminal jurisdiction. Justice courts still exist in many parts of the state, having jurisdiction over minor cases. By 1997, thirty of Oregon's thirty-six counties had district courts with sixty-three district judges. As early as the 1970s, however, efforts were underway to consolidate the district and circuit courts. In 1998, unable to withstand the mounting pressure for consolidation, the Oregon legislature abolished all district courts and transferred judicial authority and pending cases to the circuit courts. Without executive appointment or popular election, but by virtue of consolidation, all sitting district court judges became circuit judges.[6]

In 1969, the legislature created the Oregon Court of Appeals to address the overflowing supreme court docket and the multitude of criminal procedure issues and cases spawned by the decisions of the Warren Court.[7] The legislature initially provided for five judges and limited jurisdiction (criminal, domestic relations, and administrative law), and added one judge in 1973 and four more in 1977. In 1977, the legislature also removed most of the previously imposed jurisdictional limitations, routing nearly all types of cases through the court of appeals. The court operated with ten judges, as one of the busiest appellate courts in the country, until October 2013, when three new judges were seated. The current jurisdictional structure of the Oregon judicial branch is shown in figure 8.1.

The Oregon court system experienced its most dramatic change in 1981 when the legislature enacted legislation that "ended county funding of trial court operations (both circuit court and district court), replacing it with state funding . . . [and] centralized the administration of the Oregon Judicial Department in the hands of the chief justice of the Oregon Supreme Court."[8] This change addressed two major problems. First, before 1981, trial court funding depended on the county government's finances, which resulted in uneven and unpredictable financial support across Oregon's courts. Second, the trial courts suffered from "inadequate judicial administration, which affected all levels of control."[9] With the adoption of the 1981 legislation, the office of the chief justice greatly expanded, with "significantly more authority to function as

OREGON JUDICIAL DEPARTMENT
Court Jurisdiction Structure

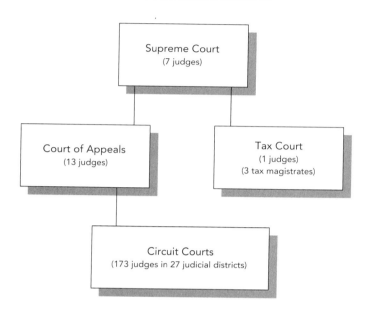

Figure 8.1. **Court jurisdiction and background.** *Oregon Judicial Department, Chief Justice's Recommended Budget, 2017-2019 Biennium (Salem: State of Oregon, 2017), 1*

head of the Oregon Judicial Department" and charged with "developing a personnel plan, a budgeting plan, and a property management plan for the courts of the state."[10]

The chief justice and the state court administrator now manage a statewide court system, consisting of 27 judicial districts, 194 independently elected judges, and nearly 1,700 employees, with a biennial budget of $586 million. As table 8.1 shows, the courts have a heavy workload. In 2016, 729,116 cases were filed in Oregon circuit

Table 8.1. Case filings in circuit courts

Case Category	2012	2013	2014	2015	2016
Civil	70,090	75,187	65,868	54,634	47,115
FED*	22,562	20,004	19,870	19,482	19,253
Small claims	76,075	70,259	78,149	67,932	54,535
Dissolution	17,397	16,790	16,219	16,337	16,116
FAPA**	10,181	9,649	9,457	9,730	9,828
Other domestic related	17,721	16,790	16,219	16,337	16,116
Felony	31,980	32,464	32,180	32,407	34,698
Misdemeanor	57,529	53,029	51,363	50,335	51,482
Violation	211,504	215,080	212,316	205,511	200,417
Juvenile	12,924	11,783	10,921	11,430	10,798
Mental health	9,459	9,582	8,619	8,512	8,308
Probate	10,196	10,642	10,553	11,312	11,423
Subtotal	547,618	542,096	532,664	504,357	479,652
Multnomah parking	247,696	264,874	253,166	269,501	249,464
Total	795,314	806,970	785,830	773,858	729,116

*Landlord/Tenant disputes; **Family Abuse Prevention Act cases
Note: Data are from two case management systems (OJIN/Odyssey), resulting in minor differences in filing counts. Source: Oregon Judicial Department, Chief Justice's Recommended Budget, 2017-2019 Biennium (Salem: State of Oregon, 2017)

courts, including 249,464 parking tickets in Multnomah County. From an organizational standpoint, Oregon's court system is a large, complex entity. Even though its courts are unified within a well-defined administrative hierarchy, physically, the judicial branch is a collection of widely dispersed courthouses, each with a unique and independent organizational culture. In addition to the functions traditionally associated with the judiciary, today the Oregon court system includes a growing array of specialized services that range from providing mediation services to solving specific community problems in nontraditional adjudicatory forums such as drug courts, family courts, mental health courts, and veterans' courts.

JUDICIAL FEDERALISM, OREGON'S CONSTITUTION, LEGISLATIVE POLICYMAKING, AND JUDICIAL POWER

"Judicial federalism" is the term for the legal principle that state courts should consider state constitutional and statutory law before turning to federal law in their legal analysis. In practice, judicial federalism means that although no state can abridge an individual's federal constitutional rights, states may expand upon them. Oregon played a special role in developing this concept and remains a leader in its applications. In 1977, Justice William Brennan published an article in the *Harvard Law Review* emphasizing the fundamental principle that US Supreme Court interpretations of the US Constitution "are not . . . dispositive of questions regarding rights guaranteed by counterpart provisions of state law."[11] Many legal scholars, such as Stewart Pollock, identify Justice Brennan's article as the starting point of the modern reemphasis on state constitutions.[12]

Beginning in 1970, however, in a series of writings and lectures, Hans Linde, then a law professor at the University of Oregon School of Law, urged state court judges to resolve constitutional questions under their own state constitution before analyzing them under the US Constitution.[13] Linde asserted that because state and federal claims are not cumulative but alternative, claims raised under the state constitution should be decided first. According to Linde, to resolve state constitutional questions before reaching federal constitutional claims, counsel and the court must give independent professional attention to the text, history, and function of state constitutional provisions.[14] Linde was appointed to the Oregon Supreme Court in 1977 and immediately began advocating in that court's opinions for the primacy of the Oregon Constitution. In 1981, in *Sterling v. Cupp*, 290 OR 611 (1981), Justice Linde succeeded in cementing Oregon constitutional primacy into Oregon law, stating, "The proper sequence is to analyze the state's law, including its constitutional law, before reaching a federal claim. This is not required for the sake of parochialism or of style, but because the state does not deny any right claimed under the federal Constitution when the claim before the court in fact is fully met by state law."[15] Today, legal scholars credit Justice Brennan and Justice Linde as reestablishing the primacy of state constitutions as independent sources of constitutional safeguards.

Consistent with Justice Linde's primacy formulation, Oregon courts today define individual rights (affording greater, not less, than those afforded by federal law) and governmental responsibilities under the Oregon Constitution, independent of federal court analysis of the US Constitution.[16] In that regard, in *State v. Isom*, 306 OR 587 (1988), the Oregon Supreme Court concluded that a defendant's statements secured in violation of the right to counsel provisions contained in Article I, Section 12, of the Oregon Constitution could not be used to impeach a defendant's trial testimony. In doing so, the court observed, "The fact that the officers admittedly were following the federal interpretation of the utility and admissibility of such statements under federal law as set forth in *Oregon v. Hass* is of no consequence. We are concerned with interpreting the Oregon Constitution on this issue and are not dependent on or restricted by federal law."[17] Similarly, in *Sterling v. Cupp*, the court relied on Article I, Section 13, of the Oregon Constitution, which guarantees that prisoners will not be "treated with unnecessary rigor"—a more cogent premise than can be found in the US Constitution.[18] In other words, Oregon courts are not bound to follow a decision of a federal court, including the US Supreme Court, when dealing with state law matters.

Although the Oregon Supreme Court's commitment to independent state constitutional interpretation is significant in the individual rights context, of equal importance are the cases in which the court is required to interpret the Oregon Constitution and how it applies to legislative processes and popular lawmaking. Cases where the courts interpret and apply constitutional provisions regarding the titling of bills, their form and nature, the amendment process, and the subjects that a bill can embrace inject the judicial branch directly into the legislative/political process.

In *McIntire v. Forbes*, 322 OR 426 (1996), for example, the Oregon Supreme Court invalidated the light-rail funding provisions of Senate Bill 1156 because Sections 1–17 of the bill violated the *one subject requirement* of Article IV, Section 20, of the Oregon Constitution. In doing so, the court observed that Article IV, Section 20, was designed to serve two purposes: (1) require that the body of each act embrace a single subject and matters properly connected therewith to avoid logrolling (combining unrelated subjects representing diverse interests in order to unite the members of the legislature who favor either, in support of all) and (2) prevent the use of the title as a means of deceiving members of the legislature and other interested persons as the bill moved through the legislative process.

Similarly, in *Armatta v. Kitzhaber*, 327 OR 250 (1998), the Oregon Supreme Court invalidated initiated Ballot Measure 40, applying the Article XVII, Section 1, *separate vote requirement* requiring that two or more amendments to the Oregon Constitution be submitted so that each amendment shall be voted on separately. Similarly, *League of Oregon Cities v. State of Oregon*, 334 OR 645 (2002), invalidated Ballot Measure 7, which required governments to compensate private real property owners for the cost of restrictive regulations that reduce the value of their real property, because it violated the Article XVII, Section 1, separate vote requirement.

Unlike the federal courts, which have little to say in how the US Congress manages its internal legislative process, the Oregon courts can and do often have significant input into state lawmaking practices and procedures, ultimately having a profound effect on the public policy of the state.

JUDICIAL SELECTION

Unlike the framers of the US Constitution, who concluded that appointing judges for life was integral to the creation of an independent judicial branch of government, the delegates to Oregon's constitutional convention of 1857—caught up in the national wave of Jacksonian populism—concluded that an election for a specified term, rather than appointment and confirmation, was the preferable method of selecting judges.[19] From statehood until 1931, judicial elections were partisan political races in which the candidates were identified with the major political parties. In 1931, the Oregon legislature accepted an Oregon State Bar proposal and passed legislation abolishing partisan elections for the judiciary, requiring that candidate names be printed on the ballot "without any party designation."[20] Today, judges at every level of the state court system are elected as nonpartisan judicial candidates for six-year terms. Justices of the Oregon Supreme Court, judges of the court of appeals, and the Oregon Tax Court judge are selected through statewide elections. With limited exceptions, circuit judges are elected by the voters of the county where they serve and reside.

As described above, the Oregon Supreme Court stands at the intersection of every important social, political, economic, and legal issue in the state. That being so, it is no wonder that special interest groups eventually recognized opportunities to influence who serves on Oregon's highest court. The importance of the courts raises the significance of two factors that help determine who is on the court: the role of gubernatorial appointment and the rise of campaign donations and spending to influence who becomes judges, particularly at the supreme court level.

Although the Oregon Constitution mandates that judges are to be selected by popular vote, most judges ascend to the bench by gubernatorial appointment. That is so because Article V, Section 16, of the Oregon Constitution authorizes the governor to appoint a judicial applicant to fill the unexpired term of a judge who resigns or retires before the end of his or her six-year term. But the same Section 16 also provides that the appointed judge must stand for election in the next regularly scheduled general election. With regard to judicial appointments, the governor's discretion is for the most part unfettered, providing the governor with the opportunity to appoint supreme court justices who have a judicial philosophy compatible with the governor's political and legal views. In 2018, for the first time in Oregon history, five of the seven justices were women, four of whom were appointed by Governor Brown. Given the age of the three senior members of the Oregon Supreme Court, it may be possible for Governor Brown to eventually appoint all seven members of that court.

Although elements of political and partisan rhetoric and notable campaign spending occurred sporadically in judicial campaigns following the change to "nonpartisan" elections, the tactics employed generally were directed against specific candidates. That strategy began to change in 1996, when Robert Tiernan, a former legislator with no judicial experience, received nearly $200,000 in campaign contributions from three conservative millionaire businessmen. Tiernan employed a "Tough on Crime" campaign, pointing out that as a legislator he had "sponsored" Measure 11, the mandatory sentencing law, and other tough-on-crime laws. Tiernan criticized the supreme court as "too liberal," and one supporter claimed in the voter's pamphlet that "too many judges let child pornographers off the hook and violent criminals [back] on the street on technicalities." Despite the Tiernan race, and at least one other supreme court race that easily eclipsed the Tiernan race in terms of spending, Oregon has, for the most part, been spared the financial arms race that typifies the funding of judicial election campaigns in many other states.[21]

Perhaps owing to the lack of success in head-to-head supreme court elections, in 2002, special interest groups critical of the makeup of Oregon's appellate courts adopted a different strategy designed to change the composition of Oregon's appellate courts. Ballot Measure 22 (the Judicial Accountability Act) would have ended state-wide elections for the supreme court and court of appeals judges. In place of state-wide elections, the measure would have created a district-based system of residency requirements. Loren Parks, the principal donor to two previous unsuccessful supreme court races, contributed nearly $1.2 million to the measure before the Oregon voters.[22] Ballot Measure 22 would have taken away the voters' right to elect the most quali-fied judicial candidate to the supreme court and the court of appeals, and limited the number of judges that voters could choose by electing only one supreme court justice or two court of appeals judges per region. Supreme court justices would have been accountable to geographic areas instead of to all Oregonians. The measure would also have driven up judicial administration costs, requiring judges to maintain offices in their district while serving on a court that transacts all business in Salem. Measure 22 lost by a margin of less than 2 percent (about 49% for to 51% against).[23]

Apparently emboldened by the narrow defeat of Measure 22, similar-minded special interests again sought an initiated constitutional amendment in the form of Measure 40, to require the election of supreme court justices and court of appeals judges by district. That measure was defeated in the 2006 general election by a margin of about 13 percent (about 43% for and 56% against).[24]

Today, judicial campaigns across the country are characterized by exorbitant spending, the involvement of national special interest groups, and a blizzard of mis-leading attack ads that mask the true interests of the sponsors.[25] Selecting judges through this kind of political process, with its inflammatory rhetoric and demagogu-ery, can erode public confidence in the impartiality of all judges. Polls consistently show that the public believes judicial campaign contributions pay off for donors. A 2010 Harris poll found that more than 70 percent of Americans believe that cam-paign contributions influence courtroom outcomes.[26]

History has shown that our constitutional system of government has endured, in part, because the public and the other branches of government acquiesce to judi-cial authority. Americans tend to have confidence and trust in the impartiality and independence of judicial decision-making. They see the courts as making decisions free of outside political and economic influence. But reformers see the special inter-est financing of judicial campaigns in states across the country as having the poten-tial not just to erode, but to destroy the public's trust and confidence in state and federal courts. Nationwide, and in Oregon, advocates of judicial campaign reform are seeking to either restrain campaign contributions or to do away with the popular election of judges to protect the impartiality and independence of the court system. Currently, the Oregon Law Commission is studying judicial selection in Oregon and will eventually provide a report to the legislature that may someday provide the basis for constitutional reform in how the state selects its judges.

COURTHOUSES AND COURT SECURITY

As part of the 1981 legislation unifying the Oregon court system, Oregon's counties retained ownership of the local courthouses, and the legislation required the counties to maintain suitable and sufficient facilities.[27] Under that relationship, many local governments felt no need to spend their limited resources on court facilities or security. By 2006, the Oregon judicial branch was conducting operations in most counties in aging facilities with little or no security. For supporters of the court system, the decline in facilities was considered harmful to the image of the courts, making the public less respectful of the law and more skeptical that justice is available to everyone.

Throughout the 1990s and early 2000s, the Oregon Judicial Department lobbied the legislature to provide suitable and sufficient court facilities. The legislative response was that the problem needed to be addressed to the counties, not to the state. Finally, in 2006, in response to a study characterizing the poor condition of Oregon's courthouses as a "public safety" issue that endangered the public and courthouse staff, the legislature agreed to fund a $1.2 million study of all of Oregon's court facilities in 2007.[28] That study, completed in 2008, confirmed that Oregon's courthouses were in dire need of repair, upgrading, or, in some cases, complete replacement.[29]

In turn, the 2009 legislative session authorized the expenditure of $12 million for immediate repairs to court facilities throughout the state. The 2011 legislative session then allocated funds from a new criminal fines bill to assist with county courthouse projects. Finally, in 2013, the legislature enacted legislation authorizing partnerships between the counties and the state for the repair, upgrade, and replacement of county court facilities.[30]

The first courthouse replaced is in Union County, where the circuit court had "temporarily" operated in an abandoned hospital for twenty years. That new courthouse was dedicated in March 2016. And, on October 25, 2016, Multnomah County broke ground on a new courthouse in Portland.

In 2005, the legislature enacted ORS 1.178, known as the State Court Facilities and Security Account. The funds accumulated in that account are dedicated for the exclusive use of the judicial branch to develop and implement a plan for courthouse security improvement and training, emergency preparedness, distributions to local court facility security accounts and capital improvement to courthouses throughout the state.[31] With these funds, the branch contracted with the National Center for State Courts in 2007 to engage in a detailed security assessment of the Oregon's court facilities. Their report provided the branch with an appropriate perspective for addressing the branch's security needs and enhancing the court security governance structure.

In 2009, the branch established the Oregon Judicial Department Security Standards for the appellate, tax, and circuit courts of the state, and authorized the implementation of a five-year security plan.[32] Implementation of that plan has resulted in security, emergency preparedness, and business continuity for all of Oregon's courts; two emergency response trailers that can provide temporary courtrooms, full video arraignment, telephone, and Internet support with sixteen laptops and two multifunction printers in an environment with full heating, ventilation, and air conditioning; a court security officer course that provides courtroom specific training for deputy sheriffs and police officers who provide security in the state's courtrooms; security cameras, access control, and duress alarm systems for all courts; a circuit court security assistance program that provides funding for additional security at high-risk trials in smaller circuit courts; personal security training for judges and court staff; a threat assessment and management program designed to mitigate targeted violence against judges and court staff; and the creation of a judicial marshal's office to head all security and emergency preparedness for the judicial branch.

In 2012, the legislature designated the marshal's office as a law enforcement unit, allowing judicial marshals to receive police training and certification through Oregon's Department of Public Safety Standards and Training.[33] Most recently, the legislature included judicial marshals within the legal definition of a peace officer,[34] which provides judicial marshals with full police powers, including arrest authority[35] and liability protection for specific use of force that may be used during any dignitary protection incidents.[36] Although many state judiciaries have some dedicated security service, the Oregon judicial branch is the first to achieve the status of peace officers.

REENGINEERING OREGON'S COURTS

One of the greatest challenges facing the Oregon court system is obtaining sustainable funding that will permit the court system to engage in research and development, and continue to modernize and meet the public's expectation for access to justice. The impediment to doing so, however, cannot be easily overcome. Although the Oregon and US Constitutions provide for decisional independence for judges, neither provides for any form of institutional independence of the judicial branch. That lack of constitutionally mandated institutional independence explains why Oregon's court system is not more insulated from funding decisions made by the other two branches of government, which reduce and expand Oregon's judicial branch funding from session to session. Until Oregonians agree on the importance, in their daily lives, of an independent, relevant, and efficient court system—or the Oregon Constitution is amended to guarantee a certain level of funding to the judicial branch—obtaining *sustainable* funding will remain difficult.

In recognition that funding the judiciary would never be a priority for the legislature, but that it had a public obligation to responsibly manage its resources and to increase public access to the courts despite the economic downturn and resulting loss of funding, the Oregon Judicial Department began in 2009 to reengineer the structure and operations of the Oregon courts. Their objective was to "shepherd [Oregon] courts through bad economic times, improve the quality of judicial services, and significantly enhance the judiciary's profile as an innovative manager of the public funds."[37]

To reengineer the structure and operations of Oregon's courts, the judicial department focused on three key target areas: (1) governance structures, (2) case administration, and (3) essential functions. It did so guided by four principles on whether the proposed change would: (1) improve litigants' convenience, (2) reduce cost and complexity for litigants, (3) improve litigants' access to justice, and (4) improve case predictability. Many of these changes reflect the embrace of managerial and technological efficiencies.

One of the ways the judiciary began moving toward a reengineered court system in Oregon was by placing greater emphasis on centralizing judicial staff functions within local courthouses. To do so, however, ran counter to one hundred and fifty years of judicial culture in Oregon. Traditionally, the "judicial unit, essentially [a] judge and his or her personal support staff," had been considered sacrosanct—the supervisory domain of the sitting judge alone. As a result, judicial staff were frequently insulated from changes that affect the courthouse's central administrative work force, changes that often include increased workloads and staffing shortages.

At the Oregon Supreme Court, the traditional concept of the judicial unit had held sway for well over one hundred years. Each justice had her or his own judicial assistant and staff resources. That organizational model made sense when judicial assistants typed opinions on Underwood typewriters with onionskin copies; it was no longer useful in today's technologically advanced world.

As a result of those early reengineering efforts, judicial assistants at the Oregon Supreme Court now share duties between multiple chambers under the supervision of a single appellate court manager rather than the court's seven justices. That format, in turn, has allowed the court's judicial assistants to take on tasks directly related to court operations that were previously performed by the Appellate Records Division. Today, the appellate court manager and three judicial assistants do the same work that a seven-member staff did, and additionally perform a great deal of the electronic case management tasks related to the supreme court's docket. The increased flexibility of that work unit effectively added the equivalent of two and a half full-time employees to the Records Division with no new funding, enabling that department to efficiently handle the increasing case management workload of the Oregon Court of Appeals, the state's busiest appellate court. The cultural shift away from the judicial unit, which was initiated in the supreme court, has now been implemented throughout most of the Oregon court system.

From a reengineering standpoint, however, this example was just a harbinger of a much larger and bolder shift toward centralized operations that were needed to more closely resemble a single enterprise. Centralized docket control, jury management, and payment systems were the next logical steps. The Oregon court system has now implemented all of those system changes in one form or another.

Centralizing common court operations has facilitated further renovation of Oregon's court governance structures by redistributing and regionalizing state courts and judges to maximize judicial resource management, staffing, and the general delivery of trial court services. One example involves Oregon's prison litigation. Oregon has fourteen prisons scattered throughout the state. By leveraging its technology, the judicial branch has centralized nearly all postconviction litigation to a special docket that is administered out of the state court administrator's office in Salem, instead of the individual counties. Nearly all postconviction litigation is handled electronically from Salem, saving millions of dollars in indigent attorney fees, security and transportation costs, and paper and postage.

Reengineering efforts have also focused on the paper-intensive method by which the courts and Oregon's citizens interfaced. Oregon courts previously handled approximately fifty million pieces of paper—or two hundred and fifty tons of documents—every year.[38] The inherent inefficiencies of that system, particularly in the face of rising judicial workloads, combined with budget-mandated staff reductions were one of the greatest impediments to the public's expectation for court access.[39] To combat the problem, the branch initiated the Oregon eCourt Program in 2006.

The statewide eCourt Program has focused on building a state-of-the-art electronic system for case management, content management, electronic filing, and e-commerce. The goal of eCourt was to transform the business operations of Oregon's courts by creating a single virtual courthouse—the largest and most accessible in the state—available twenty-four hours a day, seven days a week. Oregon eCourt now houses: (1) a website through which parties can conduct significant portions of court business online without traveling to an actual courthouse; (2) an enterprise content management system that acts as an electronic warehouse to store every court-related document—e-filed or not—centrally and in a digital format; (3) a financial management system that facilitates online payment of court filing fees, as well as fines and restitution awards; and (4) a case management system that allows court personnel to track the many matters that arise in the course of an individual case, from inception to final disposition. Oregon's eCourt is now operational in both appellate courts and in all twenty-seven judicial districts.[40]

The reengineering initiatives described so far can be summarized as follows:

- **Centralization.** Costs and local trial court workloads have been reduced in Oregon through the central processing of payables, collections, payment of traffic citations, and jury management.
- **Regionalization.** Court processes in Oregon are now managed more efficiently by looking beyond venue borders to expedite case processing or adjudication and by using specialized dockets to better utilize judicial resources statewide.
- **Leveraging Technology.** The judicial branch is committed to providing the public with the ability to pay fees and fines online—including traffic citations—as well as online access to dockets and documents. It is also using technology to promote the more efficient use of judicial resources statewide.

THE RISE OF THERAPEUTIC COURTS

No change in Oregon's judicial process has gained more attention over the last thirty years than the ascendency in Oregon of problem-solving, or therapeutic, courts. Though certain aspects of the adversarial system can still be found in these courts, it is the focus on alternative processes that provide social support systems, while simultaneously seeking to address larger underlying social causes of problems, that is the hallmark of these Oregon courts.

Problem-solving courts were established in the state to address the special needs of individuals who were not being adequately managed through traditional court procedures. Problem-solving courts are, in effect, specialty dockets within existing courts where judges, other officials, and litigants utilize alternative adjudication processes and programs to address unique litigant needs. Three elements underlie Oregon's problem-solving court approach: (1) a focus on treating the underlying problem, (2) an emphasis on outcome as opposed to output, and (3) therapeutic considerations over penal considerations. Today, these nontraditional adjudicatory forums include drug courts, family courts, mental health courts, and veterans' courts. Treatment courts now operate in twenty-eight counties (see table 8.2). A lengthy analysis of the effectiveness of Multnomah County's drug court shows that therapeutic courts can significantly reduce the recidivism rate of participants.[41]

The leadership of the judicial branch is committed to expanding these courts for more Oregonians in need of treatment and to keep pace with advanced treatment methods. As science, social norms, and knowledge march forward, expansion and changes in treatment court models will provide better outcomes for treatment court participants and society.[42]

CONCLUSION

Oregon judges no longer work only in the confines of the courthouse. Today, Oregon judges and courts interact, often in nontraditional roles, with the legislature, local governments, and community organizers to fashion court processes and programs, and

Table 8.2. Current listing of treatment courts in Oregon Circuit Courts

Circuit Court	Current Treatment Courts	Circuit Court	Current Treatment Courts
Benton	Adult Drug	Klamath	Adult Drug, Family Dependency Treatment, Juvenile Drug, Veterans
Clackamas	Adult Drug, Community, Domestic Violence, DWI, Family Dependency Treatment, Juvenile Drug, Mental Health	Lane	Adult Drug, Juvenile Drug, Veterans
Clatsop	Adult Drug, Family Dependency Treatment, Mental Health	Lincoln	Mental Health, Domestic Violence
Columbia	Adult Drug, Family Dependency Treatment	Linn	Domestic Violence, Family Dependency Treatment, Juvenile Drug
Coos	Mental Health	Malheur	Community, Juvenile Drug, Mental Health
Crook	Adult Drug	Marion	Adult Drug, Family Dependency Treatment, Juvenile Drug, Mental Health, Veterans, Other
Curry	Mental Health	Multnomah	Community, Domestic Violence, DWI, Mental Health, Veterans, Other
Deschutes	Domestic Violence, Family Dependency Treatment, Mental Health	Polk	Adult Drug
Douglas	Adult Drug, Domestic Violence	Umatilla	Adult Drug
Harney	Adult Drug	Union	DWI, Family Dependency Treatment, Juvenile Drug
Hood River	Adult Drug	Wallowa	DWI, Juvenile Drug
Jackson	Family Dependency Treatment	Wasco	Adult Drug, Family Dependency Treatment
Jefferson	Adult Drug, Mental Health	Washington	Adult Drug, Juvenile Drug, Mental Health
Josephine	Adult Drug, Mental Health	Yamhill	Adult Drug, Family Dependency Treatment, Juvenile Drug, Mental Health, Other

Note: Some Oregon circuit courts utilize drug or DUI court programs such as SAFE (Stop Addiction Forever), STOP (Sanctions Treatment Opportunity Progress), START (Success Through Accountability, Restitution, and Treatment), and DISP (DUI Intensive Supervision Program).

Source: Oregon Judicial Department, 2016 Annual Report *(Salem: Oregon Judicial Department, 2017, 42)*

to offer a wide array of services necessary to meet the needs of a modern Oregon. In doing so, the judicial branch has increased its use of technology, streamlined court processes, and developed specialty courts such as drug courts, mental health courts, family courts, and veterans' courts.

Despite the unprecedented economic challenges that Oregon's government has faced during the last decade, the *New York Times* in a 2011 editorial identified the Oregon court system as one of the two best run in the country.[43] Even with funding difficulties, the branch has worked hard to maintain the public's trust and confidence, changed century-old traditions to become more efficient, adopted statewide security standards for Oregon's courthouses to protect the public, and diligently emphasized impartiality and the court's limited role to interpret the law.

In the end, however, the independence, competency, efficiency, and relevance of the Oregon court system of the future will depend on funding. It is too often said publicly that America's court systems need to be funded at an "adequate" level. Unfortunately, "adequate" funding is usually defined at the barest, most basic level.

To supporters of an independent judiciary, providing a bare, basic level of funding is not enough. To these supporters, adequate funding for the courts must include recognition of both the duty of the court system to provide justice without delay and the responsibility of a viable separate and equal branch of government.

Finally, beyond funding, the biggest challenge confronting the judicial branch is that it must be sensitive to the relationship between technology and the future of the court system. The younger generations that use technology every day have no patience or time for what was once considered the "court norm"—wading through reams of paper and long delays to get information, much less searching for missing paper files or delayed entry of judgments. Younger Americans are now used to instantly accessing information, facts, and data from their smartphones. Given that reality, Oregon's courts must have the capacity to move forward quickly with technological opportunities to support and improve their work processes, or it will not be able to meet the needs of these citizens.

Notes

1   Gustavus Hines, *Wild Life in Oregon* (New York: Hurst & Co., 1881), 418.

2   Charles H. Carey, *A General History of Oregon Prior to 1861* (Portland, OR: Metropolitan Press, 1935), 319.

3   Hines, *Wild Life in Oregon*, 418.

4   Oregon Constitution, Article VII, Sections 1, 2, and 8. See Stephen P. Armitage, "History of the Oregon Judicial Department: After Statehood," State of Oregon Law Library, accessed April 17, 2018, https://digital.osl.state.or.us/islandora/object/osl%3A43020/datastream/OBJ/view.

5   Armitage, "History of the Oregon Judicial Department."

6   Armitage, "History of the Oregon Judicial Department."

7   ORS 2.510 (2015).

8   Armitage, "History of the Oregon Judicial Department."

9   Armitage, "History of the Oregon Judicial Department."

10 Armitage, "History of the Oregon Judicial Department."

11 William J. Brennan Jr., "State Constitutions and the Protection of Individual Rights," *Harvard Law Review* 90 (1977): 489, 502.

12 See Stewart G. Pollock, "State Constitutions as Separate Sources of Fundamental Rights," *Rutgers Law Review* 35 (1983): 707, 716, referring to Justice Brennan's 1977 article as "the Magna Carta of state constitutional law."

13 See Hans A. Linde, "Without Due Process: Unconstitutional Law in Oregon," *Oregon Law Review* 49 (1970), and idem, "First Things First: Rediscovering the States Bills of Rights," *University of Baltimore Law Review* 379 (1980): 387-96, encouraging state courts to look first to their own state constitutions in resolving state constitutional questions, thereby insulating such decisions from federal review.

14 Linde, "First Things First."

15 *Sterling v. Cupp*, 625 P.2d 123 (1981), 290 OR 611.

16 In 1984, Oregon Supreme Court Justice Hans Linde observed, "It once again is becoming familiar learning that the federal Bill of Rights was drawn from the earlier state declarations of rights adopted at the time of independence, that most protections of peoples' rights against their own states entered the federal Constitution only in the Reconstruction amendments of the 1860s, and that it took another hundred years and much disputed reasoning to equate most of the first eight amendments with due process under the fourteenth." H. Linde, "*E Pluribus*—Constitutional Theory and State Courts," *Georgia Law Review* 18 (1984): 174.

17 *State v. Isom*, 761 P.2d 524 (1988), 306 OR 587.

18 *Sterling v. Cupp*, 625 P.2d 123 (1981), 290 OR 611.

19 Oregon Constitution, Article VII, Section 3 (1857) (providing for six-year judicial terms). The delegates did not debate the choice of elected terms over appointment for life, and they appear to have assumed, like other delegates in states during that period, that judges would be elected for terms.

20 See 1931 *Oregon Revised Statutes*, chap. 347, section 6, and chaps. 607 and 610.

21 See Debra Erenberg and Matt Berg, "The Dark Knight Rises: The Growing Role of Independent Expenditures in Judicial Elections after Citizens United," *Willamette Law Review* 49 (2013): 501.

22 Janice Thompson, "As I See It," *Gazette Times*, November 1, 2002.

23 "Oregon Judicial Districts and Elections, Measure 22 (2002)," *BallotPedia*, accessed April 17, 2018, https://ballotpedia.org/Oregon_Judicial_Districts_and_Elections,_ Measure_22_(2002).

24 "Oregon Ballot Measure 40, Election of Judges by District (2006)," *BallotPedia*, accessed April 17, 2018, https://ballotpedia.org/Oregon_Ballot_Measure_40,_Election_of_ Judges_by_District_(2006).

25 "Special-interest spending in judicial elections has turned into an arms race," according to Alicia Bannon, counsel at the Brennan Center for Justice. For example, in 2011-12, a record $33.7 million was spent on television ads during the supreme court campaign, far exceeding the previous record of $26.6 million in 2007-8. Alicia Bannon, "Who Pays for Judicial Races? The Politics of Judicial Elections, 2015-16," Brennan Center for Justice, December 14, 2017, https://www.brennancenter.org/publication/politics-judicial-elections.

26 Cliff Collins, "Judicial Selection and Its Consequences," *Oregon State Bar Bulletin* (August 2012): http://www.osbar.org/publications/bulletin/12augsep/judicialselection.html.

27 See ORS 1.185 (2015).

28 Legislative Administration Committee Services, *Interim Committee on Court Facilities: Final Report* (Salem: State of Oregon, February 2009), https://www.oregonlegislature. gov/citizen_engagement/Reports/court_facilities_final_report.pdf; State of Oregon, *Oregon Court Facilities Assessment: Summary Report* (Salem: State of Oregon, 2008). See also Court Facilities Task Force, *Report on Oregon Court Facilities* (Salem: Oregon Bar Association Court Facilities Task Force, 2006), http://www.osbar.org/_docs/resources/ CourtFacilities06dec.pdf.

29 State of Oregon, *Oregon Court Facilities Assessment*, 7.

30 See 2013 *Oregon Revised Statutes*, chaps. 705 (Act Relating to State Financial Administration); and 621 (Act Relating to Critical Infrastructure Development).

31 See ORS 1.178 (2014).

32 Order Revising the Oregon Judicial Department Security Standards for the Appellate, Tax, and Circuit Courts and the Office of the State Court Administrator and Five-Year Implementation Plan, Chief Justice Order No. 10-048 (2013).

33 See ORS 181.610 (12) (a) (2013) (defining judicial marshals as a law enforcement unit) and ORS 181.640 (2013) (setting minimum training and certification standards for law enforcement units).

34 ORS 133.005 (2013).

35 ORS 133.235 (2013).

36 See generally ORS 161.095 (2013) (establishing justification as a defense to any prosecution); ORS 161.195 (2013) (defining justifiable use of force to include conduct by a "public servant in the reasonable exercise of official powers, duties or functions"); and ORS 161.235 (2013) (granting peace officers authority to use physical force to make an arrest). Liability protection for the use of force during dignitary protection incidents remains subject to limitations established for peace officers, such as the use of excessive force.

37 Paul J. De Muniz, "Oregon Courts Today and Tomorrow," *Willamette Law Review* 50, no. 3 (2014): 295.

38 Bud Borja, "Oregon ECourt: Improving Judicial Outcomes and Services," in *Future Trends in State Courts*, ed. Carol R. Flango et al. (Williamsburg, VA: National Center for State Courts, 2009), 87, http://www.imagesoftinc.com/documents/oregon_ecourt_ bud_borja.pdf.

39 Borja, "Oregon ECourt."

40 In addition, most Oregon Supreme Court arguments are streamed online and then archived for subsequent public access.

41 National Institute of Justice, *Impact of a Mature Drug Court over 10 Years of Operation: Recidivism and Costs: Final Report* (Washington, DC: National Institute of Justice, 2007).

42 Oregon Judicial Department, *2016 Annual Report* (Salem: Oregon Judicial Department, 2016), 43.

43 "Threadbare American Justice," *New York Times*, August 17, 2011, http://www.nytimes.com/2011/08/18/opinion/threadbare-american-justice.html.

9

Local Governments in Oregon

ABDULLAH HUSAIN, ETHAN SELTZER, and BRENT S. STEEL

Local governments—including cities, counties, special districts, and metropolitan areas—are often the most visible levels of government in Oregon. Whether it be public schools, streets and highways, mass transit, sewer and water, parks, land-use planning, law enforcement, hospitals, or other activities, local governments are either directly involved in offering these services or in regulating the organizations hired to provide them. From the 36 counties, 241 cities, approximately 200 school districts, and over 900 special districts, the typical Oregonian encounters multiple local government services and programs on a daily basis. There has been much continuity in local government structures and services since Oregon gained statehood, but there also have been many innovative changes. The most noteworthy of these changes is what has occurred at the regional level.

CITIES, COUNTIES, AND SPECIAL DISTRICTS

Cities, counties, and special districts are the primary providers of government services at the local level. All three of these types of local governments play an important role in meeting the needs of Oregonians. Each type of government has its own set of rules governing it and its own specific responsibilities, though in some policy areas, all three types of government may be involved. Unlike other parts of Oregon government, which have seen significant change in recent years, many of the most important changes in these local governments took place in the early to mid-twentieth century.

City Government

Unlike county governments, city governments are barely mentioned in the Oregon Constitution. Little is said about how they should be organized or their proper structure and function. Article VI of the constitution, which focuses on administrative offices and local officers, has one small section about city officers. It states: "Other officers: Such other county, township, precinct, and City officers as may be necessary, shall be elected, or appointed in such manner as may be prescribed by law." Vague and simplistic in terms of how cities should be structured and organized, this description also does not reveal the extent to which cities have developed to form and carry out a complex and important set of responsibilities around the state.

A central contributor to this organization and evolution of cities is *home rule*. The *Oregon Blue Book* states that in 1906, cities were granted "extensive" lawmaking authority with the approval of a city home rule law.[1] The state's action was consistent with the spirit of the Progressive Movement, which reshaped the state's constitution at the time to give residents as much power as possible in running their local government. County governments have also been granted the right to home rule, but city governments have been allowed greater independence than their county counterparts. This is mainly because of differences in the character of home rule charters for these two types of local government. County governments are considered complimentary to the state government in exercising authority and carrying out responsibilities, and thus have greater restrictions placed on their activities. Cities, however, are allowed more flexible approaches to governance and services offered.

The independence that cities enjoy is a product of the state laws establishing city governments. These laws include a few important components. The most important is laid out in chapter 221 of the *Oregon Revised Statutes*. This chapter establishes the regulations guiding city home rule, including how cities can be incorporated and the different powers cities can exercise. Chapter 221 provides people in any geographical area that is not incorporated the power to propose and petition to form a city if the number of people living in that area is one hundred and fifty or more.

Later in that chapter, the broad power given to city government is spelled out. Section 221.410 states: "Except as limited by express provision or necessary implication of general law, a city may take all action necessary or convenient for the government of its local affairs." This broad wording means that, unlike counties, the power of city government and its responsibilities are independent from that of the state government. These components of city home rule make it possible for cities to handle a wide range of responsibilities, such as building roads, policing, providing emergency services, and staffing fire departments. Another source of independence is their ability to levy a wider range of taxes compared with county governments.

These provisions in the Oregon Constitution regarding city government were not possible before the push from the Progressive Movement (see chapter 1) for home rule for both county and city governments. As a result of these changes to the constitution and the power granted local governments, cities—especially Portland, by far the largest city in the state—have grown in complexity and size over the past few decades in response to the state's growing urban population.

The freedom provided to cities in the constitution has also allowed them to choose how they want to structure their government. Most medium and larger cities have adopted the council-manager system in which there is an elected city council, which then hires a city manager to implement the council-approved policies. One of the few

Table 9.1. Forms of Oregon city governments

	Mayor/City Manager	Council or Commission	Administrative Departments	Location
Council-Manager	• Implements city policies. Manages administration and personnel. • Hired by and responsible to council. • Proposes city budgets. • Provides administrative support for council members.	• Manages and administers city government.	• Administers programs and reports to the city manager.	• Most of Oregon's larger cities (populations over 2,500).
Strong Mayor-Council	• Chairs city council. • Recommends policies. • Appoints most department heads. • May have veto power over city council.	• Establishes city policy. • Has veto override power.	• Administers programs and reports to mayor.	• Beaverton
Weak Mayor-Council	• Mayor is ceremonial leader of city. • Chairs council meetings. • Has weak administrative powers.	• Establishes city policy and directly runs programs.	• Administers programs and reports to council.	• Most smaller Oregon cities (populations under 2,500).
Commission Form	• Chairs commission and makes commissioner assignments. • Proposes city budgets.	• Establishes city policy and administers programs.	• Commissioners serve as department heads and administers programs.	• Portland

Source: Oregon Secretary of State, Oregon Blue Book (Salem: State of Oregon, 2016)

larger cities that has not adopted this type of system is Beaverton, which is considered to be the only strong mayor-council structure in the state. Most of the smaller cities in the state have adopted the weak mayor system, in which the mayor plays primarily a ceremonial role in leading the city. Portland is unusual in that it is one of the few cities in the nation that uses a commission form of government. Under this system, the elected city commissioners serve in a dual role, both writing laws as part of the council and serving as heads of city departments. The commission system provides for a relatively weak mayor. For the most part, the only power that Portland mayors have, beyond those of the other city commissioners, is deciding which department each commissioner will head. Table 9.1 displays the various types of city governments that can be found in Oregon, along with the powers granted the councils, managers, and mayors.

As discussed in chapter 2, Oregon experienced a sizable drop in its rural population, mainly due to the diminishing timber and natural resources industries that dominated the state's economy in the early part of the twentieth century. As a result, Oregon has one of the highest numbers of "ghost towns" compared with other states in the Union.[2] Many of these towns were once thriving logging towns. The decline in small rural towns, however, has also coincided with a growth in urban centers in the state. According to the *Oregon Blue Book* (2016), cities generate around 80 percent of the state's economy, are the sites of the state's largest universities, employ the vast majority of the police force in the state, and build most of the state's roads. They also constitute approximately 70 percent of the state's population.[3] This increase in significance by the big cities and the suburbs accompanied the growth of the high-tech economy in the state, especially in the Portland Metro area.[4] This growth started in the 1980s and continues to this day, despite the decline the tech sector suffered from during the dot-com bubble of 2001.[5] Table 9.2 shows the population size of the seven biggest cities in Oregon and the percentage change of their population size since 1980.

There are a number of conclusions that can be drawn from table 9.2. The first is that population growth has been rapid, especially in the three cities surrounding Portland. The second is that this increase has solidified Portland as the main urban center in the state. Beaverton, Gresham, Hillsboro, and Portland are all part of the Portland Metro area, and together they comprise almost a quarter of the state's population. Not only did this concentrated population growth increase Portland's influence in the state's politics, but it also meant that the role of city government in Portland has increased significantly over the past thirty-five years to meet the demands of this increasing population, especially when it comes to policing, the fire department, and building roads (discussed below in "The Portland Metro").

Table 9.2. Oregon's largest cities

City	Population Size in 1980	Population Size in 2015	Change since 1985, %	Share of State Population Today, %
Portland	366,383	632,309	72.58	15.73
Salem	89,091	164,549	84.70	4.09
Eugene	105,664	163,460	54.70	4.07
Gresham	33,005	110,553	234.96	2.75
Hillsboro	27,664	102,347	269.96	2.55
Beaverton	31,962	96,577	202.16	2.40
Bend	17,260	87,014	404.14	2.16

Source: Oregon Secretary of State, Oregon Blue Book *(Salem: State of Oregon, 2016)*

County Government

Counties were a central element of the state's governmental structure even before Oregon achieved statehood. Not long after western European immigrants began settling Oregon, counties were created to take care of services such as building roads, operating courts, and collecting taxes. They remain an important institution today, but there have been significant changes in their structure and responsibilities. Most of the changes occurred in the twentieth century, as counties in the western part of the state adapted to increases in population, the rise of the new "postindustrial" economy, and growing demands for services. (As discussed in chapter 2, postindustrial economies are characterized by a dominant service sector that requires highly trained and educated employees.) In the less populous, rural areas of the state, many counties still have the same government structures and continuity in many of the services provided.

After Oregon officially became a state, the new constitution provided a distinction between responsibilities of the local government and the state government. Article VI of the Oregon Constitution, which was ratified in 1859, outlined the different administrative departments in the state. Article VI, Section 6, explicitly recognized county officers, including county clerks, treasurers, and sheriffs. But the Oregon Constitution only allowed county governments to function as agents of the state government at this time, which meant that county functions had to be authorized by the state.

While these historical county roles persist, much has changed since the nineteenth century in terms of defining county government in the state and their functions. These changes are primarily a result of the Progressive Movement in the early part of the twentieth century, which reshaped attitudes about the role of local government in Oregon, including county government. Progressive reformers sought more effective local government, one that would have the ability, resources, and expertise to address local problems. The most prominent change the Progressive heritage brought to county government was the result of the home rule amendment, which was added to the state constitution in 1958 to provide a process by which counties received the authority to act independently in addressing local concerns, though they would have to follow certain formal steps to enjoy those powers, including putting forward a revised county charter to voters for approval. The availability of home rule was then expanded even further in 1973 when the state adopted a law that gave both home rule and non–home rule counties greater authority. These changes in Oregon law have given considerable freedom to county governments to operate independently from the state, which represents a significant switch from the country's role as an agent of state government, as was originally intended by Oregon's constitution.

While only nine counties have adopted formal home rule charters based on the 1958 constitutional amendment, the passage of the 1973 statute means that all counties enjoy considerable authority in tackling local concerns. According to Association of Oregon Counties Director Mike McArthur, Oregon counties "enjoy two kinds of

Table 9.3. Oregon counties

County	Year Established	Population in 2014	Percentage Population Change, 2010-16	Type of County
Washington	1843	560,465	10.2	home rule
Yamhill	1843	100,550	5.8	general law
Marion	1843	326,150	5.9	general law
Clackamas	1843	391,525	7.7	general law
Clatsop	1844	37,495	3.2	home rule
Polk	1845	77,735	5.7	general law
Benton	1847	88,740	6.7	home rule
Linn	1847	119,705	4.8	general law
Lane	1851	358,805	4.0	home rule
Douglas	1852	109,385	2.5	general law
Jackson	1852	208,375	5.2	home rule
Tillamook	1853	25,480	2.7	general law
Coos	1853	62,900	0.2	general law
Columbia	1854	50,075	2.9	general law
Multnomah	1854	765,775	7.5	home rule
Wasco	1854	26,105	5.9	general law
Curry	1855	22,355	1.1	general law
Josephine	1856	83,105	2.4	home rule
Umatilla	1862	78,340	5.3	home rule
Baker	1862	16,325	2.3	general law
Union	1864	26,485	3.9	general law
Grant	1864	7,425	−0.5	general law
Lake	1874	7,990	1.5	general law
Crook	1882	20,780	2.9	general law
Klamath	1882	66,910	1.6	general law
Morrow	1885	11,525	5.1	general law
Gilliam	1885	1,975	5.8	general law
Malheur	1887	31,470	1.3	general law
Wallowa	1887	7,070	1.9	general law
Sherman	1889	1,785	1.7	general law
Harney	1889	7,2605	−1.4	general law
Lincoln	1893	46,890	3.7	general law
Wheeler	1899	1,440	1.7	general law
Hood River	1908	23,730	10.7	home rule
Jefferson	1914	22,205	4.9	general law
Deschutes	1916	166,400	12.0	general law

Source: Oregon Secretary of State, Oregon Blue Book (Salem: State of Oregon, 2016)

home rule": one based on the constitutional amendment ("home rule counties") and the other on the 1973 statute ("general law counties"). Combined, these two forms of home rule have been so important, McArthur wrote, that "the U.S. Advisory Commission on Intergovernmental Relations concluded in a 1981 report that Oregon counties have a greater degree of local discretionary authority than counties in any other state."[6] Table 9.3 provides a list of the counties, showing their legal form as well as their population and the year in which they were established.

Today, county governments in Oregon have evolved to exercise a degree of authority that is unmatched anywhere else in the nation.[7] Yet the counties still share responsibilities with the state in many areas, including in health and human services, public safety, natural resources and recreation, transportation, land use, and economic development. Table 9.4 summarizes the distribution of responsibilities between state and county governments. While the number of programs and responsibilities that are handled only by county governments is a small fraction of the chart, the list of shared state/county services and county services makes it clear that counties are involved in the majority of government functions, either by solely carrying them out or by sharing the responsibility with the state government.

There are five types of county governments in Oregon: county manager, county administrative officer, elected executive, county court system, and board of commissioners. Table 9.5 provides an overview of these types of county governments and how they function in Oregon.

According to the *Oregon Blue Book*, the county court system is the oldest form of county government in Oregon.[8] All thirty-six counties once had a county court; however, only eight counties have a county court today, and the county judge primarily attends to administrative affairs, rather than presiding over the county court, which has limited judicial authority. Also interesting is that county courts are only found in counties on the eastern side of the Cascade Mountains, which have experienced the smallest population increases in the state. In other parts of Oregon, as the population increased over the decades, the counties adopted other, more complex forms of governing structures, and the use of county courts declined.

For those counties that have board of commissioner form of government, the executive position is often rotated among the three to five commissioners and is mostly a ceremonial role. For county manager governments, the manager is hired by the county commissioners and is much like a city manager, by being responsible for implementing policies passed by the county board or council. Similarly, in the counties with a county administrative officer structure, the administrative officers are also appointed by and responsible to the board or council. County boards and councils establish policy, but the administrator is responsible for implementation of policies and oversight of administrative department heads. Only Multnomah County has a directly elected executive who chairs the board and directly supervises administrative department heads.

Table 9.4. Shared state-county services

Health and Human Services	Public Safety	Natural Resources and Recreation	Transportation, Land Use, and Economic Development	Other Community Services
STATE-PROVIDED SERVICES				
• Child protection • Housing • Mental health hospitals	• appellate court • state police • state prison • attorney general	• state parks • state lands • water regulation • wildlife regulation	• state highways • state fair	• administrative services
STATE/COUNTY SHARED SERVICES				
• Aging/senior services • Alcohol/drug treatment • Alcohol/drug prevention • Children and family services • Services for the developmentally disabled • Mental health services • Oregon Health Plan services	• trial courts • district attorney • 911/emergency communications • emergency management • homeland security • community corrections • court security • juvenile services • marine patrol • drug courts • county law library	• county forest trust lands/ state forest management • habitat restoration • wildlife/predator control • federal land policy • noxious weed control • water master	• land-use planning and coordination • land-use permitting • highway and road system • senior and disabled transportation • energy development • engineering • building permits and inspection • economic development • county fair • infrastructure development	• assessment and taxation • PERS • employee/ labor relations • elections • extension service • telecommunications
COUNTY-PROVIDED SERVICES				
• Solid waste management • Recycling programs	• sheriff patrol • animal control • justice courts • search and rescue • county jail	• county forest management • county parks • vector control • soil and water conservation	• surveying • county transportation system	• administrative services • procurement • recording public documents • county library • county museums • county services district

Source: Association of Oregon Counties

As discussed above, population change has been a major drive behind the adoption of new forms of county government, because they are viewed as being more capable of handling the complex responsibilities placed on counties today. Table 9.3 shows the percentage change in population size over the past two decades. Five out of the eight counties that have retained a county court as their form of government have

Table 9.5. Forms of Oregon county governments

	Executive	Board or Council	Administrative Departments	Location
County Manager	• Implements county policies. • Manages administration and personnel. • Hired by and responsible to board. • Proposes county budgets. • Provides administrative support for board members.	• Board size varies and set by charter. • Establishes county policy and oversees administration.	• Administers programs and answers to manager.	• Home-rule counties (Clatsop and Hood River).
County Administrative Officer	• Appointed by and responsible to board. • Implements board policies. • Appoints and dismisses administrative department heads. • Supervises county budget.	• Board size varies and is set by charter. • Establishes county policy and oversees administration. • May share administrative responsibilities with administrator.	• Administers programs and may answers to officer.	• Home-rule counties (Benton, Jackson, Josephine, Lane, Umatilla, and Washington).
Elected Executive	• Executive is independently elected and chairs the board. • Implements board policies. • Appoints and dismisses administrative department heads. • Supervises county budget.	• Board size varies and is set by charter. • Establishes county policy and oversees administration.	• Reports to elected executive, except for independently elected offices; administers programs.	• Home-rule county (Multnomah).
County Court System	• Chief executive is county judge who chairs court. • Oversees administration and may perform some judicial duties.	• County court consists of county judge and two other elected commissioners. • Establishes county policy and oversees administration.	• Reports to county court, except for independently elected offices; administers programs.	• General law counties (Crook, Gilliam, Grant, Harney, Malheur, Morrow, Sherman, Wasco, and Wheeler).
Board of Commissioners	• Rotated among board members; some are elected. • Chairs board meetings. • May have administrative authority over departments.	• Typically three- to five-member boards. • Commissioners are elected. • Establishes county policy and oversees administration.	• Administers programs and reports to board, except for independently elected offices.	• General law counties • (all others).

Source: *Oregon Secretary of State,* Oregon Blue Book *(Salem: State of Oregon, 2016)*

experienced population decline since the 1980s, when their population was already small.[9] Moreover, none of the counties with the county court structure has a population over thirty-two thousand. The lack of growth and small population in these counties help to explain why they have retained the more traditional county court structure, while many of the largest counties have adopted new government forms.

Special Districts

A special district usually has a population of residents occupying a specific geographic area, features a legal governing authority, possesses the power to levy taxes to pay for its services, maintains a legal identity separate from any other governmental authority, and exercises considerable autonomy. Special districts are created to provide a specific service for a local area; for instance, a watershed district aims at promoting the beneficial use of water, and a rural hospital district works to maintain health-care services to a sparsely populated area. While the vast majority of the special districts in Oregon perform a single function, a small proportion of them provide two or more services.

State law allows the creation of twenty-eight different kinds of special districts in Oregon, including education, water improvement, cemeteries, parks and recreation, soil and water conservation, insurance, transportation, sanitary, water supply, fire, irrigation, and port districts (see chapter 17 for discussion of education districts).[10] According to the Special Districts Association of Oregon, there were over 900 special districts in Oregon in 2016, up from 835 special districts in 1992.[11] Unlike with public school districts, which went through widespread consolidation in the latter half of the twentieth century, other types of special districts in Oregon have continued to grow in a variety of diverse policy areas. For example, as Oregon developed into a postindustrial society, special districts emerged in new areas consistent with postmaterialist values (see chapter 2), such as in governing parks, recreation, and environmental issues.

Using Benton County (home of Oregon State University) as an example of the types and number of special districts that can be found in an Oregon county, there is one education service district, two community college districts, seven public school districts, nine rural fire protection districts, one park and recreation district, two water control districts, one cemetery district, one social and water conservation district, and eleven road districts. This is a total of thirty-five special districts for a county with a population of approximately eighty-nine thousand people.

Special districts can be funded through fees for services, property taxes, or some combination of both. Most special districts have an elected board of commissioners that oversees operations.

Regional Government

The more interesting story about change in local government in Oregon is not about cities, counties, and service districts. It is about what has happened at a higher level:

Oregon has adopted the most powerful regional government in the nation, and the only one with an elected governing council. The creation of the regional government did not begin in recent years, but rather dates to the latter half of the twentieth century.

THE PORTLAND METRO

Until the early twentieth century, urbanization in the United States resulted in the growth of relatively large, central cities surrounded by smaller suburban bedroom communities and small towns. Centrally located downtown areas were the locations for essential financial, insurance, and other services, including the manufacturing base for metropolitan and often state and regional economies. This was clearly the case in Oregon, where Portland served as the financial, services, manufacturing, and market center for communities located throughout the Columbia River basin. It was no accident that the Pacific International Livestock Exhibition, the premier annual livestock exhibition for Oregon, took place in Portland in facilities specially built for that purpose. By 1930, the center built for the exhibition, now known as the Expo Center in north Portland, was the largest center of its kind on the entire West Coast.[12]

But this strong tendency to favor cities over state and regions was soon to come to an end. By the 1920s, the profound impact of the automobile on residential settlement patterns was already apparent. Though slowed by the Great Depression and the Second World War, rapid suburban development became the driving force for metropolitan area expansion, fueled by massive federal investment in infrastructure, mortgage insurance, and the devastating effects of urban renewal on central cities.

By the mid-1950s, the unintended consequences of what became known as "suburban sprawl" led to new federal initiatives to encourage, through the provision of cash incentives, metropolitan regional planning and intergovernmental coordination. Federal planning assistance to municipalities, first provided through Section 701 of the 1954 Housing Act and continued through subsequent housing acts until 1981, enabled jurisdictions across the nation to develop local comprehensive plans, often for the first time.

In Oregon, planning funds from the US Department of Housing and Urban Development led (known as HUD 701 funds) to the creation of the Mid-Willamette Valley Planning Council in 1957, involving Marion and Polk Counties, the Salem School District, and the City of Salem. All of these initiatives laid the groundwork for a Compact of Voluntary Intergovernmental Cooperation with the state of Oregon in 1959, one of the first such intergovernmental compacts in the nation.

In a 1994 work, Allan Wallis, a leading expert on metropolitan regional government and the former director of research at the National Civic League, described the evolution of regional governance, in Oregon and throughout the nation, as amounting to several successive "waves" of activity.[13] The first wave occurred in the latter part of the nineteenth century and the first half of the twentieth century. It was the product of reform efforts meant to address the impacts of rapid urbanization on mostly mono-centric city regions—the great industrial centers of the United States. Governmental consolidations were promoted as part of these efforts to address the emerging needs and challenges of institutions created at a scale needed to meet these needs and solve those problems. During this period, the city we know today as Portland was created through the consolidation of Albina, East Portland, Portland, Sellwood, and St. Johns.

According to Wallis, the second wave of regional governance began to emerge in the mid-1950s and 1960s, as the federal and state governments began to get involved in this process.[14] Where the first wave of regional governance was largely voluntary and the product of local leadership and conditions, the second wave brought federal money to local communities to encourage coordinated programs of comprehensive planning and subsequent action. In particular, the Housing Act of 1961, the Federal Highway Act of 1962, and the Urban Mass Transit Act of 1964, among others, required comprehensive planning as the basis for the distribution of program funds. After the election of Ronald Reagan in 1980 and the elimination of HUD 701 planning, along with a wide range of federal programs to incentivize local action using federal funds, regional planning and governance associated with this second wave came to an abrupt halt. As Martha Derthick reported in her 1974 report on regional governance for the Brookings Institution: "There has never been a sustained movement for regional orga-nization that left its impress across the United States."[15]

Despite the withdrawal of federal involvement that incentivized regional gover-nance, the growth of distinctive metropolitan economies in the 1970s and 1980s led to the emergence of what Wallis has called the third wave of regional governance in the United States.[16] Fueled by a growing sense of the interlocking fortunes for central cit-ies and surrounding suburbs, a revival of civic engagement at the regional scale began to become evident, even in places where regional governance had been declared dead.

All these waves of regional governance in the United States are evident in Oregon, particularly in the Portland metropolitan region. Carl Abbott, the state's leading urban historian, and Margery Post Abbott, a Portland-based researcher and writer, have writ-ten a succinct history of the Portland Metro, which explains how the state's regional government developed.[17] As Abbott and Abbott suggest, regional governance in the Portland metropolitan area can be described as having unfolded in four waves. The first, up through World War II and ending in the mid-1950s, was, like Wallis's first wave, a response to rapid and extraordinary growth. They trace the roots for the Portland Metro as a regional planning agency back to the 1920s, and a study commit-tee that was created by the state to investigate the governance and the fragmentation of local government in the Portland region.

By 1944, the inefficiency of fragmented governmental responsibilities coupled with what Abbott and Abbott call the "extraordinary war boom" led to a call by the League of Oregon Cities for legislation to authorize regional planning districts in

Oregon.[18] But the legislature instead responded by authorizing county planning and zoning, something that Oregon had put in place for cities in 1919.

As with Wallis's first wave, this first wave of metropolitan planning and governance in the Portland region came to an end with a 1956 report from the Oregon legislature's Joint Interim Committee on Local Government.[19] This report called for the use of traditional tools for metropolitan expansion—annexation, special districts, coordinated planning—as a means for addressing the challenges posed by fragmented governance and rapid growth. If the word "sprawl" was in common usage at the time, it would have been invoked.

Abbott and Abbott's second wave coincided with the efforts at the federal level to catalyze metropolitan planning and governance through planning paid for by HUD 701 funds.[20] As in other regions, metropolitan planning initiatives got under way through a series of projects created to take advantage of the federal funding, and initiated both by the state of Oregon and by local agreements. As Abbott and Abbott report, the first two regional agencies, the Portland Metropolitan Planning Commission (1957) and the Portland-Vancouver Metropolitan Transportation Study (1959), were created at this time.

The League of Women Voters and other business and community groups drew new attention to wasteful and inefficient service delivery in the Portland region, as well as to the lack of accountability for improvement accompanying escalating governmental fragmentation. The league issued a report in 1961 that led the Oregon legislature to establish an interim committee to study the problem. The 1963 session of the legislature saw the creation of the Portland Metropolitan Study Commission to confront the issues of service delivery and governance unable to be effectively addressed by single jurisdictions. As Abbott and Abbott report, the initial report of the Study Commission, issued in 1966, proposed the creation of a single "super city" for the region.

This proposal met significant opposition in the Oregon legislature and was replaced by what Abbott and Abbott described as a "'market basket' approach of incremental changes."[21] Out of this approach came the creation in 1970 of the Portland Metropolitan Service District (MSD), a special district created to take on the provision of specific services, like the management of solid waste, on which all jurisdictions depended but that no single jurisdiction could provide.

Among those incremental changes was the replacement of the Portland Metropolitan Planning Commission by a more broad-based Council of Governments, the Columbia Regional Association of Governments (CRAG), modeled on the Mid-Willamette Valley Council of Governments and its more inclusive representation of smaller cities. The creation of CRAG in 1967 and its subsequent assumption of the role as a metropolitan planning organization (MPO) for the Portland region needed to continue the flow of Section 701 planning monies, marked the beginning of the activity that led to the creation of the Portland Metro some ten years later.

While MSD struggled to realize its promise as a collector of regional-scale service responsibilities, CRAG found itself leading planning efforts with little or no authority to make needed changes. In 1973, the same year that it created Oregon's landmark and mandatory statewide land-use planning program, the legislature also adopted Senate Bill 769, making local government membership in CRAG mandatory. This bill also weighted votes on the CRAG council by population, thereby granting Portland an enhanced role in CRAG decision-making.

In 1975, the National Academy for Public Administration issued a request for proposals to explore new governmental forms for metropolitan regions. The call for proposals came to the attention of A. McKay Rich, former director of the Portland Metropolitan Study Commission. He convened a group of academics, civic leaders, and directors of regional initiatives to prepare a response. The National Academy ultimately awarded a $100,000 grant to the proposal from the Portland region, matched by $50,000 in cash and in-kind contributions from Portland State University, the Portland Metropolitan Area Local Government Boundary Commission, and local businesses. A sixty-five-member committee was created to oversee the effort, and the entire effort took place under the auspices of what became known as the Tri-County Local Government Commission.

It was the Tri-County Commission that proposed combining CRAG and its planning responsibilities with MSD and its role as a service provider in order to create a more streamlined and authoritative regional entity. It also proposed the direct election of governing body members as a means for escaping the inevitable conflicts that local elected officials face between their local interests and the area-wide focus of a council of governments. This proposal for directly elected and therefore directly accountable regional government garnered the support of the major newspapers in the state for the proposal.

The legislature adopted enabling legislation for the proposal made by the commission but required it to go before the voters of the region before being adopted. In addition, rather than including all of Clackamas, Multnomah, and Washington Counties, it was limited to the smaller, urbanized portions of the three counties. Finally, the legislature required that this new jurisdiction, to be called the Portland Metropolitan Service District, would have to secure a tax base prior to taking on any regional-scale service responsibilities.

In May 1978, the measure went before area voters and was approved. But the ballot title—"Reorganize the Portland Metropolitan Service District, Abolish CRAG"—was, as Abbott and Abbott report, confusing to many, and led to the supposition that it was approved largely as a means to eliminate the prior agencies rather than to make them more effective. Nonetheless, the third wave of regional governance began, according to Abbott and Abbott, with the approval of this measure by local voters, and pivoted away from a council of governments, CRAG, toward a directly elected unit of government, the Portland MSD, the only such entity in the United States then or now.

Since the 1973 passage of Oregon's landmark land-use planning program, all urban areas in the state have been required to establish growth boundaries. In 1989, the MSD Council adopted a proposal for the creation of a regional growth management strategy as part of the periodic review of the metropolitan area's urban growth boundary. That action resulted in the adoption of the Regional Urban Growth Goals and Objectives in 1991, and led to the creation of the Region 2040 Growth Concept, now the region's guiding vision for metropolitan urban growth management. Also in the late 1980s, MSD led the effort that created the Regional Land Information System (RLIS), a collaborative venture involving MSD and local government, and recognized internationally as a path-breaking accomplishment.

The adoption of the Regional Urban Growth Goals and Objectives, the Region 2040 Growth Concept, and the creation of RLIS and MSD, by then referred to simply as "the Portland Metro," constituted what Wallis has identified as the third wave of regional governance activity in America. In addition to its directly elected structure, the Portland Metro also had unprecedented planning powers. Since 1978, the Portland Metro has had the authority to adopt regional "functional" plans, plans addressing a single or narrow scope of functions at a regional scale, and to require that local plans be modified to embrace and be consistent with the aims of these regional plans.

No other regional entity in the country has this kind of power. Particularly in Oregon, where comprehensive plans have specific legal meaning and guiding authority for all land-use decision-making, the Portland Metro's functional planning authority stands as a remarkable and distinctive authority granted to a regional agency. Especially in the Oregon context, but nationally as well, the Portland Metro's planning powers are unmatched. Despite the presence of these powers in the Portland Metro's enabling legislation for the first twelve years of its existence, however, the politics of regional governance remained fragile. Like other regions, the Portland Metro had to build up its planning capacity and role through a collaborative process, one engaging citizens, local and state government, and key business and civic leaders. As in other regions described by Wallis as engaging in a third wave of regional planning and governance, so, too, did the Portland Metro region depend not on its statutory authority, but on the strength of the collaborative planning process.[22]

Today, the Portland Metro's charter, adopted in 1992, has been updated three times by voters, in 2000, 2002, and 2014. The charter focuses on planning, sustainability, and efficient and effective service provision—all at the scale of the region. It pledges to work cooperatively with local government and underscores the notion of accountability that underlies the creation of a directly elected regional government for the Portland area in the first place.

Chapter IV of the Portland Metro's charter lays out its form of government. This chapter identifies the powers, duties, and composition of the Portland Metro council, which consists of six councilors elected from districts and one council president elected at-large. Chapter IV also specifies the powers and duties of the council's presiding officer, who is elected from among the council members, as well as those of the council president. This section also identifies the Portland Metro auditor, to be elected at-large and to "make continuous investigation of the operations of the Portland Metro." In Chapter V, procedures for elections, compensation, and filling vacancies are specified, among other details.

Significantly, Section 26 of the charter, found in Chapter V, identifies the creation of the Portland Metro Policy Advisory Committee. According to the charter, this committee has a standing role in both the Portland Metro's planning functions as well as in the Portland Metro's process for the assumption of additional functions or services of regional concern. In addition, Section 27 calls for the creation of a Portland Metro Office of Citizen Involvement to "develop and maintain programs and procedures to aid communications between citizens and the Council." With these sections, the charter goes beyond the specification of duties to describing, structurally, how the Portland Metro shall be established to continue working cooperatively with local governments and to substantially ensure that direct citizen engagement, the promise of a directly elected government, is sustained.

The Portland Metro has now been operating according to its charter for fourteen years. It maintains an active and robust planning program, along with the other regional services tasks assigned to it by the charter. Despite having what is arguably the most developed and powerful regional form of local government in the nation, the Portland Metro has relied substantially on partnerships to carry out its work. Although the Portland Metro is charged by its electors with planning and policymaking as its primary tasks, it is the other local governments in the region—cities and counties—that implement those plans and policies through the policies they adopt.

The Portland Metro's success or failure as a planning agency is ultimately up to the numerous implementing and planning decisions made daily by cities and counties. Consequently, the Portland Metro's success is ultimately a product of the quality of the relationships it is able to cultivate and sustain with its local government partners. As Abbott and Abbott noted, the Portland Metro is now firmly engaged in a fourth wave of regional governance in this region. Structurally, the Portland Metro Charter works as a living document to describe the powers, duties, and processes for the jurisdiction.

COUNCILS OF GOVERNMENT

In addition to the Portland Metro, Oregon has seven regional councils of government (COGs), which are multijurisdictional and multipurpose voluntary associations composed of local governments. COGs often work on policy issues and problems that cross county and city boundaries. The seven COGs in Oregon are: Central Oregon Intergovernmental Council, Lane COG, Mid-Columbia COG, Mid-Willamette Valley COG, Northwest Senior and Disability Services, Oregon Cascades West COG, and

Rogue Valley COG. COGs have both an executive director and professional staff, and are typically governed by a board of directors that includes city councilors, mayors, county commissioners, and other administrative officers. Funding for COG programs comes from the member local governments as well as from various state and federal sources.

Examples of the types of programs and services offered by the Oregon Cascades West COG, which represents Benton, Lincoln, and Linn Counties and cities, include: senior and disability services (e.g., adult protective services, aging and disability, food security, veterans' services); transportation (e.g., park and ride, Pedal Corvallis, Albany Area Metropolitan Planning Organization); and community development (e.g., planning and interjurisdictional collaboration, community facilities development, comprehensive economic development strategy). According to the Lane Council of Governments, COGs are an "association of local governments dedicated to helping area cities, the county, educational and special-purpose districts achieve their common goals."[23]

CONCLUSION: A DARK FUTURE?

Oregon's local governments are responsible for many services and programs that affect all Oregonians every day of the year. They build and maintain roads, highways, and bridges; provide water and sewage services; offer fire and police protection; decide how communities will be planned and zoned; raise taxes and decide how to spend the money; work collaboratively with other state and local governments to co-offer services and programs; and much, much more. Local government is also an important entry point for those citizens who want to begin careers in public service, either through public participation processes or through elected office.

While local governments are central in providing these many services, there are some looming concerns for Oregon's local governments, regarding both their budgets and ability to deliver those services and programs. Before the passage of Measure 5 in 1991 (see chapter 18), property taxes were the largest source of revenue for most local governments in Oregon. In 1991-92, when Measure 5 was just beginning to be phased in, property taxes still accounted for almost 40 percent of all local government general revenue. By 1998-99, however, they accounted for only 24 percent of revenue.[24] The decline in property tax revenues has meant that local governments have had to scale back on programs and services over the last two decades and to look for alternative sources of funding. With the passage of Measure 50 in 1997, which further reduced property tax revenues, Oregon's local governments continue to have financial difficulties and are having to cope with drastically increasing costs of the Public Employee Retirement System (PERS), the state's unwillingness to adopt new taxes while relying too heavily on personal income tax, below-average per capita income, and a crumbling infrastructure.

According to a 2011 ECONorthwest report, property tax limitations and rising retirement costs are not the only problems going into the future for local governments: "Street fund revenues have lagged behind growth in incomes and the overall economy, making it difficult to maintain Oregon's transportation system. Cities have struggled to keep up with the demand for capital expenditures, and construction costs are increasing at an above-average rate. Oregon cities do not have sufficient funds to replace aging facilities and invest in new infrastructure to accommodate growth."[25] Without some type of tax reform or new, innovative approaches for service delivery, continuity in local government service and program delivery may well change for the worse.

Notes

1   Oregon Secretary of State, *Oregon Blue Book* (Salem: State of Oregon, 2016), http://bluebook.state.or.us/default.htm.
2   "Ghost Towns," Pacific Northwest Photoblog, accessed April 18, 2018, http://pnwphotoblog.com/ghost-towns/.
3   Oregon Secretary of State, *Oregon Blue Book*.
4   Joseph Cortright and Heike Mayer, *Overview of the Silicon Forest, Regional Connections Working Paper 1* (Portland, OR: Institute for Portland Metropolitan Studies, Portland State University, 1999), https://www.brookings.edu/wp-content/uploads/2016/06/06_metro_hightech_mayer.pdf.
5   Mike Rogoway, "As Other Tech Hubs Grow, Will Portland Fall Behind?," *Oregonian*, July 26, 2017.
6   Telenor and Associates, *County Home Rule in Oregon* (Salem: Association of Oregon Counties, 2005), http://www.hugoneighborhood.
7   Oregon Secretary of State, *Oregon Blue Book*.
8   Oregon Secretary of State, *Oregon Blue Book*.
9   Oregon Secretary of State, *Oregon Blue Book*.
10 Oregon Secretary of State, *Oregon Blue Book*.
11 "2012 Census of Governments," US Census Bureau, accessed April 18, 2018, https://www.census.gov/programs-surveys/cog.html.
12 "The Expo Story," Portland Expo Center, accessed April 18, 2018, http://www.expocenter.org/about-expo/the-expo-story.
13 Allan Wallis, "Inventing Regionalism: The First Two Waves," *National Civic Review* 83 (1994): 159-75; idem, "The Third Wave: Current Trends in Regional Governance," *National Civic Review* 83 (1994): 290-310.
14 Wallis, "Inventing Regionalism"; idem, "Third Wave."
15 Martha Derthick, *Between State and Nation: Regional Organizations of the United States* (Washington, DC: Brookings Institution, 1974).
16 Wallis, "Inventing Regionalism"; idem, "Third Wave."
17 Carl Abbott and Margery Post Abbott, "A History of the Portland Metro," Oregon Metro, May 1, 1991, https://www.oregonmetro.gov/history-metro.
18 Abbott and Abbott, "History of the Portland Metro."
19 Wallis, "Inventing Regionalism."
20 Abbott and Abbott, "History of the Portland Metro."

21 Abbott and Abbott, "History of the Portland Metro."

22 Wallis, "Inventing Regionalism"; idem, "Third Wave."

23 "About Us," Lane Council of Governments, accessed May 24, 2018, http://www.lcog. org/101/About-Us.

24 Legislative Revenue Office, *New Direction of the Oregon Property Tax System under Measure 50* (Salem: Oregon Legislative Assembly, 2017), https://digital.osl.state.or.us/ islandora/object/osl:4510.

25 ECONorthwest, *Fiscal Challenges for Oregon's Cities* (Portland, OR: ECONorthwest, 2011), http://www.orcities.org/Portals/17/Publications/SpecialPubs/Fiscal_ Challenges_for_Oregon_Cities_FINAL.pdf.

10
Tribal Government
Maintaining and Advancing Sovereignty through Advocacy
JUSTIN MARTIN AND MARK HENKELS

In the 1950s, the federal government, under President Eisenhower and former Oregon governor Douglas McKay, his secretary of interior, decided that tribal communities were preventing the advancement of Native Americans and the efficient use of tribal lands. Accordingly, they terminated the Klamath Tribe and all tribes located in western Oregon. Today, that policy has largely been reversed, and Oregon has nine federally recognized tribes that play a highly visible role in their communities and state government. This chapter describes the current context of Indian affairs in Oregon, first examining the historical experience and demographics of Oregon's nine recognized tribes and then the four key drivers of change in Oregon's Indian Country today: gambling, shifts in tribal legal jurisdiction, the enhanced political capacity of tribes, and a strong commitment to state-tribal collaboration.

Historically, state and tribal relations were marked by conflict, as states would interfere in what tribes considered their proper jurisdiction. They also competed for control over tribal land resources and the flow of federal money and services to Native Americans, tribal areas, and tribal governments. The historical animosity was such that the US Supreme Court deemed states to be the tribes' "deadliest enemies."[1] Since 1970, more positive and creative collaborative relationships between states and tribes have developed owing to changes in federal policies and better recognition of their shared interests.[2] Oregon is among the leaders in developing these positive relationships, whose fates hinge on continued state and tribal good will, tribal political efficacy, and federal support.

GENERAL BACKGROUND OF THE OREGON NATIVE AMERICAN EXPERIENCE
The active and passive destruction of Native American people, tribes, and culture has been chronicled extensively, as has their ability to survive. The following broad brush of history, which parallels the analysis of Stephen Pevar, one of the nation's leading experts on federal law regarding American Indians, cannot do justice to the unique experience of each region and tribe, but it provides the context needed to appreciate how things are today.[3]

Before Oregon's statehood, Native American contact with whites not only meant a complex mix of trade and competition, but also decimation through disease. Already ravaged by previous smallpox epidemics, outbreaks of non-native malaria reduced the Native American population of the Willamette Valley and the lower Columbia from 13,940 in 1830 to 1,175 in 1840.[4] American settlers overwhelmed the tribes of western Oregon, and early treaties could be ignored or renegotiated with impunity. Tribes in other parts of the state retained much larger sections of land over time, their resilience reinforced by their less desirable land and relative isolation from disease and conflict.

Throughout America, and in Oregon, many tribes experienced their own "trails of tears" as they were forcibly moved from their ancestral homes under great duress. Western Oregon tribes were pushed to reservations in the early 1850s. The Paiutes of central Oregon and the Modocs of southern Oregon and California, who had members violently resist or respond to white intrusions, were completely removed from their homelands in the 1860s and 1870s.[5] The federal government consolidated many different tribal groups together in the reservations. Today, all Oregon tribes, except the Cow Creek Band and the Burns Paiute, are composites of diverse Native American tribes and bands. For example, the Grand Ronde are officially known as the Confederated Tribes of the Grand Ronde, and their emblem features five feathers that represent the five core groups of their complex heritage.

Stating that it was for the tribes' own good, and to enable whites to better use Native American lands, the federal government in 1887 passed the Dawes Act authorizing the dismantling of reservations. This breakup had two dimensions. First, tribal members were "allotted" parcels for personal ownership that theoretically would extinguish the native lifestyle by transforming them into farmers. This policy generally failed because Native Americans lacked the knowledge, capital, land base, and cultural interest to succeed in the idealized life of a small farmer.

The second side to allotment was the auctioning of "surplus lands" to whites. In the Grand Ronde's case, for example, thirty-three thousand acres went to tribal members (and later slipped out of Indian ownership), while twenty-six thousand acres of "surplus" prime timberland went to private parties for about $1 per acre.[6] This era also featured the creation of American Indian schools, such as Chemawa in Salem, and the removal of Indian children from their families in an attempt to eradicate tribal languages and socialize them into white culture.[7]

Native American autonomy had a brief reprieve under President Franklin Roosevelt. The 1934 Indian Reorganization Act sought to reinvigorate tribal government by allowing some land restoration and promoting tribal government reforms. Although only the Warm Springs Tribe adopted a formal constitution in the 1930s, other Oregon tribes reorganized themselves, and some received land and more resources. The end result was the significant modernization of tribal government, education, and economic structures.

In the 1950s and 1960s, President Eisenhower's government returned to the earlier belief that American Indians must leave their traditions and isolation behind. In 1953, Congress adopted "termination," the legal elimination of tribes as political entities, as the center of its Native American policy. This policy was a disaster for many Oregon tribes. Secretary of Interior Douglas McKay led the way by terminating all Oregon tribes west of the Cascades, selling their lands to private parties and distributing minimal payments to members.[8] The Klamath Tribe was also terminated, ultimately with a payment of $44,000 per member for the loss of 590,000 acres of timberland, ending the legal existence of one of the country's wealthiest tribes.[9] Tribal culture and cohesion were further disrupted by policies that sent Native Americans to distant cities to be integrated further into white culture and that encouraged white families to adopt Indian children. A final notable federal law of the era was Public Law (PL) 280, passed in 1953, which gave states criminal jurisdiction in Indian Country throughout most western states. In Oregon, only the Warm Springs Tribe was excluded from this erosion of tribal sovereignty.

The pendulum of Native American policy swung again in favor of tribal sovereignty in the late 1960s and early 1970s. Native American activism and pride was inspired by, and fed into, the broader civil rights movement of this era. Native and tribal interests were advanced by national organizations loosely identified as the "Red Power" movement, such as the American Indian Movement (AIM), highly visible actions such as the nineteen-month occupation of Alcatraz Island near San Francisco in 1969-71, and by increasingly sophisticated legal and political strategies.[10] According to Stephen Cornell, a leading scholar of American Indian politics, this "movement was the movement of a whole population—a huge collection of diverse, often isolated, but increasingly connected Indian communities—into more active political engagement with the larger society, seeking greater control over their lives and futures."[11]

Oregon's Native American communities fully engaged in political activism at this time, most significantly by pushing hard to regain federal recognition and the associated tribal rights. In 1977, the Siletz became the second tribe in the country to successfully obtain restoration as a federally recognized tribe. Restoration, while a great accomplishment for tribes that had lost nearly everything, stopped short of restoring their previous lands or hunting and fishing rights. In fact, the Klamath Nation acquired only about three hundred acres, approximately one-tenth of one percent of their previous land holdings.

In the 1970s and 1980s, the federal government tried to rectify past wrongs and to make tribes more effective communities. The Indian Child Welfare Act (ICWA), passed in 1978, sought to reverse the disproportionate removal of tribal children from their communities by providing American Indian families, extended families, and tribal authorities prioritized consideration in decisions about foster care or adoption for tribal children. Another notable law was the Indian Self-Determination and

Educational Assistance Act of 1978, which empowered tribal governments to directly administer educational and other federal programs, rather than channeling all federal grants through the Bureau of Indian Affairs or states. Perhaps the most visible and important federal endorsement of tribal autonomy was the Indian Gaming Regulatory Act (1988), which dramatically altered the economic conditions of some tribes, as discussed below.

OREGON'S NINE TRIBES

Although Oregon's nine federally recognized tribes dominate the state's contemporary Native American politics and policy, the state's Native American experience is much broader. Before contact from the West, innumerable tribal groups lived or migrated throughout the state. In the Columbia Gorge, Celilo Falls was once an epicenter for salmon fishing and regional Native American trade. Travelers through the gorge today can see that the Celilo-Wyam, a nonfederally recognized intertribal Indian community, retains joint use of trust land property near The Dalles dam that flooded the falls. Another distinct community can be found in the portion of the Fort McDermitt Paiute-Shoshone Indian Reservation, which is centered in Nevada but extends into

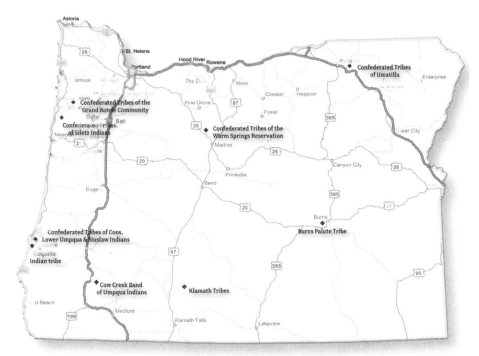

Figure 10.1. Reservations of Oregon's federally recognized tribes. Tribal headquarters are in rural parts of the state, in communities ranging in population from 735 to 16,780. Besides the areas noted on this map, most tribes have land parcels that are not contiguous to these principal locations. *Source: Northwest Portland Area Indian Health Board*

Oregon. Other tribes have disappeared or left, perhaps most notably the Nez Perce, who were scattered from northeast Oregon to various reservations in Idaho and Washington after a brave but futile eighteen-hundred-mile fighting retreat toward Canada in 1877.[12]

There is also a large concentration of "urban Indians" living in and around Portland. Individuals among the approximately thirty thousand self-identified Native Americans are separated from their home tribes and services. Politically, some view these "urban Indians" as a "hidden minority," and their lack of access to health care is notable.[13] Members of Oregon's nine recognized tribes are legally identified and enjoy whatever rights and privileges the tribe or other governments confer on their citizens. As figure 10.1 illustrates, tribal reservations are in rural areas and are often quite small. The review below provides a simple overview of each tribe's distinctive qualities.

The Burns Paiute Tribe

The approximately 349 members of the Burns Paiute Tribe descend from the Wadatika band of Paiute, who seasonally migrated from the Cascades in central Oregon to the Payette Valley north of Boise, Idaho, and from southern parts of the Blue Mountains, to the desert south of Steens Mountain. In 1873, a 1.8-million-acre Malheur Reservation was formed in southeastern Oregon only to be greatly reduced soon after. In the winter of 1879, after some tribal members participated in the Bannock War, over five hundred Paiute were forced to relocate on the Yakama Reservation and Fort Vancouver. Many of those at Fort Vancouver were subsequently moved to the Warm Springs Reservation.

Many members of the Wadatika band on the Yakama Reservation moved back to Burns. In 1928, a local land company gave the Burns Paiute ten acres of land just outside the city. In 1969, after a thirty-five-year-long court case, the tribe was awarded a small sum of money for the lands taken from the Malheur Reservation. In 1972, the Burns Paiute were recognized as an independent American Indian tribe. Today, the Burns Paiute reservation covers 770 acres just north of the city of Burns.

The Confederated Tribes of the Coos, Lower Umpqua, and Siuslaw Indians

The Coos, Lower Umpqua, and Siuslaw Indians are three tribes organized into a single confederation of 953 members. They occupied southwest Oregon coastal areas along the three major rivers named after the tribes. In 1855, coastal tribes signed a treaty with the US government, but a year later, the Rogue River War broke out south of Coos Bay and the US Army, in a preemptive strike, rounded up the Coos Indians and forced them to live in an encampment. The Lower Umpqua Indians were soon forced in as well. Both tribes later refused to relocate to the Siletz Reservation and instead joined the Siuslaw Indians. In 1918, the three tribes formed a confederation and pursued land claims they were entitled to under the 1855 treaty.

After termination in the Eisenhower administration, the Confederated Tribes of Coos, Lower Umpqua, and Siuslaw Indians had their tribal status restored in 1984. In 2004, the Coos, Lower Umpqua, and Siuslaw opened the Three Rivers Casino off Highway 126, one mile east of Florence, and added a hotel in 2007.[14] In 2015, they opened a fifteen-thousand-square-foot class II casino in Coos Bay. (Class II gambling allows for bingo-based games, which can include machines that look like regular slot machines but operate according to bingo rules. Class II also allows for card gambling so long as it is only between the players themselves and the house does not have a stake in the game. Class III gambling includes all forms of regular gambling.)

Coquille Indian Tribe

The Coquille Indian Tribe descended from people who inhabited the Coquille River watershed on the southern Oregon coast. The tribe signed treaties with the US government in 1851 and 1855, ceding seven hundred thousand acres of ancestral territory. But Congress never ratified the treaties, so the Coquille were denied a permanent homeland. The tribe was terminated by the Eisenhower administration in 1954 but subsequently restored by Congress in June 1989. The Coquille Indians then acquired several land parcels. The Coquille Indian Tribe has 1,041 members and owns the Mill Casino-Hotel and the Mill RV Park in North Bend, Oregon, overlooking the Coos Bay waterfront.[15]

Cow Creek Band of Umpqua Tribe of Indians

The Cow Creek Band, with a current population of about 1,722 members, has occupied the inland areas of today's Douglas County, Oregon, for over a thousand years. In 1853, soon after the discovery of gold in southwest Oregon, the tribe entered into a treaty that ceded their land to the federal government for 2.3¢ an acre—a fraction of the market value at that time. The Cow Creek never received the reservation or the services their treaty promised. Although the federal government tried to move the Cow Creek Band to the Grand Ronde Reservation, tribal members remained in their homelands and continued their community activities without significant support or interference for over a century. In 1954, Congress terminated the Cow Creek Band, only to restore it in 1982.[16]

After restoration, the tribe fought the federal government over the 1853 land claims and received about $1.3 million. In 1991, the Cow Creek Band constructed a bingo hall, which later became the Seven Feathers Hotel and Casino Resort on Interstate 5.[17]

Confederated Tribes of Grand Ronde

The Confederated Tribes of the Grand Ronde (CTGR) of Oregon is composed of over thirty tribes and bands whose traditional homelands extend from northern

California to the north shore of the Columbia River. It is the largest tribe in Oregon, with more than fifty-four hundred members. The many treaties signed by Grand Ronde tribes include the Willamette Valley Treaty of January 22, 1855, which ceded the entire Willamette Valley Basin. The various tribes and bands were forced to the Grand Ronde Reservation by executive order on June 30, 1857. The reservation covered approximately sixty thousand acres on the eastern side of the Coast Range, land that was mostly lost owing to the Dawes Act and other federal actions.

Termination in 1954 left the Grand Ronde with little more than a ten-acre cemetery and maintenance shed. The tribal community successfully obtained federal restoration in 1983. Five years later, President Ronald Reagan restored 9,811 acres of the original reservation to the confederation.

The Grand Ronde Tribe owns and operates Spirit Mountain Casino, the largest casino in Oregon. Each year, the tribe dedicates 6 percent of the casino profits to the Spirit Mountain Community Fund, which has given nearly $70 million to Oregon nonprofits and civic institutions since 1995, the largest such donations among Oregon tribes.[18]

The Klamath Tribes

The Klamath Basin of southern Oregon is the traditional homeland of the Klamath Tribe, the Modoc Tribe, and the Yahooskin Band of Snake Indians, who form the contemporary Klamath Tribes. After decades of hostilities, the tribes ceded 23 million acres in 1864 and moved to a 1.8-million-acre reservation. The Klamath Tribes built highly successful cattle and lumber operations and by the 1950s were one of the wealthiest tribes in the country. That came to an abrupt end when the US Congress passed the Klamath Termination Act. Although tribal members were compensated, the tribe lost all tribal lands and legal recognition.

The Klamath Tribes were restored in 1986, but their land was not returned. In early 2009, they owned 890 checker-boarded acres in trust. Gradually, the Klamath Tribes are rebuilding their economy. In 1997, they opened their first business since termination—the Kla-Mo-Ya Casino in Chiloquin, named for an acronym of the three tribes. In 2010, to encourage more travelers to visit, the Klamath Tribes opened the seventy-eight-hundred-square-foot Crater Lake Junction Travel Center, which sells fuel, convenience items, food, and services for truck drivers.[19] The Klamath have about thirty-seven hundred members.

Confederated Tribes of Siletz Indians

The Siletz are a federally recognized confederation of many bands originating from northern California, western Oregon, and southwest Washington. In 1856, they ceded nineteen million acres to the United States and agreed to confederate on the Siletz Reservation on the central Oregon Coast. In 1865 and 1875, nine hundred thousand acres of the "permanent reservation" were opened to white settlement. Additional lands were lost through allotment and forced fee policies.

The Confederated Tribes of Siletz Indians were terminated in 1954-56, but in 1977, the Siletz became the first tribe in Oregon and second in the United States to gain restoration. The Siletz have a 3,666-acre reservation in Lincoln County and 5,080 members. The Confederated Tribes of Siletz Indians operate the Chinook Winds Casino in Lincoln City. They recently acquired and renovated a large oceanfront hotel next to the casino and have added a golf course and RV park to their visitor amenities.[20]

Confederated Tribes of the Umatilla Indian Reservation

The Confederated Tribes of the Umatilla Indian Reservation, or CTUIR, was established in 1855 by a treaty signed by the US government and the Cayuse, Umatilla, and Walla Walla Tribes. The three tribes occupied over 6.4 million acres of the Columbia River Plateau of southeastern Washington and northeastern Oregon. Of the 510,000 acres that were set aside in the 1855 treaty as the Umatilla Indian Reservation, only 174,874 acres remain part of the reservation, and non-Indians own 40 percent of that. Tribal enrollment is about 3,016.

Because of their significant lands and treaty rights, the CTUIR government provides a broad array of services to members and the region, including police, fire, and emergency response services; a natural resources department; a science and engineering department that oversees cleanup of the Hanford Nuclear Reservation and the Umatilla Chemical Depot; the Yellowhawk Tribal Health Clinic; and the Nixya'awii Community School, which gives reservation students a culturally sensitive high school education. The CTUIR also owns and operates the Wildhorse Resort and Casino near Pendleton, the Tamástslikt Cultural Institute, and the Arrowhead Travel Plaza. The tribal government employs approximately 450.[21]

Confederated Tribes of Warm Springs

The Confederated Tribes of Warm Springs consist of three distinct tribes. The Wasco and Walla Walla (later called the Warm Springs) bands lived along the Columbia River and its tributaries. These two groups traded with one another but had separate cultures and languages. The Paiute occupied the high deserts of southeastern Oregon and rarely had contact with the Wasco or Warm Springs.

In 1855, the US government and the Wasco and Warm Springs Tribes signed a treaty that created the Warm Springs Reservation east of Mt. Hood on the Deschutes River. Starting in 1879, Paiute Indians were moved from Fort Vancouver onto the Warm Springs Reservation. The three tribes organized themselves as the Confederated Tribes of Warm Springs Reservation of Oregon in 1937. Enrollment is 4,306.

The Warm Springs built forest products and tourism businesses on their reservation. In 1964, they opened Kah-Nee-Ta Village near natural hot springs deep in Indian

Head Canyon, about fourteen miles from Highway 26. In 1972, they opened the Kah-Nee-Ta Lodge, adding a casino to this facility in 1995. Kah-Nee-Ta closed in September 2018, partially because in early 2012, the Warm Springs moved their gaming operations to a new and larger casino right off Highway 26. Although it lacks a hotel, the new Indian Head Casino's better location attracts more visitors than the old one.[22]

MAJOR ELEMENTS OF CHANGE IN OREGON'S INDIAN COUNTRY TODAY

Change is the only certainty in Indian Country. Political environments strongly influence what changes are likely. For Oregon's tribes today, there is a generally favorable political environment, built upon their deliberate political effort and the rise of a positive political sensitivity to their cause. In the 1970s, Oregon's tribes benefited from the support of Senators Mark Hatfield and Bob Packwood as they pursued recognition and other objectives controlled by the federal government, setting a positive tradition of congressional support for Oregon's tribes. Oregon state government itself has been a leader in building uniquely direct relations with the tribes, starting with the creation of the Legislative Commission on Indian Services in 1975 to advise the Oregon Legislative Assembly and other Oregon officials and agencies on the needs of American Indian people in the state. In the past twenty years, Governor John Kitzhaber supported positive relations between the tribes and the state itself. On May 22, 1996, Kitzhaber signed Executive Order 96–30, directing state agencies to operate on a government-to-government basis with Oregon tribes. These direct relationships were further affirmed in 2001, when the Oregon legislature and Governor Kitzhaber approved Senate Bill (SB) 770, making Oregon the first state to have a formal legal government to government relationship with regional tribes.[23]

Four factors seem likely to particularly influence Oregon tribal affairs in the coming decade: tribal gaming, greater recognition of tribal sovereignty in Oregon's legal system, increased tribal political capacity, and the development of collaborative models of governance with Oregon's state and local governments.

Tribal Gaming

For most Americans, tribal casinos epitomize the modern resurgence of Native American fortunes.[24] The passage of the Indian Gaming Regulatory Act (IGRA) in 1988 provided many tribes with previously unthinkable amounts of fiscal resources. The impact on the tribes is highly variable, though, because casino success depends upon location, management, and marketing.

The IGRA does not give tribes unfettered permission to sponsor gaming. Tribes must create a compact with their states and cannot offer any games the state forbids. The Cow Creek Bingo Hall that opened in April 1992 was Oregon's first Indian gaming facility. Indian gambling developed alongside the rise of Oregon's state-sponsored gambling, the Oregon Lottery. On April 29, 1994, Cow Creek's bingo hall was replaced

Market Shares of Oregon Gaming, 2015
TOTAL GAMBLING REVENUE: $1.585 billion

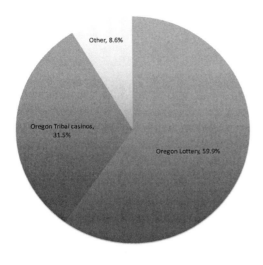

Figure 10.2.
Market shares of Oregon gaming, 2015.
*Source: Robert Whelen and Jared Rollier,
"The Contributions of Indian Gaming to
Oregon's Economy in 2014 and 2015,"*
ECONorthwest, *October 4, 2017, 33*

with a casino containing video lottery terminals (or VLTs) similar to those operated by the Oregon Lottery, and basically the same modern slot machines found in Las Vegas casinos. All Oregon tribes had casinos by 2004, although the Burns Paiute's Old Camp Casino closed in 2012 and has not been replaced.

The initial gaming compacts limited tribes to only one type of casino table game: blackjack. In January 1997, the Grand Ronde negotiated permission to install roulette, craps, and other casino table games in exchange for funding a charitable foundation with a share of the casino's profits. Since then, the Coos, Lower Umpqua, and Siuslaw, the Siletz, Cow Creek, Coquille, and Umatilla have similarly amended their compacts.

Tribal gaming has three layers of oversight: the federal government, the Oregon state police, and tribal gaming commissions. Collectively, $32.6 million was spent on all gaming regulation in 2015. Tribes picked up nearly $25.1 million in gaming regulation costs, even though they account for less than 32 percent of Oregon's gaming. The Oregon State Lottery accounted for 60 percent of the $1.585 billion in total gaming conducted in Oregon in 2015. Figure 10.2 shows how the gambling market is divided in Oregon.

Casinos are major drivers of the rural Oregon economy. In 2015, an estimated 7.46 million visits were made to Oregon casinos, filling 425,695 hotel room nights. Including everything from wages to infrastructure, Indian gaming generated nearly $1.53 billion dollars in total economic output in Oregon in 2015, and directly supported 5,422 jobs and $253.5 million in wages and benefits. Earnings from gaming operations were used to pay for $151 million in tribal government services and $98.6 million for tribal community services, including health care, education, and housing. The distribution of tribal gambling proceeds is shown in figure 10.3.

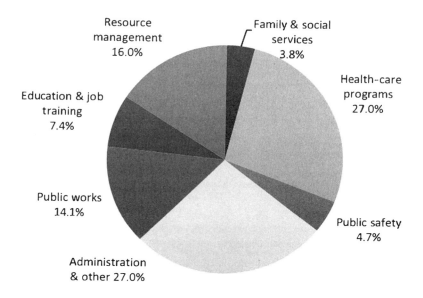

Figure 10.3. Allocation of tribal gaming receipts, 2015. *Source: Robert Whelen and Jared Rollier, "The Contributions of Indian Gaming to Oregon's Economy in 2014 and 2015,"* ECONorthwest, *October 4, 2017, 19*

The benefits of Indian Gaming include the $109.1 million that tribes have donated to local communities and to civic and nonprofit organizations. Income taxes paid by the workers and businesses that directly or indirectly service the industry are the greatest fiscal impact of tribal gaming, bringing over $139.2 million in revenues to federal, state, and local governments in 2015.

Tribal Legal Jurisdiction

The legal implications of tribal sovereignty continually evolve. The US Supreme Court recognized that the federal government can do what it wants in Indian Country under Congress's so-called plenary power. The termination policy of the 1950s dramatically demonstrates this principle. Plenary power also enabled Congress to designate major crimes involving nontribal members in Indian Country to be under federal jurisdiction in 1885. In the 1950s, Congress chose to give states criminal jurisdiction in Indian Country through the abovementioned PL 280. PL 280 sought to reduce federal law enforcement commitments in Indian Country by having states take on that responsibility, without consulting tribes.[25] The law did not give states any more resources, however, and therefore created a vacuum of police protection in affected tribal areas.[26] The Warm Springs Reservation was exempted from PL 280, so the state has no criminal jurisdiction there.

Table 10.1. Criminal jurisdiction on reservations not affected by PL 280

Indian Status	Major Crime	All Other Crimes
Indian perpetrator, Indian victim*	federal (under MCA) and tribal jurisdiction	tribal jurisdiction
Indian perpetrator, non-Indian victim**	federal (under MCA) and tribal jurisdiction	federal (under the General Crimes Act) and tribal jurisdiction
Non-Indian perpetrator, Indian victim	federal jurisdiction (under the General Crimes Act)***	federal (under the General Crimes Act) jurisdiction***
Non-Indian perpetrator, non-Indian victim	state jurisdiction	state jurisdiction

Note: The Warm Springs Tribe was always excepted from PL 480. The Burns Paiute and Umatilla Tribes gained some exceptions to PL 480 since the 1970s. A major crime is defined as such by the Major Crimes Act (MCA). There is federal jurisdiction in Indian country for crimes of general applicability.

*If the offense is listed in the MCA, there is federal jurisdiction, exclusive of the state, but not the tribe. If the listed offense is not otherwise defined and punishable by federal law in the special maritime and territorial jurisdiction of the United States, state law is used in federal courts. See section 1153(b). If not listed in the MCA, the tribal jurisdiction is exclusive.

** If listed in the MCA, there is federal jurisdiction, exclusive of the state, but probably not the tribe. If the listed offense is not otherwise defined and punishable by federal law applicable in the special maritime and territorial jurisdiction of the United States, state law is used in federal courts. If not listed in the MCA, there is federal jurisdiction, exclusive of the state, but not of the tribe, under the General Crimes Act. If the offense is not defined and punishable by a statute within the special maritime and territorial jurisdiction of the United States, state law is used in federal courts under 18 U.S.C. § 13. The United States can prosecute an Indian for a non-MCA crime, provided the tribe has not prosecuted.

*** Tribal jurisdiction for crimes under the Violence Against Women Act (VAWA) 2013 Title IX, when the tribe has opted in to Special Domestic Violence Criminal Jurisdiction (SDVCJ).

Source: "General Guide to Criminal Jurisdiction in Indian Country," Tribal Law and Policy Institute, accessed April 24, 2018, http://www.tribal-institute.org/lists/jurisdiction.htm

At least two aspects of Indian Country law enforcement have changed since the 1950s. First, the Umatilla and Burns Paiute Tribes obtained "recissions," which reversed PL 280 and reestablished their sovereignty over criminal jurisdiction. As tables 10.1 and 10.2 illustrate, PL 280 had a powerful influence over state jurisdiction on tribal lands. What the tables do not show, however, is that the limited area of western Oregon tribal reservations makes the sharing of jurisdiction with the state not as significant as it might seem. For the tribes with small land bases, collaborative relationships with local and state authorities are of more practical importance.

Second, Oregon took a unique step in 2011 when the legislature passed SB 412, which granted properly trained tribal police authority equal to other state and local police. The new power granted to tribal police reflects the development of, and new respect for, the tribal administrative and court systems, since qualifying tribal police forces must "guarantee that tribal courts will hear a civil case against its police."[27]

Tribal Political Development and Collaborative Governance

Passage of bills such as SB 412 was possible because Oregon's tribes have fundamentally transformed their political abilities. Over half of Oregon's tribes have

Table 10.2. Criminal jurisdiction where PL 280 applies.

Indian Status	Major Crime	All Other Crimes
Indian perpetrator, Indian victim*	state and tribal jurisdiction	state and tribal jurisdiction
Indian perpetrator, non-Indian victim*	state and tribal jurisdiction	state and tribal jurisdiction
Non-Indian perpetrator, Indian victim*	state jurisdiction**	state jurisdiction**
Non-Indian perpetrator, non-Indian victim	state jurisdiction	state jurisdiction

Note: PL 280 applies to most Oregon tribes. A major crime is defined as such by the Major Crimes Act (MCA). There is federal jurisdiction in Indian country for crimes of general applicability.

*Under the Tribal Law and Order Act (TLOA), a tribal government may request federal concurrent jurisdiction over crimes in PL 280 states, subject to approval by the US Attorney General.

** Tribal jurisdiction for crimes under the Violence Against Women Act (VAWA) Title IX, when a tribe has opted in to Special Domestic Violence Criminal Jurisdiction (SDVCJ).

Source: "General Guide to Criminal Jurisdiction in Indian Country," Tribal Law and Policy Institute, accessed April 24, 2018, http://www.tribal-institute.org/lists/jurisdiction.htm

professionals working on intergovernmental relations, with a strong focus on state-level issues, a move away from the "federal government only" practices of the past. This strategy has greatly benefitted Indian Country, the state, and local communities. Tribes adopted a strategy emphasizing long-term intergovernmental relationships based on trust, negotiation, and tribal sovereignty. Five strategic principles guide contemporary tribal advocacy: communication, education, cooperation, contributions, and presence.

This more assertive and collaborative tribal problem-solving is demonstrated by the Confederated Tribes of the Grand Ronde's institutionalization of advocacy in the late 1990s. To protect its hard-earned sovereignty, the tribe deliberately built a presence in local, regional, state, and federal policy affairs. In 1997, CTGR created the Intergovernmental Affairs Department to facilitate its government to government relationships. The sophistication of Grand Ronde's approach is notable. The department uses a legislative tracking system to identify state and national bills and initiatives that could affect the tribe's interest, sending a categorized list of concerns to the tribal council every two weeks. Council members return a prioritized list to the Intergovernmental Affairs staff, which works with the council's legislative committee to create strategic responses to key legislative initiatives. The system fosters targeted, proactive advocacy. At the state level, undoubtedly the arena of Grand Ronde's greatest success, the number of bills opposed by the tribe dropped from nineteen in 1997 to only three in 1999. Tribal leaders were no longer treated as ordinary lobbyists, but as representatives of a respected independent government. The state government treats the CTGR as a partner in resolving important regional issues.[28]

Other Oregon tribes developed similar political capacities simultaneously. The late 1990s were a critical turning point in state–tribal relations. The 1997 Oregon legislative session featured many bills that would significantly interfere with tribes and their gaming operations. Some would have prohibited all state and tribal gambling and stopped the VLTs that both Oregon and the tribes desired. Tribal lobbying killed these bills and dramatically reduced other hostile measures within just a two-year period. This educational effort emphasized the common interest of tribes as well as state and local communities, and greatly improved their relationships. According to the *Oregon Ethics Commission Lobbying Report*, there were ten different tribal-related groups with lobbyists representing them in the 2015 legislative session.[29]

The 2001 Oregon legislature passed much legislation that helped establish the foundation for today's positive state–tribal relationships. The most important of these acts was SB 770, which codified the Kitzhaber administration's executive orders supporting collaborative relationships with tribes into state law. According to a report of the National Conference of State Legislatures (NCSL), this agreement was the "first of its kind."[30]

The 2001 Oregon legislature also passed SB 690, directing the Teacher Standards and Practices Commission to establish the American Indian Language Teaching License and confirming tribal rights to develop and implement standards for evaluating and certifying their own language teachers. The session also passed a bill that allowed tribes to enter into contractual relationships with Oregon's Division of Mental Health and Developmental Disabilities, a prohibition of using the derogatory term "squaw" in the naming of a public property, and a law regulating trade in illegally held archeological objects.

One recent example of tribal political success in Salem is the abovementioned SB 412, passed in 2011, which granted tribal police officers the powers and protections provided to all other Oregon law enforcement officers under certain conditions.[31] SB 1509 from 2014, which gives tribes a central role in determining the use of Native American mascots or symbols by public schools, also exemplifies tribal political efficacy.

Native American tribes have had a particularly visible role in the areas of fisheries and water rights. Tribal rights in these areas are typically based on guarantees in the peace treaties of the nineteenth century and vary greatly between tribes. Some tribes, such as the Siletz and Grand Ronde, lost their hunting and fishing rights with termination. The mid-Columbia tribes (the Nez Perce, Umatilla, Warm Springs, and Yakama) have long-standing fishing rights on the Columbia and its tributaries above Bonneville Dam.

When the states of Oregon and Washington contested these rights in the 1960s, the tribes sued, and a federal court held in 1974 that the treaty tribes were legally entitled to 50 percent of the salmon taken above Bonneville. Today, those four tribes collaborate on the management of the Columbia River fisheries through the Columbia River Inter-Tribal Fish Commission (CRITFC) and have agreements with the states of Washington and Oregon on long-term conservation and harvesting measures for these fish runs.[32] In recent years, the courts have granted these tribes more legal leverage on a range of issues affecting salmon, including the siting of coal terminals on the Columbia River.[33]

Since the state of Oregon recognized its extensive water rights on the Klamath River, the Klamath Tribe has been deeply involved in building consensus on how to preserve and enhance Native American fisheries while meeting the water needs of white farmers.[34] After over a decade of negotiation among farmers, the states of California and Oregon, federal agencies, PacifiCorp (operator of four major dams on the Klamath), the Klamath, and several California tribes agreed to support the Klamath River Restoration Agreement, only to face congressional opposition. The 2016 revision allows most of the agreement to be launched without congressional support, at least initially.[35]

A key element of contemporary Native American political strategy in Oregon today is the construction of a special relationship with other governments, especially that of the state. Avoiding the typical interest group lobbying seeking favors from the state, Oregon's tribes have pursued a government-to-government approach that recognizes each side's distinct legitimacy and interests. State actions have mirrored this approach.

Governor Kitzhaber's Executive Order 96-30 (1996), "State/Tribal Government-to-Government Relations," incorporates these principles. EO 96-30 requires state agencies to (1) develop a departmental statement recognizing when state policies affect tribal interests and (2) to identify agency "key contacts" responsible for coordination with tribal governments. EO 96-30 also requires an annual meeting between the governor, leaders from each of the nine federally recognized tribes, and other key state representatives. The Legislative Commission on Indian Services provides an archive of the reports filed as part of this process.[36]

As noted above, SB 770 made Kitzhaber's executive actions state law in 2001. The aforementioned NCSL report noted that Oregon's implementation of SB 770 included the "innovative tool" of "policy cluster groups," state/tribal work groups that collaborate on natural resources, cultural resources, public safety and regulation, economic and community development, health and human services, and education.[37]

CONCLUSION:
ISSUES THAT MAY DRIVE CHANGE IN OREGON'S INDIAN COUNTRY

Four elements may particularly affect whether Oregon's tribes can extend their recent accomplishments into the future. First, gambling revenues are not certain in the future. In 2017, the Hartmann Group identified four challenges to casino gambling that Oregon's tribes must mind: (1) new casinos, (2) millennials, (3) Internet gaming, and (4) other entertainment.[38] The Cowlitz Tribe of Washington is currently building a casino just fifteen miles from Portland, which could cost the Grand Ronde Tribe alone an estimated $100 million per year. The Cowlitz project is still being challenged in court because its location is not on historic Cowlitz lands, but the Portland market is always tempting casino investors.[39] The success of the Grand Ronde–led effort to defeat Measure 82 in 2012, which would have legalized private casino gambling in Portland, illustrates the commitment and effectiveness of the tribes in defending their interests, at least in Oregon. This vital source of funds is also threatened by the fact that millennials gamble much less than their elders.[40] Internet gaming and other entertainment provide alternatives for individuals who might otherwise spend money at tribal casinos.

Second, Oregon's tribes are all located away from the metro area, generally in smaller rural settings. Tribes face the same uncertainty confronting Oregon's other timber and agricultural communities, as the economy favors high-tech and urban life-styles, and these communities share in the economic stagnation and poverty of these areas.[41] Oregon's Native American communities may help lead some rural localities into new prosperity through their own economic development and the investment of revenues raised through gambling.

Third, tribes face internal struggles connected to membership and identity issues. Tribes set and enforce their own rules for tribal citizenship, and these laws vary among them. Only recognized members receive the benefits of being in the tribe, and the recent economic success of some tribes creates new incentive for enrollment. But membership can be complicated in a society whose few members frequently marry and have children with unenrolled members. Controversies over where to draw lines for tribal citizenship will never go away for some tribes.[42]

Fourth, tribes are natural allies in most respects, but there are issues where they compete or disagree on what strategy is best. Efforts by tribes to move casinos toward the Portland area can create fears among others that they will lose market share. The potential for division also arises from the unavoidable fact that each tribe, and all tribal members, have distinct values and interests. Long-term success for Indian Country will require that tribes remain in basic agreement on the core principles that should guide state and federal and tribal relations.

Oregon tribes are better prepared to face these challenges than ever before. This positive situation arose from the individual and collective vision of tribes and of state and federal leaders to build a new set of relationships incorporating mutual respect and collaborative problem-solving. The benefits of these positive relations is well illustrated in a speech made by Grande Ronde tribal chair Reyn Leno to commemorate the passage of SB 1509, which integrated tribes into the approval process for Native American mascots and symbols in 2014:

> I am very proud of the work we have done, and want to continue to discuss communication, education and how we can keep working together to build

a better future for all Oregonians. Let's use this issue as an opportunity to start educating our children about the nine federally recognized tribal governments in Oregon, why we are relevant and why we make the fabric of Oregon so unique.

Notes

1   Erich Steinman, "American Federalism and Intergovernmental Innovation in State-Tribal Relations," *Publius* 34, no. 2 (Spring 2004): 95.

2   Steinman, "American Federalism," 96-98.

3   This review of Oregon tribal history roughly follows the historical stages identified by Stephen Pevar in *The Rights of Indians and Tribes*, 4th ed. (New York: Oxford University Press, 2012), 1-15.

4   "Lesson Seven: The Changing World of Pacific Northwest Indians," Center for the Study of the Pacific Northwest, accessed April 19, 2018, www.washington.edu/uwired/outreach/cspn/Website/Classroom%20Materials/Pacific%20Northwest%20History/Lessons/Lesson%207/7.html.

5   Laura Berg, ed., *The First Oregonians*, 2nd ed. (Portland: Oregon Council for the Humanities, 2007), 47-48 and 153.

6   Berg, *First Oregonians*, 135.

7   Annalee G. Good, "'Unconscionable Violence': the Federal Role in American Indian Education, 1890-1915," *Studies in the Humanities* 33, no. 2 (Dec. 2006).

8   David G. Lewis, "Termination of the Confederated Tribes of the Grand Ronde Community of Oregon: Politics, Community, Identity" (PhD diss., University of Oregon, 2009).

9   William G. Robbins, "Termination," Oregon History Project, last updated March 17, 2018, https://oregonhistoryproject.org/articles/termination/#.WB54KYUfnE8.

10 Stephen Cornell, "The New Indian Politics," *Wilson Quarterly* 10, no. 1 (1986): 113-31.

11 Cornell, "New Indian Politics," 131.

12 Robert H. Ruby, John A. Brown, and Cary C. Collins. *A Guide to the Indian Tribes of the Pacific Northwest*, 3rd ed. (Norman: University of Oklahoma Press, 2010), 204-10.

13 Bill Graves, "Portland-Area Native Americans Burdened by Health Hurdles Generation after Generation," *Oregonian*, May 2, 2012.

14 Robert Whelan, *The Contributions of Indian Gaming to Oregon's Economy in 2014 and 2015: A Market and Economic Impact Analysis for the Oregon Tribal Gaming Alliance* (Portland, OR: EcoNorthwest, October 4, 2017), 8, http://otga.net/wp-content/uploads/FINAL-2014-2015-OTGA-Report-1.pdf.

15 Whelan, *Contributions of Indian Gaming*, 9.

16 "The Cow Creek Story," Cow Creek Band of Umpqua Tribe of Indians, accessed April 19, 2018, http://www.cowcreek.com/tribal-story/.

17 Whelan, *Contributions of Indian Gaming*, 9.

18 Whelan, *Contributions of Indian Gaming*, 9-10.

19 Whelan, *Contributions of Indian Gaming*, 10-11.

20 Whelan, *Contributions of Indian Gaming*, 11.

21 Whelan, *Contributions of Indian Gaming*, 11-12.

22 Whelan, *Contributions of Indian Gaming*, 11-12.

23 "ORS 182.162-168: Oregon's State Tribal Government-to-Government Law," Oregon
    Legislative Commission on Indian Services, accessed April 19, 2018, https://digital.osl.
    state.or.us/islandora/object/osl%3A4679/datastream/OBJ/view.
24 All material in this following section is drawn from Whelan, *Contributions of Indian
    Gaming*.
25 "General Guide to Criminal Jurisdiction in Indian Country," Tribal Court Clearinghouse,
    accessed April 19, 2018, www.tribal-institute.org/lists/jurisdiction.htm.
26 Sarah N. Cline, "Sovereignty under Arrest? Public Law 280 and Its Discontents" (master's
    thesis, Oregon State University, May 13, 2013), tloa.ncai.org/files/New%20Study%20
    on%20Impact%20of%20PL%20280%20on%20Umatilla%20Reservation.pdf.
27 Jayme Fraser, "New State Law Expands Authority of Tribal Police, Fills Gaps in State Law
    Enforcement," *Oregonian*, August 14, 2011.
28 "Enhancing Government to Government Relationships Intergovernmental Affairs
    Department: The Confederated Tribes of Grand Ronde (Grand Ronde, Oregon)," in
    Honoring the Nations 2000 (Cambridge, MA: John F. Kennedy School of Government,
    Harvard University, 2000), 21-22, hpaied.org/sites/default/files/publications/
    Enhancing%20Government%20to%20Government%20Relationships.pdf.
29 Compiled by the authors from "Public Records: Client/Employer Lists," Oregon Ethics
    Committee, March 2, 2015, www.oregon.gov/ogec/pages/index.aspx.
30 Susan Johnson, Jeanne Kaufmann, John Dossett, and Sarah Hicks, updated by Sia Davis,
    Models of Cooperation between States and Tribes (Denver: National Conference of State
    Legislatures, 2009), 39.
31 "SB 412C Staff Measure Summary," House Committee on Rules, June 27, 2011, https://
    olis.leg.state.or.us/liz/2011R1/Downloads/MeasureAnalysisDocument/16863.
32 John Harrison, "Indian Fishing," Northwest Power and Conservation Council, accessed
    May 24, 2018, https://www.nwcouncil.org/history/IndianFishing.
33 Felicity Barringer, "In the Pacific Northwest, Native Fishing Rights Take on a Role as
    Environmental Protector," Bill Lane Center for the West, December 7, 2016, https://
    west.stanford.edu/news/blogs/and-the-west-blog/2016/pacific-northwest-native-
    fishing-rights-take-role-environmental-protector. See also "CRITFC Mission & Vision,"
    Columbia River Inter-Tribal Fish Commission, accessed April 19, 2018, www.critfc.org/
    about-us/mission-vision/.
34 Scott Learn, "Water Squeeze in Oregon's Klamath Basin Pits Ranchers against Tribes,
    Both with Strong Ties to the Land," *Oregonian*, July 6, 2013.
35 Dennis Theriault, "Klamath Basin: Revived Water Pact Could See Aging Dams Taken
    Down," *Oregonian*, February 2, 2016.
36 "Government to Government Annual Reports," Legislative Commission on Indian
    Services, Oregon State Legislature, accessed April 19, 2018, www.oregonlegislature.gov/
    cis/Pages/Gov-to-Gov-Annual-Reports.aspx.
37 Johnson et al., *Models of Cooperation*, 38.
38 Jeff Hartmann, "The Biggest Threats to Tribal Gaming," presented at the 2017 Global
    Gaming Expo, *thehartmanngroup.net/wp-content/.../G2E17_THG-Presentation_brand-
    REVISED.pdf*.
39 Dana Tims, "Cowlitz Casino on Track, Still Stirring Controversy," *Oregonian*, June 25,
    2016.
40 Elaine Povich, "State Gambling Revenue Takes Hit as Millennials Bring New Habits to
    Casinos," *Stateline*, September 15, 2015,
41 http://www.pewtrusts.org/en/research-and-analysis/blogs/stateline/2015/09/15/
    state-gambling-revenue-takes-hit-as-millennials-bring-new-habits-to-casinos.

42 Caitlyn M. May, "Who's In and Who's Out: Tribal Courts and Boards Feud over Membership," *Statesman Journal*, September 20, 2016.

11

Collaborative Governance

EDWARD P. WEBER AND CASEY TAYLOR

Collaborative governance involves "governing arrangement[s] where one or more public agencies directly engage non-state stakeholders in a collective decision-making process that is formal, consensus-oriented, and deliberative and that aims to make or implement public policy or manage public programs or assets."[1] Put differently, collaborative governance involves shared authority for decisions with a broad cross section of stakeholders, an openness to different forms of knowledge (e.g., scientific, practical, and cultural), reliance on continuous deliberation and consensus, and commitment to the production of mutually beneficial outcomes for participants versus the win-lose outcomes of adversarial settings. In short, it is a paradigm shift away from top–down, expert led, adversarial, command-and-control style of government decision-making to a more bottom–up, citizen-led, place-based approach to managing public problems.[2]

Initially developed as an alternative method for resolving difficult and complex collective action problems in both the international arena and in small-scale, stateless societies, the idea of collaborative governance is that groups of interdependent actors can and often do succeed in managing the function of governance without resorting to the creation of governments in the conventional sense.[3] In larger-scale, strong state societies such as the United States, European Union, and Japan, collaborative governance joins together governments, nonprofits (or NGOs, nongovernmental organizations), and private sector stakeholders to tackle public problems in policy areas as diverse as policing, welfare management, disaster management, homeland security, rebuilding broken urban neighborhoods, reforming public education, creating and maintaining environmentally sustainable communities, reducing drug abuse, building affordable urban housing, and managing ecosystems and watersheds.[4] Growth in community-based collaborative governance arrangements has been especially pronounced. Jules Pretty, writing in *Science* in 2003, claimed there are more than two hundred thousand examples across the globe, while David Western and Guy Salmon described their emergence in Africa, New Zealand, and Scandinavia.[5]

The importance of collaborative governance arrangements as an alternative policymaking venue—"the institutional locations where authoritative decisions are made concerning a given issue"—is now such that Lubell et al. and others regularly consider

collaboratives as a fourth major venue in addition to the traditional legislative, judicial, and administrative policymaking venues.[6] Moreover, the authoritative *Oxford
Handbook of Governance* notes that "collaborative governance has come to represent
for many policymakers, managers, and community members an elixir to the business
as usual approach to policymaking which privileges hierarchy and order over inclusion and innovation" and finds that "scores of public and private sector entities employ
collaborative governance . . . recent trends that suggest collaborative governance is
gaining in popularity as a superior method of policy redress."[7]

The state of Oregon has joined the trend toward the greater use of collaborative
governance for addressing critical public problems. Its use is found in numerous policy
areas. The Public Health Division of Oregon's Health Authority has long embraced a
philosophy of collaborative governance and has succeeded in establishing a high level of
collaboration between the state and local levels in the public health domain.[8] There are
numerous examples of human services policy collaboration, too.[9] For example, Oregon's
Washington County Vision Action Network is a private nonprofit agency designed "to
be a champion, catalyst, incubator, and facilitator for collaborative efforts to improve
life for people throughout [the] county."[10] As well, Oregon has employed a collaborative model for senior and disabled services, specifically seventeen Area Agencies on
Aging that work with diverse governments, notably councils of governments and private groups, while mixing federal, state, local, and private funding in an effort to create a
systemic approach to community-based care for this important demographic.[11] Natural
resources management in Oregon has experienced a surge in collaborative governance,
whether it is the all-lands approach to forestry management, watershed management,
marine reserves along the Oregon coast, or endangered species, to name a few.

After discussing how collaborative governance differs from traditional governance approaches and explaining why different political actors choose collaboration,
this chapter examines two key cases involving watershed restoration and endangered
species (greater sage-grouse). These cases illustrate empirically how and why different federal and state-level government agencies—the Oregon Department of Water
Resources and the Oregon Watershed Enhancement Board, the US Fish and Wildlife
Service (FWS), and the Oregon Department of Fish and Wildlife—along with many
different stakeholders are employing collaborative governance arrangements to tackle
difficult, complex public problems.

CHOOSING COLLABORATIVE GOVERNANCE

There is a pragmatic element to why public, private, and nonprofit stakeholders from
across the spectrum choose collaboration. The literature offers substantial evidence
that the voluntary decision to participate in collaborative efforts is heavily influenced
by individuals' incentives to participate. Some research shows that stakeholders in collaborative settings often make decisions and act on the basis of an internal calculus

comparing anticipated benefits (or cost savings) and losses (or costs), including the transaction costs associated with institutional arrangements,[12] while others find that actors behave in a boundedly, or intentionally, rational manner, with "competing tendencies to cooperate and act selfishly."[13]

Beyond such calculations, there is a general expectation that the collaborative approach can address or at least minimize the problems associated with existing, top–down, hierarchical governance systems. See table 11.1 for key differences between these models. The basic idea is that collaboration can deliver improved governance performance, especially over the long term. Chief among the expected advantages of collaboration over the traditional model are:

- It facilitates the resolution of severe policy problems (e.g., biodiversity loss, persistent drought, ecosystem change) that hamper the ability of individual stakeholders to maximize the achievement of their primary goals[14] because it (1) improves trust and relationships among stakeholders with disparate interests and policy preferences, and (2) increases the likelihood of creative, solutions that leave all participants better off than before (i.e., stronger environmental protection, lower compliance costs, improved social relationships, etc.). This is the idea of positive sum or mutual gain (win-win-win) outcomes.[15]
- It creates a supportive climate for policy implementation and reduces litigation, conflict, and delay because it gives more people a voice in decisions, which translates into ownership of results. This can lead to more durable solutions that are able to weather future change given the broad, consensus-based support.[16]
- It increases the capacity of participants by leveraging the resources of many different organizations. The incentive for cooperation among stakeholders is amplified to the extent that the "problem severity" in question is high and no one organization can successfully solve it on their own.[17]
- It facilitates shared interpretations of science, risk, and uncertainty and increases the influence of science and "rational solutions" in policymaking, while also taking the politics of problem-solving into explicit consideration.[18]
- It, along with networks and bottom–up coordination, is better matched than traditional bureaucratic institutions to complexity and dynamic associated with "wicked" problems such as sustainability, watershed restoration, or ecosystem-based forestry.[19]

WATERSHED COUNCILS IN OREGON

The 1990s were the decade when collaborative watershed councils in the Pacific Northwest started to form and find broad political support. As part of a broader national push toward ecosystem-based management, the councils were designed to improve land stewardship; restore ecological and water quality; help recover at-risk

Table 11.1. Comparing hierarchical and collaborative governance types

Component	Traditional Hierarchical Model	Collaborative Governance
General style	adversarial, zero sum (win-lose)	cooperative, mutual gain
Policy focus	narrow; single policy area (e.g., water, air, forestry)	broad; environment, economy, and community
Types of boundaries	traditional legal-jurisdictional, both policy and political	ecological (e.g., watershed) and social, boundary-spanning across traditional jurisdictions
Public engagement/ participation	limited and directed, controlled by government officials; less dialogue than "one-way listening" exercises by government officials	robust public participation; more cooperative decision-making; back-and-forth dialogue in deliberative forums is key
Decision style/rules	experts in charge; agencies make decisions after consultation with public and nongovernmental organizations	government experts are among many stakeholders integrally involved in decision process; consensus/near-consensus is decision rule
Problem-solving and management approach	fragmented, separated bureaucratic problem-solving and management silos	systems (integrated, holistic, cross-cutting) problem-solving and management approach
Rules vs. results	agency focus primarily on rules and proxies vs. on-the-ground results	explicit focus on results
Temporal problem solving approach	short-term problem solving focus; legal compliance key	building relationships and developing long-term problem-solving capacity; legal compliance still important
Role of science	scientific expertise is authoritative and dominant	scientific expertise critical, but practice-based and cultural expertise also needed for long-term solutions

species, especially salmon and steelhead; and, more generally, to improve the effectiveness of environmental protection policies. They also focused on supporting rural, natural resource-based economies and communities.

Beginning with individual efforts such as the Willapa Alliance in Washington State and the Applegate Partnership in Oregon, by the end of the 1990s, California, Idaho, Oregon, and Washington had all passed state legislation to support and promote this new collaborative "environment, economy, and community" model for natural resource governance. Among them, Oregon led the way, passing legislation in 1992 encouraging watershed council formation, followed by a unanimously passed 1995 state law offering further guidance, but making clear that the best solutions were likely to be local in origin and ceding the authority to form collaborative watershed councils to local governments, with no state approval required. The legislature did, however, require broad representation in each council from "a balance of interested and affected persons within the watershed," and encouraged collaborative problem-solving partnerships between the local councils, private and public property owners, and key government (federal and state) land, resource, and water management agencies.[20]

In 1997, the Oregon Salmon and Watersheds Plan, pushed by Governor John Kitzhaber in response to the dramatic declines in salmon stocks throughout the state and the desire to prevent more stringent federal policies from being imposed, reinforced the earlier initiatives by creating and funding the seventeen-member Oregon Watershed Enhancement Board (OWEB). OWEB's mission was "to help create and maintain healthy watersheds and natural habitats that support thriving communities and strong economies."[21] Drawn from the ranks of tribes, federal and state natural resource agencies, private property interests, environmentalists, and the public at large, OWEB immediately became the central power broker in Oregon watershed restoration efforts, given their statutory authority as primary funder of watershed councils (WCs) and the fact that restoration grants required the use of scientific criteria by councils when "decid[ing] jointly what needs to be done to conserve and improve rivers and natural habitat."[22]

The citizens of Oregon responded quickly to these initiatives, and by 1999 there were 87 active watershed councils, 157 in operation by 2001, and 91 as of 2016.[23] The lower number in 2016 represents consolidation, where small watersheds banded together into larger partnerships (e.g., Partnership for the Umpqua Rivers and the Klamath Watershed Partnership). Funding for watershed councils grew rapidly after passage of the "Parks and Salmon" Measure 66, which amended the state constitution to give OWEB a permanent stream of state lottery proceeds. By 2001, OWEB was awarding over two hundred grants each year and investing approximately $20 million annually in restoration activities. Helped by the requirement of a 25 percent match by awardees, OWEB restoration spending tripled between 2001 and 2002.[24] Funding increased until the Great Recession in 2009, when OWEB's budget of $96 million in the 2007-9 biennium fell to about $73 million in 2011-13 and then rose to a legislatively approved $108 million in 2015-17.[25]

Despite the statewide embrace of the collaborative governance concept for watershed management, the fragmented manner in which watershed restoration grant requests were being awarded increasingly frustrated OWEB officials. They felt that more *integrated, strategic, long-term* collaboration was needed in many areas of the state in order to tackle the complex problems facing each watershed. This perspective eventually led to the Focused Investment Partnership (FIP) starting in 2007. These investments provide capacity-building funding for collaborative partnerships, with grants being awarded according to four criteria:

1. Address a board-identified focused investment priority of significance to the state;
2. Achieve clear and measurable ecological outcomes;

3. Use integrated, results-oriented approaches strategic action plan;
4. Is implemented by a high-performing partnership.

In 2008, the first FIP funding was awarded to a partnership in the Willamette River Basin and to the Deschutes Partnership (DP), an amalgam of four groups: Upper Deschutes Watershed Council (UDWC), Deschutes River Conservancy (DRC), Deschutes Land Trust (DLT), and Crooked River Watershed Council. The Deschutes Partnership offers a good perspective on how these watershed-based collaboratives operate and what they have been able to achieve.

In the run-up to and immediately after the 1999 listing under the Endangered Species Act (ESA) of Deschutes River steelhead as threatened, members of the Deschutes Partnership began collaborating in ad hoc fashion and by 2005 had come to the same conclusion as OWEB: their initial, largely separate and fragmented responses were inadequate to the overarching goal of habitat restoration in support of successful fish reintroduction. As a result, the partnership adopted a mission of integrated, strategic watershed restoration and focused their initial efforts on the forty-mile-long Whychus Creek drainage. Whychus Creek was an easy choice given that sections of the stream were often dewatered in the summer. The choice was also driven by the fact that eighteen miles of stream channelization by the US Army Corps of Engineers destroyed what had historically been one of the river's most productive nursery habitats for steelhead. Hence the biological potential for recovering healthy habitat and fish populations listed as threatened was high.

The preference for collaborative action did not occur in a vacuum. In fact, a key reason the DP chose collaboration involves the facilitation efforts of Todd Reeve, the leader of the Bonneville Environmental Foundation (BEF), and Mary Voss of the National Forest Foundation (NFF). In 2005 and 2006, Reeve and Voss worked to overcome the limited trust among the groups.[26] At the same time, the two facilitators were not disinterested parties. They had a stake in helping the organizations adopt a collaborative approach precisely because their home organizations (foundations) wanted to fund and test such approaches.[27] The BEF's Model Watershed Program requirement that funds go only toward strategic plans with measurable long-term objectives and monitoring programs enabled the Deschutes Partnership to win FIP designation from OWEB in 2008 (including indefinite funding of $2 million per year), and convinced the Pelton Dam Mitigation Fund technical team to move beyond their fragmented approach, which resulted in another $6 million for Whychus Creek restoration.[28]

DP also included other major stakeholders on Whychus Creek restoration, such as the US Forest Service (the primary upstream landowner), the US Bureau of Reclamation, Confederated Tribes of Warm Springs, the City of Sisters, the Deschutes County Commission, private landowners, and key state agencies. But perhaps most critical to successful restoration was the involvement of the Three Sisters Irrigation District (TSID), which controlled nearly all water rights in the Whychus. This is because the core restoration problem was the lack of water in the creek during irrigation season, particularly late summer, and successful restoration required that a significant amount of water be placed back into the stream to facilitate fish passage.

Knowing this, the partnership also recognized that a principle important to success was for the costs of providing improved habitat and streamflow to be shared among all stakeholders. Instead of forcing all the costs onto one group, in this case farmers, DP's successful search for funding allowed for significant cost sharing to occur.

Yet while the cost-sharing initiative from DP started the conversation, TSID, under the leadership of Marc Thalacker, was highly motivated to act. The 1999 ESA listing of steelhead would likely strip them of control over a significant portion of their water rights if they were not proactive. Further, modernizing their water delivery infrastructure to be more efficient, hence economically viable, made sense given that 45–55 percent of all water in the system was regularly lost to evaporation and ground infiltration. A new $50 million pressurized, piped water delivery system, in place of fifty miles of traditional open canals, meant that irrigators, including junior water rights holders, would have guaranteed full water rights while also reducing economic outlays for electric pumps used to bring water to crops. Further, putting a portion of the roughly 50 percent of "saved" water *back into the stream* reaped significant revenues for TSID, since they could lease or sell "new" water shares to willing buyers, which included the state of Oregon. Finally, the new pressurized system created opportunities for two small hydroelectric power plants to generate additional electricity at low cost, while simultaneously generating a new revenue stream for TSID. Taken together, the hydropower revenues and water sales help to pay off the principal and interest on the piping system construction loans.[29]

To be considered successful, however, collaborative governance arrangements must produce positive sum, or win-win-win, outcomes, not just economic benefits important to some stakeholders. In fact, the new efficiencies in TSID's irrigation system were essential to the Deschutes Partnership's overarching goal of watershed restoration for three reasons. First, the collaborative deal with TSID reserved half of all "saved" water, or 25 percent of the total water right being delivered, for permanent, year-round instream flows. This initial added streamflow of twenty-four cubic feet per second (cfs) satisfied the Oregon Department of Fish and Wildlife (ODFW) mandate specifying the amount of water required to meet ecological needs.[30] Second, the old irrigation system relied on six water diversions along Whychus Creek, each of which blocked fish passage. The pressurized pipe system allowed for all six to be removed. Third, at the point of diversion for the new pressurized irrigation system, TSID installed a new, state-of-the-art, fish-friendly screen that stops fish from getting into the system and thus complies with ESA requirements.[31]

This effort also succeeded in producing significant contributions to the overall ecological health of the Whychus Creek watershed.[32] These accomplishments included, but were not limited to:

- installing ten new fish screens on 83 percent of all diverted water;
- using preserves and conservation easements to protect almost five thousand acres adjacent to the stream;
- more consistently meeting federal Clean Water Act stream temperature requirements;
- reintroducing more than 1.5 million steelhead and chinook salmon to Whychus Creek since 2007;
- reestablishing the historical "natural" stream path over 1.7 miles in Camp Polk Meadows (this area contains the creek's premier steelhead rearing and spawning habitat); and
- restoring native vegetation, wetlands, and other natural riparian zone habitat over several miles of stream (with another nine miles of similar restoration activities currently in the planning stages).[33]

AVOIDING A LISTING: HARNEY COUNTY'S COLLABORATIVE APPROACH TO SAGE GROUSE PRESERVATION

The holistic, large-scale watershed approach to collaboration in Oregon has been complemented by corollary efforts to protect and recover rare or endangered species such as the gray wolf and the greater sage-grouse. While the collaborative approach in both cases has not been conflict-free, wolf populations in the state recovered enough by 2015 that the ODFW formally delisted them as an endangered species in eastern Oregon. (Oregon's policy approach to wolf restoration is discussed extensively in chapter 12.) The greater sage-grouse story, however, is still unfolding, and it shows how collaboration can be used to forestall an ESA listing.

Greater sage-grouse habitat extends across almost two hundred million acres of high mountain sagebrush desert in eleven western US states and two Canadian provinces. Populations have declined by up to 90 percent over the past one hundred years, from over fifteen million to an estimated three hundred thousand to five hundred thousand today. Evidence also indicates that sage-grouse are an umbrella species—protecting them will likely result in the protection of hundreds of other sagebrush species.[34] They are sagebrush obligates, meaning they depend on the large, undisturbed expanses of the high-desert sagebrush-steppe habitat. Key to this habitat are lekking grounds, or breeding areas that are extremely sensitive to fragmentation and other disturbances such as energy development (e.g., oil, gas, wind), certain grazing practices, wildfires, and invasive species.

The massive decline in sage-grouse populations led environmental advocacy groups to pressure the US Fish and Wildlife Service to list the sage-grouse under the federal ESA. In 2010, after years of lawsuits, the FWS announced that although the species warranted ESA protection, it was precluded from listing owing to limited agency resources and higher-priority species requiring agency attention. More lawsuits ensued, and in 2011, a legal settlement with environmental organizations required the FWS to address the sage-grouse decision by September 2015.[35] The 2011 settlement created an opportunity for stakeholders across the western United States to take up sage-grouse conservation on their own terms in order to avoid the stringency and costs of a future ESA listing.[36] A variety of collaborative efforts arose in Colorado, Idaho, Nevada, Oregon, Utah, and Wyoming. Some were led by state governments or federal agencies, while others were initiated and pushed forward by local governments and private landowners. A particularly notable example of this latter style of local-level collaboration emerged from rural Harney County in southeastern Oregon.

The effort began in the spring of 2011, when concerned ranchers began asking Oregon State Extension agents about options in the event that the greater sage-grouse were listed under the ESA, and in particular about a program offered by the FWS called Candidate Conservation Agreements with Assurances (CCAAs).[37] This growing program was developed under Section 10 of the act, which provides for incentives for voluntary conservation efforts. Specifically, in exchange for specific conservation actions, CCAAs offer regulatory relief under the ESA in the form of permits that protect a participating landowner from additional regulations in the event the species is listed as threatened or endangered. With interest in the program evident among local ranchers, a small group of extension staff, landowners, and local officials began meeting to explore the possibility of developing programmatic CCAAs for Harney County, which would allow any interested landowner to participate without going through the process of developing their own individual agreement with the FWS. By August, the group had formally created the Harney County CCAA Steering Committee to develop the agreement.[38] The committee included several landowners and representatives of Harney County Court and the Soil and Water Conservation District (SWCD), Oregon State Extension, the Eastern Oregon Agriculture Research Center, the Nature Conservancy, the FWS, and a host of other state and federal agencies involved with sage-grouse management.

The steering committee, chaired by Harney County rancher Tom Sharp, began meeting regularly at the county courthouse to explore the threats to sage-grouse and to consider possible conservation strategies to incorporate into the agreement. These courthouse meetings achieved somewhat legendary status among participants, as several noted the length and duration of the discussions that spread out over years until the completion and signing of the agreement in May 2014. Overall, those discussions were generally positive, though difficult and tense at times. There was no shortage of disagreement, but participants resolved those conflicts productively and avoided derailing the overall agreement.[39]

Many of those participating, even if they disagreed on specific pieces of the agreement, had the advantage of strong existing relationships as a result of recent collaboration involving an update for the Comprehensive Conservation Plan (CCP) at the nearby Malheur National Wildlife Refuge.[40] That collaborative effort, which developed from decades of conflict over refuge management, created a CCP that saw no legal challenges upon implementation—a near-impossibility among federal land management plans.[41] Just as valuable, they were able to learn from the cautionary tale of the first sage-grouse CCAA effort, in west central Idaho. After years of planning, miscommunication and divergent goals for the Idaho CCAA led to a breakdown in trust between local landowners, state-employed consultants, and the FWS.[42]

Certainly, the Harney County effort benefited from having the Natural Resource Conservation Service (NRCS) and the SWCD play a buffering role between land-owners and the FWS, which organizationally had less experience working directly with community members.[43] Early on, it was decided that the Harney County Soil and Water Conservation District should act as the permit holder for the CCAA, since that agency had strong existing relationships with area landowners and administrative resources, as well as the ability to maintain a higher level of privacy regarding individual ranching operations.[44] Later, FWS officials commented that this had been the ideal course of action, as the agency would not have had the resources to manage the hugely popular agreement and the number of landowners who participated.[45]

Central to these discussions was the question of how to approach the sage-grouse issue. The ESA, perhaps notoriously, has traditionally taken a species-centered approach to conservation that has been challenged for both its lack of efficiency and effectiveness in the face of systemic threats like drought, wildfire, and climate change. Ecologists from the Eastern Oregon Agricultural Research Center (EOARC), participating as technical advisors to the steering committee, proposed an alternative perspective that was more holistic and focused on addressing the threats to the sagebrush ecosystem as a whole. Declines in sage-grouse, they argued, were only a symptom of these larger problems. Further, by taking an ecosystem perspective, they argued, ranchers could be enlisted as partners in common cause rather than simply an industry to be regulated.[46] After all, the main threats to sage-grouse—wildfire and invasive species—were threats to ranching operations as well.

The EOARC scientists pointed to the state-and-transition models that they had been developing, which illustrated patterns in land-cover change that led to a self-reinforcing cycle of widespread invasive species and increasing wildfire. If conservation efforts focused on limiting or preventing that cycle, there would be a chance to do much more for struggling sage-grouse populations than any narrowly focused interventions on grazing practices to improve sage-grouse habitat features could. After working through the data and evidence and exploring hypothetical scenarios for a full year, the EOARC scientists had most of the steering committee on board with this perspective.[47] State and federal agency biologists, however, were concerned the innovative approach would be rejected by senior FWS officials or be challenged in the courts. These concerns were mitigated by the program's resemblance to the CCP process for the Malheur National Wildlife Refuge and the strong support by Paul Henson, FWS state supervisor.[48]

The novel ecosystem approach that the steering committee adopted for the CCAA was not the only element causing concern about legal challenges. Ranchers worried that if information about their individual enrollment agreements, called site-specific plans, were made public, it would create an opening for litigious environmental organizations to file lawsuits against individual landowners. This was why they had wanted the SWCD to hold the CCAA permits in the first place, but SWCDs were not immune to Oregon's open records laws.[49] Eventually, the steering committee received assistance in this area, when, in support of the CCAA effort, the Oregon legislature passed a bill, signed by Governor John Kitzhaber, that designated the associated documents exempt from Oregon public records laws.[50] This component, predictably, concerned some environmental advocates, who argued that it would be impossible to hold permit holders and enrolled landowners accountable if the plans were not available to the public.[51]

With celebration and fanfare, the Harney County CCAA was signed and adopted by the FWS in May 2014. Meanwhile, other Oregon counties with sage-grouse populations had been watching with interest, and wondering whether they could develop similar agreements for their landowners. Key members of the steering committee—including Harney SWCD's Marty Suter-Goold, NRCS District Conservationist Zola Ryan, and Tom Sharp—began taking "CCAA road trips" to share their experiences and advice for interested stakeholders.[52] As a result, by December, only months after the Harney County CCAA was signed, CCAAs modeled after the Harney County model were adopted and signed by all remaining Oregon sage-grouse counties.[53]

The Harney County CCAA is considered by most to be a success. In total, at least fifty-three landowners enrolled around 320,000 acres of sage-grouse habitat under the plan in the county, agreeing to manage their lands to minimize threats to the bird.[54] In addition, much more land has been enrolled in the other seven Oregon counties that have adopted versions of the Harney County plan. In total, the agreement enrollments cover around 1.5 million acres of private land. The Oregon Department of State Lands, which manages state-owned lands, also adopted a modified version of the Harney County plan to cover its own sage-grouse habitat, amounting to about 633,000 acres. The total acreage of sage-grouse habitat covered by the agreements (i.e., eligible for future enrollments) exceeds 4 million acres.[55]

Several factors contributed to the successful collaboration that produced the Harney County agreement. The encroachment of juniper trees into sagebrush habitat is a threat both to sage-grouse and livestock forage, and the extent of encroachment in Harney County created common cause among ranch management and sage-grouse conservation. Institutionally, the Harney County Steering Committee was also operating in a context of established trust and ongoing relationships, both as a result of the Malheur National Wildlife Refuge CCP process and the overall shift toward collaboration in Oregon land management conflicts. Effective leadership at multiple levels also played a substantial role in the effort's success. Within the steering committee, Chair Tom Sharp and SWCD's Marty Suter-Goold helped to keep skeptical landowners at the table and moving discussions forward. Scientists from the EOARC, committed to their community, took an active and engaged role in the plan's development, working through the scientific evidence with the steering committee with the aim of integrating a larger, ecosystem-centered perspective that would be relevant to future species declines as well as to sage-grouse. For the FWS, local officials as well as state leadership were comfortable and capable engaging openly in the process. For his part, State Supervisor Paul Henson was prepared to make a gamble on the CCAA in order to create stronger working relationships with grazing stakeholders.

CONCLUSION

Collaborative governance appears to be gaining a significant foothold across the world as a method for multiple, conflicting interests to pursue more lasting, positive-sum resolutions to complex environmental, social, and economic problems. The same is true for Oregon, whether it involves environmental protection and natural resources, health policy, quality of life, or other issues, including the integration of minority populations. These new governance arrangements are spurred by pragmatism on the part of stakeholders; they expect a more effective problem-solving process that will protect and enhance their own interests, while also providing outcomes benefitting the broader public interest. The case studies of watershed councils and greater sage-grouse conservation illustrate how collaborative governance can and does work to produce the expected positive-sum "win-win-win" outcomes.

But these examples of success should not be interpreted as the way collaboration will work in every case. They are exemplars that demonstrate the possibilities associated with choosing collaboration. This is because collaboration is, in general, hard to do, and not every case will have the benefit of the abovementioned factors that influenced the successful outcomes in the Whychus Creek restoration or the sage-grouse efforts in Harney County. A key case in point is the Klamath Basin. After fifteen years of negotiations, breakdowns, and politicization, a tenuous agreement over watershed management among tribes, farmers, environmentalists, power companies, and state and federal interests has just emerged in Oregon's Klamath River Basin.

For these reasons, and despite the growing interest in and use of collaborative governance, the dominant forms of policy implementation still involve the traditional hierarchical model of governance, and conflict will still pervade many, if not most, public policy discussions. An example of the forces that push toward the traditional hierarchical and politicized forms of governance is how the Trump administration, under the leadership of Secretary of Interior Ryan Zinke, has chosen to reconsider the outcomes of all collaborative efforts to address sage-grouse restoration.[56] At the same time, the experience to date—namely, the ability of collaborative governance arrangements to produce broad public interest outcomes—is likely to be enough that the change to collaborative governance in Oregon and elsewhere remains an important new policymaking and policy implementation venue for managing and resolving complex public problems.

Notes

1   Chris Ansell and Alison Gash, "Collaborative Governance in Theory and Practice," *Journal of Public Administration Research and Theory* 18, no. 4 (2008): 544.

2   See, e.g., Thomas Dietz and Paul Stern, *Public Participation in Environmental Assessment and Decision Making* (Washington, DC: National Academies Press, 2008); Paul Sabatier et al., eds., *Swimming Upstream: Collaborative Approaches to Watershed Management* (Cambridge: Massachusetts Institute of Technology Press, 2005); Edward P. Weber, "A New Vanguard for the Environment: Grass-Roots Ecosystem Management as a New Environmental Movement," *Society and Natural Resources* 13, no. 3 (2000): 237-59.

3   Elinor Ostrom, *Governing the Commons: The Evolution of Institutions for Collective Action* (New York: Cambridge University Press, 1990); Oran R. Young, "Rights, Rules, and Resources in International Society," in *Rights to Nature: Ecological, Economic, Cultural, and Political Principles of Institutions for the Environment*, ed. S. Hanna, C. Folke, and K. G. Maler (Washington, DC: Island Press, 1996), 245-64.

4   Ansell and Gash, "Collaborative Governance"; Robert Agranoff and Michael McGuire, "Multinetwork Management: Collaboration and the Hollow State in Local Economic Policy," *Journal of Public Administration Research and Theory* 8, no. 1 (Jan. 1998); Don Kettl, "Managing Indirect Government," in *The Tools of Government: A Guide to the New Governance*, ed. Lester M. Salamon (Oxford: Oxford University Press, 2002); Edward P. Weber and Anne M. Khademian, "Wicked Problems, Knowledge Challenges, and Collaborative Capacity Builders in Network Settings," *Public Administration Review* 68, no. 2 (2008): 334-49; Edward P. Weber, *Bringing Society Back In: Grassroots Ecosystem Management, Accountability, and Sustainable Communities* (Cambridge: Massachusetts Institute of Technology Press, 2003).

5   Jules Pretty, "Social Capital and the Collective Management of Resources," *Science* 302, no. 5652 (2003): 1912-14; David Western and R. Michael Wright, *Natural Connections: Perspectives in Community-Based Conservation* (Washington, DC: Island Press, 1994); and Guy Salmon, "Collaborative Approaches to Sustainable Development—Lessons from the Nordic Countries" (presented at the 9th Southeast Asian Survey Congress on Developing Sustainable Societies, Christchurch, New Zealand, October 31, 2007).

6   Frank R. Baumgartner and Bryan D. Jones, *Agendas and Instability in American Politics* (Chicago: University of Chicago Press, 1993), 32; Mark Lubell, Adam Douglas Henry,

and Mike McCoy, "Collaborative Institutions in an Ecology of Games," *American Journal of Political Science*, April 9, 2010, doi:10.1111/j.1540-5907.2010.00431.x

7   Alison Gash, "Collaborative Governance," in *Handbook on Theories of Governance*, ed. Christopher Ansell and Jacob Torfing (Northampton, MA: Edward Elgar, 2016), 455-55.

8   National Opinion Research Center, *Oregon: Engaging the Public Health System in Collaborative Governance* (Chicago: University of Chicago Press: May 2012).

9   Margaret Banyan, "Civic Capacity Assessment Framework," in *New Public Governance*, ed. D. F. Morgan and B. J. Cook (Armonk, NY: M. E. Sharpe, 2014), 101.

10   Don Bohn, "Civic Infrastructure and Capacity Building," in *New Public Governance*, 145.

11   "Area Agencies on Aging Overview," State of Oregon, accessed September 24, 2017, www. oregon.gov/DHS/SENIORS-DISABILITIES/SUA/Documents/Agency_Type_ Overview.pdf.

12   Douglas C. North, *Institutions, Institutional Change, and Economic Performance* (Cambridge: Cambridge University Press, 1990); Edward P. Weber, *Pluralism by the Rules: Conflict and Cooperation in Environmental Regulation* (Washington, DC: Georgetown University Press, 1998).

13   Bryan D. Jones, *Politics and the Architecture of Choice: Bounded Rationality and Governance* (Chicago: University of Chicago Press, 2001), 127.

14   Ostrom, *Governing the Commons*; Sabatier et al., *Swimming Upstream*.

15   Ansell and Gash, "Collaborative Governance"; Weber, *Bringing Society Back In*.

16   Weber, *Pluralism by the Rules*.

17   Ostrom, *Governing the Commons*; Weber, *Pluralism by the Rules*.

18   Thomas Dietz, "Bringing Values and Deliberation to Science Communication," *Proceedings of the National Academy of Sciences* 110, suppl. 3 (2013): 14,081–87.

19   Edward P. Weber and Anne M. Khademian, "Wicked Problems, Knowledge Challenges, and Collaborative Capacity Builders in Network Settings," *Public Administration Review* 68, no. 2 (2008): 334-49; Edward P. Weber, Denise Lach, and Brent Steel, eds., *New Strategies for Wicked Problems: Science and Problem Solving in the 21st Century* (Corvallis: Oregon State University Press, 2017).

20   "The Oregon Watershed Enhancement Board," Oregon.gov, accessed April 19, 2018, www.oregon.gov/OWEB/pages/index.aspx.

21   "Oregon Watershed Enhancement Board."

22   Funding came from state lottery proceeds, custom "preserve salmon" license plates, and matching funds from several federal government programs. Quote from "Oregon Watershed Enhancement Board."

23   "Oregon Watershed Enhancement Board."

24   A 2001 study of the OWEB grant program concluded that 80¢ of every project dollar is spent in the county where the project is located, and that more than 95¢ of every project dollar is spent in Oregon. The study also concluded that between $1.65 and $2.50 in additional spending occurs indirectly in the local economy as project dollars are re-spent multiple times. "Oregon Watershed Enhancement Board Sustainability Plan," Oregon Watershed Enhancement Board, March 2004, accessed October 5, 2017, https://www. oregon.gov/OWEB/docs/pubs/oweb_sustainability_plan_2004.pdf.

25   Oregon Department of Administrative Services, *2017-2019 Governor's Budget: Watershed Enhancement Board* (Salem: Oregon Department of Administrative Services, April 2017), https://olis.leg.state.or.us/liz/2017R1/Downloads/ CommitteeMeetingDocument/115234.

26 Edward P. Weber, interviews with stakeholders in the Whychus Creek, Oregon, collaborative restoration effort.

27 Edward P. Weber, interviews with stakeholders in the Whychus Creek, Oregon, collaborative restoration effort.

28 The Pelton Dam Mitigation Fund was set up under the Federal Energy Regulatory Commission relicensing agreement negotiated with Portland General Electric and the Confederated Tribes of Warm Springs and was aimed at ensuring effective fish reintroduction. It contained over $20 million.

29 "McKenzie Pipeline," Three Sisters Irrigation District, accessed April 19, 2018, http://www.tsidweb.org/siteProjects/PJ-McKenzie.aspx; Edward P. Weber, "Integrated Hydro-Irrigation-Restoration Systems: Resolving a Wicked Problem in the Whychus Creek Watershed," *Journal of Sustainable Development* 10, no. 2 (2017): 104–15.

30 Efficiencies have since allowed an additional thirteen cubic feet per second (cfs) of streamflow back in the creek starting in 2017. Upper Deschutes Watershed Council, *2012 Whychus Creek Monitoring Report* (Bend, OR: Upper Deschutes Watershed Council, 2013), 110 pp.

31 Weber, "Integrated Hydro-Irrigation-Restoration Systems."

32 Weber, "Integrated Hydro-Irrigation-Restoration Systems."

33 The supporting data for these items can be found at "Accomplishments: Whychus Creek," Deschutes Partnership, accessed April 19, 2018, www.deschutespartnership.org/accomplishments/whychus-creek/; L. Mork and R. Houston, eds., *2014 Whychus Creek Monitoring Report* (Bend, OR: Upper Deschutes Watershed Council, Dec. 2015) 141; "Accomplishments: Whychus Creek"; and Weber, "Integrated Hydro-Irrigation-Restoration Systems."

34 Edward P. Weber, *Changing Philosophies and Policies: Endangered Species across the Years* (Santa Barbara, CA: ABC-CLIO, 2016).

35 "Overview of Greater Sage-Grouse and Endangered Species Act Activities," US Fish and Wildlife Service, accessed October 5, 2017, www.fws.gov/greatersagegrouse/.../Primer4SGOverviewESAActivities.pdf.

36 Assuming no change in sage-grouse status from the FWS's earlier "warranted but precluded" decision, state and local governments had four years to design and establish conservation policies to bolster bird populations and habitat and thereby preclude more restrictive ESA protections.

37 Casey L. Taylor, "The Challenges and Opportunities of a Proactive Endangered Species Act: A Case Study of the Greater Sage Grouse" (PhD diss., Oregon State University, 2016), interview 3.

38 Taylor, "Challenges and Opportunities of a Proactive Endangered Species Act."

39 Taylor, "Challenges and Opportunities of a Proactive Endangered Species Act."

40 "Record of Decision for the Malheur National Wildlife Refuge Final Comprehensive Conservation Plan," US Fish and Wildlife Service, Department of Interior, accessed March 1, 2016, https://www.fws.gov/refuge/Malheur/what_we_do/conservation.html.

41 Taylor, "Challenges and Opportunities of a Proactive Endangered Species Act," interview 9.

42 Taylor, "Challenges and Opportunities of a Proactive Endangered Species Act."

43 Taylor, "Challenges and Opportunities of a Proactive Endangered Species Act."

44 Taylor, "Challenges and Opportunities of a Proactive Endangered Species Act," interviews 9 and 10.

45 Taylor, "Challenges and Opportunities of a Proactive Endangered Species Act," interview 7.

46 Taylor, "Challenges and Opportunities of a Proactive Endangered Species Act," interview 5.

47 Taylor, "Challenges and Opportunities of a Proactive Endangered Species Act," interview 5.

48 Taylor, "Challenges and Opportunities of a Proactive Endangered Species Act," interview 21.

49 Taylor, "Challenges and Opportunities of a Proactive Endangered Species Act," interview 10.

50 C. Collins, "New Conservation Law in Place," *Baker City Herald*, March 28, 2014.

51 Taylor, "Challenges and Opportunities of a Proactive Endangered Species Act," interview 14.

52 Taylor, "Challenges and Opportunities of a Proactive Endangered Species Act," interviews 3, 10, and 11.

53 Taylor, "Challenges and Opportunities of a Proactive Endangered Species Act," interview 3.

54 "Oregon Sage Grouse: A Model for Lasting Partnerships," US Fish and Wildlife Service, March 25, 2016, www.usfwspacific.tumblr.com/post/114586973540/oregon-sage-grouse-a-model-for-lasting.

55 E. Mortenson, "Oregon Expands Sage-Grouse Conservation Agreements," *Capital Press*, March 17, 2015, www.capitalpress.com/Livestock/20150317/oregon-expands-sage-grouse-conservation-agreements.

56 George Plavan, "Oregon Cattlemen Urge Changes to BLM Sage Grouse Management Plan," *Capital Press*, January 22, 2018; Courtney Flatt, "Reopening the Sage Grouse Debate Has Ranchers, Conservationists Weighing Risk and Reward," *Capital Press*, November 10, 2017, http://www.capitalpress.com/California/20171110/reopening-the-sage-grouse-debate-has-ranchers-conservationists-weighing-risk-and-reward.

III

Public Policies

12

Environmental Policy
The Challenge of Managing Biodiversity in Oregon
JOE BOWERSOX

In the waning days of 2015, armed militants occupied the Malheur National Wildlife Refuge in remote Harney County, Oregon. Citing a diverse set of grievances ranging from the erosion of personal liberties to the purported unconstitutionality of federal ownership of the refuge itself, the forty-one-day standoff ultimately ended in bloodshed and the arrest and prosecution of the occupation's ringleaders.[1] Though not endorsed by the majority of residents of Harney County, their actions once again drew attention to the outsized role played by federal entities in many local or state environmental and natural resource issues in the western United States. With nearly 52 percent of the state's landmass under federal ownership and management, the federal presence in Oregon is pronounced and pervasive, and with particular regard to the state's biodiversity policies, Oregon's actions today are largely reactive to, and heavily shaped by, federal policies. Examining instances of state biodiversity policy reveals not only the ongoing tensions within federalism exacerbated by environmental and natural resource issues, but also the extent to which Oregon environmental politics and policy are driven as much by exogenous forces as by internal factors.

FIRST SOME CONTEXT: OREGON'S ENVIRONMENTAL LEGACY
As noted throughout this book, Oregon's national reputation is closely linked to its real and perceived role as a state innovator in environmental and natural resource policy, postindustrial environmental values, quality of life, and sustainability efforts. Indeed, much of the legacy of Oregon's Golden Era (1954-78) noted in chapter 1 is related to critical, largely bipartisan, efforts to address pollution, environmental and natural resource degradation, and community livability spearheaded by the political rivalry between Republican Tom McCall and Democrat Bob Straub.[2]

But in fact Oregon's environmental and natural resource innovations started much earlier: in 1874, Governor LaFayette Grover pushed the state legislature to protect the state's salmon runs and establish fish ladders to improve salmon passage and habitat, leading to construction at Willamette Falls of one of the first fish ladders in North America.[3] Oregon was the first state—in 1915—to statutorily recognize the environmental and aesthetic value of water left in-stream and to prohibit new water diversions from some critical waterbodies, and was also the first (in 1955) to pass legislation establishing perennial minimum in-stream flows. This in turn laid the groundwork for passage (in 1987) of Senate Bill (SB) 140, which established the first statute in the country creating in-stream water rights held by the state for the public good to benefit fish, water quality, and recreation.[4]

Oregon's early leadership in water quality is legendary: journalist Tom McCall's documentary *Pollution in Paradise* chronicled the "foul smelling masses of filth" degrading the Willamette River. During his political career—first as secretary of state and then governor—McCall initiated a massive cleanup of the Willamette and other Oregon waterbodies via aggressive regulation of point source pollution from wastewater treatment plants and industrial facilities, foreshadowing the central strategy of the 1972 federal Clean Water Act.[5] In 1986, responding to challenges from environmental activists, the state's Department of Environmental Quality became a national leader in addressing nonpoint water pollution like streamside use of fertilizers, pesticides, and herbicides, erosion, and vegetation removal.[6]

Oregon has also led the way in comprehensive land-use planning. Oregon provided authority for municipal planning and enforcement in 1919, long before McCall's famous crusade to protect against "sagebrush subdivisions, coastal condomania and . . . the grasping wastrels of the land."[7] Channeling growing public frustration with sprawl's impact upon farm and forestland and community livability, McCall utilized his 1970 gubernatorial reelection campaign to expand upon earlier planning efforts, culminating in passage of 1973's SB 100, establishing the state's Land Conservation and Development Commission (LCDC) and a statewide land-use planning process guided by nineteen goals, ranging from citizen participation to protecting saltwater estuaries. Despite numerous legal and legislative challenges, SB 100's basic structure remains intact and popular.[8] Recent studies of its impact on restraining urban sprawl and protecting Oregon's farm and forestlands demonstrate its positive, if complex effects.[9]

Oregon has also achieved national prominence for declaring all of the state's ocean shoreline public property (first in 1913) and then protecting public access to (nearly) all of Oregon's beaches via statute (1967). Oregon passed the nation's first enforceable beverage container deposit, or "bottle bill," in 1971. The state continues to be a national leader in waste recovery, diversion, and materials management with the passage of SB 263 (2015), upping statewide enforceable waste recovery/diversion targets to 55 percent by 2025, while specifically addressing food and plastic waste recovery and requiring more comprehensive public outreach and education.[10]

Such historical efforts and the state's continued focus on livability and sustainability (chapter 2), stewardship of natural resources, renewable energy and climate change (chapter 13), and earth- and community-friendly food and agricultural systems (chapter 16) contribute to Oregon's prominence in recent rankings of the "greenest states." Kiernan,[11] compiling data from seventeen different measures, ranks Oregon third overall (after Vermont and Massachusetts), and first in "eco-friendly" behaviors (see table 12.1 below).

Oregon's environmental record is much more complex, however. This chapter examines two key case studies in biodiversity policy to illustrate instances where internal and exogenous factors drive Oregon environmental politics and policy and constrain innovation and response. Though one should not generalize broadly from these two case studies, it is worth noting that other state environmental dilemmas outside of biodiversity policy evince similar characteristics. For instance, in 2016, US Forest Service researchers published a study conducted in Portland, Oregon, that showed toxic concentrations of cadmium and arsenic in the vicinity of two stained-glass manufacturers already subject to state monitoring and controls.[12] The ensuing controversy revealed that the Oregon Department of Environmental Quality (DEQ) had failed to act to reduce atmospheric concentrations that were 159 times the state threshold mandated by the federal Clean Air Act.[13] Also in 2016, in light of the national controversy surrounding lead contamination of drinking water in Flint Michigan, DEQ once again drew fire from federal and other state authorities for inadequately addressing the presence of lead in municipal water supplies across the state, particularly in schools.[14] In both instances, external forces significantly affected internal actors and state responses.

After a brief discussion of contemporary scholarship regarding internal and external factors affecting state policy efforts, case studies in Oregon biodiversity

Table 12.1. Top ten greenest state scores, 2017

Overall Rank	State	Total Score	"Environmental Quality" Rank	"Eco-Friendly Behaviors" Rank	"Climate-Change Contributions" Rank
1	Vermont	78.88	1	2	9
2	Massachusetts	71.39	4	12	6
3	Oregon	71.25	9	1	24
4	Washington	70.23	3	7	20
5	Connecticut	68.96	7	22	3
6	Maine	68.77	11	6	10
7	Minnesota	68.23	2	5	31
8	New York	67.14	12	11	5
9	New Hampshire	66.29	29	10	2
10	Rhode Island	65.72	15	16	4

Source: After John S. Kiernan, "2017's Greenest States," WalletHub, April 17, 2017, https://wallethub.com/edu/greenest-states/11987/

policy—wolf management and state forestry policy—help to illustrate how Oregon's environmental legacy and leadership of the 1970s, which are often hailed as unique and exceptional, may also often be driven and bracketed by nonstate actors and objectives.

FACTORS AFFECTING STATE RESPONSES

It is useful to contextualize Oregon within the broader literature regarding factors affecting state environmental policymaking. These factors are often divided by scholars into (1) internal determinants[15] and (2) policy drivers from external sources.[16]

The primary *internal determinants* of state environmental policy are political culture, socioeconomic factors, interest group activity, and legislative and administrative professionalism. In general, the literature on state-level environmental policymaking finds that states with liberal political cultures, as measured by mass citizen ideologies[17] or partisan legislative control,[18] are more likely to adapt stricter, greener environmental policies compared to states with more conservative political cultures.[19] Similarly, states with more economic resources tend to enact more stringent environmental controls.[20] Other scholars have found that interest group activity by well-organized interests are often determinative, with business predominance associated with weaker environmental policy and high citizen participation in environmental groups correlating with stronger policies.[21] Some also suggest that state legislative and administrative professionalism positively affect environmental policy adoption.[22]

In contrast to such internal determinants of environmental policy, scholars also note that *external influences and drivers* affect policy development, adoption, and implementation. These external influences can in turn be divided into two classes: the role of the federal government in establishing and mandating state policy responses, and policy diffusion and learning from other states, particularly those in geographic proximity.

The federal government affects state environmental policy in several ways. While it is clearly unconstitutional for Congress or the executive branch to directly demand or *commandeer* states to address environmental and natural resource issues like biodiversity within our dual federalist system,[23] the powers found in the US Constitution provide ample tools for promoting/persuading/sanctioning state efforts. For example, Congress and federal agencies can *preempt* or preclude state regulation under the Supremacy Clause (see Article VI) when states tread in areas where existing federal legislation is pervasive, or where the Constitution explicitly demands national efforts, such as in policies affecting interstate commerce.[24] Federal supremacy (as in interstate commerce) can in turn significantly affect state policies, as they must conform to federal requirements and court decisions.[25] Congress and federal agencies also can offer *inducements* (both monetary and nonmonetary) to encourage and channel state policy responses, or *sanctions* (loss of funding, penalties, or the threat of federal preemption) when states fail to regulate or protect. Adler notes that the combined effects of these inducements and sanctions may be overwhelming: for instance, under the Clean Air Act, states like Oregon receive significant funds and expertise for creation of State Implementation Plans (SIPs) to address ambient and hazardous air pollutants.[26] Failing to create an adequate SIP may lead to the loss of lucrative federal highway funds or the imposition of a more stringent and demanding Federal Implementation Plan (FIP).[27]

In addition to these more direct ways of affecting state policy, the federal government can indirectly affect state responses through *agenda-setting*, which can draw legislative and public attention to a particular issue, *facilitating* state efforts (e.g., via data collection, research underwriting, information dissemination), and *signaling* or *crowding out* certain potential state responses by establishing and encouraging particular standards or guidelines while discouraging others.[28]

As seen in the following case studies of wolf recovery and the state's approach to regulating private and state timberlands, these internal determinants and external influences affect state biodiversity policy formation. Additionally, there may be evidence in the twenty-first century that those broader federal influences significantly channel state responses by sanctioning or crowding out policy choices proffered by various internal determinants, whether they be interest groups or state agency professionals.

BIODIVERSITY: GRAY WOLVES IN OREGON

Oregon's history with gray wolves is both complicated and checkered. Ubiquitous across the state prior to European settlement, wolves thrived in the state's varied landscapes, from the high desert, to the upper Cascades, to the dense forests of the Coast Range. Wolves benefitted from a wary caution and sacred respect conferred on them by the native peoples of the region; wolves were considered both extended family and competitor for game.[29] European trappers and settlers in the eighteenth and nineteenth centuries brought with them European prejudices and fears regarding the species, seeing wolves as an existential threat to human life and livelihood. Wolves were dangers to adults and children, and to the livestock necessary for trade and farming. Fairy tales reinforced such fears, and just as large-scale efforts had been waged to eradicate wolves from the British Isles in the 1500s and the North American colonies in the seventeenth and eighteenth centuries, so too did the new arrivals in the Pacific Northwest soon begin to rid the landscape of wolves.[30] In fact, the initial local political organizations in Oregon Country were "wolf meetings" and "wolf committees." Formed in the early 1840s, these committees preceded the establishment of the provisional government in 1843.[31] Bounties became the primary tool of extirpation, and they remained in place even after the last known wolf was killed in the Umpqua watershed in 1946.[32] Between 1946 and 1999, no other sightings or killing of wolves in Oregon were recorded, with the exception of four animals glimpsed between 1974 and 1980, which wildlife officials later recorded as domesticated wolves or wolf-dog hybrids.[33]

Wolves Return to Oregon Country

Wolf recovery and reintroduction elicit the strongest of reactions from stakeholders and affected parties. On the one hand, scientists and conservationists argue that
returning this apex predator to the landscape fundamentally enhances the function of
degraded ecosystems, ranging from healthier ungulate herds to restored riparian vegetation and improved anadromous fish populations.[34] Many environmentalists make
the case for wolf recovery or reintroduction upon more ethical grounds.[35] On the
other hand, ranchers and livestock owners fear economic loss and the loss of their way
of life as wolves stalk cattle and sheep on private and public rangeland.[36] In states like
Minnesota and Idaho, ranchers and livestock owners have faced significant hardship
as wolves have expanded into grazing areas, with reports of depredation increasing by
over 400 percent.[37] Thus the appearance of wolves inevitably leads to political conflict
and controversy.

The first verified sighting of a gray wolf in Oregon in over sixty years occurred in
January 1999 in northeastern Oregon. Wolf B-45, a radio-collared female from Idaho,
had crossed the Snake River and Interstate 84 and ventured into the Blue Mountains.
B-45's journey elicited alarm from ranchers and celebration among environmentalists.[38] Though a state survey commissioned that year by Oregon Natural Desert
Association found that 70 percent of Oregonians favored wolf return and recovery,[39]
ranchers and the livestock industry pressured the Oregon Department of Fish and
Wildlife (ODFW) and the US Fish and Wildlife Service to capture B-45 and return her
to Idaho.[40] Two other male wolves crossed into Oregon the following year, with one
shot near Pendleton in May and the other struck by a car near Baker City in October.
It was now clear to Oregon policy makers that the wolves were coming, regardless of
whether they were ready or willing to deal with the issue.[41]

That wolves were on the state's policy agenda at the dawn of the twenty-first century was itself a reflection of federal influence. Gray wolves were listed as endangered
under the US Endangered Species Act (ESA) (16 U.S.C. § 1531-1544) in 1974, and
the US Fish and Wildlife Service (FWS) completed its wolf recovery plan for the
northern Rocky Mountains in 1987. The federal recovery plan recognized the desire
for natural repopulation of three targeted areas (northern Montana, central Idaho,
and the Yellowstone National Park) by southern dispersal of Canadian wolves, but
anticipated translocation of Canadian wolves under the 1982 ESA amendments establishing experimental populations.[42] By the early 1990s, natural dispersal had clearly
failed. Under pressure from scientists, tribes, and environmental groups, the FWS and
the Nez Perce Tribe translocated 66 gray wolves from British Columbia and Alberta
in 1995 and 1996; 35 were released in central Idaho and 31 in Yellowstone National
Park.[43] Just four years later, these "non-essential experimental populations" had
expanded to 115 wolves in central Idaho and 110 in Yellowstone, with young males
and females like B-45 dispersing to new territory.

In these first years of wolf sightings, Oregon wildlife officials and politicians sought to do the same as they had done with B-45: call the FWS to trap and deport the "problem wolf" back to Idaho. Federal officials were loath to assume this costly service, which in fact violated Oregon's own state Endangered Species Act.[44] Indeed, in these early years, state actors seemed incapacitated and caught between conservationists on the one hand and the livestock industry on the other. Both were mobilized and active. State representatives from eastern and central Oregon introduced a bill in the 2001 legislature to remove wolves from the state ESA and reclassify them as a nuisance predator. In response, the Oregon Natural Desert Association and other conservation groups petitioned the ODFW and the Oregon Fish and Wildlife Commission to develop wolf survival guidelines they believed were mandated by the state ESA.[45] Despite some internal debate over whether such efforts were indeed mandatory, in March 2003, the commission voted to move forward with wolf management plan development after receiving extensive testimony from around the state.[46] Feeling pressure from both the livestock industry and conservationists, the commission ultimately endorsed a stakeholder model for plan development, hopeful that conservationists, ranchers, farmers, and other stakeholders together could produce a politically and biologically viable management plan. The newly formed Wolf Advisory Committee began its work in January 2004.

A Unique Policy Response

The commission and Oregon's Wolf Advisory Committee (WAC) took a different approach to planning compared to neighbors like Idaho and Montana, or others like Michigan, Minnesota, and Wisconsin. Working from objectives and principles provided by the commission, the WAC sought a middle ground: to "ensure the long-term survival and conservation of gray wolves as required by Oregon law while minimizing conflicts with humans, primary land uses and other Oregon wildlife." The plan would not consider wolf reintroduction but merely management of arriving wolves, and would expressly provide for financial relief of livestock depredation and consider "flexibility mechanisms" for population management.[47]

Oregon's planning efforts were further complicated by a broader context: at the federal level, the George W. Bush administration was trying to completely delist gray wolves from the federal ESA, while neighboring states were permitting game-hunting and citizen predator control of wolves.[48] In this uncertain context, the commission and the WAC created a unique management plan that gained broad (if somewhat grudging) support from most participating stakeholders. In fact, as conservative legislators sought to short-circuit the compromise embodied in the plan through preemptive delisting of the wolf in the 2005 legislature, the commission and WAC members lobbied hard to keep the listing and plan intact. In December 2005, the commission formally adopted the plan, and rulemaking began.[49]

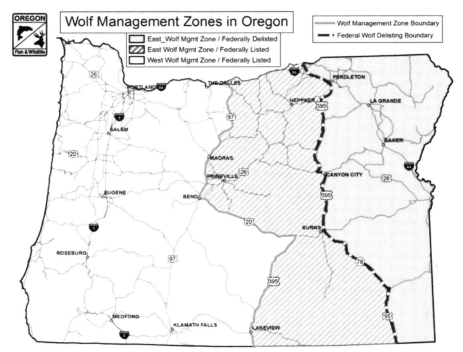

Figure 12.1. Oregon wolf management zones and federal Endangered Species Act status in Oregon.
Copyright 2016 Oregon Department of Fish and Wildlife. Used by permission

The resulting plan was a political result driven by both internal factors and external influences. The benchmarks for species survival and recovery had no basis in conservation biology, but rather reflected significant compromise among stakeholders. Wolf advocates on the WAC agreed to low population thresholds for conservation success (four breeding pairs for three consecutive years in both eastern and western Oregon), while livestock and ranching interests agreed to significant restrictions on depredation management (e.g., priority to nonlethal means conducted by agency personnel and permitted private individuals). The commission would consider state delisting at the "four breeding pair" threshold, and controlled hunts could be considered at the "seven breeding pair" level.[50] The management plan received cautious praise from both the environmental and livestock communities, addressing concerns of affected industries and landowners yet providing significantly greater species protection than neighboring states.

In 2008, state biologists confirmed the first reproducing wolf pack in Oregon, north of LaGrande. It consisted of two adults and two pups.[51] By 2011, there were 29 wolves in northeastern Oregon in four packs, with at least one breeding pair. The state's first lethal removal of livestock depredating wolves occurred in 2011 as well, when two adults from the Imnaha pack were killed by state Fish and Wildlife personnel.[52] By January 2017, a minimum of 112 wolves in eleven packs were confirmed throughout Oregon, and eight of those eleven packs had breeding pairs, all in northeastern Oregon, though one pup was born in southwestern Oregon (fig. 12.1).[53]

Such success led the state Fish and Wildlife Commission to delist wolves throughout the state. This move, however, was roundly opposed by environmental groups and scientists as premature and in violation of the state's own policies. Fearing lawsuits, and in an unprecedented step, Democratic majorities in both chambers of the state legislature passed House Bill (HB) 4040, which effectively blocked legal challenges to the delisting decision. Democratic Governor Kate Brown signed the bill in March 2016.[54] At present, wolves are still subject to monitoring and potential state relisting, while they remain under federal protection only west of US 395 / US 95, since federal delisting of other population units of gray wolves was finalized in 2014.[55] Despite HB 4040, lawsuits surrounding the listing and delisting of wolves on the Oregon ESA continue.[56]

CONSERVING BIODIVERSITY IN OREGON'S PRIVATE AND STATE FORESTS

Forestry and biodiversity protection on forestlands is often associated with federal forests owned and managed by the US Forest Service and the Bureau of Land Management, which together comprise over 57 percent of the total forestland within Oregon. Those lands have been at the center of highly contentious and visible conflicts over threatened and endangered species, whether they be spotted owls, coho salmon, marbled murrelets, or pacific fishers. Nevertheless, private industrial and nonindustrial timberlands make up roughly 38 percent of the state's forest base, while forests owned directly by the state and other local governments make up an additional 4 percent (see table 12.2). Though federal endangered species protection reaches these lands, Oregon regulates the daily operations of private industrial and nonindustrial forest lands through the state's forest management policies and also controls the operation of state-owned forests.

MANAGING BIODIVERSITY ON PRIVATE INDUSTRIAL
AND NONINDUSTRIAL FOREST LANDS

Often hailed as the first comprehensive state forest management law in the United States, Oregon's Forest Practices Act (FPA) was passed in 1971 and signed into law by Governor Tom McCall in 1972.[57] The 1972 FPA also reflected the power and

Table 12.2. Average annual harvest, 1990–2015, by sector

	Private Industrial	Private Non-industrial	Native American	State of Oregon	US Bureau of Land Mgmt.	US Forest Service
1990s	2,633	602	78	151	234	742
2000s	2,479	322	66	284	106	226
2010s*	2,558	424	58	260	176	378

Note: Values given in million board feet, Scribner scale; * Years are 2011 to 2015 only.
Source: Oregon Department of Forestry Annual Reports

economic importance of the private timber industry in Oregon. As a result, and much like other natural resource management approaches at the time, it was unsurprisingly responsive to industry's desire to have management rules that facilitated growth and economic productivity by emphasizing preharvest planning and postharvest reforestation at industrial densities.[58] Its provisions addressing the ecological impacts of timber harvesting were largely aspirational, with directives regarding riparian buffers, green tree retention, and water quality either recommended, voluntary, or subject to waivers when determined to be economically impractical.[59] Industry dominance was further assured because six of nine Board of Forestry seats (responsible for oversight of the Department of Forestry and its implementation of the FPA) were allocated to industry and its allies. This often meant that the concerns of citizens groups, environmental organizations, and even other state agencies regarding FPA transparency, implementation, and enforcement were routinely ignored.[60]

Nevertheless, as with the case of gray wolf management and recovery, internal state developments and external influences coalesced in the mid-1980s to influence forest policies, eventually leading to significant reform of Oregon's FPA and increased biodiversity protection on private forestlands. Federal regulators at the US Environmental Protection Agency (EPA), US Fish and Wildlife Service, and National Marine Fisheries Service placed increasing pressure on Oregon's Department of Environmental Quality and Department of Fish and Wildlife to address federal Clean Water Act (CWA) and Endangered Species Act compliance on private forestlands and adjacent streams. Additionally, the state commission in charge of overseeing Oregon's comprehensive land-use planning, the Land Conservation and Development Commission, issued a report to the state legislature that was critical of both the Department of Forestry and the FPA itself.[61] Finally, the political and organizational strength of local environmental groups and their national counterparts was increasing rapidly during this time, which led to a growing influence on the state legislature.

Such external and internal factors led to passage of HB 3396 during the 1987 legislative session, the first major overhaul of the FPA since 1971.[62] The industry-dominated Board of Forestry became a seven-member citizen's board appointed by the governor, with no more than three to have economic interests in forestry. HB 3396 established more stringent and enforceable regulations for riparian buffers on larger, fish-bearing streams, green tree retention and distribution, and road building.[63] While some forestry professionals claimed that these reforms nearly tripled the cost of timber operations,[64] environmentalists believed they did not go far enough, as industry pressure during bill negotiations significantly reduced the mandated stream buffers and left smaller streams and wetlands unprotected.[65]

Despite these reforms, over the past few decades, the Board of Forestry has displayed a general reluctance to incorporate additional biodiversity and ecological concerns within the FPA. During the 1990s, the board rebuffed concerted efforts to address the impacts of road-building and clear-cutting on water quality, in-stream habitat, and landslides.[66] The early 2000s saw challenges (including a statewide ballot measure) regarding the FPA's capacity to prevent nonpoint source pollution and habitat destruction.[67] Indeed, peer-reviewed analyses commissioned by the Board of Forestry itself found FPA standards and riparian buffers to be inadequate for meeting state water quality and ambient water temperature requirements, parameters deemed necessary for healthy fish habitat and municipal water supplies.[68]

In January 2015, the National Oceanic and Atmospheric Administration (NOAA) and the EPA issued a joint finding that Oregon's nonpoint source pollution control program was insufficient and noncompliant with the CWA and the Coastal Zone Act Reauthorization Amendments (CZARA) of 1990. The finding specifically singled out the FPA's insufficient provisions for protecting water quality from multiple sources, including harvests, roads, and chemical applications.[69] In addition, and as part of an adaptive management review process started in 2012, the Board of Forestry proposed an expansion of the riparian management areas (RMAs) by ten feet, to sixty feet on small and eighty feet on medium "salmon, steelhead, bulltrout" (SSBT) bearing streams, with a "no-cut" buffer of twenty feet within all RMAs.[70]

The new SSBT classification covers between 25 and 35 percent of forested fish streams. This modification—supported by some industry and nonindustry representatives on the board—was viewed as a meaningful yet costly compromise.[71] NOAA's National Marine Fisheries Service, however, declared it insufficient.[72]

STATE FOREST LANDS

Controlling just over 3 percent of the state's forest base, authorizing legislation crafted in 1945 mandated that state forests be managed by the Department of Forestry for the "greatest permanent value (GPV)," with timber revenues supporting county coffers and the state's Common Schools Fund.[73] Given Oregon's statutory requirements to maximize economic value (GPV), it is not surprising that well into the 1990s state forests emphasized intensive silvicultural techniques incorporating single-species (predominantly Douglas-fir), single-aged rotations with significant chemical inputs. Other values for state forestlands (biodiversity, water quality, or even recreation) were largely overlooked and were in fact excluded from calculations of GPV.[74] It was not until 1998 that the Board of Forestry developed language suggesting that GPV might include both economic and noneconomic benefits.[75] This slight shift was a delayed admission of the much more complex social, political, and ecological context within which state forestlands were operating.

As the local and national debates over federal forest management in the Pacific Northwest raged in the 1980s and 1990s, managers of Oregon state forestlands found themselves in a difficult position. The state's three largest forests—the Elliott, the Clatsop, and the Tillamook—were all in the Oregon Coast Range, the center of much of the controversy regarding forestry impacts upon threatened and endangered species like the northern spotted owl, marbled murrelet, and coho salmon. Furthermore, as state forestlands had been managed so intensively for GPV for more than six decades, their condition and structure were more akin to private timberlands maximizing timber revenue than the more structurally diverse multiple-use forests of the US Forest Service and US Bureau of Land Management.[76] Though not formally subject to the federal Northwest Forest Plan (NWFP) or individual species' federal recovery plans,[77] habitat considerations and takings prohibitions[78] for federally listed species did reach to state forests, consequently affecting their management.

Reflecting the GPV mandate, Oregon's response to this more complex policy environment was different in most respects from its neighbor Washington State. Instead of adopting a comprehensive statewide Habitat Conservation Plan under the federal ESA, which gave state managers considerably more management flexibility as well as more credibility with that state's environmental community,[79] the Board of Forestry's primary approach involved a piecemeal "takings avoidance" strategy, which did not fundamentally alter state management objectives (e.g., GPV) or processes.[80] It only created a Habitat Conservation Plan (HCP) for the ninety-five-thousand-acre Elliott State Forest in 1995. By the late 1990s, however, this strategy was facing strong internal pressure from the state legislature as well as from state environmental groups to manage state forests for values other than timber production.

In response to this political pressure, the Board of Forestry initiated a comprehensive planning process to develop management strategies for state forests that embodied a new "holistic" interpretation of GPV. The selected strategy, called by some "sustainable forestry, Oregon style,"[81] embraced a dynamic, structure-based silvicultural model mimicking natural succession and disturbance regimes across forest landscapes.[82] While the NWFP governing federal forests in the Pacific Northwest utilized the traditional Forest Service framework of land-use allocations (LUAs) and habitat reserves,[83] this structure-based management system would move age classes (from newly planted stands to old-growth stands) across the landscape over time, with no anchor habitats or reserves, but dramatically increasing the variability of the forest mosaic and significantly boosting (at least theoretically) the volume of older age classes within the state forests—and thereby theoretically helping old-growth-dependent species like the northern spotted owl and the marbled murrelet.[84]

At the time, structure-based management was new and untried, but the board utilized the model on 95 percent of the 848,000 acres of state forestland it managed. Implementation of the structure-based management plan faced legal and administrative challenges: federal agencies responsible for threatened and endangered species believed it inadequate for protecting habitat, forcing Oregon to remain focused on "takings avoidance" in all operations. In 2004, environmental activists and fisheries groups took the case directly to the voters via Measure 34, which would have removed

50 percent of the 518,000 acres within the Clatsop and Tillamook State Forests from all harvests / active management.[85]

Despite voters' overwhelming rejection of Measure 34 by 71 to 29 percent, environmentalists and fisheries activists have filed more lawsuits targeting Oregon's Forest Practices Act. These actions have succeeded in disrupting planned harvest and other activities on the Elliott State Forest, cutting timber receipts in half between 2011 and 2014, leading to a recurring $3 million annual operating deficit. In 2015, the inability of the State Land Board, the owner of the Elliott Forest, to discharge its constitutional responsibility to transfer revenue from the Elliott to the state school trust fund led it to announce its intent to sell the Elliott in order to provide such funds.[86] With only one bid as of November 2016, Democratic Governor Kate Brown, using her position on the State Land Board, ordered the Department of Forestry to examine other options, including public management of the Elliott and a potential state bond sale to keep the Elliott as state land.[87] In May 2017, the fate of the Elliott appeared settled, as the State Land Board voted unanimously to keep the Elliott State Forest in public ownership and pursue other financing strategies.[88]

CONCLUSION

Oregon's efforts to manage returning wolves and enhance biodiversity conservation on state and private forestlands illustrate the influence of both internal and external factors upon state policy development and implementation. Internally, state policy makers faced significant pressure from members of the environmental community as well as the affected industry. In the case of wolf management, collaborative processes provided space for development of a (at least temporarily) viable political compromise, giving both wolves and humans time to acclimate to coexistence. In the case of state forest practices, both state statutory requirements (GPV) and industry dominance have inhibited substantive incorporation of biodiversity concerns in regulation and management.

Yet, as the case of private and state forestland amply illustrates, federal mandates and pressure now set the state agenda and signal the necessity of much more significant riparian protection (with regards to the FPA), and crowd out innovative state efforts (like structure-based management) that provide insufficient anchor habitats and reserves. At least regarding these two case studies in biodiversity policy, Oregon more closely approximates political scientist James Lester's[89] "delayer" rather than "progressive" category of state policy actors, as Oregon exhibits limited commitment despite having significant capacity to affect policy change. As such, the vision of Oregon as a national leader in environmental policy may need some qualification.[90] But early indications suggest that Oregon's citizens and political leaders will not sit idly by as the Trump administration pulls out of international climate change agreements, permits offshore oil and gas drilling, rolls back clean water protections, and removes wilderness and national monument designations. Such efforts threaten many of Oregon's core commitments to sustainability and livability. Oregon seems poised to find common cause with other "green states" in reinitiating state leadership in environmental stewardship, and in so doing reclaim much of its well-deserved reputation.[91]

Notes

1   Bradley W. Parks, "41 Days and 8 Months Later: Dissecting the Oregon Standoff Trial," *Oregon Public Broadcasting*, October 30, 2016.

2   Richard A. Clucas, "The Political Legacy of Robert W. Straub," *Oregon Historical Quarterly* 104, no. 4 (2003): 462-77.

3   See LaFayette Grover, "Biennial Message, 1874," Messages and Documents, Biennial Message of Gov. LaFayette Grover to the Legislative Assembly, September 1874, Oregon State Archives, Salem; Ian McCloskey, "The Hidden World of Oregon's Overlooked Falls," *Oregon Public Broadcasting*, December 6, 2017.

4   Janet Neuman, Anne Squier, and Gail Achterman, "Sometimes a Great Notion: Oregon's Instream Flow Experiments," *Environmental Law* 36 (2006): 1125-55.

5   Brent Walth, "Tom McCall and the Language of Memory," *Oregon Historical Quarterly* 113 (2012): 570-83; idem, *Fire at Eden's Gate: Tom McCall and the Oregon Story* (Portland: Oregon Historical Society, 1994).

6   Joe Bowersox, "From Water Development to Water Management: Federal Agency Opportunism in an Era of Policy Devolution," *American Behavioral Scientist* 44, no. 4 (2000): 599-613.

7   Tom McCall quoted in Walth, "Tom McCall and the Language of Memory," 581.

8   Walth, "Tom McCall and the Language of Memory"; see also Carl Abbott and Deborah Howe, "The Politics of Land-Use Law in Oregon: Senate Bill 100, Twenty Years After," *Oregon Historical Quarterly* 94 (1993): 4-35.

9   Hannah Gosnell, Jeffrey D. Kline, Garrett Chrostek, and James Duncan, "Is Oregon's Land Use Planning Program Conserving Forest and Farm Land? A Review of the Evidence," *Land Use Policy* 28 (2011): 185-92.

10 Walth, *Fire at Eden's Gate*; Nikolas J. Themelis and Dolly Shin, "Survey of MSW Generation and Disposition in the US," *MSW Management Magazine* (Nov.–Dec. 2015); "Oregon's Recycling Laws," Department of Environmental Quality, accessed April 20, 2018, http://www.oregon.gov/deq/mm/Pages/Oregon-Recycling-Laws.aspx.

11 John S. Kiernan, "2017's Greenest States," *WalletHub*, April 17, 2017, https://wallethub.com/edu/greenest-states/11987/.

12 Geoffrey Donovan et al., "Using an Epiphytic Moss to Identify Previously Unknown Sources of Atmospheric Cadmium Pollution," *Science of the Total Environment* 559 (2016): 84-93.

13 Cassandra Profita, "EPA: Portland Glassmakers Should Have Had Pollution Controls," *Oregon Public Broadcasting / EarthFix*, April 13, 2016.

14 Amelia Templeton, "Why the EPA Worries about Lead in Water at Portland Schools and Day Cares," *Oregon Public Broadcasting*, June 3, 2016.

15 James P. Lester and Emmett. M. Lombard, "The Comparative Analysis of State Environmental Policy," *Natural Resources Journal* 30 (1990): 301-19.

16 Dorothy Daley, "Public Participation and Environmental Policy: What Factors Shape State Agency's Public Participation Provisions?," *Review of Policy Research* 25 (2008): 21-35.

17 William Berry, Evan J. Ringquist, Richard C. Fording, and Russell L. Hanson, "The Measurement and Stability of State Citizen Ideology," *State Politics and Policy Quarterly* 7 (2007): 111-32.

18 Thomas P. Lyon and Haitao Yin, "Why Do States Adopt Renewable Portfolio Standards? An Empirical Investigation," *Energy Journal* 31, no. 3 (2010): 133-57.

19 Joshua G. Wiener and Tomas M. Koontz, "Extent and Types of Small-Scale Wind Policies in the U.S. States: Adoption and Effectiveness," *Energy Policy* 46 (2012): 15-24.

20 Wiener and Koontz, "Extent and Types of Small-Scale Wind Policies."

21 Evan J. Ringquist, *Environmental Protection at the State Level: Politics and Progress in Controlling Pollution* (Armonk, NY: M. E. Sharpe, 1993).

22 Tomas Koontz, "State Innovation in Natural Resources Policy: Ecosystem Management on Public Forests," *State and Local Government Review* 34, no. 3 (2002): 160-72.

23 Jonathan H. Adler, "When Is Two a Crowd: The Impact of Federal Action on State Environmental Regulation," *Harvard Environmental Law Review* 31 (2006): 67- 114.

24 Nancy K. Kubasek and Gary S. Silverman, *Environmental Law*, 8th ed. (Boston: Pearson, 2014).

25 Kubasek and Silverman, *Environmental Law*.

26 Adler, "When Is Two a Crowd."

27 Denise Scheberle, *Federalism and Environmental Policy: Trust and the Politics of Implementation* (Washington, DC: Georgetown University Press, 1997).

28 John Kingdon, *Agendas, Alternatives, and Public Policies* (New York: Harper Collins, 1996). See also Jesse Abrams, Dennis Becker, Jordan Kudma, and Cassandra Moseley, "Does Policy Matter? The Role of Policy Systems in Forest Bioenergy Development in the United States," *Forest Policy and Economics* 75 (2017): 41-48.

29 Oregon Department of Fish and Wildlife (ODFW), *Oregon Wolf Conservation and Management Plan* (Salem: ODFW, 2005 [updated 2010]).

30 Luigi Boitani, "Wolf Conservation and Recovery," in *Wolves, Behavior, Ecology, and Conservation*, ed. L. David Mech and Luigi Boitani (Chicago: University of Chicago Press, 2003).

31 Hubert H. Bancroft, *History of Oregon*, vols. 29 and 30, *Works* (San Francisco: History Co., 1888).

32 ODFW, *Oregon Wolf Conservation and Management Plan.*

33 ODFW, *Oregon Wolf Conservation and Management Plan.*

34 Robert L. Beschta and William J. Ripple, "The Role of Large Predators in Maintaining Riparian Plant Communities and River Morphology," *Geomorphology* 157-58 (2012): 88-98.

35 Dave Foreman, *Rewilding North America* (Washington, DC: Island Press, 2004).

36 Aime L. Eaton, *Collared: Politics and Personalities in Oregon's Wolf Country* (Corvallis: Oregon State University Press, 2013).

37 Idaho Legislative Wolf Oversight Committee (ILWOC), *Idaho Wolf Conservation and Management Plan* (Boise: Idaho Legislative Wolf Oversight Committee, 2002).

38 Kim Murphy, "Conservationists Elated, Ranchers Irritated By Wolf's Comeback," *Los Angeles Times*, June 6, 1999.

39 Davis & Hibbitts, Poll Commissioned by the Oregon Natural Desert Association (ONDA) and paid for by ONDA, Defenders of Wildlife, Oregon Natural Resources Council, and Predator Defense Institute, April 1999.

40 Eaton, *Collared*.

41 Michael Milstein, "Genetic Tests Show Animal Shot Dead in Eastern Oregon was a Wild Wolf," *Oregonian*, February 3, 2001, D1.

42 US Fish and Wildlife Service (USFWS), *Northern Rocky Mountain Wolf Recovery Plan* (Denver, CO: USFWS, 1987).

43 Jim Holyan, Kari Holder, Jeff Cronce, and Curt Mack, *Wolf Conservation and Management in Idaho: Progress Report 2010* (Lapwai, ID: Nez Perce Tribe Wolf Recovery Project, March 2011).

44 Michael Milstein, "Groups Spar over Returning Wolves," *Oregonian*, June 11, 2002, B5.

45 Milstein, "Groups Spar over Returning Wolves."

46 Oregon Fish and Wildlife Commission, *Draft Minutes, March 20-21, 2003* (Salem: ODFW, 2003).

47 ODFW, *Oregon Wolf Conservation and Management Plan*, 2.

48 ILWOC, *Idaho Wolf Conservation and Management Plan*.

49 ODFW, *Oregon Wolf Conservation and Management Plan*.

50 ODFW, *Oregon Wolf Conservation and Management Plan*.

51 Michael Milstein, "Biologists Confirm First Breeding Wolf Pack in Oregon," *Oregonian*, July 21, 2008.

52 Russ Morgan, *Oregon Wolf Conservation and Management Plan 2011: Annual Report* (La Grande: ODFW, 2011).

53 ODFW, *Oregon Wolf Conservation and Management: 2016 Annual Report* (Salem: ODFW, 2017).

54 Kelly House, "Gov. Kate Brown Signs Bill Blocking Legal Review of Gray Wolf Protections," *Oregonian*, March 15, 2016.

55 ODFW, *Oregon Wolf Conservation and Management: 2016 Annual Report*.

56 Hilary Corrigan, "Wolves in Oregon Are Not Native, Agriculture Groups Contend," *Bend Bulletin*, January 11, 2017.

57 John J. Garland, "The Oregon Forest Practices Act: 1972-1994," *Proceedings of the FAO/ UFRO Meeting of Experts on Forest Practices* (1994): 33-43.

58 Ruth Langridge, "When Do Challengers Succeed? Nongovernmental Actors, Administrative Agencies, and Legal Change: Shifting Rules for Oregon's Private Forests," *Law and Social Inquiry* 36 (2011): 662-93.

59 Peggy Hennessey, "Oregon Forest Practices Act: Unenforced or Unenforceable?," *Environmental Law* 17 (1987): 717-737.

60 Langridge, "When Do Challengers Succeed?"

61 Hennesey, "Oregon Forest Practices Act." See also Edward J. Sullivan and Alexia Solomou, "Preserving Forest Lands For Forest Uses—Land Use Policies for Oregon Forest Lands," *Journal of Environmental Law and Litigation* 26 (2011): 179.

62 Garland, "Oregon Forest Practices Act."

63 Langridge, "When Do Challengers Succeed?"

64 Garland, "Oregon Forest Practices Act."

65 Langridge, "When Do Challengers Succeed?"

66 Langridge, "When Do Challengers Succeed?"

67 Nobuya Suzuki and Deanna H. Olson, "Options for Biodiversity Conservation in Managed Forest Landscapes of Multiple Ownerships in Oregon and Washington, USA," *Biodiversity Conservation* 16 (2007): 3895-917.

68 Oregon Department of Forestry (ODF), *Riparian Function and Stream Temperature (RipStream) Project: Background, Analysis, Approach, Initial Findings, and Future Analysis* (Salem: ODF, August 1, 2009), August Meeting Agenda Item 5, Attachment 1. See also Jeremiah D. Groom, Liz Dent, Lisa J. Madsen, and Jennifer Fleuret, "Response of Western Oregon (USA) Stream Temperatures to Contemporary Forest Management," *Forest Ecology and Management* 262 (2011): 1618-29.

69 "NOAA/EPA Finding that Oregon Has Not Submitted a Fully Approvable Coastal Nonpoint Program," National Oceanic and Atmospheric Administration / Environmental Protection Agency, January 30, 2015, https://coast.noaa.gov/czm/pollutioncontrol/media/ORCZARAdecision013015.pdf.

70 ODF, *Riparian Management Area Widths for Streams of Various Sizes and Beneficial Uses,* OAR 629-635-0310 (Salem: ODF, August 12, 2016), September Meeting Agenda Item 7, Attachment 7d_1. See also idem, "Notice of Proposed Rulemaking Hearing," Filed with Office of the Oregon Secretary of State, December 15, 2016.

71 Jes Burns and Llam Moriarty, "Oregon's Updated Streamside Logging Rules Get A Chilly Response," *EarthFix / Oregon Public Broadcasting,* December 26, 2016.

72 National Marine Fisheries Service, *Recovery Plan for Oregon Coast Coho Salmon Evolutionarily Significant Unit* (Portland, OR: National Marine Fisheries Service, West Coast Region, 2016).

73 *Oregon Revised Statutes* 530.050.

74 Tim G. Wigington, "Wading Out of the Tilla-Muck: Reducing Timber Harvests in the Tillamook and Clatsop State Forests, and Protecting Rural Timber Economies through Ecosystem Service Programs," *Environmental Law* 42 (2012): 1275-338.

75 Michael A. Bordelon, David C. McAllister, and Ross Holloway, "Sustainable Forestry: Oregon Style," *Journal of Forestry* 98 (2000): 26-34.

76 Richard H. Waring and Jerry F. Franklin, "Evergreen Coniferous Forests of the Pacific Northwest," *Science* 204 (1979): 1380–86. See also Suzuki and Olson, "Options for Biodiversity Conservation."

77 16 U.S.C. § 1533.

78 16 U.S.C. § 1538.

79 Washington State Department of Natural Resources, *Final Habitat Conservation Plan: September 1997* (Seattle: Washington State Department of Natural Resources, 1997). See also Suzuki and Olson, "Options for Biodiversity Conservation."

80 Suzuki and Olson, "Options for Biodiversity Conservation."

81 Bordelon et al., "Sustainable Forestry."

82 Chad D. Oliver and Bruce C. Larson, *Forest Stand Dynamics* (New York: John Wiley and Sons, 1996). See also Andrew B. Carey et al., *Washington Forest Landscape Management Project—A Pragmatic, Ecological Approach to Small Landscape Management,* Report No. 2 (Olympia: Washington State Department of Natural Resources, 1996).

83 US Department of Agriculture Forest Service, *Record of Decision for Amendments to Forest Service and Bureau of Land Management Planning Documents within the Range of the Northern Spotted Owl* (Washington, DC: US Department of Agriculture Forest Service, April 13, 1994).

84 Bordelon et al., "Sustainable Forestry."

85 Michael Milstein, "Future Uses of State Forests Ride on Fate of Measure 34," *Oregonian,* October 16, 2004, A1.

86 "State Land Board Votes to Support Ownership Transfer of Elliott State Forest," Oregon
    Department of State Lands News Release, August 13, 2015.

87 Cassandra Profita, "Oregon Governor Calls for A 'Plan B' for the Elliott State Forest,"
    Oregon Public Broadcasting / EarthFix, December 13, 2016.

88 "Land Board Votes to Retain Public Ownership of the Elliott State Forest, Continue
    Common School Fund Distribution Policy," Oregon Department of State Lands News
    Release, May 9, 2017.

89 James P. Lester, "Federalism and State Environmental Policy," in *Environmental Politics
    and Policy: Theories and Evidence*, 2nd ed., ed. James P. Lester (Durham, NC: Duke
    University Press, 1995).

90 See Walth, *Fire at Eden's Gate*.

91 See, e.g., Zach Dundas, "Oregon's Fierce Response to Trump's Climate Move Is Just the
    Beginning," *Portland Tribune*, June 2, 2017.

13

Oregon Energy Policy

DAVID BERNELL, WARDA AJAZ, AND DANIEL GRAY

Energy policy in Oregon has for many years reflected the state's increasingly "blue state" politics.[1] Considered one of the more liberal states in the nation, with ongoing support for legislation that emphasizes sustainability and environmental stewardship, Oregon is not surprisingly at the forefront in developing energy policies that seek to diminish reliance on fossil fuels while simultaneously favoring the use of renewable energy, along with efficiency and conservation measures.[2] And while the state has long benefitted from abundant and inexpensive hydropower, since the 1990s, Oregon has encouraged the development of other renewable energy sources, particularly wind and solar power.

In fact, in 1997, Oregon was the first US state to adopt carbon dioxide emissions standards for new energy facilities, while the city of Portland in 1993 adopted its own Global Warming Reduction Strategy at the same time the international Kyoto Protocol was being negotiated.[3] At the end of the decade, the state approved a surcharge on consumers' electricity and natural gas bills to establish and fund the Energy Trust of Oregon, a quasi-governmental nonprofit organization that provides cash incentives and technical support for individuals and organizations investing in renewable energy and energy efficiency equipment. Oregon also passed a net metering law in 1999 to incentivize distributed (primarily solar) generation.

At the same time, Oregon promoted renewables and efficiency, as well as energy conservation measures, establishing a Renewable Energy Action Plan and expanding efficiency standards for state-owned buildings and home appliances. Significant milestones were achieved in 2007, when the legislature passed the Oregon Renewable Energy Act to implement a renewable portfolio standard, adopt a renewable fuel standard, and expand a key tax incentive for renewables known as the Business Energy Tax Credit (BETC). In 2009, legislators adopted a solar feed-in-tariff, and in 2012 Governor Kitzhaber's office issued the 10-Year Energy Action Plan, which contained three "core strategies."

1. Meeting 100 percent of new electric load growth through energy efficiency and conservation.

2. Enhancing clean energy infrastructure development by removing finance and regulatory barriers to attract new investment and pursue promising new technologies.

3. Accelerating the market transition to a more efficient, lower-cost, and cleaner transportation system, including strategies for fleet vehicle conversion and access to cleaner-burning and more efficient vehicles.[4]

More recently, Oregon's 2016 Clean Energy and Coal Transition Act strengthened the state's Renewable Portfolio Standard (RPS) and phased in a statewide ban on using coal for energy generation.

In short, the policy agenda in Oregon reflects not only political support for renewable energy and sustainability, but also the fact that markets, costs, consumer behavior, and profitability provide a great deal of continuity in the types of energy sources that individuals and businesses use. Policy has acted as a catalyst for change in energy markets because without them, such changes in production and consumption of sustainable energy resources would be far less likely, according to Oregon policy makers.

OREGON'S ENERGY PROFILE

Oregon is supplied by a diversity of energy sources (fig. 13.1) and, in particular, is well known for its vast hydropower resources. Beginning in the 1930s, federal agencies constructed dams and hydroelectric plants along the Columbia River and throughout the

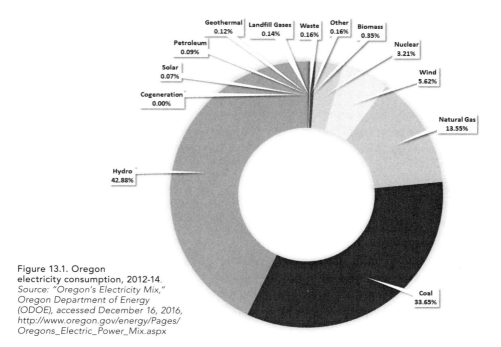

Figure 13.1. Oregon electricity consumption, 2012-14. *Source: "Oregon's Electricity Mix," Oregon Department of Energy (ODOE), accessed December 16, 2016, http://www.oregon.gov/energy/Pages/Oregons_Electric_Power_Mix.aspx*

region, with the largest at Bonneville, The Dalles, and John Day. Hydropower plants in Oregon have a combined 8,525 megawatts of generating capacity, and they account for two-thirds of all the electricity generated in the state, though only about 40 percent of the electricity used in the state.[5] Oregon's hydropower facilities provide electricity through the Bonneville Power Administration, a federal agency based in Portland, which provides power not only to Oregon, but also to California, Washington, and several other states. The abundance of inexpensive hydropower contributes to low electricity prices in the state. The average retail price is 8.6¢ per kilowatt-hour, compared to 10.4¢ nationally, and 15¢ to 17¢ in places such as New York, Massachusetts, and Connecticut.[6]

Coal accounts for one-third of the electricity used in the state despite the fact that there is only one coal-fired power plant in Oregon, with a capacity of 585 megawatts, and it is scheduled to cease operations in 2020. By comparison, natural gas-fired plants in Oregon provided 3,830 megawatts of generating capacity in 2015, which was almost one-quarter of the state's total capacity. Oregon also has the only field in the Pacific Northwest that produces natural gas, providing one billion cubic feet per year.[7]

Usage of renewable energy resources such as wind, solar, geothermal, and biomass has increased greatly in Oregon during recent years. From 2007 through 2014, electricity generation from nonhydroelectric renewables more than quadrupled.[8] This change has been quite rapid and is consistent with national trends. Wind power is by far the largest source of these newer renewable resources, with more than 3,150 megawatts of generating capacity in Oregon, most of it sited near the Columbia River Gorge. As with hydropower, Oregon produces more wind energy than it consumes in state, accounting for 12 percent of the state's electricity generation in 2014, but only about 6 percent of consumption.[9] Solar, biomass, and geothermal, however, while increasing their share of the state's energy portfolio, have experienced far more limited development (see table 13.1).

In contrast to the increasing diversification of energy sources fueling the electric power sector, the transportation sector has seen far less change, as it remains heavily

Table 13.1. Oregon's electricity generation capacity

Fuel Source	Generation Capacity (megawatts)
Hydropower	8,525
Natural gas	3,830
Wind	3,158
Coal	585
Biomass	308
Solar	100
Geothermal	27

Source: "Existing Nameplate and Net Summer Capacity by Energy Source, Producer Type and State," Energy Information Administration, accessed May 15, 2017, https://www.eia.gov/electricity/data/state/

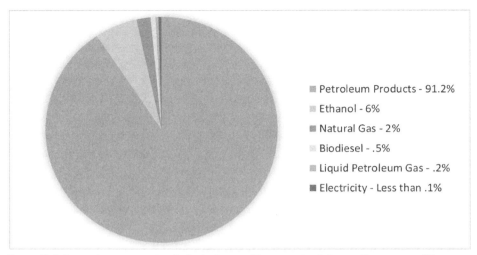

Figure 13.2. Oregon's transportation fuel mix. *Source: "Transportation," Oregon Department of Energy, accessed June 5, 2018, https://www.oregon.gov/energy/energy-oregon/Pages/Transportation.aspx*

reliant on one source: oil. This is similar to other states, as petroleum, mostly in the form of gasoline and diesel, provides more than 91 percent of all energy used for moving people and goods in the state (see fig. 13.2).[10] This energy profile for transportation has significant consequences for Oregon's goals regarding climate change. While Oregon's size and vast hydropower resources—and its minimal use of coal—mean that the state emits fewer greenhouse gases than many other states (both overall and per person), roughly 85 percent of the state's greenhouse gas emissions are energy related.

OREGON'S ELECTRICITY: YES TO RENEWABLES, NO TO COAL

Oregon adopted a number of policy measures in the 2000s to spur the use of renewable energy sources and significantly alter the state's energy profile. Two items that were expected to have a large impact were the Business Energy Tax Credit and the renewable portfolio standard. The BETC, similar to the 30 percent federal investment tax credit (ITC), allowed commercial purchasers of qualifying technologies—solar photovoltaic, solar water and space heating, wind turbines, geothermal and biomass, as well as energy efficiency and conservation projects—to claim a tax credit over five years equaling 50 percent of installation costs. Combined with the federal ITC and an additional cash rebate from the Energy Trust of Oregon, the BETC provided a substantial incentive to consumers. Residential customers also received an additional tax credit incentive up to $6,000 for the installation of solar or other qualifying technologies, along with rebates from the Energy Trust. This led to a high rate of solar PV installations for several years. The high cost of the BETC, however—roughly $1 billion in tax credits—and concerns with its administration ultimately led to the end of the program in 2014.[11]

Oregon's Renewable Portfolio Standard, enacted in 2007, was also designed to increase renewable energy use. It required investor-owned utilities to ensure that 25 percent of the electricity they sold came from renewable resources by 2025. Although there is no national RPS, twenty-nine states in the United States currently employ an RPS, either as mandates or goals, ranging from 2 to 100 percent.[12] Unlike the BETC or other incentives, an RPS is a legislative mandate that requires utilities to meet a specified goal or face a financial penalty. After the demise of the BETC in 2014, Oregon focused on the RPS as the primary instrument for expanding renewable energy use. This led in March 2016 to the passage of the Clean Energy and Coal Transition Act (Senate Bill [SB]1547), which sought to transform the electricity sector by expanding the RPS mandate to 50 percent. With this change, Oregon's RPS target matches the targets of California and New York, which are now exceeded only by Hawaii (100 percent) and Vermont (75 percent).

The Clean Energy and Coal Transition Act also included a first-of-its-kind provision that both represented a major departure from past practice in the state and set Oregon apart from all other US states: a complete ban on coal-fired power. The trajectory in Oregon energy policy since the 1990s had been to encourage the use of renewable energy. But policy makers had also recognized the importance of fossil fuels in the state's electricity mix. The passage of SB 1547 marked a significant change from past practice by singling out one particular fuel source and prohibiting its use. With respect to carbon dioxide emissions, coal is a dirty fuel, and while its mining and burning are heavily regulated, coal still has substantial environmental impacts. Importantly, the RPS and ban on coal apply *only to the large investor-owned utilities*—Portland General Electric (PGE) and Pacific Power—and not to municipal or consumer-owned utilities, or other small entities (see table 13.2). Yet, because coal use by these smaller utilities is negligible, their exemption from the ban has little practical impact.

The law is expected to affect PGE less than it does Pacific Power. PGE relies on coal-fired power for less than a quarter of the electricity it provides to customers. Currently, PGE owns 90 percent of the Boardman Generating Station, a coal plant near Boardman, Oregon. This facility supplies PGE with 585 megawatts of generation capacity, but the company is already on track to shut down the coal generator by the

Table 13.2. Entities subject to compliance with SB 1547

Electric Service Providers	50% Renewables	Ban on Coal
Portland General Electric	yes	yes
Pacific Power	yes	yes
Eugene Water and Electric Board	no	no
Municipal/consumer-owned/other small utilities	no	no

Source: Senate Bill 1547, Oregon Legislative Assembly, 2016 Regular Session

end of 2020. PGE also owns a share of the Colstrip Generating Station in Montana, and it receives electricity from other generators (independent power producers not owned by PGE) that supply 296 megawatts of coal-fired power.[13] The company will now have to plan for ending its use of electricity from these suppliers.

Pacific Power is more heavily reliant on coal power than PGE. Almost two-thirds of the electricity it sells comes from coal (natural gas, hydro, and wind are its other major sources), so it will have to make far greater changes to its operations in order to comply with the law.[14] Pacific Power acquires electricity for its Oregon customers from plants it owns or through power purchase agreements from eleven sites in Arizona, Colorado, Montana, Utah, and Wyoming.[15]

As part of the effort to facilitate the use of renewable energy, SB 1547 also addresses the development of community solar. Community solar refers to projects in which many customers share the ownership and benefits of a single PV generation system, which may not be sited on any of the properties where the energy consumers actually live or work. This type of arrangement is often useful for renters, condominium owners, and small businesses that may not be able to install solar on their own property. Oregon residential and commercial customers will now be permitted to credit electricity received from off-site solar projects directly to their utility bills.

Owing to the sweeping nature of the law, SB 1547 also includes a provision that exempts the utilities from these RPS requirements if the cost of purchasing RPS-compliant renewables exceeds 4 percent of a utility's annual revenue requirement (this is the amount of revenue needed to provide the services it is required to provide, plus a profitable rate of return; this sum is determined and approved by the Public Utilities Commission in the rate-making process). The law also provides for two "reality checks" to gauge the impacts of the legislation. One measure authorizes the Public Utilities Commission (PUC) to investigate whether compliance with the RPS could conflict with the utilities' obligation to comply with mandated reliability standards. Another provision directs the PUC to conduct a study about the impact of the law on rates, greenhouse gas emissions, grid reliability and operations, and the risks faced by consumers and the utilities.

POLITICS AND POLICY: ANTICIPATED IMPACTS

SB 1547 generated a great deal of debate on the way to its passage, owing to the lack of certainty about its impacts. Advocates claimed that the law would meet both environmental and economic goals, helping to reduce greenhouse gas emissions and combat air pollution, with little impact on the cost of electricity. By contrast, opponents argued that the legislation would result in higher costs for consumers, while jeopardizing grid reliability and having a negligible impact on environmental quality. The votes in the Oregon legislature were divided along party lines, passing in the senate by a vote of 17 to 12 that included all but one Democrat and no Republicans voting for the measure.

In the house, the vote was 38 to 20, with all the Democrats and four Republicans voting for the bill.[16]

Among those crafting the legislation, there was a surprising amount of unity. Supporters in the Democratic-controlled senate and house were joined by the governor, environmental groups, ratepayer advocates, and, most surprisingly, the utilities themselves. The Public Utilities Commission, which is responsible for regulating electric power services, contributed little to the process and expressed opposition to both the plan and the fact that it was largely left out of the bill's development.

The environmental community was particularly pleased. The executive director of the Oregon Environmental Council said, "Kissing coal goodbye and doubling renewable energy will give Oregon some of the cleanest power in the country."[17] At the same time, even Pacific Power, which relies heavily on coal and had opposed the legislation when it was originally introduced in 2015, offered its support and participated in crafting the final version of the bill. As Stefan Bird, the chief executive officer of Pacific Power, stated upon passage of the law, "Our company has been reducing reliance on coal generation and expanding our renewable energy portfolio for the past ten years as market forces, regulation and evolving customer preference continue to drive change in the way electricity is generated and delivered."[18]

The law could potentially affect electricity generation elsewhere. Because Oregon's utilities acquire power from outside the state, the reduced demand for "imported" coal power may reach into other jurisdictions and might eventually be the catalyst (or at least a contributor) to reduced overall demand from the coal plants now serving Oregon customers. The Natural Resources Defense Council, one of the larger environmental organizations in the United States, argued, "This bill does everything Oregon has legal authority to do to cut the market out from underneath coal plants from other Western states . . . And it's very likely as a result to bring about retirement and reductions at those coal facilities."[19]

Critics of the law point out that this expectation is unlikely to be realized. They argue that coal usage will only be shifted out of Oregon to other states. Coal plant operators throughout the western United States that would have otherwise sold electricity to Pacific Power will simply reallocate their coal-fired energy to customers in other states. The president of the National Association of Regulatory Utility Commissioners, Travis Kavulla, stated as much, pointing out, "It's pretty clear that this law won't actually reduce carbon emissions, despite that being the ostensible purpose of it."[20] Moreover, substituting coal power with wind and solar power would arguably increase rates for customers, as new generation facilities will have to be built to meet the state mandates. Both PGE and Pacific Power have stated that the new requirements are likely to raise prices. PGE has estimated that increases will be small, telling its customers that the law may increase rates an average of 1.5 percent a year between 2017 and 2040.[21]

Although the impacts of this legislation are as yet unclear, what is certain is that Oregon is pursuing a path in the electricity sector that exhibits both continuity with its past, developing an energy policy that is ambitious in its environmental and sustainability goals, and change, by aggressively moving the state toward a future with high levels of renewable energy and no coal in the electric power sector.

TRANSPORTATION AND FUELS

Transportation accounts for approximately one-third of energy use both in Oregon and the United States, while also accounting for approximately one-third of Oregon's greenhouse gases.[22] Taxes on fuels also raise millions of dollars in annual revenue for the Oregon Highway Fund. Given these competing, often contradictory, environmental and economic impacts, Oregon has tried to vary its approach to transportation energy policy. The state has sought to foster change in the transportation sector, toward alternative fuels and diminished environmental impacts, while recognizing that petroleum will continue to be the state's primary transportation fuel and an important source of tax revenue for a long time to come. To that end, Oregon has initiated a renewable fuel standard and a low-carbon standard, while also increasing the gasoline tax and testing alternative taxation mechanisms. The result has been a decline in fossil fuel use for transportation purposes from 98 percent in 2005 to only 91 percent in 2013. Further, biofuels—primarily ethanol and biodiesel—now account for almost 9 percent of total fuel use.[23]

Renewable Fuels Standard

The major reason behind the reduction in fossil fuel usage has been the legal requirement to use renewable fuels. A renewable fuels standard (RFS) is a mandate specifying that a certain amount of the fuel being used must come from renewable sources. These biofuels are produced primarily from plant materials and vegetable oils, and are blended with conventional gasoline or diesel. Renewable fuels have some advantages over petroleum in that they emit fewer greenhouse gases when produced and combusted (though this can vary greatly depending upon how these fuels are produced and distributed). They also can improve public health because they do not emit harmful pollutants into the air, and contribute to US energy security by reducing reliance on imported oil.

In 2007, Oregon enacted an RFS with the passage of House Bill (HB) 2210. Conventional gasoline was to be blended with at least 10 percent ethanol (designated as E10), while diesel fuel was to be blended with at least 5 percent biodiesel (designated as B5). These requirements were tied to Oregon's domestic production of ethanol and biodiesel, and did not kick in until Oregon produced forty million gallons of ethanol per year and fourteen million gallons of biodiesel. The required ethanol level was reached in 2007, and the biodiesel level was reached in 2010.[24] The state has also created several tax incentives for producers and distributors of biofuels. The adoption of an RFS by the state was preceded by a similar measure in 2006 by the City of Portland, which mandated that all gasoline and diesel sold in the city contain 10 percent biofuel.[25]

These developments in Oregon mirrored national policy at the time, as the country was engaged in a war in Iraq, reigniting concerns about energy security, while the threat of global climate change had garnered increased calls for action. At the federal level, the Energy Policy Act of 2005 created a nationwide RFS, and this was expanded by the Energy Independence and Security Act of 2007, which mandated that thirty-six billion gallons of biofuels—including advanced biofuels that have greater energy and environmental benefits than ethanol—must be blended into conventional transportation fuels by 2022. Annual targets, however, have been adjusted downward by the Environmental Protection Agency since 2011 to account for actual supply and demand of these fuels.[26] Owing to the federal legislation that was enacted, an increased level of renewable fuels would have come into use in Oregon, even without the state RFS mandate.

Clean Fuels Program

The Oregon Clean Fuels Program was initiated in 2009 with the passage of HB 2186. The program seeks to reduce by 10 percent the carbon intensity associated with transportation fuels over a ten-year period. Carbon intensity is a measure of the greenhouse gasses emitted in the production, distribution, and combustion of a fuel per unit. Fuels such as ethanol, biodiesel, hydrogen, electricity, and biogas have substantially lower carbon intensity than petroleum. In 2016, the Oregon Department of Environmental Quality (DEQ) fully launched the program, which requires fuel providers to report all their sales, including fuels that do not meet the standard (termed deficits) and those that do (credits). Credits must exceed deficits in order for fuel suppliers to be in compliance with the law. As of mid-2016, DEQ reported that vendors were in compliance with the law, and that ethanol and biodiesel accounted for more than 99 percent of the credits generated under the program.[27]

The Clean Fuels Program has faced strong opposition since its inception. This has come from Republicans in the state legislature along with interest groups such as the Oregon Fuels Association, which have sought to repeal the program, arguing that the standard raises costs but provides little benefit. Though the program was extended in 2015, a major $343 million transportation bill making its way through the legislature in the same year included a compromise to scrap the Clean Fuels Program in exchange for an increase in gasoline taxes, which would be used to pay for needed repairs and improvements to roads throughout the state. While the GOP was a minority in both houses at the time, it had enough votes to block any tax increases, such as the gas tax, which require a 60 percent majority to pass. In exchange for Republican support for the tax increase, Democrats would have had to agree to end the Clean Fuels Program. Although Governor Kate Brown and many Democratic members of the Oregon House and Senate were initially supportive of the deal, resistance by a number of legislators who strongly supported the Clean Fuels Program made agreement unattainable, leading to a collapse of the negotiations and no legislation on transportation funding.[28]

Gasoline Tax, Mileage Tax

Oregon was the first state in the nation to enact a gasoline tax (1¢ per gallon in 1919) and to use the funds for roads and transportation infrastructure. It has raised the tax many times since then, and in 2017 passed a bill that raised the fuel tax by 4¢ per gallon to a total of 34¢, and then will raise taxes by 2¢ per gallon in 2020, 2022, and 2024.[29] Notably, the same law made Oregon "the first state in the nation to tax the sale of higher-end bicycles, with $15 tacked onto the sale price of bikes costing more than $200 or having a wheel diameter of more than twenty-six inches."[30] While the cost of maintaining roads continually increases, prompting increases in the gasoline tax, it is also the case that the use of increasingly fuel-efficient vehicles has resulted in diminished fuel use and thus fewer tax revenues (eventually, a large number of electric cars on the road may have a similar impact). The state legislature directed a task force to study the issue, collect public feedback, and test alternative revenue collection measures. Ultimately, the task force recommended adoption of a mileage tax, where drivers pay according to miles driven on Oregon roads.[31]

The task force recommendation led to the creation in 2015 of the OreGo program, a trial project consisting of up to five thousand volunteers using either an odometer device or a Global Positioning Satellite (GPS) tracker to monitor miles driven. Participants pay 1.5¢ per mile driven. They pay the regular fuel tax at the gas pump, and then, at the end of the month, they receive either a refund or a bill based on the mileage tax rate.[32] The project is the first of its kind in the country, and because the state is working with private vendors to supply mileage trackers and gather the data, it has raised concerns regarding privacy, reliability, and security of information. To address these concerns, the state and private vendors must destroy records of locations and daily use after thirty days, and law enforcement will not be able to access the data unless a court order is issued.[33]

Alternative Motor Fuels and Electric Cars

One of the ways that Oregon has sought to diminish the use of petroleum is through the promotion of alternative motor fuels and electric cars via tax incentives and loans. The Oregon Department of Energy (ODOE) administers these programs, which provide businesses with a 35 percent tax credit to purchase alternative-fuel vehicles (this includes electric cars) or the infrastructure needed to charge or fuel the vehicles. ODOE also provides loans to help with the purchase of the vehicles. Residential customers can also receive tax credits up to $750 for charging stations.[34] These programs are designed to increase the number of cars, trucks, buses, and other vehicles, often used as part of a fleet that can run on fuels such as electricity, natural gas, or bio-fuels. There is strong emphasis on the potential of electric vehicles, and there are more than one thousand charging stations throughout the state. Oregon has also partnered with British Columbia, California, and Washington to create the West Coast Electric Highway, a network of fast-charging stations for electric vehicles along I-5 and a number of state highways that will span the distance from Canadian to the Mexican border with public fast-charging locations every twenty-five to fifty miles. Oregon's portion of the highway is already completed.[35]

EMERGING ISSUES AND OPPORTUNITIES

A number of emerging and ongoing issues have become increasingly salient in Oregon energy politics and policy. In particular, these issues address the question of supplying a variety of energy resources—including natural gas, coal, ocean energy, and nuclear power—and the role that Oregon will play in their availability. Oregon has historically been a large provider of energy in the form of hydropower, but it now has the potential to play a larger role in the supply chain for many other energy sources.

Liquefied Natural Gas

The availability and development of plentiful supplies of inexpensive natural gas in Pennsylvania, North Dakota, Texas, and other states have prompted efforts to boost natural gas exports. Doing this requires the construction of terminals to cool and liquefy the natural gas so that it can be loaded onto ships and transported, along with pipelines to send the gas to the terminals. There have been numerous proposals to construct many of these liquefied natural gas (LNG) terminals and pipelines throughout the country, including two on the Oregon Coast, one at Coos Bay, and another at Warrenton.

LNG facilities require a variety of permits for construction, land use, and environmental protection from several federal and state agencies. The Federal Energy Regulatory Commission (FERC) is responsible for deciding where to allow a liquefied natural gas facility to operate. As of late 2016, FERC had approved plans to build ten LNG export terminals in Georgia, Louisiana, Maryland, and Texas (though not without noteworthy local opposition), and had proposals for an additional fifteen terminals.[36] If a facility gains federal approval, Oregon requires that several state agencies also review and approve the permit applications.

The project in Coos Bay was proposed in 2007 and approved by FERC two years later, but the decision was reversed in 2011 when the project was revised. FERC denied the application in 2016, citing that the need had not been sufficiently demonstrated, and that harm from the project to local landowners and environmental interests would outweigh its economic benefits. Jordan Cove LNG, the project developer, continued to pursue the project with revisions, and in 2017 began the process of submitting a new application to FERC. The project planned for Warrenton, Oregon, faced even more significant opposition than did the project at Coos Bay, as local, state, and federal officials opposed it. One month after FERC denied the application at Coos Bay, the company proposing the terminal in Warrenton canceled the project.[37]

Coal and Oil Transport

The low price of natural gas and increasing regulation of coal have resulted in several coal plant retirements, and little investment in new plants. At the same time, in 2015, the US Congress ended the nation's fifty-year ban on the export of crude oil. These developments have led to increased exports of both coal and oil, with increased rail traffic of oil through Oregon and Washington along the Columbia Gorge, along with proposals to further increase the export of coal and oil from the West Coast to Asia.

The oil production boom in the Bakken Shale of North Dakota has already led to the transport of petroleum through Oregon, with oil train traffic in the Columbia River Gorge going from none in 2012 to sixty million gallons a week in 2016.[38] Coal is also shipped through the gorge, and the level of shipments through the region will increase if proposals to build coal export terminals in Washington and British Columbia are approved. In response, environmental interest groups such as Friends of the Columbia Gorge have sought to block or limit the volume of these shipments. The City of Portland went so far as to pass a resolution in 2015 opposing the transshipment of oil through the city, though it could not stop such shipments. The fears of opponents of oil transport through the state were realized when a derailment in Mosier in 2016 led to forty-seven thousand gallons of oil being spilled, causing a massive fire and seepage of oil into the Columbia River.[39]

With regard to coal, which is shipped in open-top rail cars, dust blows out of the rail cars and is deposited along the route. While state agencies have limited authority over rail transportation, Oregon does regulate the facilities that handle coal or oil in the state. For example, a coal export facility planned for Boardman, Oregon, received permits from the DEQ regarding air and water quality, but in 2014 the Division of State Lands rejected a permit, saying that it would interfere with long-established tribal fisheries in the area. This denial eventually led to cancellation of the project in 2016.

Alternative Energy Sources

The state of Oregon is playing a role in the development of new, alternative energy resources. Its coast is an ideal location for using energy from ocean waves and tides to generate electricity. To that end, federal agencies such as the US Department of Energy, the Bureau of Ocean Energy Management, and FERC are partnering with California, Oregon, and Washington to evaluate the potential benefits and impacts of ocean energy, and to develop plans and regulations for this effort. In Oregon, the Pacific Marine Energy Center has been established to conduct research at test sites along the coastline, support technology commercialization, and assess the economic, environmental, and community impacts.[40]

In addition to playing a key role in ocean energy, Oregon is also home to the development of a new generation of nuclear energy. A partnership between the US Department of Energy and Oregon State University in the early 2000s to research the potential for small nuclear power plants led to the creation of a company called NuScale Power in 2007. NuScale is developing a small modular reactor (SMR), a self-contained nuclear reactor that can generate forty-five megawatts of electricity. SMRs, which are under development by more than a dozen companies around the world, are far smaller than typical nuclear energy reactors (a nuclear power plant is usually one thousand to fifteen hundred megawatts), and they are scalable so that multiple SMRs can be grouped together. Built in a plant and then transferred to a site for installation, SMRs are designed to be safer and more efficient than earlier generations of nuclear power, with less waste. And because there is no handling of nuclear materials outside of the manufacturing plant, there can be fewer concerns with security and proliferation. NuScale is one of several companies in the United States that is currently partnering with the US Department of Energy to develop and commercialize SMRs.[41]

CONCLUSION

The state of Oregon is continuing on a long-established path to incorporate a greater proportion of sustainable energy sources into its energy portfolio. The state can expect continued rapid change from its electric power sector, incorporating higher levels of renewable energy while removing coal from the electricity mix. Transportation, on the other hand, can expect only slow change, as alternatives to oil are not on the horizon. These efforts are taking place in a context in which there are expected to be changes in energy policy at the national level. After many years of strong support for renewable energy by the Obama administration, including several new regulations that affect the use of coal in power plants, the Trump administration is placing greater emphasis on development of the country's fossil fuel supplies. In March 2017, President Trump issued an executive order calling upon federal agencies to "review all existing regulations, orders, guidance documents, policies, and any other similar agency actions (collectively, agency actions) that potentially burden the development or use of domestically produced energy resources, with particular attention to oil, natural gas, coal, and nuclear energy resources." The aim is to "suspend, revise or rescind" those regulations that pose such a burden.[42]

One of the key elements in any policy measure is the extent to which it can support an industry to help make it economically feasible. While the markets for oil and natural gas are less likely to be affected by national policy, coal may fare differently under President Trump, who has taken action to do away with the Clean Power Plan and to reverse environmental regulations that have adversely affected the coal industry. Notwithstanding these potential developments at the national level to boost traditional energy sources, these actions may not significantly affect Oregon in terms of its electric power consumption and production. The coal plant at Boardman is already set to be closed, the state's RPS will remain in place, and the ban on coal power remains in force. Because many other states continue to have RPS requirements that call for more renewable energy use in the future, while natural gas prices remain low, Oregon and other parts of the country may find that greater demand for renewable energy sources and natural gas will continue to transform the energy sector.

Notes

1   Blue states are those that reliably favor the Democratic Party and liberal/progressive policies, while red states are those considered more Republican and conservative. This distinction is particularly true for presidential elections.

2   Art Swift, "Wyoming Residents Most Conservative, D.C. Most Liberal," *Gallup*, January 31, 2014, http://www.gallup.com/poll/167144/wyoming-residents-conservative-liberal. aspx#1.

3   City of Portland and Multnomah County, *Local Action Plan on Global Warming* (Portland, OR: April 2001).

4   Governor John Kitzhaber, *10-Year Energy Action Plan* (Salem: State of Oregon, December 14, 2012), 11-13.

5   "Oregon Profile Analysis," U.S. Energy Information Administration (EIA), accessed December 9, 2016, http://www.eia.gov/state/analysis.cfm?sid=OR.

6   "State Electricity Profiles," EIA, accessed December 16, 2016, http://www.eia.gov/ electricity/state/.

7   "Oregon Profile Analysis."

8   "Oregon Electricity Profile 2014," EIA, accessed December 9, 2016, https://www.eia. gov/electricity/state/oregon/.

9   "Oregon's Electricity Mix," Oregon Department of Energy (ODOE), accessed May 3, 2018, http://www.oregon.gov/energy/energy-oregon/Pages/Electricity-Mix-in-Oregon. aspx. Natural gas plants and wind turbines have similar levels of capacity in Oregon to generate electricity. But there is a sizable difference between the amount of electricity actually generated by these two sources. The reason is that wind turbines produce electricity only when the wind is blowing, while natural gas plants can operate at any time.

10 "Oregon's Energy Profile," ODOE, accessed December 16, 2016, http://www.oregon. gov/energy/Pages/Oregon%27s-Energy-Profile.aspx.

11 Marsh Minick Consulting Services, *Report of Findings: Business Energy Tax Credit Program Investigative Examination* (Portland, OR: Marsh Minick Consulting Services, September 7, 2016), http://sos.oregon.gov/audits/Documents/2016-20.pdf. This independent audit of the BETC, which was prepared for the Oregon Secretary of State, revealed that numerous projects received tax credits in excess of the maximum allowed, some projects were never or only briefly operational, Department of Energy recordkeeping was

inconsistent or incomplete, and many of the credits issued "seemed improper, violated statutes or rules, or exhibited suspicious activity."

12 "Renewable Portfolio Standards Policies," Database on State Incentives for Renewables and Efficiency (DSIRE), accessed April 20, 2018, http://www.dsireusa.org/resources/detailed-summary-maps/.

13 "Where Your Electricity Comes From," Portland General Electric (PGE), accessed December 10, 2016, https://www.portlandgeneral.com/our-company/energy-strategy/how-we-generate-electricity.

14 "Fuel Source and Environmental Impact," Pacific Power, accessed December 10, 2016, https://www.pacificpower.net/ya/po/otou/fsei.html.

15 "Coal Plants Currently Serving Oregon," Citizens' Utility Board (CUB) Policy Center, accessed December 10, 2016, http://cubpolicycenter.org/coal/oregon.

16 "Senate Bill 1547," Oregonian, accessed December 10, 2016, http://gov.oregonlive.com/bill/2016/SB1547/.

17 "Oregon Governor Kate Brown Signs Historic Coal Transition Bill into Law," Sierra Club, March 11, 2016, http://content.sierraclub.org/press-releases/2016/03/oregon-governor-kate-brown-signs-historic-coal-transition-bill-law.

18 "Oregon Governor Kate Brown."

19 Julia Pyper, "Oregon Passes Bill to Cut Coal Purchases, Double Renewable Energy by 2040," Greentech Media, March 4, 2016, http://www.greentechmedia.com/articles/read/oregon-passes-bill-to-cut-coal-purchases-double-renewable-energy-by.

20 "Oregon Bill to Curb Coal, Set 50% RPS Heads to Governor after Senate Passage," Utility Dive, March 3, 2016, http://www.utilitydive.com/news/oregon-bill-to-curb-coal-set-50-rps-heads-to-governor-after-senate-passag/414933/.

21 "Oregon Legislature Sets New Renewable Energy Standard," PGE, March 2, 2016, https://www.portlandgeneral.com/our-company/news-room/news-releases/2016/03-02-2016-oregon-legislature-sets-new-renewable-energy-standards#.

22 "Oregon's Energy Profile."

23 "Oregon's Energy Profile."

24 Oregon Legislative Committee Services, Background Brief on Renewable Fuels (Salem: State of Oregon, September 2014), https://www.oregonlegislature.gov/citizen_engagement/Reports/BB2014RenewableFuels.pdf.

25 Motor Vehicle Fuels, Portland City Code, chap. 16.60.

26 "Renewable Fuel Annual Standards," Environmental Protection Agency, accessed May 15, 2017, https://www.epa.gov/renewable-fuel-standard-program/renewable-fuel-annual-standards.

27 "Clean Fuels Program: Second Quarter 2016 Data Summary," Oregon Department of Environmental Quality, accessed May 3, 2018, http://www.oregon.gov/deq/FilterDocs/cfp2016q2summary.pdf .

28 Ian Kullgren, "How the Legislature's $343.5 Million Transportation Package Fell Apart," Oregonian, June 26, 2015.

29 Christian Hill, "New Oregon Laws to Kick In Jan. 1; Taxes and Fees to Increase," Eugene Register-Guard, December 30, 2017.

30 Gary A. Warner, "Oregon Has Some New Car Laws, Bend Bulletin, December 28, 2017.

31 Oregon Department of Transportation (ODOT), Road Usage Charge Pilot Program 2013 (Salem: ODOT, May 2014), http://www.myorego.org/wp-content/uploads/2017/07/RUCPP-Final-Report.pdf.

32 "OreGo," ODOT, accessed December 20, 2016, http://www.myorego.org/about/.

33 Oregon Legislative Assembly, Senate Bill 810, 2013 Regular Session.

34 "Alternative Fuel Vehicle Charging and Fueling," ODOE, accessed December 20, 2016, https://www.oregon.gov/energy/TRANS/Pages/hybridcr.aspx.

35 "Electric Vehicles and Infrastructure Program," ODOT, accessed December 20, 2016, http://www.oregon.gov/ODOT/HWY/OIPP/Pages/inn_ev-charging.aspx; West Coast Electric Highway website, accessed December 20, 2016, http://www.westcoastgreenhighway.com/electrichighway.htm.

36 "North American LNG Import/Export Terminals," Federal Energy Regulatory Commission, accessed December 20, 2016, https://www.ferc.gov/industries/gas/indus-act/lng/lng-approved.pdf.

37 "Oregon LNG Cancels Plans for Warrenton Terminal," *Oregonian*, April 15, 2016, http://www.oregonlive.com/environment/index.ssf/2016/04/company_cancels_plan_for_warre.html.

38 "Crude Oil Transport Through the Columbia Gorge," Friends of the Columbia Gorge, accessed December 10, 2016, https://gorgefriends.org/protect-the-gorge/crude-oil-transport.html.

39 "Mosier Union Pacific Railroad Derailment," DEQ, accessed December 20, 2016, http://www.deq.state.or.us/Webdocs/Forms/Output/FPController.ashx?SourceIdType=11&SourceId=6115.

40 See the website of the Pacific Marine Energy Center at Oregon State University, accessed May 15, 2017, http://nnmrec.oregonstate.edu/.

41 Dan Yurman, "NuScale Announces Roadmap for SMR Operation at Idaho Site by 2024," *Energy Collective*, May 1, 2016.

42 President Donald Trump, "Presidential Executive Order on Promoting Energy Independence and Economic Growth," March 28, 2017, https://www.whitehouse.gov/the-press-office/2017/03/28/presidential-executive-order-promoting-energy-independence-and-economi-1.

14

Oregon Health Policy
The Struggles of an Innovating State
MELISSA BUIS MICHAUX

Most Americans do not realize that the United States ranks at the bottom of many measures of health system quality among industrialized countries. The problem is not just about access to health insurance, which lags that of other countries even after the 2010 passage of the Patient Protection Affordable Care Act (shortened here to ACA). Compared to other systems, health care in the United States is less safe, less coordinated, and much more expensive.[1] These problems have been well known among health policy researchers for decades, but the systemic issues have few easy solutions, given the complex and fragmented nature of our health insurance market and health delivery system. The current system is complicated by having public and private components, and federal and state dimensions. Oregon's health policy system reflects the complexity of the American approach. To capture Oregon's current health policy context, this chapter examines the basic design of the American health policy system, Oregon's distinctive health-care experiments with rationed care and coordinated care, and the vulnerabilities of the system that might determine its sustainability and future directions.

THE AMERICAN HEALTH POLICY SYSTEM

The American health policy system relies on a variety of sources in the private and public sectors. Nationally, just under half of people in the United States get some form of health insurance through their employer in private group plans.[2] Employers increasingly share the costs with their employees by requiring contributions to monthly premiums or by offering plans that increase co-payments or other out-of-pocket expenses. Employer-sponsored plans help consumers because the benefits are not taxed as income by the federal government, and they tend to pool risk across a large population of healthier workers. Since 1965, Americans aged 65 and older get insurance from the federal government in the form of Medicare, which is funded through a payroll tax. Another 20 percent of Americans get their insurance from a federal-state program for poor families called Medicaid.[3] In Oregon, the percentage of people covered by Medicaid is even higher; 24 percent of all Oregonians are enrolled

Table 14.1. Insurance coverage in the United States and Oregon, 2015

Insurance Type	Whom It Covers	National Share %	Oregon %
Employer-based (group market)	employees and their families	49	46
Medicare	over age 65	14	14
Medicaid	poor (determined by state eligibility standards)	20	24
Individual private market	everyone else	7	7
Uninsured		9	7

Source: Data from the Current Population Survey Annual Social and Economic Supplement (CPS ASEC), Jessica C. Barnett, and Marina S. Vornovitsky, Health Insurance Coverage in the United States: 2015 (Washington, DC: US Census Bureau, September 13, 2016)

in the Oregon Health Plan, which is Oregon's version of Medicaid.[4] Both Medicare and Medicaid are government programs, forms of socialized insurance. Finally, 7 percent of the US population gets health insurance from individual insurance plans purchased from private insurers, some portion of which are eligible for federal subsidies for those earning up to 400 percent of the federal poverty line through the ACA's health-care exchanges. Another 9 percent remain uninsured. See table 14.1 for a comparison of coverage rates in the United States and Oregon.

What few Americans appreciate is that nearly all forms of health coverage in the United States involve some level of government support. This governmental support is direct and more obvious in the case of public programs like Medicare and Medicaid, and is partially visible with federal subsidies in the state exchanges under the ACA. But not taxing health-care benefits paid to employees is another form of governmental expenditure that costs the federal government about $150 billion in annual revenue; combined with other tax exclusions, this kind of spending represents almost one-third of the total amount that the federal government spends on health care, the largest percentage of which goes to the wealthiest Americans.[5] Health-care expenditures are also a significant portion of Oregon's total budget, as in other states, but since much of this is federal money, state general fund-spending in this area pales in comparison to education funding, which represents over 50 percent of all general fund and lottery fund budgeted expenditures.[6] In fact, 59 percent of funding for the Oregon Health Authority comes from the federal government in various grants and matching funds. These federal dollars are only provided if Oregon puts up its matching share, so cuts in state spending can result in dramatic losses in federal revenues or penalties.[7] Further, spending on health care can reduce future costs in terms of lost worker productivity and chronic illnesses, meaning that cuts in state health-care spending may not be the best way to reduce overall government spending.

State governments are not just constrained by federal program rules and requirements. Conditions in the private health insurance market also make it difficult to maintain or increase insurance coverage. As a 2016 Congressional Budget Office report shows, private sector insurance in recent years has been marked by increasing costs and more cost-sharing, affecting affordability for companies and individuals in the private market.[8] A broader consolidation of insurance companies also limits the range of options for individual coverage. Thirty-two states have one health insurer that has captured more than 50 percent of the individual insurance market.[9] Using the Herfindahl-Hirschman Index (HHI) to measure a market's competitiveness by examining market share distribution, only three states rank as highly competitive. Oregon's individual insurance market is relatively competitive, better than Washington State but not as competitive as California.[10] Fewer insurers and less competition means that a small number of dominant players have a great deal of power to set terms of engagement in the face of regulations or attempts to influence price. Because health insurance companies are regulated at the state level, the health of the insurance market across states creates serious disparities for consumers on price and coverage. Despite these challenges, Oregon has long been a leader among states in health-care reform, a role that was accelerated by the ACA's passage in 2010.

HISTORY OF HEALTH POLICY INNOVATION

Oregon began serious health-care reform in 1989 with the creation of the Oregon Health Plan (OHP), which sought to increase coverage among the "working poor" whose incomes were too high to qualify for Medicaid by rationing care, creating a culture of innovation around health policy, and developing health policy expertise both in and out of government. Although the original Oregon Health Plan fell victim to political pressures in debates about rationed care and fiscal shortfalls, the process of creating OHP in the first place set Oregon apart from other states. Statewide conversations in the late 1980s about health reform prepped a variety of participants—from physicians to insurers—to think more creatively and boldly about health care. Oregon is a small state, with various health-care policy leaders moving around to different positions, but many of the actors stay the same across time. The shared experiences, lessons learned, and general familiarity with the personalities and policy preferences of the participants help to create a cohesive policy community, which has included significant involvement from those in the medical field.

The ultimate leader of this policy community was Dr. John Kitzhaber, an emergency room physician turned politician from southern Oregon who touted his experience with the health-care system and campaigned as a health-care innovator. Kitzhaber was the chief legislative leader and visionary for OHP enactment as a state senator, senate president in 1989, and then as governor from 1995 to January 2003. Kitzhaber put health-care reform on the agenda for Oregon and shepherded it through each of the subsequent policy process stages: alternative specification or formulation, legitimation, implementation, and evaluation. Although there were many policy actors involved in each stage of the process, his leadership and political skill on health-care reform were essential.

Governor Kitzhaber returned to the executive office in January 2011, just in time to again take up the health reform mantle. In between his second and third terms in office, Kitzhaber launched the Archimedes Movement in 2006, designed to engage civic leaders in community conversations about reforming health care. Archimedes Movement participants created a set of principles and a framework for a new way to deliver health care and endorsed the "Triple Aim" goals: improve health, lower costs, and create a better health-care experience.[11] In a single year, the Archimedes Movement could boast of sixty-five hundred members across the state, organized into thirty-eight chapters.[12] Looking more like a social activist than a former governor, Kitzhaber and his Archimedes Movement sponsored rallies at the state capitol, introduced legislation, lobbied legislators, and spoke around the state at various civic venues. As both a political pragmatist and a doctor who understood the system well, Kitzhaber's experience and knowledge of health-care issues emboldened reformers on health-care issues both within and outside government.

The fundamental idea of the original Oregon Health Plan was to achieve universal coverage of poor Oregonians (everyone up to 100 percent of the federal poverty line) by providing a health benefit package that was more limited than Medicaid but smarter, ranking treatments on the basis of clinical and cost-effectiveness with decisions being made by the Health Service Commission, composed of five physicians (including one doctor of osteopathy), one public health nurse, and one social worker, with the remaining four members representing purchasers and consumers of health care. The plan was controversial because OHP would cover more people, but not provide less efficient or less effective treatments covered in the original Medicaid. Some people would actually lose some forms of health care. The original design of OHP was that health care for the poor would be rationed on the basis of need and the best use of limited health-care dollars using evidence-based research. Based on his experience as an emergency room physician, Kitzhaber was passionate about reforming the health-care system and endeavored to educate the public and other legislators about inequities in the health-care system.[13] Still, it was a difficult path, first to get federal approval for the waiver and second to ensure that the prioritized list truly represented the best available data and not the priorities of individual lawmakers or the better-financed lobbyists. Further, OHP sought to control costs by enrolling Medicaid recipients into managed care programs. The idea animating managed care is that consumers can get better-quality care and reduce medical overuse if they have regular contact with a primary care physician who assesses their needs and makes referrals to specialists only when necessary. In the optimal scenario, the primary care physician coordinates a patient's medical needs. In practice, patients often feel that physicians primarily keep costs down by being a gatekeeper to higher-cost services. Still, early studies of OHP were largely positive, and Oregon's experiment launched a national conversation about health reform through the 1990s.[14]

But subsequent attempts to expand OHP were less successful, and the program of cost-effective care began to erode. In fact, OHP was cut into two plans with different benefit levels, which undermined the claim of universality. In addition, state-level revenue shortfalls led the Oregon legislature to cut program funding by $40 million and institute cost-sharing in the form of higher premiums and co-pays; enrollment dropped by 75 percent in 2007, raising the uninsured rate from a low of 11 percent in 1996 to 17 percent after OHP2 changes went into effect.[15] Policy makers failed to realize how price-sensitive poor Oregonians would be to these changes, as many were willing to go without insurance altogether once there were fees and co-pays.[16] Other than dropping expensive services, OHP and the state of Oregon could do little to control the overall increase in medical costs, which were increasing 2.7 percent faster than gross domestic product during this period.[17] Writing in 2007, Jonathan Oberlander found:

> OHP is now covering both fewer services and fewer people, and the elimination of entire benefit categories and rollback in enrolled beneficiaries looks more like the arbitrary cuts common in other states than the rational and equitable model of prioritization to which Oregon aspired. The state is trying to hold onto its core principles in health reform, but its grip has weakened considerably. Indeed, the environment in Oregon today resembles that in the years preceding OHP's enactment, as the state has fallen into the very cycle—rising costs, growing numbers of uninsured people, Medicaid eligibility cuts, increased emergency room use, and cost shifting—that OHP was created to avoid.[18]

A subsequent study found that although increasing access to OHP produced "increased access to and utilization of health care, substantial improvements in mental health, and reductions in financial strain," it did not reduce emergency room use or produce better health outcomes, such as "reductions in measured blood-pressure, cholesterol, or glycated hemoglobin levels."[19] As originally envisioned, OHP proved to be unsustainable given both health-care economics and political pressures. With the nation's highest unemployment rate (7.4% from 2001 to 2003), fiscal imperatives in Oregon were impossible to curtail. Further, the pressure on state legislators to cover specific diseases or treatments was difficult to resist with the help of a media environment willing to publicize the drama of individual cases.[20] Ultimately, reformers had to start anew.[21]

BUILDING STATE CAPACITY

The next phase of health policy reform emerged in the wake of the failure of OHP and was made possible through a series of legislative steps that first enhanced the capacity of health-care reformers in state government. In 2007, the Oregon Health Policy Commission created the Road Map for Health Care Reform, which called for a new Oregon Health Authority (OHA) as a permanent structure outside of the Department of Human Services (DHS).[22] Given the Democratic Party's hold on the executive branch in Oregon since 1987, health-care reformers enjoyed a level of continuity for planning and strategic engagement that few state officials enjoy.

Creation of the Oregon Health Authority as a separate entity was an important step for achieving health-care transformation in 2012. DHS was considered an unwieldy bureaucracy with many responsibilities for a variety of complicated social welfare programs like Temporary Assistant to Needy Families (TANF), the Supplemental Nutrition Assistance Program (SNAP), and foster care and refugee services. During an early House Health Care Committee hearing, Representative (and Chair) Mitch Greenlick explained that he used to teach organizational theory and said, "I think DHS is simply too big to manage."[23] But the authorizing legislation for creation of OHA and its policy board was more than just an administrative right-sizing. House Bill (HB) 2009 was intended to create a new approach to improving health in the state by joining health care, mental health, insurance and hospital regulation, addiction services, and public health in one agency for better policy coordination. As the director of DHS explained at the time, policy coordination would be matched with a consolidation of state purchasing power for health care and health insurance. The broader vision and structural power embodied in HB 2009 excited the more liberal members of the House Health Care Committee and worried the free-market advocates. As one Republican representative noted at the time, "This is a shift in power . . . This is a fundamental structure change in how we do business in the state of Oregon, let alone how we do health care."[24] In addition to creating a separate agency, the legislation directed the organization to develop a variety of plans for: improving health information technology; reducing expensive treatments for chronic conditions; generating new reporting requirements for hospitals, insurers, and ambulatory surgical centers; and conducting comparative effectiveness research. If the state's role in health care had previously been "diffuse and unclear," as one participant noted, the creation of the OHA was designed to enhance state power under a unified vision. The agency has provided an effective, consistent, and coherent guiding vision of what priorities should define Oregon's health-care system.

The vote in the 2009 Oregon House in support of OHA and the new vision for health was 38-22, almost exactly along party lines. Only two Republicans joined Democrats in supporting the legislation. With overwhelming Democratic margins in the house, Republicans were not key players.[25] The partisan disagreement here highlights that this was a contentious bill subject to almost thirty public hearings over the course of nearly five months of legislative work. Preceding the passage of the ACA, HB 2009 was buoyed and informed by the national conversation on health reform. Indeed, public hearings featured frequent references to the likelihood of federal reform. Within two years, OHA would propose the broader transformation of health care with the help of the passage of the ACA.

IMPLEMENTING THE AFFORDABLE CARE ACT

Although headlines touted the passage of national health-care reform in 2010, few policy areas escape a prominent role for the states. The promises and pitfalls of federalism and separation of powers have been on display in the implementation of the ACA. Originally projected to cover an additional seventeen million uninsured, low-income adults, the ACA's effect on the uninsured was curtailed when the US Supreme Court ruled that the Health and Human Services secretary could not withdraw all Medicaid funding if the states failed to expand eligibility up to the required 133 percent of the federal poverty line (FPL).[26] As of 2017, thirty-one states plus the District of Columbia accepted Medicaid expansion, leaving many people uninsured in states that rejected expanded eligibility. Eighteen states continue to have no coverage at all

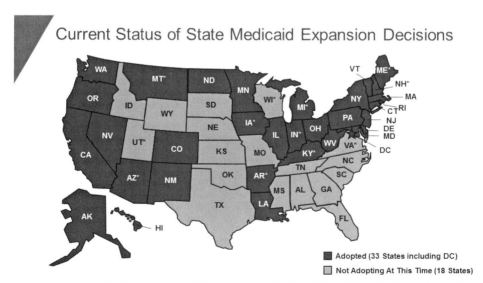

Figure 14.1. Current status of state Medicaid expansion decisions. *Source: Kaiser Family Foundation, Status of State Action on Medicaid Expansion Decision, KFF State Health Facts (San Francisco: Kaiser Family Foundation, January 1, 2017)*

for poor childless adults, and twelve states only cover parents with dependent children up to 50 percent of the FPL (see fig. 14.1).[27] All the states that have not expanded Medicaid have Republican governors except for Virginia and North Carolina, which have Republican-controlled state legislatures. About three million adults fall into this coverage gap created when states did not expand coverage; more than half of those uninsured are people of color, especially African Americans who are more likely to reside in Southern states that are not covered.[28]

In addition to the expansion of the Medicaid program, the ACA increased coverage through an individual mandate (requiring everyone to buy insurance) and with national subsidies up to 400 percent of the FPL for people purchasing insurance through state exchanges or marketplaces. The exchanges turned out to be far more controversial and difficult to implement than most policy makers anticipated. First, Republican-controlled states refused to create state insurance exchanges so that the federal government had to step in and run twenty-eight different federally facilitated marketplaces.[29] Second, even states like Oregon, which was eager to implement the exchange through an advanced Internet marketplace called "Cover Oregon," experienced major technical difficulties linking all the necessary data. In a major failure for the OHA, the Cover Oregon project spent $300 million but was never operational.[30] Third, new ACA requirements for insurance plans, deemed "essential health benefits," raised costs for insurers that contributed to premium increases, especially for healthier and younger consumers who are effectively subsidizing sicker and older enrollees. So, the high costs of insurance continue to be a primary reason individuals report being uninsured.[31] Despite the difficulties, one in five of the uninsured (about 5.3 million people) are eligible for subsidies through the insurance exchanges, so it is a significant component of attempts to make health care more affordable.[32]

The OHA would not have been able to carry out many of its plans despite its enhanced structural power if the US Congress had not passed the ACA in March 2010. The expansion of Medicaid in the ACA with financial support from the federal government significantly freed the new state agency to tackle payment alternatives, global budgeting, and quality metrics. Oregon, long a leader in health-care reform, embraced the opportunity the ACA provided. Oregon transformed its Medicaid program through a federal waiver designed to tackle cost containment and change the delivery of health care through the creation of coordinated care organizations (CCOs). While these changes primarily affect the Medicaid population, the state plans to spread this model to health insurance for government employees and teachers, and ultimately to private insurers.

OREGON'S WAIVER: COORDINATED CARE ORGANIZATIONS

While much of the nation was focused on debates over the ACA and whether states would expand Medicaid or build their own health-care exchanges, Oregon was laying the groundwork for dramatically changing the delivery of health care, not just increasing access to insurance. At the core of the transformation was the creation of coordinated care organizations: local networks of health-care providers charged with improving health outcomes for OHP recipients. The move to CCOs promised a reduction of health-care costs with an increase in quality outputs by better addressing the root problems of medical expenses, especially poorly managed chronic conditions and expensive emergency room use.

CCOs are like a massive managed care system where the overarching organization is responsible for health outcomes subject to global budget caps and standards of care. The goal was to transform the system away from just delivering services to achieving measurable results. Accomplishing this level of reform required a waiver from the Centers for Medicare and Medicaid Services (CMS). Oregon, in effect, reached a kind of grand bargain with CMS where Oregon promised to reduce health-care spending by 2 percent per year without cutting beneficiaries or quality of care; in exchange, CMS provided $1.9 billion to fund the transformation. Oregon reasoned that it could reach significant savings through payment reform to realign incentives for unnecessary services; integration of physical, behavioral, and oral health; administrative simplification; increased flexibility in what is considered a legitimate health-care cost; and learning through decentralized experimentation and information sharing.[33]

Sixteen CCOs formed across the state, just in time for the broad expansion of Medicaid eligibility through the ACA. A little over a million Oregonians now receive health care through the state's Medicaid program.[34] Given that Oregon's population is not quite four million, Medicaid beneficiaries account for a substantial portion of the insured population in the state. Early reports on the effectiveness of CCOs have been positive. The Oregon Health Authority highlighted the following results from 2014:[35]

- Emergency room use decreased 21 percent compared to baseline year of 2011.
- Hospital admissions for diabetes complications fell 9.3 percent.
- Hospital stays for patients with chronic respiratory diseases dropped 48 percent.

These positive results occurred without increasing per capita costs and despite the influx of a significant number of newly insured patients. The 2014 report details outcomes on thirty-three state performance metrics and seventeen incentive metrics. Policy makers can make comparisons across CCOs, across various demographic groups, and now across time. There is significant variation across the CCOs in terms of outcomes and innovation. Not all CCOs are engaging in the kind of flexible payment or public health initiatives the bill sponsors imagined. But the state provides a variety of resource and technical assistance to CCOs to enhance learning and outcomes. While a few critics insist that compromises reached in the political process mean that CCOs are not as transformative as they should be, many outside observers agree that the Oregon reform is significant and a remarkable shift in health-care delivery.[36] A recent study comparing Oregon and Colorado found that Oregon's reform was associated with improvements in utilization, access, and quality, especially with regard to mental health coverage.[37] The debate is likely to continue as implementation and evaluation proceeds.

Historically, the greatest impediment to changing the delivery of health care to more cost-effective means has been the opposition of hospital and doctor groups that have made personal and business investments in the existing system. Such opposition never fully materialized in Oregon, and helps to explain why the state's health policy looks different in comparison.

THE ROLE OF THE MEDICAL COMMUNITY

Traditionally, the most powerful forces favoring the status quo in health care have been insurance companies, pharmaceutical companies, doctors, and hospitals. This is well documented at the national level.[38] In the Oregon case, insurance and pharmaceutical companies were not directly in play with the creation of CCOs. Doctors and hospitals put up surprisingly little resistance given the uncertainties that CCOs generated, especially its global budgeting plan and incentive payment structure using quality metrics. Instead, doctor and hospital groups constructively engaged in the policy process, working through a complicated bill, compromising, and largely supporting the measures.

In the fall of 2010, as various proposals were being considered by the Health Policy Board of the OHA, Oregon Medical Association (OMA) President Dr. John Evans warned its members that the OHA and its board "have numerous committees producing possible tectonic changes, some quite extensive, changing the landscape for how we practice medicine today and into the future."[39] As Evans details the various committees and the reforms proposed, he notes the physicians active in the deliberations. Each policy subcommittee had at least one and sometimes as many as four doctors. He concludes: "The ground may feel unstable under our feet, but as physicians and care providers we must stand for *our patients'* best interests."[40] It is clear from OMA reporting that physicians were intimately involved early in the policy process, that various proposals were openly discussed and debated, and that the OMA saw its role as protecting patients, not just physicians. This focus on protecting patients has a rhetorical use if, for example, the primary way physicians want to protect low-income access to health care is to fight any provider payment cuts.[41] But the OMA embraced CCOs, at least in part, for the perceived benefits they promised to patients. The OMA newsletter from Fall 2012 featured a story about how care for a woman with congestive heart failure and diabetes would change under CCOs in ways that would both improve her health and provide more than enough cost coverage for her doctor.[42] The author, a past president of the OMA, concluded: "I understand that Mary is hypothetical and this is a rosy story, but I have seen a real enthusiasm on the part of local doctors to use the CCO model of care to improve care and control costs."[43]

Physicians and hospitals were supportive of reform partly because the dire budget predictions meant that provider cuts were inevitable, the old system was largely indefensible, and bipartisanship resulted in no place to go for those opposing reform. Doing nothing meant that doctors and hospitals were facing significant cuts; they were all standing on a "burning platform" and needed to work together to put out the fire. Policy makers made it clear that the consequences of standing still were severe. Additionally, physicians were involved in the policy process, two physicians-turned-legislators were deeply involved in the legislative process, and many physician groups lobbied, including the Coalition for a Healthy Oregon (COHO), an association of managed care groups that supported health-care transformation and the creation of CCOs. The existence of COHO is a reminder that the OMA does not necessarily dominate medical groups the way it once did, and that the political arena reflects changes in the nature of the provider system.

From at least the 1970s to the early 2000s, the OMA was dominated by specialists with high incomes who were paid for providing services, not necessarily for improving health outcomes. The OMA during that time was the overriding force in legislative lobbying and practiced old-style, behind-the-scenes, protect-your-money politics. By the early 2000s, primary care physicians began to have an increasing role in the OMA, while specialists declined in numbers and influence. In a relatively short period of time, the OMA went from a closed network dominated by specialists who asserted tremendous political power to one led by primary care physicians with different priorities for health reform. Meanwhile, the Oregon Academy of Family Physicians (OAFP) began to get more political and in 2006 increased their dues to pay for a contract lobbyist. OAFP's tactics were different. They claimed to represent patients, not just doctors, and they argued for changes based on better outcomes for patients. So, the OMA evolved and competitor physician groups moved into the political space, diluting OMA power. The divide in the medical community, however, was not just limited to type of physician but also included type of business model.

The managed care organizations (MCOs) were in the best position to take advantage of the new CCO structure. So, COHO—a coalition of MCOs—lobbied in support of the transformation. In fact, given the high rates of managed care for Medicaid patients in Oregon, physicians may have been less concerned about the changes than they would have been in another state. The national average for managed care in Medicaid is 80 percent, but that number masks large variation across the states.[44] About 98 percent of Medicaid patients in Oregon were in managed care by 2011, compared to reportedly none in Alaska and New Hampshire, 64 percent in Wisconsin, and 88 percent in Washington.[45] MCOs were concerned throughout the legislative process about various details embedded in the implementation plans; the hearings are full of

technical amendment requests from various groups. But this kind of policy engagement was largely supportive of the overall measures.

Governor Kitzhaber did make a commitment to medical liability reform, an
issue dear to nearly every doctors' group. Senate Bill 1580 included a requirement to
develop a liability reform proposal for the next legislative session.[46] But the biggest
concessions were probably to hospitals in the form of the governing structures for the
CCOs. Hospitals struggled initially with the CCO proposal because one of the goals
of the CCOs is to keep people out of the hospital. In fact, Salem Hospital filed suit
against its CCO for low reimbursement rates and then got local legislators to file a bill
that would end the dispute in their favor before eventually settling the matter on their
own.[47] Although the state of Oregon enhanced its authority with the creation of the
OHA, the creation of CCOs devolved power, so that a great deal of decision-making
takes place at the local level. The state holds CCOs responsible for meeting various
benchmarks and rewards them for good health outcomes, but CCOs can still operate
as fee-for-service entities with contracts to all the traditional provider groups. Those in
the legislature who were strongly committed to payment reform felt that CCOs should
be mandated to get rid of fee-for-service. Further, more liberal reformers argued that
the governing boards are largely dominated by stakeholders, especially hospitals, who
will resist truly innovative reform and operate in their self-interest.

In their work examining health-care reform in the 1990s and early 2000s, Gray
et al. found that the influence of health interests at the state level varied according to
the nature of the specific policy proposed, but that interest groups usually have a high
impact on policies that represent a major departure from the status quo or represent
regulatory changes—both of which were in play with the creation of CCOs.[48] The
cooperation of the doctors and hospitals, then, is surprising and at least unusual. In
one of the health policy areas they studied, Gray et al. also found that states with more
crowded health interest communities were less likely to achieve reform.[49] Oregon,
however, ranks in the middle for health interest group density—not particularly high
but not low either.[50] That health interest groups cooperated is beyond question; why
they cooperated is harder to determine. It is difficult to understand the engagement of
doctor and hospital groups in the creation of CCOs without understanding the larger
bureaucratic and legislative structure in which they operated. Doctor and hospital
groups formulated and pursued their interests in reform within the context of an open
policymaking process, largely facilitated by the bureaucracy.

THE POLICYMAKING PROCESS

Health-care transformation in 2011-12 was achieved with bipartisan support because
the legislature is rather weak compared to the increasingly professionalized bureaucracy that has developed the expertise for long-range planning as well as a parallel
political process that brings stakeholders together to hammer out differences before

legislation is ever introduced. This does not mean that the legislative process is irrelevant, but rather that crucial policy compromises were reached outside the normal legislative process. The work of the state agencies in formulating reform and bringing together stakeholders is vital for transformation given the limitations of what has largely remained a citizen legislature.

Policy participants from the agency side do not feel particularly powerful. They are demonstrably deferential to legislative authority and offices. When the legislature is in session, policy makers are often at the beck and call of legislators who ask them to provide information, data, and testimony, sometimes with little notice. The bureaucracy, like the rest of state government, is also at the mercy of a permissive initiative process that frequently forces its will on policy in the state.[51] And legislative leaders who are caught in the throes of getting bills heard and passed, often with great difficulty, and who spend countless hours negotiating various compromises and attending meetings with lobbyists, citizen groups, and various stakeholders, do not believe they play a subordinate role. What is more, the legislature contained a number of skilled Democratic leaders in the health-care field: Representative Mitch Greenlick, who has been a professor of public health at the School of Medicine at Oregon Health Sciences University (OHSU) and involved with Oregon health policy on various committees and task forces for decades; Senator Alan Bates, practicing physician and health policy leader who had served in the state legislature since 2001;[52] and Senator Elizabeth Steiner-Hayward, a practicing physician and associate professor of family medicine at OHSU are three standout leaders with health-care expertise, and there are others. But it would have been extremely difficult for health-care transformation to pass the Oregon legislature without the extralegislative work of the Oregon Health Authority.

The Oregon health-care bureaucracy follows a pattern of open access and citizen involvement. In the case of health-care transformation, the Oregon Health Authority came up with an Action Plan for Health, fostered an enormous public education campaign, sought feedback from communities and various stakeholder groups, and facilitated a crucial set of public meetings in support of the CCO implementation plan prior to the 2012 legislative session. Even the first of these important contributions, creating an eighty-page "action plan," was the result of a public process begun in 2007 and 2008; the Oregon Health Policy Board met with 300 people who served on "20 committees, subcommittees, workgroups, task forces and commissions" and held six community meetings across the state attended by more than 850 people.[53] After HB 3650 passed in 2011 and the OHA began to formulate plans for implementing CCOs, the agency launched "Road Trip 2011," which brought the conversation to medical providers, community leaders, and other stakeholders in eight Oregon cities—Astoria, Bend, Eugene, Florence, Medford, Pendleton, Portland, and Roseburg—reaching about one thousand Oregonians. These community meetings included a presentation from the director of OHA or a health policy advisor to the governor, followed by someone from the local health-care community, breakout into small groups for discussion, and then reporting back concerns and issues. An additional 133 Oregonians participated in four formal workgroups that at least one participant described as a "robust exchange of ideas."[54] However, nearly every policy participant cited the importance of the "Wednesday night" meetings for bringing together diverse and discordant stakeholders and legislators around a compromise plan for CCOs.

The Wednesday night meetings were held in the fall of 2011 at Willamette University (just across the street from the statehouse) when the legislature was not in session and were hosted by the governor's office and staffed by the OHA. Approximately forty-five stakeholders and policy makers met once weekly for nine to ten weeks. Participants report that it was crucial having these face-to-face exchanges. Often Governor Kitzhaber or his chief of staff was in the room, along with key policy personnel from OHA. One Republican lawmaker felt the Wednesday night meetings educated him about health policy; he appreciated hearing candid talk from health experts. The meetings were not recorded and had an informal air, with participants sharing best practices, asking questions, and formulating ideas. The Wednesday night meetings seem to have reassured stakeholder groups that no one would absorb all the costs of transformation, that everyone would have "skin in the game," and that everyone would work together to produce a better, more rational system. Of course, not everyone was brought along. The long-term care component dropped out of the reform proposal because those interests never bought into the vision and felt that they had too much to lose. These meetings provided the bridge between legislative sessions to enhance coalitions in support of reform. Disagreements were aired and explored with a focus on data and expert advice. Participants experienced these meetings as apolitical, by which they meant outside of the usual partisan divides, because coalition-building and problem-solving are deeply political.

AN (UN)SUSTAINABLE POLICY REGIME?

Why was Oregon able to move forward with bipartisan transformation of its health-care system? Like most "breakthrough" policies, the creation of CCOs benefitted from a long-range planning process that built state capacity and created and fostered a coherent policy community. This policy community engaged meaningfully with stakeholder groups, namely, doctors and hospitals who would have been most likely to oppose reform but did not. Proposals for reform also adapted to opposition. The institutional structure of a part-time legislature and a full-time professionalized bureaucracy created the conditions for a policy process that could escape the usual partisan divides. Reformers did not use this institutional imbalance to shut out political considerations. Instead, they engaged in coalition-building in order to provide support for passage and implementation of the policy. The success of such an undertaking, given the complications of the health arena, should not be underestimated.

The demise of the original Oregon Health Plan, however, is a cautionary tale for CCO advocates. Ambitious reforms frequently unravel.[55] The current transformation benefits from significant financial support from the federal government—not only the 100 percent reimbursement for the Medicaid expansion but also the additional federal dollars secured for Oregon in promise of delivering reduced health-care costs through the CCO waiver. Federal reimbursement rates for the Medicaid expansion dropped to 90 percent after 2016 and may be subject to further cuts in a changed national administration.

President Trump and congressional Republicans have vowed to repeal the ACA. Current estimates are that repeal of the individual subsidies and the Medicaid expansion along with the mandate would double the number of uninsured, dramatically increase uncompensated medical costs for doctors and hospitals, and result in employment reductions in health care and other sectors. A George Washington University analysis concluded that repeal of the ACA without a replacement policy would cost Oregon forty-five thousand jobs in 2019 and generate a cumulative loss for state and local revenue of more than $800 million over five years.[56] Republican replacement proposals vary widely but generally seek to reduce federal spending on health care, which will create new fiscal pressures for states.

Health-care transformation involved long-range planning, sustained over successive Democratic state administrations and supported by a Democratic national administration. Although a dogged defender of health reform was found in Governor Kitzhaber, he is out of office again, replaced by a Democrat who is sympathetic to health reform but may not be a champion of it. Finally, the bureaucracy and its health policy experts have enjoyed an unusual level of continuity, even as governors changed. That kind of continuity may not be possible in the future. Given the need for sustained investment in health-care reform as well as the inherent complexity of the mesh of federal and state policies, public and private components, and competing interests, transformative policies encounter difficulties regardless of the leadership. Potential changes in federal policy and broad uncertainty in the market make state-level policies newly vulnerable.

Notes

1   Karen Davis, Kristof Stremikis, David Squires, and Cathy Schoen, "Mirror, Mirror on the Wall, 2014 Update: How the U.S. Health Care System Compares Internationally," *Commonwealth Fund*, June 16, 2014, http://www.commonwealthfund.org/publications/fund-reports/2014/jun/mirror-mirror.

2   "Health Insurance Coverage of the Total Population: 2015," Kaiser Family Foundation, accessed April 21, 2018, kff.org/other/state-indicator/total-population/?currentTimeframe=0.

3   "Health Insurance Coverage."

4   Over one million Oregonians were enrolled in OHP in 2016. Oregon Health Authority, *Quarterly Legislative Report, Q1 2016* (Salem: Oregon Health Authority, September 1, 2016), http://www.oregon.gov/oha/HPA/ANALYTICS/Documents/Legislative-Report-Q1-2016.pdf.

5   John Iselin and Philip Stallworth, "Who Benefits from Health-Care Related Tax Expenditures?," Tax Policy Center of the Urban Institute and Brookings Institution, August 22, 2016, http://www.taxpolicycenter.org/taxvox/who-benefits-health-care-related-tax-expenditures.

6   "Government Finance: State Government," Oregon Blue Book website, accessed April 21, 2018, bluebook.state.or.us/state/govtfinance/govtfinance01.htm.

7   Legislative Fiscal Office, *2015-2017 Legislatively Adopted Budget Detailed Analysis* (Salem: State of Oregon, October 2015), www.oregonlegislature.gov/lfo/Documents/2015-17%20LAB%20Detailed%20Analysis.pdf.

8   Congressional Budget Office, *Private Health Insurance Premiums and Federal Policy* (Washington, DC: Congressional Budget Office, February 2016), https://www.cbo.gov/sites/default/files/114th-congress-2015-2016/reports/51130-Health_Insurance_Premiums.pdf.

9   "Individual Insurance Market Competition," Kaiser Family Foundation, public use file for 2014, as of October 7, 2015, kff.org/other/state-indicator/individual-insurance-market-competition/?currentTimeframe=0&sortModel=%7B%22colId%22:%22Location%22,%22sort%22:%22asc%22%7D.

10   "Individual Insurance Market Competition." Oregon's HHI is 2,942 out of a scale of 10,000, with 10,000 being no competition. Any score over 2,500 is considered a highly concentrated market.

11   "Expanded History," We Can Do Better, accessed March 18, 2015, www.wecandobetter.org/who-we-are/history/expanded-history/.

12   "John Kitzhaber at the Rally for the Oregon Better Health Act," YouTube video, 9:45, posted by archimedesmovement, March 26, 2007, www.youtube.com/watch?v=noLbqHptOd8.

13   John Kitzhaber and Mark Gibson, "The Crisis in Health Care—The Oregon Health Plan as a Strategy for Change," *Stanford Law and Policy Review* 3 (1991): 64-72.

14   Janet B. Mitchell, Susan Haber, Galina Khatutsky, and Suzanne Donoghue, "Impact of the Oregon Health Plan on Access and Satisfaction of Adults with Low Income," *Health Services Research* 37, no. 1 (2002): 11-31; Thomas Bodenheimer, MD, "The Oregon Health Plan—Lessons for the Nation—First of Two Parts," *New England Journal of Medicine* 337, no. 9 (1997): 651-56.

15   Philip Perry and Timothy Hotze, "Oregon's Experiment with Prioritizing Public Health Care Services," *American Medical Association Journal of Ethics* 13 (2011): 244; Jonathan Oberlander, "Health Reform Interrupted: The Unraveling of the Oregon Health Plan," *Health Affairs* 26, no. 1 (2007): 102.

16   Philip A. Perry, MSJ, and Timothy Hotze, "Oregon's Experiment with Prioritizing Public Health Care Services," *American Medical Association Journal of Ethics* 13, no. 4 (April 2011): 244, and Oberlander, "Health Reform Interrupted," 99.

17   "How Much Does the U.S. Spend on Health and How Has It Changed?," Kaiser Family Foundation, May 1, 2012, www.kff.org/report-section/health-care-costs-a-primer-2012-report/.

18   Oberlander, "Health Reform Interrupted," 102.

19   Katherine Baicker, PhD, et al., "The Oregon Experiment—Effects of Medicaid on Clinical Outcomes," *New England Journal of Medicine* 368, no. 18 (May 2, 2013): 1721.

20 Perry and Hotze, "Oregon's Experiment," 241-47.

21 Oberlander, "Health Reform Interrupted," 100.

22 Oregon Health Policy Commission, *Road Map for Health Care Reform: Creating a High-Value, Affordable Health Care System*, submitted to Governor Kulongoski, July 2007.

23 "House Health Care Committee Public Hearing on HB 2009," Oregon State Legislature, January 26, 2009, https://olis.leg.state.or.us/liz/2009R1/Committees/HHC/2009-01-26-15-00/Agenda.

24 "House Health Care Committee Public Hearing on HB 2009."

25 The Oregon Senate vote attracted a handful of additional Republicans along with the support of every Democratic senator.

26 *National Federation of Independent Business v. Sebelius*, 567 U.S. (2012).

27 "Where Are States Today? Medicaid and CHIP Eligibility Levels for Adults, Children and Pregnant Women," Kaiser Family Foundation, January 19, 2017, kff.org/medicaid/fact-sheet/where-are-states-today-medicaid-and-chip/.

28 Samantha Artiga, Anthony Damico, and Rachel Garfield, "The Impact of the Coverage Gap for Adults in States Not Expanding Medicaid by Race and Ethnicity," Kaiser Family Foundation, October 26, 2015, kff.org/disparities-policy/issue-brief/the-impact-of-the-coverage-gap-in-states-not-expanding-medicaid-by-race-and-ethnicity/.

29 "State Health Insurance Marketplace Types, 2018," Kaiser Family Foundation, accessed May 25, 2018, http://kff.org/health-reform/state-indicator/state-health-insurance-marketplace-types/.

30 "Cover Oregon Is Dead; Brown Signs Bill Eliminating Troubled Exchange," *Associated Press*, March 6, 2015.

31 "Key Facts about the Uninsured Population," Kaiser Family Foundation, September 29, 2016, https://www.sandersinstitute.com/blog/key-facts-about-the-uninsured-population.

32 Garfield et al., "Estimates of Eligibility."

33 K. John McConnell et al., "Oregon's Medicaid Transformation: An Innovative Approach to Holding a Health Care System Accountable for Spending Growth," *Healthcare*, August 7, 2013.

34 Oregon Health Authority, *Oregon's Health System Transformation: 2014 Mid-Year Report* (Salem: Oregon Health Authority, January 14, 2015), http://www.oregon.gov/oha/HPA/ANALYTICS/MetricsScoringMeetingDocuments/2014-Mid-Year-Report.pdf.

35 Oregon Health Authority, *Oregon's Health System Transformation*.

36 Sarah Kliff, "Can Oregon Save American Health Care?," *Washington Post*, January 18, 2013.

37 K. J. McConnell et al., "Early Performance in Medicaid Accountable Care Organizations: A Comparison of Oregon and Colorado," *JAMA Internal Medicine* 177, no. 4 (April 1, 2017): 538-45. See also McConnell et al., "Oregon's Medicaid Reform and Transition to Global Budgets Were Associated with Reductions in Expenditures," *Health Affairs* 36, no. 3 (March 2017): 451-59.

38 Steven H. Landers and Ashwini R. Sehgal, "Health Care Lobbying in the United States," *American Journal of Medicine* 116 (April 1, 2004): 474-77.

39 John Evans III, MD, "The Map of Health Care Is Changing," *Medicine in Oregon* (Fall 2010): 4, emphasis original.

40 Evans, "Map of Health Care Is Changing," 5.

41 Joanne Bryson, "Deep Budget Deficits Drive Legislative Session," *Medicine in Oregon* (Spring 2011): 6.

42 Bob Dannenhoffer, MD, "A Reform Story: How We'll Care for Mary," *Medicine in Oregon* (Fall 2012): 21-22.

43 Dannenhoffer, "Reform Story," 22.

44 Centers for Medicaid and Medicare Services and Mathematica Policy Research, *Medicaid Managed Care Enrollment and Program Characteristics, 2015* (Baltimore, MD: Centers for Medicaid and Medicare Services, Winter 2016), https://www.medicaid.gov/medicaid/managed-care/downloads/enrollment/2015-medicaid-managed-care-enrollment-report.pdf.

45 "Total Medicaid Managed Care Enrollment," Kaiser Family Foundation, accessed April 21, 2018, kff.org/medicaid/state-indicator/total-medicaid-mc-enrollment/.

46 Bob Dannenhoffer and John Moorhead, "Liability Reform: The Oregon Opportunity," *Medicine in Oregon* (Fall 2012): 20.

47 Saerom Yoo, "Salem Hospital Drops Suit against CCO," *Statesman Journal*, July 9, 2013.

48 Virginia Gray, David Lowery, and Jennifer Benz, *Interest Groups and Health Care Reform across the States* (Washington, DC: Georgetown University Press, 2013), 166-67.

49 Gray et al., *Interest Groups*, 165.

50 Gray et al., *Interest Groups*, 184.

51 Richard Ellis, "Direct Democracy," in *Oregon Politics and Government: Progressives versus Conservative Populists*, ed. Richard A. Clucas, Brent Steel, and Mark Henkels (Lincoln: University of Nebraska Press, 2005).

52 Senator Bates died on August 5, 2016, while holding office.

53 Oregon Health Authority, *Oregon's Action Plan for Health* (Salem: Oregon Health Authority, December 2010), 7, http://www.oregon.gov/oha/actionplan/rpt-2010.pdf.

54 Oregon Health Authority, *Transforming the Oregon Health Plan* (Salem: Oregon Health Authority, September/October 2011).

55 Eric Patashnik, *Reforms at Risk: What Happens after Major Policy Changes are Enacted* (Princeton, NJ: Princeton University Press, 2008).

56 Leighton Ku, Erika Steinmetz, Erin Brantley, and Brian Bruen. *The Economic and Employment Consequences of Repealing Federal Health Reform: A 50 State Analysis* (Washington, DC: Center for Health Policy Research, George Washington University, January 5, 2017), publichealth.gwu.edu/sites/default/files/downloads/HPM/Repealing_Federal_Health_Reform.pdf.

15

Oregon Social Policy
The Safety Net
LEANNE GIORDONO AND MARK EDWARDS

Extending from the edges of tall buildings under construction, one can see safety nets, which are intended to protect workers and members of the public from potential harm. Without such nets, a long fall will result in death or permanent injury to either workers or people below. Similarly, the US federal social safety net, and the Oregon version of it, is intended to catch people from "falling" into poverty and to protect low-income individuals, families, and communities from hardship. But the strength, weave, resilience, and positioning of the safety net have changed substantially over time.

In 2014, 15 percent of Americans were living in poverty, meaning that for those individuals, total pretax family income[1] was lower than the poverty threshold (adjusted for size of family and number of related children under age 18). In Oregon, the average poverty rate for individuals in 2013-15 was about the same as in the United States as a whole (13% vs. 14%, respectively), and child poverty in Oregon (for those under age 6) also resembled that of the rest of the United States, around 25 percent.[2] During a similar timeframe (2009-13), poverty rates for households varied considerably among Oregon counties, from 9.8 percent in Clackamas County to 27 percent in Malheur County.[3]

The social safety net includes some of the largest and best-known poverty alleviation programs, such as Temporary Assistance for Needy Families (TANF, often called "welfare"), the Earned Income Tax Credit (EITC), Supplemental Security Income (SSI), the Supplemental Nutrition Assistance Program (SNAP, formerly known as food stamps), and "Section 8" Housing Choice Vouchers.[4] In 2015, approximately $362 billion, or 10 percent of the 2015 federal budget, was allocated to safety net programs, including income security (5% of the federal budget), food and nutrition assistance (3%), housing (1%), and unemployment compensation (1%).[5]

At any given time, the percentage of Americans receiving funds from any of these programs is relatively low (1% receiving TANF, 4% receiving housing aid, and 13% receiving SNAP). From 2009 to 2012, however, over 25 percent of Americans participated in one or more major means-tested programs for one or more months.[6] Demographers estimate that 58 percent of all American adults will have experienced at least one year of poverty at some point in their lives, and nearly two-thirds will have spent some time in a household receiving help from a social safety net program.[7] While most safety net programs are "means-tested" (i.e., subject to eligibility rules), program rules, benefits, and expected outcomes can vary substantially by program type and jurisdiction.

The term "social safety net" dates back to the early 1980s, when it was popularized by President Ronald Reagan's administration.[8] However, the federal tradition of providing income support and other forms of poverty relief through public policy and programs began decades earlier with adoption of the Social Security Act of 1935, launched by President Roosevelt as part of the New Deal initiative. The term "safety net" is now widely used by researchers and policy makers alike to describe the whole of poverty alleviation efforts. While an interest in poverty alleviation is neither inherently conservative nor liberal, debate has been predictably political over expanding or shrinking traditional safety net programs. In Washington, DC, as well as in many state capitals, decision makers have vigorously debated the form and function of the safety net, asking questions such as:

- Who should be eligible for assistance?
- How poor should one be to be eligible for assistance?
- How long should people rely on public assistance?
- How often should recipients prove their eligibility?
- What types of assistance should be provided?
- What kinds of requirements should be imposed on recipients?

In this chapter, we summarize the evolution and key elements of the federal approach to "catching" those who fall into poverty and describe how Oregon policy makers, advocates, and nonprofit groups have creatively tended to the safety net within the context of the federalist system. We describe Oregon's approach to four discrete poverty alleviation areas: income, food, housing, and caregiving. Our descriptions of Oregon's approach to income, food, and housing assistance show how Oregon has addressed needs traditionally associated with poverty alleviation strategies. We include caregiving assistance to illustrate Oregon's response to pressing new issues related to the changing workforce, economic growth, and changes in the approach to poverty alleviation itself.

Oregon's approach to tending the state's social safety net reflects a distinctive weave of strategies that leverage federal opportunities and funding, incorporate input from advocacy groups and researchers, and respond to the state's changing economic and social circumstances. Oregon leaders have, by necessity, turned to innovative and collaborative strategies to maintain a level of support for Oregonians that preserves state-level priorities within the context of the larger federal system. While Oregon has participated in, and even contributed to, the growing policy emphasis on individual responsibility (in lieu of government support), the state has maintained a strong commitment to supporting families and individuals during times of crisis, economic downturns, and longer-term demographic and economic shifts, reflecting a generally progressive approach to social programs. The recent political dominance by Democrats and a pro-welfare political climate have helped contribute to the overall level of support for a strong social safety net.

THE FEDERAL SAFETY NET:
AN EVOLVING APPROACH TO POVERTY ALLEVIATION

The earliest New Deal poverty alleviation programs, launched in 1935, included unemployment insurance, old-age assistance, aid to dependent children, and an early version of food stamps. Amendments to Social Security during the 1950s and early 1960s included President Lyndon Johnson's 1964 declaration of a "War on Poverty," which launched additional assistance programs and institutionalized the "welfare state" more broadly. Anti-poverty strategies have evolved considerably since then, shifting from cash transfers toward programs emphasizing labor market participation and in-kind transfers.[9] For example, the 1970s saw the development of the Earned Income Tax Credit (EITC) for low-income workers, as well as the growth of the Food Stamps Program, which dedicated funds to food assistance. Throughout the 1980s and 1990s, the emphasis on labor force participation continued, with multiple expansions of the EITC and introduction of legislation to increase work incentives among welfare recipients and low-income individuals. Similarly, the Personal Responsibility and Work Opportunity Act of 1996 resulted in major welfare reforms, including strict work requirements and lifetime limits on benefits.

The role of states in safety net programs and policy has also evolved over time, especially during the 1980s and 1990s, when the federal government shifted from issuing categorical grants to states (i.e., grants with narrowly defined purposes and specific spending requirements) to block grants (i.e., grants with broad provisions for expenditures).[10] Known as "new federalism," this shift in federal policy sought to give states more freedom by allowing states to play a much more active "weaver" role in determining spending priorities and consolidating duplicative programs. Even among programs funded by categorical grants, such as Medicaid, the federal government has offered more flexibility in the last several decades, via waivers (i.e., formal exceptions to legislated priorities). Other programs, including SNAP, remain fully federally funded (i.e., benefits pass directly to individuals), but states administer the programs via contract, and can also take advantage of waivers to federal program rules.[11]

Given the federal system's level of complexity, the social safety net concept is an apt metaphor for the connectedness and comprehensiveness of those programs and policies. However, the shifts in priorities, program designs, and funding instruments also suggest that the safety net is an evolving system that reflects both federal- and state-level changes in priorities and interests. Indeed, Oregon's approach to weaving the safety net echoes federal priorities and design, while retaining unique qualities reflective of Oregon's own needs and preferences.

INCOME ASSISTANCE
Broad Context

Income assistance programs redistribute income to specific groups of people, either via direct cash benefits or tax credits. Eligibility for income support programs is typically based on characteristics such as age or disability (categorical programs) or income level (means-tested programs). Income support programs have evolved considerably since the initial adoption of the Social Security Act of 1935, which introduced the first systematic income support programs. While early income support programs were focused on providing unconditional cash benefits, the late twentieth-century reforms shifted income support toward work-dependent and time-limited cash benefits, as well as income-related tax credits, all aimed at increasing the incentive for welfare recipients to work.

Currently, three major federal income redistribution programs are directly aimed at providing income supports to individuals in poverty in the United States.[12] Two of these programs, Supplemental Security Income (SSI) and Temporary Assistance for Needy Families (TANF), are delivered as cash benefits. The third program, the Earned Income Tax Credit (EITC), is delivered as a federal tax credit. Multiple states have adopted their own EITC as a supplement to the federal EITC.

Supplemental Security Income provides cash benefits to low-income seniors, adults with a disability, and children with a disability from low-income families. SSI is distinct from both Social Security retirement benefits and Social Security Disability Income (SSDI), which are contingent on prior work history; in contrast, there are no limits or work requirements associated with SSI receipt. SSI is closely associated with Medicaid health insurance participation because most SSI recipients are "categorically" eligible for Medicaid. The federal government is responsible for funding SSI, setting SSI policies, and administering SSI payments, which leaves states with little room for flexibility.

Temporary Assistance for Needy Families provides cash and selected other benefits to low-income families, contingent on meeting work requirements. TANF eligibility is means-tested, and TANF participants are subject to a lifetime limit on benefits receipt. While federal legislation determines broad policy, federal TANF funds are provided to states via block grants, which gives states flexibility with respect to eligibility determination, work requirements, and benefits packages but limits the amount of federal funds available to states. To receive federal funds, states are required to achieve state-specific work participation rates among TANF recipients.

The Earned Income Tax Credit, which was first introduced in the 1970s and significantly expanded in the 1990s, provides a federal tax credit to working families to offset the household's tax liability. The EITC is refundable, so if the EITC exceeds the worker's tax liability, the Internal Revenue Service will repay the balance in the form of a lump-sum check. The EITC targets low- and moderate-income working families with dependent children, although some individuals without partners or dependents are also eligible to receive the tax credit. The EITC is designed to incentivize labor force participation, increase take-home earnings, and provide additional assistance to raise living standards.

Oregon Approach

Oregon's approach to income assistance is largely reflective of federal policies and guidelines, but the state has taken advantage of the flexibility of federal policy to make distinctive choices, demonstrating the state's capacity to innovate within the bounds of federal priorities and guidelines, as well as its willingness to "buck the trend." However, the state's history also demonstrates some inconsistency and sensitivity to fiscal pressures. Table 15.1 provides a snapshot of the prevalence of poverty among Oregonians, as well as Oregon participation in TANF and EITC.

Table 15.1. Oregon social policy: Income assistance

Indicator	Key Data
People living in Oregon (2016)[a]	4,093,465 persons
Children >18 years old living in Oregon (2016)[a]	867,815 children
People living in poverty in Oregon (2016)[b]	538,169 persons
	13% of all persons
Children <18 years old living in poverty (2016)[b]	146,609 children
	17% of all children
Federal poverty threshold for family of four (2016)[c]	$24,250
Oregonians receiving TANF per month (2016)[d]	36,985 persons
	1% of all persons
Children receiving TANF per month in Oregon (2016)[d]	26,666 children
	3% of all children
Oregon taxpayers claiming federal EITC (2016)[e]	286,000 claims
Average federal EITC claim among Oregonians[e]	$2,110

a. "Quick Facts Oregon," US Census Bureau, accessed December 20, 2017, https://www.census.gov/quickfacts/OR.
b. "Small Area Income and Poverty Estimates," US Census Bureau, accessed December 20, 2017, https://www.census.gov/programs-surveys/saipe.html.
c. "2015 Poverty Guidelines: 09/03/15," US Department of Health and Human Services, September 5, 2015, https://aspe.hhs.gov/2015-poverty-guidelines.
d. "TANF Caseload Data 2015," Office of Family Assistance, June 24, 2016, https://www.acf.hhs.gov/ofa/resource/tanf-caseload-data-2015.
e. "Statistics for 2016 Tax Returns with EITC," US Internal Revenue Service, accessed December 20, 2017, https://www.eitc.irs.gov/eitc-central/statistics-for-tax-returns-with-eitc/statistics-for-2016-tax-year-returns-with-eitc.

Even prior to 1996 welfare reform, Oregon had begun to invest in employment-focused strategies and was considered an innovator among the states with respect to promoting self-sufficiency and reducing TANF caseloads in the early 1990s.[13] During the remainder of the decade, however, overall inflation-adjusted spending on self-sufficiency programs (i.e., cash as well as work-related, child care, and emergency assistance) declined owing to fiscal pressures, decreasing caseloads and flexibility in TANF guidelines, and diversion of TANF funds to other programs.[14]

In alignment with 1996 welfare reforms, the proportion of TANF funding spent on basic cash assistance had declined to 25 percent by 2005.[15] With the onset of the recession in 2008, however, Oregon placed a renewed emphasis on increasing access to cash assistance, in contrast with other states' efforts to reduce spending on cash assistance.[16] During the recession, as unemployment rose steeply, Oregon absorbed the growing need for income assistance by increasing contributions from the state's general fund, yielding increased expenditures on cash assistance, increased case manager workloads, decreased expenditures on other client services (e.g., job training and childcare subsidies), and decreased attention to TANF work requirements and time limits.[17] At the end of the recession in 2010, Oregon experienced the lowest work participation rate among TANF recipients compared to all other states, at 8 percent,[18] although the rate steadily increased to almost 52 percent in 2014.[19] These controversial steps underscore Oregon's willingness to adjust cash assistance levels during an era of economic hardship, although the decision came at the cost of work-related assistance and, relatedly, employment outcomes.

Oregon is among twenty-six states that offer a state EITC, illustrating Oregon's interest in supplementing the safety net.[20] Initially adopted in 1997 as a nonrefundable credit (i.e., the worker would only receive a credit equal to the tax liability), the Oregon Earned Income Credit (OEIC) was made refundable in 2006, similar to the federal EITC, so that workers with tax liability lower than the credit receive a rebate equal to the balance. Like most other states, the Oregon tax credit is determined as a percentage of the federal tax credit; the proportion has grown from 5 percent in 1997 to 11 percent for families with children under age 3 and 8 percent for all other families in 2016.[21] Despite these efforts, Oregon families have one of the lowest rates of federal EITC participation in the nation, suggesting that there may be unique barriers to access among low-income working families.[22]

Oregon's approach to income assistance is generally progressive and illustrates the state's willingness to innovate within the constraints of the federal system, to supplement federal programs, and to resist federal guidance and national trends, in response to perceived needs and changing circumstances. Oregon's approach also suggests that income assistance is sensitive to fiscal pressures that can limit the types, amounts, and consistency of resources available to low-income individuals and families.

HUNGER AND FOOD INSECURITY
Broad Context

In a nation that produces more food than it can eat, and that pays its farmers to produce less than they could, it often comes as a surprise that tens of millions of people struggle to get enough food to lead a productive, healthy life. Since the mid-1990s, the US Department of Agriculture has sought to reduce the level of "food insecurity" among American households. A household is food insecure if it shows several indications of difficulty obtaining enough healthy food.[23] If a family shows many more indications of this difficulty, then it is categorized as having "very low food security" (sometimes still referred to by advocates as "hunger").

The federal government has focused on three main safety net strategies to ensure that low-income American households are adequately fed: (1) distributing excess commodities such as cereals (rice, corn, etc.), beef (canned), cheese, milk, and orange juice; (2) providing targeted cash benefits (SNAP and WIC, also known as Special Supplemental Nutrition Assistance Program for Women, Infants and Children) for food purchases; and (3) providing meals in public schools.[24] The excess commodities are provided to states through The Emergency Food Assistance Program (TEFAP) and are often distributed through the network of food pantries coordinated nationally by the nonprofit organization Feeding America. SNAP and WIC provide dedicated food money for families and individuals, with WIC focusing on prenatal health as well as young children and their mothers, and SNAP providing for a wide variety of household and family types.

In 2008, during the midst of the recession, SNAP enrollment had already begun to grow to 31.4 million people (14.1 million households).[25] That number continued to grow throughout the recession and, despite the economic recovery, remained high at 43.5 million people (21.4 million households) in 2016.[26] Historically, enrollments in SNAP roughly tracked with unemployment rates, but since the recession, SNAP participation remains high even among families that have part-time jobs or low-paying full-time jobs. In contrast, WIC enrollment peaked at 9.2 million women in 2010 but, somewhat inexplicably, declined by about 10 percent by 2016.[27]

Oregon Context

Since 1999, Oregon, despite its strong agricultural sector, has consistently had one of the highest levels of "very low food security" in comparison to other states. This high level of distress for families has puzzled researchers, who note that Oregon does not have especially high levels of poverty. New evidence suggests that recent rises in rent, as a proportion of prevailing wages, in combination with fluctuating, high unemployment and a concentration of low-income people in a high-rent location (Portland), has contributed to Oregon's food insecurity.[28] Moreover, among remote rural communities that experience even more volatile seasonal unemployment rates, the struggle

Table 15.2. Oregon social policy: Addressing hunger and food insecurity

Indicator	Key Data
People experiencing food insecurity per year (2014-16)[a]	560,000 persons
	14% of all persons
People experiencing very low food security per year (2014-16)[a]	238,000 persons
	6% of persons
Oregonians receiving SNAP per month (2017)[b]	510,000 persons
	13% of persons
Median amount of time on SNAP for a recipient in Oregon (2008-9)[c]	11 months
National average SNAP monthly benefit (2017)[d]	
one-person household	$142
two-person household	$253
three-person household	$379
four-person household	$465

a. Mark Edwards, "Food Insecurity in Oregon and the U.S.: Uneven Recovery in the Midst of Overall Improvement (2014-2016)," Oregon State University School of Public Policy and the Rural Studies Program, accessed December 20, 2017, https://appliedecon.oregonstate.edu/sites/agscid7/files/oregonhungerreport_28oct2017.pdf
b. Oregon Department of Human Services, SNAP Caseload Report, accessed December 20, 2017, http://www.oregon.gov/DHS/ASSISTANCE/Branch%20District%20Data/SNAP%20Flash%20Figures%20for%20September%202017.pdf.
c. Mark Edwards, Suzanne Porter, and Bruce Weber, "The Great Recession and SNAP Caseloads: A Tale of Two States," Journal of Poverty 20, no. 3 (2016): 261–77, doi:10.1080/10875549.2015.1094770.
d. "A Quick Guide to SNAP Eligibility and Benefits," Center on Policy and Budget Priorities, accessed December 20, 2017, https://www.cbpp.org/research/a-quick-guide-to-snap-eligibility-and-benefits.

to consistently feed a family throughout the year remains a considerable challenge for families throughout the state. Table 15.2 shows keys indicators related to food insecurity, including prevalence and program participation by Oregonians.

Nonetheless, Oregon's food security situation would likely be worse if it were not for Oregon's policy environment, which fosters collaboration and innovation by state agencies and nonprofit organizations.[29] In 1990, the Oregon legislature declared that freedom from hunger was a human right, and lawmakers vowed to pursue the elimination of hunger from the state,[30] which resulted in creation of the Oregon Hunger Task Force (OHTF), a diverse group of representatives from state agencies, nonprofits, and other sectors. Since the mid-1990s, the OHTF has convened regularly to discuss opportunities for collaboration and coordination, eliminating "silos" and yielding service improvements. For example, the OHTF has supported a service-oriented approach to providing SNAP and pilot programs to expand emergency food distribution throughout the state.[31] The Oregon Food Bank (OFB), a nonprofit organization that coordinates and distributes emergency food throughout the entire state, regularly testifies in the capitol and participates in the OHTF.

The OHTF has prioritized bringing in federal dollars to address Oregon's high hunger rate. Because SNAP is a federal program administered by states, the state must abide by federal policies, while deciding when and how to take advantage of various waivers (i.e., exceptions that permit the state to avoid doing something prescribed or to try a new approach that is not prohibited). For example, Oregon's Department of Human Services was among the first state agencies that took advantage of an opportunity to make more people eligible for SNAP through "broad-based categorical eligibility," whereby a person who was found to be qualified for TANF or for the Low-Income Home Energy Assistance Program (LIHEAP) was automatically qualified, and received, SNAP.

Oregon's efforts to identify, recruit, and qualify more SNAP participants has yielded a nationally exemplary (top five) rate of program participation among eligible individuals.[32] In many states, between half and three-quarters of eligible people receive the SNAP benefits for which they are eligible, but Oregon remains among the most effective at enrolling residents with nearly 100 percent participation (as calculated by the US Department of Agriculture). During the recession, while many other states' human services agencies were unprepared for the rapid rise of newly poor Americans, Oregon invested resources to expand personnel and outreach throughout the state and enrolled record numbers.[33]

The Oregon story about addressing hunger is one of sometimes unexpected contrasts, innovative bureaucratic maneuvering, and institutionalized collaboration. Nationally recognized success at SNAP enrollment suggests that available safety net solutions can indeed be implemented, yet moderate to high food insecurity rates reveal that SNAP alone is insufficient for solving the problem. Leadership within the state has contributed to public awareness, while also bringing in federal dollars and using available waivers have increased Oregon's visibility among legislatures, state agencies, and nonprofits.

HOUSING
Broad Context

Since the Great Depression of the 1930s, federal housing policy has focused on expanding home ownership through such major government-sponsored mortgage enterprises as Fannie Mae and Freddie Mac. Home ownership is a significant part of the typical American family's wealth portfolio, with housing wealth equaling about half of household net worth in America.[34] The US homeownership rate peaked in 2005 at 69 percent, but the collapse of the housing market "bubble" resulted in a sharp drop in homeownership during and after the recession, with a disproportionate impact on low-income and minority families.[35] During that period, the overall rate of homeownership in the United States fell to 64 percent, similar to the 1980s.[36]

While the public and private mortgage markets clearly influence homeownership trends, they are supplemented by other federal efforts to influence homeownership and rental housing availability and affordability. The federal US Department of Housing and Urban Development (HUD) is the primary source of support for affordable housing and related community investments, funded through Community Development Block Grants (CDBG) and managed at the state and local levels. Since the 1970s, there has been little construction of publicly managed and owned affordable housing, with most housing funds targeting public investment in affordable housing and rent subsidies, which enable families to rent from private landowners.

HUD defines families who pay more than 30 percent of their income for housing as "cost burdened."[37] As of 2014, over half of renter households, and over 80 percent of the lowest-income renter households, were considered cost burdened in 2014.[38] These trends have been exacerbated by a shortage of affordable housing influenced by high land and wage costs as well as land use and planning decisions, especially in urban areas, illustrating the need for creative solutions to complex problems.

Oregon Context

The Oregon housing story echoes the overall US experience. After a 2005 peak home-ownership rate of 69 percent, the decline associated with the collapse of the housing bubble and the recession brought the rate back to 61 percent, similar to Oregon low points in the mid-1980s and mid-1990s.[39] On average, renter households in Oregon spend just over 30 percent of their family income on housing, but the lowest-income groups have been substantially more cost burdened.[40] Table 15.3 displays selected indicators of Oregon housing burden experience and related program participation.

Like other states, Oregon's effort to address housing affordability and availability for low-income individuals and families is characterized by a multifaceted approach that combines federal assistance with state and local initiatives. Oregon's strategy, spearheaded by Oregon Housing and Community Services (OCHS), relies on a

Table 15.3. Oregon social policy: Addressing housing inequality

Indicator	Key Data
Oregon households experiencing housing burden (2007-11)a	200,000 households
	15% of all households
Oregon households receiving housing vouchers (2016)b	43,000 households
	3% of all households
Total federal housing voucher funds for Oregon (2016)b	$406 million
Estimated number of homeless persons in Oregon in any given month (2017)c	13,953 persons

a. "Housing Statistics Comparison Table: 2007-2011 American Community Survey," Oregon Housing and Community Services, accessed December 20, 2017, http://www.oregon.gov/ohcs/Pages/research-multifamily-housing-demographics-data.aspx.

b. "Oregon Fact Sheet: Federal Rental Assistance," Center on Budget and Policy Priorities, accessed December 20, 2017, https://www.cbpp.org/sites/default/files/atoms/files/4-13-11hous-OR.pdf.

c. "2017 Point-in-Time Estimates of Homelessness in Oregon," Oregon Housing and Community Services, accessed December 20, 2017, http://www.oregon.gov/ohcs/ISD/RA/2017-Point-in-Time-Estimates-Homelessness-Oregon.pdf.

number of longstanding federal and state programs to address housing stability issues, but the growing concern about housing affordability (renting or purchasing), especially in urban areas, has provided fertile ground for new investments and innovations.

Beyond the work of OHCS, the Oregon legislature passed Senate Bill 1533 in 2016, rescinding a seventeen-year-old prohibition on inclusionary housing and allowing cities to offer tax incentives or other concessions (e.g., building height) in exchange for requiring developers to set aside new low-income multifamily units.[41] In response, the Portland metropolitan region passed a 1 percent new construction tax in 2016, which is expected to raise $12 million for affordable housing.[42] Oregon cities, through collaboration between government agencies, developers, local service providers, and grassroots activists, have also developed active strategies to develop creative solutions to local housing challenges. In the City of Wilsonville, for example, funds from the sale of the Dammasch State Hospital (a former state-run mental institution) were used to develop seventy-five integrated housing units for individuals with serious mental health issues in the privately developed Villebois Community.[43]

Housing affordability issues often include concerns about homelessness. Oregon's homeless population was estimated at 13,628 in 2016, less than 1 percent of the total population. That said, Oregon has one of the highest rates (61%) of unsheltered homeless individuals in the country.[44] The issue of homelessness is complex, with diverse causes ranging from poverty, to high housing burden, to mental health and addiction issues. In part, the complexity reflects the underlying heterogeneity of the homeless population. In Oregon, the largest share of homeless individuals are people in families with children (41%), followed closely by those experiencing chronic homelessness (33%), with the remainder almost equally divided between veterans (14%) and unaccompanied youth (13%).[45] The barriers faced by these populations frequently include poverty, unemployment, mental health, and addiction.

There is no designated federal or Oregon-specific "homelessness" policy or funding stream. In 2003, however, a national call to end homelessness, accompanied by a ten-year plan, highlighted concerns about homelessness throughout the country. That effort gave rise to ten-year plans throughout the country, including in Oregon and among Oregon municipalities (e.g., Bend, Corvallis, Eugene, Medford, Portland, etc.). The Oregon plan includes a range of strategies, including prevention and intervention, permanent housing with supportive services, and system improvements, which are aligned with federal recommendations.[46] The federal Opening Doors initiative, adopted in 2010 and amended in 2015, called for system-wide strategies to address homelessness.

Oregon housing support policy is more focused on strategies that respond to, and influence, the broader housing market, rather than strategies that provide direct assistance to individuals, reflecting federal priorities to meet housing needs via markets rather than public housing investment and assistance to individuals. But the nature of housing markets, which are subject to a variety of local and regional forces (e.g., land-use policies, urbanization, etc.), has provided numerous opportunities for Oregon leaders (public, private, and nonprofit) to innovate in ways that address the rapidly changing housing environment.

MEETING CAREGIVING NEEDS
Broad Context

Although caregiving is not traditionally associated with the safety net programs, multiple factors have contributed to a growing recognition of the role of both caregiving services and supports in providing support to low-income and working families. First, the late twentieth-century rise in women's labor force participation and use of regular childcare arrangements, shifts in federal welfare and childcare policies, and growing evidence about the benefits of early care have yielded an interest in policy options for ensuring access to high-quality, affordable childcare among low-income families.[47] In 2011, at least 61 percent of children under the age of 5 were in a regular childcare arrangement, including almost 33 percent receiving care from nonrelatives.[48] Families below the federal poverty line with children under age 5 are less likely to use nonrelative childcare, but they spend a higher proportion of household income on childcare arrangements, with over 30 percent of their income spent on childcare in 2011.[49]

Second, in the United States and across the developed world, a "silver tsunami" is anticipated during the upcoming decades.[50] The combination of the swell from an aging baby boomer population and longer life expectancies is expected to change the age structure of the country, with the number of individuals aged 65 and over anticipated to double between 2012 and 2050, growing from 14 percent of the overall population to 21 percent.[51] Increased labor participation among women, who have traditionally served in caregiving roles for aging and disabled individuals, has also contributed to the growing need for alternative caregiving arrangements.

In the United States, strategies for addressing caregiving needs among low-income families are characterized by a combination of tax credits, means-tested supports, and subsidies, frequently delivered through distinct agencies and funding streams. At the federal level, Child and Dependent Care Credits (also known as the Elderly Dependent Care Credit, or the Aging Parent Tax Credit) can be used to defray expenses associated with childcare, home care, or adult supports for dependent adults.[52] Similarly, Head Start and Early Head Start are federally administered pre-kindergarten programs operated by local contractors; although these programs are means-tested, parental employment is not required. The major federal-state cooperative programs that fund caregiving assistance are the Child Care Development Fund (CCDF) and Medicaid Long Term Services and Supports (LTSS), which target childcare and long-term adult supports, respectively.[53]

While the CCDF is a block grant to states for operating childcare subsidy programs for working parents, Medicaid is operated as a categorical grant to states.

Despite those differences, state governments are required to provide matching funds for CCDF and have substantial discretion over CCDF rulemaking and program operations.[54] Similarly, the Medicaid LTSS program operates under broad federal guidelines but is financed jointly by federal and state funds.[55] Both programs rely on a network of private and nonprofit service providers that operate under state and federal guidelines.

Oregon Approach

The Oregon approach reflects a record of innovative and collaborative policy development within the broad constraints of federal policy and funding regulations, as well as strong leadership for the nation as a whole. Table 15.4 introduces key demographic and participation indicators related to caregiving supports for the state of Oregon.

Oregon has long been at the forefront of a nationwide evolution in publicly funded long-term services and support for low-income and dependent adults, reflecting state leadership, advocacy group activism, and participation in federally funded demonstration projects.[56] Early Oregon participation in the Medicaid 1915(c) waiver program and assisted-living innovations during the 1980s led to nationwide deinstitutionalization movements.[57] Several decades of reform and expansion resulted in a steady increase in the share of Oregon LTSS expenditures for home- and community-based care, from 1 percent in 1981 to 79 percent in 2014.[58] Most recently, Oregon was

Table 15.4. Oregon social policy: Meeting caregiving needs

Indicator	Key Data
People age 65 years and older (2016)[a]	687,702 persons
	17%
People with a disability, under 65 years old (2016)[a]	417,533
	10% of persons
People receiving Medicaid long-term supports and services (October 2017)[b]	34,809 persons
	1% of all persons
Households receiving Employment-Related Day Care subsidies (October 2017)[c]	8,613
Total amount of Oregon Earned Income Tax Credit and Working Family and Dependent Care Credits, combined (2014)[d]	>$66 million

a. "Quick Facts Oregon," US Census Bureau, accessed December 20, 2017, https://www.census.gov/quickfacts/OR.

b. "Monthly Caseload Variance Report, Department of Human Services, Aging and People with Disabilities," Oregon Department of Human Services, accessed December 20, 2017, http://www.oregon.gov/DHS/BUSINESS-SERVICES/OFRA/ofradocuments/APD%20Caseload%20Variance%20Report%20May17.pdf

c. "Monthly Caseload Variance Report, Department of Human Services, Self Sufficiency Programs," Oregon Department of Human Services, accessed December 20, 2017, http://www.oregon.gov/DHS/BUSINESS-SERVICES/OFRA/ofradocuments/SSP%20Caseload%20Variance%20Report%20Dec17.pdf.

d. "Oregon Personal Income Tax Statistics: Characteristics of Filers: 2016 Edition/Tax Year 2014," Oregon Department of Revenue, accessed December 20, 2017, http://www.oregon.gov/DOR/programs/gov-research/Documents/Oregon-personal-income-tax-statistics-2016.pdf.

among the early adopters of a new state plan (the K Plan) under the Affordable Care Act of 2010, which is expected to expand the types of services available to eligible individuals, retain the focus on service delivery in home- and community-based settings, and increase federal government investment by 6 percent.[59]

Oregon's interest in childcare support is a similarly long-standing effort marked by collaborative policymaking and research-based investments. Since 1987, Oregon has engaged in the Oregon Child Care Research Partnership, a long-term research partnership between state policy makers, childcare resource and referral agencies, childcare practitioners, university-based researchers, parents, and other stakeholders. The partnership convenes regularly to "define, create, and disseminate research on child care dynamics" and inform state policymaking.[60] The partnership has developed a variety of childcare research tools and guides (e.g., Market Rate Study Guidebook), establishing Oregon's status as a model for other states.[61]

Federal CCDF funds support operation of the state Employment-Related Day Care (ERDC) program, which provides childcare subsidies to low-income working families. In 2007, Oregon legislators supported a sizable increase in the generosity of CCDF subsidy payments related to legislation that increased funding by $40 million, yielding decreased copayment requirements, an increased income eligibility ceiling, and increased maximum reimbursement rates for providers.[62] Since 2007, Oregon has set payment rates so that families have access to almost 75 percent of the care in their community.[63]

Oregon has also offered a state-specific tax credit for childcare and dependent care since 1975, as well as a childcare credit targeting low-income families since 1997.[64] In 2016, Oregon combined separate state-specific tax credits for childcare and dependent care into one Working Family Child and Dependent Care Tax Credit.[65] Importantly, the state tax credit is "refundable," which means that families who are eligible for a credit exceeding the amount of owed taxes will receive a payment from the government amounting to the difference between the credit and taxes owed.[66]

In addition to innovating and investing in strategies to increase the availability and affordability of caregiving and support options for low-income families within the context of federal guidance, Oregon has shown a singular willingness to supplement federal funds and to experiment, characteristics that are associated with a high level of advocacy, fiscal pressures, strong leadership, and strong participatory policy discourse.

CONCLUSION

In the context of new federalism, commitments to buoy the poor broadly define the overall federal approach to the safety net, while state-level budgets shape and express politically and financially viable solutions within the existing federal constraints. In Oregon, leaders have leveraged new federalism to express ideals and concerns, actively experiment and innovate, and to demand or even neglect requirements. At the state level, local leadership, creativity, collaboration, and even courage have yielded a tighter and more expansive safety net. Oregon state agency and legislative leaders—as well as advocacy groups, nonprofit organizations, and other stakeholders at the local and state level—have influenced the social environment of low-income individuals, families, and communities.

The federal safety net has evolved over time, with direct (cash) support replaced by earnings (e.g., EITC) and in-kind benefits (e.g., SNAP). While the nation's official poverty rate has stayed flat since the War on Poverty was launched in 1965, the supplemental poverty rate, which includes noncash and tax-related benefits, has declined during the same period, especially among selected populations (e.g., elderly, blacks), suggesting that poverty alleviation policies have had a measurable influence on overall poverty.[67] That said, the supplemental poverty rate among children has increased and deep poverty rates have not been affected, suggesting that the safety net has not "caught" everyone.[68]

In the absence of clear evidence of impacts at the state level, it is challenging to demonstrate that the safety net is either adequate or effective at addressing the root causes of poverty, hunger, housing burden, and family care needs. However, Oregon's investment in strengthening the social safety net, even during the recession, illustrates that states can weave a safety net that leverages federal policy opportunities and transcends federal constraints. In time, we may find twentieth-century safety net institutions insufficient for addressing shifting demographic, economic, and political realities, necessitating further evolution at both the federal and state levels. If so, Oregon's history of innovation and collaboration may serve as a source of both inspiration and leadership.

Notes

1   Total pretax family income is all income excluding tax credits, noncash benefits, and capital gains/losses.

2   "Oregon: Early Childhood Profile," National Center for Children in Poverty, accessed April 21, 2018, www.nccp.org/profiles/OR_profile_16.html; "Income and Poverty in the United States: 2015: Inter-Relationships of 3-Year Average State Poverty Rates: 2013-2015," US Census Bureau, accessed May 7, 2018, census.gov/data/tables/2016/demo/income-poverty/p60-256.html.

3   "Oregon Poverty Rate by County," IndexMundi, accessed April 21, 2018, www.indexmundi.com/facts/united-states/quick-facts/oregon/percent-of-people-of-all-ages-in-poverty#map.

4   Health-care policy is also a traditional element of the safety net. Melissa Michaux discusses that topic in chapter 14.

5   "Policy Basics: Where Do Our Federal Tax Dollars Go?," Center on Budget and Policy Priorities, updated October 4, 2017, www.cbpp.org/research/federal-budget/policy-basics-where-do-our-federal-tax-dollars-go.

6   Shelley K. Irving and Tracy A. Loveless, *Dynamics of Economic Well-Being: Participation in Government Programs, 2009-2012: Who Gets Assistance?*, Household Economic Studies

(Washington, DC: US Census Bureau, May 2015), www.census.gov/content/dam/ Census/library/publications/2015/demo/p70-141.pdf; Mark R. Rank and Thomas A. Hirschl, "The Likelihood of Poverty across the American Adult Life Span," *Social Work* 44, no. 3 (May 1999): 201–16.

7   Mark R. Rank and Thomas A. Hirschl, "Welfare Use as a Life Course Event: Toward a New Understanding of the U.S. Safety Net," *Social Work* 47, no. 3 (July 2002): 237–48.

8   Krissy Clark, "How Did the Social Safety Net Get Its Name?," *Marketplace*, April 2, 2013, www.marketplace.org/2013/04/02/wealth-poverty/show-us-your-safety-net/how-did-social-safety-net-get-its-name; David E. Rosenbaum, "Reagan's 'Safety Net' Proposal: Who Will Land, Who Will Fall," *New York Times*, March 17, 1981, www.nytimes. com/1981/03/17/us/reagan-s-safety-net-proposal-who-will-land-who-will-fall-news-analysis.html.

9   Robert Haveman et al., "The War on Poverty: Measurement, Trends, and Policy," *Journal of Policy Analysis and Management* 34, no. 3 (June 1, 2015): 593–638, doi:10.1002/pam.21846.

10   Robert Jay Dilger and Eugene Boyd, "Block Grants: Perspectives and Controversies," *Congressional Research Service*, July 15, 2014, www.fas.org/sgp/crs/misc/R40486.pdf.

11   Dilger and Boyd, "Block Grants."

12   Jonathan Gruber, *Public Finance and Public Policy* (New York: Macmillan, 2013).

13   Susan Scrivener et al., *National Evaluation of Welfare-to-Work Strategies: Implementation, Participation Patterns, Costs, and Two-Year Impacts of the Portland (Oregon) Welfare-to-Work Program* (New York: Manpower Demonstration Research Corporation, May 1998), www.mdrc.org/sites/default/files/full_400.pdf.

14   Scrivener et al., *National Evaluation of Welfare-to-Work Strategies.*

15   "TANF Financial Data Archives," Administration for Children and Families, accessed May 7, 2018, archive.acf.hhs.gov/programs/ofs/data/archives.html.

16   Oregon Secretary of State, *Temporary Assistance for Needy Families: High Expectations, Stronger Partnerships, and Better Data Could Help More Parents Find Work* (Salem: Oregon Secretary of State, April 2016), sos.oregon.gov/audits/Documents/2014-08A.pdf.

17   Oregon Secretary of State, *Temporary Assistance for Needy Families.*

18   Oregon Secretary of State, *Temporary Assistance for Needy Families.*

19   "Work Participation Rates—Fiscal Year 2014," Office of Family Assistance, Administration for Children and Families, July 26, 2016, www.acf.hhs.gov/ofa/resource/work-participation-rates-fiscal-year-2014.

20   "Policy Basics: State Earned Income Tax Credits," Center on Budget and Policy Priorities, updated August 23, 2017, www.cbpp.org/research/state-budget-and-tax/policy-basics-state-earned-income-tax-credits.

21   Ed Lazere, "State Earned Income Tax Credits Build on the Strengths of the Federal EITC," Center on Budget and Policy Priorities, February 19, 1998, www.cbpp.org/archives/219steic.htm; "Tax Credits for Working Families: Earned Income Tax Credit (EITC)," National Conference of State Legislatures, April 17, 2018, www.ncsl.org/research/labor-and-employment/earned-income-tax-credits-for-working-families.aspx.

22   "Last in EITC Participation: Oregon Leaves Millions on the Table," Oregon Center for Public Policy, November 5, 2015, www.ocpp.org/2015/11/05/fs20151105-oregon-eitc-participation/.

23   "Definitions of Food Security," US Department of Agriculture (USDA), Economic Research Service, accessed April 21, 2018, www.ers.usda.gov/topics/food-nutrition-assistance/food-security-in-the-us/definitions-of-food-security/.

24 The national school meals program (which provides lunch, breakfast, etc., to schoolchildren) is described in the discussion of food and agriculture policy in chapter 17.

25 "Supplemental Nutrition Assistance Program (SNAP)," USDA, Food and Nutrition Service, April 17, 2018, www.fns.usda.gov/pd/supplemental-nutrition-assistance-program-snap.

26 "Supplemental Nutrition Assistance Program."

27 "WIC Program," UUSDA, Food and Nutrition Service, April 6, 2018, www.fns.usda.gov/pd/wic-program.

28 Mark Edwards, Suzanne Porter, and Bruce Weber, "The Recession and SNAP Caseloads: A Tale of Two States," *Journal of Poverty* 20, no. 3 (2016): 261–77, doi:10.1080/1087554 9.2015.1094770.

29 Mark Evan Edwards, "Food Insecurity in Western US States: Increasing Collaboration between State Agencies and Nonprofit Organizations," *Food, Culture & Society* 15, no. 1 (2012): 93–112.

30 "ORS 458.530 (2015): Policy on Hunger," OregonLaws.org, accessed April 21, 2018, www.oregonlaws.org/ors/458.530.

31 Edwards, "Food Insecurity in Western US States," 93–112.

32 Karen E. Cunnyngham, "Reaching Those in Need: Estimates of State Supplemental Nutrition Assistance Program Participation Rates in 2012," Mathematica Policy Research, February 10, 2015, EconPapers.repec.org/RePEc:mpr:mprres:fa0eae05467a4 ef7a1a12b8e09dd6221.

33 Edwards et al., "Recession and SNAP Caseloads," 261–77.

34 "Homeownership Rate for the United States," Federal Reserve Bank of St. Louis, July 1, 2016, https://fred.stlouisfed.org/series/RHORUSQ156N.

35 Gregory Sharp and Matthew Hall, "Emerging Forms of Racial Inequality in Homeownership Exit, 1968–2009," *Social Problems* 61, no. 3 (2014): 427–47, doi:10.1525/sp.2014.12161.

36 "Housing Vacancies and Homeownership (CPS/HVS): Historical Tables," US Census Bureau, accessed April 21, 2018, www.census.gov/housing/hvs/data/histtabs.html.

37 "Affordable Housing," US Department of Housing and Urban Development, accessed April 21, 2018, portal.hud.gov/hudportal/HUD?src=/program_offices/comm_planning/affordablehousing/.

38 "The State of the Nation's Housing 2016," Joint Center for Housing Studies of Harvard University, accessed October 24, 2016, http://www.jchs.harvard.edu/sites/jchs.harvard.edu/files/jchs_2016_state_of_the_nations_housing_lowres.pdf.

39 "Homeownership Rate for Oregon," Federal Reserve Bank of St. Louis, January 1, 2015, fred.stlouisfed.org/series/ORHOWN.

40 Oregon Housing and Community Services and Community Action Partnership of Oregon, *Moving from Poverty to Prosperity in Oregon: 2015 Report on Poverty* (Salem: State of Oregon, November 2015), www.oregon.gov/ohcs/pdfs/2015-report-on-poverty.pdf.

41 Denis C. Theriault, "Landmark Housing Bill Wins Final Approval from Oregon Legislature," *Oregonian / Oregon Live*, March 3, 2016, www.oregonlive.com/politics/index.ssf/2016/03/affordable_housing_mandates_wi.html.

42 Brad Schmidt, "Portland OKs Construction Tax to Pay for Affordable Housing," *Oregonian / Oregon Live*, June 29, 2016, www.oregonlive.com/portland/index.ssf/2016/06/portland_oks_construction_tax.html.

43 I. R. Macrae and National Alliance on Mental Illness of Clackamas County, "Wilsonville's Villebois Community Integrates Housing for Mentally Ill," *Oregonian / Oregon Live*, October 8, 2013, www.oregonlive.com/wilsonville/index.ssf/2013/10/wilsonvilles_villebois_communi.html.

44 Macrae and National Alliance on Mental Illness of Clackamas County, "Wilsonville's Villebois Community."

45 Macrae and National Alliance on Mental Illness of Clackamas County, "Wilsonville's Villebois Community."

46 Oregon Housing and Community Services, *A Home for Hope: 10 Year Plan to End Homelessness in Oregon* (Salem, OR: Ending Homelessness Advisory, June 2008), www.oregon.gov/ohcs/pdfs/report-ehac-10-year-action-plan.pdf.

47 Taryn W. Morrissey, "Child Care and Parent Labor Force Participation: A Review of the Research Literature," *Review of Economics of the Household*, March 23, 2016, 1–24, doi:10.1007/s11150-016-9331-3; Jack P. Shonkoff and Deborah A. Phillips, *From Neurons to Neighborhoods: The Science of Early Childhood Development* (Washington, DC: National Academies Press, 2000), http://www.nap.edu/catalog/9824; Roberta B. Weber, Deana Grobe, and Elizabeth E. Davis, "Does Policy Matter? The Effect of Increasing Child Care Subsidy Policy Generosity on Program Outcomes," *Children and Youth Services Review* 44 (September 2014): 135–44, doi:10.1016/j.childyouth.2014.06.010.

48 Lynda Laughlin, *Who's Minding the Kids? Child Care Arrangements: Spring 2011*, Household Economic Studies (Washington, DC: US Census Bureau, April 2011), www.census.gov/library/publications/2013/demo/p70-135.html.

49 Laughlin, *Who's Minding the Kids?*

50 Megan Comlossy and Jacob Walden, "The Silver Tsunami," *State Legislatures* 39, no. 10 (December 2013): 14–19.

51 Jennifer M. Ortman, Victoria A. Velkoff, and Howard Hogan, *An Aging Nation: The Older Population in the United States* (Washington, DC: US Census Bureau, May 2014), https://www.census.gov/prod/2014pubs/p25-1140.pdf.

52 "How Does the Tax System Subsidize Child Care Expenses?," Urban Institute and Brookings Institution, accessed April 21, 2018, http://www.taxpolicycenter.org/briefing-book/how-does-tax-system-subsidize-child-care-expenses.

53 Because of the close association with the Medicaid managed care system, long-term care is frequently described within the context of health-care policy. But LTSS are also expected to play an integral role in maintaining quality of life, supporting self-determination and reducing disparities for low-income adults, and aligning them with key expectations of safety net policies.

54 Karen Schulman and Helen Bank, *Turning the Corner*: State Child Care Assistance Policies 2014 (Washington, DC: National Women's Law Center, 2014), http://www.nwlc.org/sites/default/files/pdfs/nwlc_2014statechildcareassistancereport-final.pdf; Weber et al., "Does Policy Matter?," 135–44.

55 Robert Jay Dilger and Eugene Boyd, "Block Grants: Perspectives and Controversies," *Congressional Research Service*, July 15, 2014, http://www.fas.org/sgp/crs/misc/R40486.pdf.

56 Oregon Senior Forums, *A History of Oregon's Unique Long-Term Care System* (Salem: State of Oregon, May 2013), https://www.oregon.gov/LTCO/docs/Senior%20History%20project%20final%20full%20copy%206-2013.pdf.

57 Oregon Senior Forums, *History of Oregon's Unique Long-Term Care System*; Keren Brown Wilson, "Historical Evolution of Assisted Living in the United States, 1979 to the Present," *Gerontologist* 47, suppl. 1 (December 1, 2007): 8–22, doi:10.1093/geront/47.

Supplement_1.8; Audra Wenzlow, Steve Eiken, and Kate Sredl, *Improving the Balance: The Evolution of Medicaid Expenditures for Long-Term Services and Supports (LTSS), FY 1981-2014* (Baltimore, MD: Centers for Medicare and Medicaid Services, June 3, 2016), https://www.medicaid.gov/medicaid/ltss/downloads/evolution-ltss-expenditures.pdf.

58 Wenzlow et al., "Improving the Balance."

59 "State of Oregon: K Plan," Oregon Department of Human Services, accessed April 21, 2018, http://www.oregon.gov/dhs/seniors-disabilities/KPLAN/Pages/index.aspx.

60 "Oregon Child Care Research Partnership (OCCRP)," Oregon State University, accessed June 28, 2016, http://health.oregonstate.edu/sbhs/family-policy-program/occrp.

61 "Tools for State Child Care," Oregon State University, accessed November 30, 2017, http://health.oregonstate.edu/sbhs/family-policy-program/occrp-tools-state-childcare-publications.

62 Weber et al., "Does Policy Matter?," 135–44.

63 Weber et al., "Does Policy Matter?"

64 Legislative Revenue Office, *2016 Expiring Tax Credits*, research report (Salem: State of Oregon, February 2015), https://www.oregonlegislature.gov/lro/Documents/RR%20 2-15%202016%20Expiring%20Tax%20Credits%202.pdf.

65 "Tax Credits," Oregon Department of Education, accessed June 28, 2016, https://www.oregon.gov/OCC/Pages/taxcredits.aspx.

66 "Tax Credits."

67 Robert Haveman et al., "The War on Poverty: Measurement, Trends, and Policy," *Journal of Policy Analysis and Management* 34, no. 3 (June 1, 2015): 593–638, doi:10.1002/pam.21846.

68 Haveman et al., "War on Poverty."

16

Exporting Products and Ideas
Oregon Agriculture and Food Systems Politics
CHRIS KOSKI

> Is the chicken local?
> —Fred Armisen, *Portlandia*

Blessed with mild temperatures, diverse topography, and progressive policy, Oregon has been at the forefront of agricultural policy innovation over the past half century. The state has made significant strides in protecting farmland, promoting niche agricultural markets, and acting as a key partner in the burgeoning local food movement. At the same time, however, the state's largest value crops are traditional commodities, and the state remains a significant agricultural exporter of raw and processed foods.[1] Oregon agricultural policy thus typifies the theme of this edited volume—continuity and change—in the importance of agriculture as part of the state's shifting cultural and economic identity.

Agriculture is but one part of the broader story of food politics and policy in Oregon. A new cultural and political understanding of food issues has broadened the political landscape regarding food issues from growers to eaters. While one episode of the television series *Portlandia* may have painted an extreme picture of Portlanders' attitudes toward food when Fred Armisen and Carrie Brownstein ask about the treatment of the chicken on the menu, it captured a part of the newer dynamic of Oregon agricultural politics. This new understanding incorporates the importance of the process of growing food, while also including issues of access, environmental protection, nutrition, health, and disposal. As a result, and responding to pressures from constituents, policy makers have attempted to create policy that accommodates these new demands, continues to serve the political needs of existing interests, and seeks the kind of common ground that attempts to bring these interests together.

Food and agricultural politics affect the political fabric of every community in Oregon: dairies on the Oregon coast, filbert groves in the Willamette Valley, ranches in the Harney Basin, pear trees in Hood River, potato farms along the Columbia Basin, and backyard chicken coops in Portland (see fig. 16.1 for an overview). Many citizens of Oregon, urban or rural, think of themselves as stakeholders in food policy. The mass politics of food differs significantly from the particularistic policies associated with agriculture. The past and future of Oregon agriculture and food policy represent both the synergies and conflicts of these expanded demands on Oregon policy makers.

To start, this chapter considers the history of Oregon food and agriculture. Interests that initially dominated the state, such as ranching and wheat production, are still important today, while others have faded with shifts in market trends or declines in natural resources.[2] Next, the chapter describes the current landscape of Oregon food and agriculture policy, with a particular focus on the role of government in responding to demand and shaping policy. The chapter also includes a case study on Oregon GMO (genetically modified organism) politics. The chapter concludes with thoughts on how Oregon political institutions might change to balance traditional agricultural interests with new stakeholders. In other words, this chapter considers how Oregon political institutions can balance continuity and change in food systems.

HISTORY

Agriculture has long played a central role in Oregon's history. Meriwether Lewis and William Clark would have found their journey impossible without assistance from local Pacific Northwest tribes who had extant forms of agriculture (Wapato root) and access to significant salmon runs. Later, pioneers came to the Oregon Territory in such numbers that Oregon achieved statehood prior to the civil war in 1859. Next to the enormous economic value of Oregon's old growth forests, agricultural production was a key draw for early settlers, as well as for major commercial interests.

Federal support for agriculture was crucial in the early days of the state and remains important, though less so than in the past. Land ownership and use in Oregon, as in the rest of the western United States, is almost entirely a function of early federal allocation.[3] Settlement of lands within the state of Oregon was driven in part by the Homestead Act of 1862, which gave citizens an opportunity to claim 160 acres (a quarter of a square mile) for a modest fee if the land was successfully worked as a farm, ranch, or family forestland. The arid and semiarid eastern part of the state was further distributed to early settlers through the Desert Land Act of 1877, which allowed for individuals to purchase 320 acres (couples could purchase 640 acres, a square mile) provided that the settlers irrigated the land.

Though many of these claims failed because of the region's aridity, the pattern of private land ownership over much of eastern Oregon is a direct function of the claims made under the authority of these two laws. Additionally, it is hard to understate the importance of the Homestead and Desert Land Acts in promoting a particular kind of settlement in Oregon—an inherently agricultural one. The Desert Land Act also promoted irrigated agriculture, creating a legacy of water usage and water rights that would ultimately create severe political, cultural, and environmental conflict, such as in the Klamath Basin (see chapter 10).

Oregon Agriculture Regions

Oregon Department of Agriculture | www.oregon.gov/ODA | info@oda.state.or.us

WILLAMETTE VALLEY

Perhaps the most diverse agricultural region on earth, this region produces more than 170 different crops including grain, hay, grass seed and specialty seeds of all kinds. Fresh and processed vegetables, tree fruits, berries, hazelnuts, wine grapes, and hops are grown in the valley, too, along with nursery products, Christmas trees, dairy and beef cows, as well as poultry.

MID-COLUMBIA

Nestled in among the foothills and northern valleys of Mt. Hood, this remarkable area is famous for its high quality tree fruit. Hood River traditionally grows more pears than any other area of the country. Sweet cherries prosper in this region. Apple trees are plentiful with cider production a growing trend.

COLUMBIA PLATEAU

This is Oregon's principal wheat production area. Irrigation along the Columbia River has transformed what was once sagebrush and desert into some of the nation's most productive farmland where you can find potatoes, onions, a variety of vegetables for processing, watermelon, tree fruit, and alfalfa. One of the nation's largest dairies is located in the region as well.

NORTHEAST OREGON

Beef cattle, hay, potatoes, and mint grow in this scenic area of the state. But the most intensive production is found in the Treasure Valley along the Idaho border where much of the nation's onion production takes place. Other irrigated crops include sugar beets and a variety of vegetables.

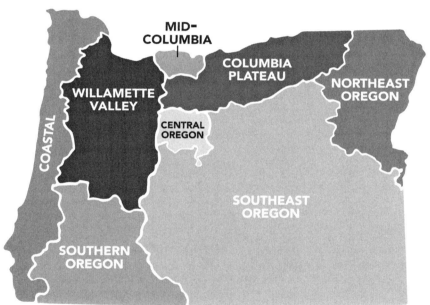

COASTAL OREGON

The bounty of the Pacific is found here in full splendor, offering a delicious menu that includes salmon, halibut, Dungeness crab, oysters, mussels, clams and more. Coastal dairy farms are famous for their cheeses. Specialty crops in this region include cranberries and lily bulbs.

SOUTHERN OREGON

Sheep and cattle graze in mountainous, hilly areas of this region. The Rogue River Valley produces pears and other high quality tree fruit. Wine production is coming on strong. The Klamath Basin is home to beef cattle, alfalfa and other hay varieties, and lots of potatoes.

CENTRAL OREGON

Tucked in the middle of the state, this popular recreational region produces a variety of specialty seed crops to go along with garlic, hay, and beef cattle. An increasing urban population in Bend has also led to a growth in local production of fresh vegetables.

SOUTHEAST OREGON

The livestock industry dominates this region. Most of Oregon's cattle graze on thousands of acres of private and federal rangeland. Because of low rainfall, most hay fields and pastures must be irrigated. Major crops include onions, potatoes, and sugar beets.

Figure 16.1. Growing regions of Oregon. *Source: "Oregon Agriculture Regions," Oregon Department of Agriculture, July 2017, https://www.oregon.gov/ODA/shared/Documents/ Publications/Administration/ORGrowingRegions.pdf*

In addition to direct divestment of federal lands to private interests, the federal government allowed for grazing of federal lands for decades, formally establishing grazing rights after a series of conflicts between grazers—notably, cattle and sheep in eastern Oregon—in the Taylor Grazing Act of 1934. And similar to the use of irrigated, semiarid farmland, the legacy of federal grazing in Oregon has contributed to contentious political relations between agricultural interests, environmentalists, and the federal agencies that manage public lands in Oregon. Concerns about federal power broadly speaking, but specifically perceived encroachments on historical rights to graze on federal land, prompted armed ranchers and other private property "constitutionalists" from surrounding western states to occupy the Malheur National Wildlife Refuge in 2016 (see chapter 4).

Food traditions and cultures that predate white settlement in Oregon by roughly nine thousand years have continually clashed with efforts to convert the land from long-established proto-agrarian and hunter-gatherer societies to increasingly industrial modes of production.[4] For example, salmon fishing was crucial for many tribes along the Columbia River and its tributaries, as well as near coastal rivers and the Klamath River Basin in southern Oregon.[5] Food-gathering and trading created opportunities for tribes to interact.[6] Local tribes were rich in food sources not because of the land on which they sat, but because of the great salmon runs. Tradition and societal organization revolved around this important food source. Salmon continue to be part of many tribes' identity and source of political power, but also high levels of controversy when tribes assert their historic rights under a variety of treaties (see chapter 10).

THE CURRENT AGRICULTURAL LANDSCAPE

Oregon's agriculture is diverse in many ways. While ranching and wheat production have historically been at the heart of Oregon agriculture, the number of products that Oregon produces both for food and for aesthetics is vast owing to the varied landscape of the state. The state is a premier producer for berries and for seed, much of it grown within the Willamette Valley. More Christmas trees are farmed in Oregon than any other state. The locavore movement has increased the diversity of farms in and around western Oregon metro areas, particularly Portland. Fertile, proximate, and protected by the urban growth boundary, these farmlands have allowed for a wider range of new farmers and farms that produce a more diverse range of products. Thus, while ranching and wheat remain significant industries, farming, farmers, and consumers have changed. Changes in the industry have brought changes in politics. Where the larger farms in rural parts of the state once dominated agricultural politics, the range of groups has expanded. Oregon State administrative structures have evolved to accommodate a systemic approach to food and agriculture. Ultimately, however, there are simply more players involved in the food politics of today than in the agricultural politics of yesterday.

State Agricultural Political Institutions

The politics of agricultural policy are generally what renowned political scientist Theodore Lowi characterizes as "distributive."[7] Distributive politics are usually low in conflict because the amount of resources distributed is relatively small for the larger group from which resources are drawn, but large in comparison to the small group to be benefitted. In the case of agriculture, the federal and state governments—the larger group—provides the resources, which benefit farmers, a much smaller segment of society. Oregon farmers benefit from the support of many federal and state programs, such as price supports for certain commodities and subsidized crop insurance from the federal government, as well as marketing and technical advice from the state and Oregon State University (OSU) extension services.[8] In general, agriculture forms what scholars refer to as a strong policy subsystem, which means that relatively few stakeholders control problem definitions and, by extension, solutions.

Issues associated with agriculture are, in broad strokes, similar to the initial governmental forays into agricultural policy dating to the nineteenth century. Farmers rely on state programs for assistance with farming techniques, compliance with federal regulations, financial assistance, marketing transparency, access to water, environmental concerns, promotion of goods, and financing future generations of farmers. The key state agency involved in Oregon agricultural programming is the Oregon Department of Agriculture (ODA). Similar to the origin of most government agencies, the ODA emerged to create a coherent policy response to agriculture, making sense of a series of related but variably implemented agricultural policies. Early responses (ca. 1900) to particular issues such as food safety, pest and disease prevention, and livestock inspection were handled by independent entities and officials such as the dairy and food commissioner, the State Horticultural Board, and the Livestock Sanitary Board. In 1931, the Oregon legislature elected to consolidate these and other independent efforts into a single agency to take a more coordinated approach to an increasingly important and complex industry.[9]

Government support and intervention into agricultural practices have grown over time, but the mission of serving farmers and consumers is the same. Similar to its federal partners, the ODA finds much of its statutory authority and organizational mission devoted to technical and marketing assistance to farmers. On the side of technical assistance, the ODA acts as an interface between new federal programs, such as the Food Safety and Modernization Act, and agricultural producers in the state. This kind of policy action on the part of the ODA can be characterized as distributive politics, which is generally not viewed as controversial, and indeed most of the debate about ODA programming occurs within the subsystem itself, rather than in the larger political context. Schneider and Ingram go on to say that advantaged groups in societies generally receive such capacity-building tools.[10] While the face of agriculture may have changed over time, its strength in securing favorable policy outcomes has not.

The Oregon Department of Agriculture also plays a key regulatory role, primarily regulating markets and ensuring transparency. This is a potentially problematic position for the agency given that its primary political constituencies are agricultural producers, even though agricultural consumers benefit from most of the regulations.

Additionally, the ODA has a significant role in regulating safety in food processing, animal welfare, and pesticide use. These powers give the ODA regulatory authority to significantly affect issues related to the environment and public health. A recent example occurred in June 2013, when sixty Oregonians gathered in a Wilsonville Target parking lot to mourn the mysterious death of more than fifty thousand honeybees.[11] The department determined that a common class of pesticides, neonicotinoids, sprayed on decorative linden trees in the parking lot was to blame. The department quickly issued a temporary ban on neonicotinoids to protect bees and later, in 2015, promulgated a rule banning neonicotinoid derivatives dinotefuran, imidacloprid, thiamethoxam, and clothianidin for use on certain tree species.[12]

The ODA also is responsible for regulating confined animal feeding operations (CAFOs).[13] In general, CAFOs are regulated by state departments of environmental quality rather than agriculture, given that the regulatory rationale for government intervention is the potential for environmental harm.[14] CAFOs produce significant quantities of untreated animal wastewater in addition to a number of air-quality impacts, including emissions of small particulate matter, methane, and hydrogen sulfide.[15] Yet, because the Oregon Department of Environmental Quality has delegated regulatory authority to the ODA, the agency has a key role in rural environmental health, which means that the ODA is both a proponent for, and regulator of, the same industry.[16]

Food Systems

The state's agricultural sector demonstrates the themes offered in this book. The ODA continues to be the most important agency in addressing other important dimensions of food issues outside of agriculture, namely, consumer protection, the support of local marketing, and environmental protection. The landscape of interest groups in Oregon food politics has changed significantly, however. Additional partners in food systems are the Departments of Human Services (restaurant safety, nutrition, and food assistance programs); Land Conservation and Development (urban growth boundary issues); and Environmental Quality (nonpoint source pollution from farming). In addition to these, a host of nonprofits and local government agencies are active partners in the food system. The interest group environment associated with these institutional shifts has moved away from one represented by larger farms in rural parts of Oregon to one that includes environmental, social justice, urban, and other economic advocacy concerns.

Academics and, increasingly, policy makers have begun to understand the politics and policy of food as part of a broader system of laws, rules, and priorities that include, but are certainly not limited to, modes of agricultural production.[17] Today's food system is the result of an amalgam of policy priorities regarding food production, manufacturing, agro-environmental health, access, nutrition, labeling, marketing, safety, and food insecurity. Each of these parts of the food system hitherto has been affected by specific, often unrelated, policies that have fostered distinct, rather than connected, communities of interest. Systemic thinking about food continues to involve agricultural interests in Oregon food politics but also changes the dynamic of policymaking to include other players.

Food Access and Nutrition

Food access and nutrition are spread across many agencies with distinct organizational missions. The primary agencies involved in food access and nutrition are the Department of Human Services, the Oregon Health Authority, and the Department of Education. But nonprofits are also integral to food access. The Department of Human Services is responsible for a variety of anti-hunger programs, and notably for implementation of the Supplemental Nutrition Assistance Program (SNAP). The program, known locally by the Oregon Trail electronic benefits transfer (EBT) cards, is the single broadest anti-hunger program in America. The SNAP program is a "means-tested" program, meaning that individuals need to meet certain criteria to be eligible for benefits.[18] Eligibility and benefits have changed over time and are provided on a scale according to need, and benefits are limited in their use. The national SNAP program is administered by the US Department of Agriculture, a holdover from an era when the solution to food access was in part solved by creating an additional market for surplus American commodities.[19] Some farmers markets in Oregon match a dollar amount of SNAP funds (typically around $5), but these are essentially charitable donations on the parts of individual markets.[20] The Oregon Health Authority (OHA) is responsible for implementing the Women, Infants, and Children (WIC) special supplemental nutritional assistance program. This program, as the title implies, is directed at expectant and recent mothers as well as their children.

An oft-forgotten player in the food system is education. Public and private schools are understated players in the delivery of nutrition and food education in America.[21] A full discussion of the two most popular school-based programs—the National School Lunch Program (NSLP) and the School Breakfast Program (SBP)—is beyond the scope of this chapter. The Oregon Department of Education administers these federal programs. Their administrative structure provides a framework through which states can implement other nutrition and education programs that go beyond issues of basic nutrition. For Oregon, this has meant thinking about schools as places to educate students about farming, engage students in gardening, and provide students with "local" food. In 2011, both houses of the Oregon legislature unanimously approved House Bill (HB) 2800, which established the Oregon Farm to School (OFS) and School Garden

(SG) Programs. The bill, which Governor John Kitzhaber signed into law, originally appropriated $1.2 million; later, Section 110 of omnibus legislation (Senate Bill 5507) in 2015 increased the appropriation to $3.3 million. Administratively, the bill directs the Department of Education to collaborate with the Department of Agriculture. Of the funds appropriated, at least 80 percent are to be used for reimbursements related to food.[22]

Organic or Local

Oregon's populist political culture, which is often wary of large corporations and big government, coupled with the fertile Willamette Valley and small farms, helped foster an early organic movement.[23] Organic agriculture in Oregon—notably, organic certification from the Oregon Tilth—provided the foundation for changes in federal policy that would have profound impacts on organic agriculture in the United States. The passage of the federal Organic Foods Production Act (OFPA) of 1990 codified what many Oregonians were already experiencing and expecting from agriculture.

While the OFPA represented a significant opportunity to create consistency and certainty in a new agricultural market for producers and consumers, the legislation ultimately focused on only one component of the organic movement. The OFPA transformed the inherently local social movement of organic agriculture into an environmental policy by defining organic in the language of pesticides and soil amendments.[24] The result is a federal policy that focuses almost exclusively on organic agriculture from an environmental protection perspective, leaving issues of public health and the political economy of agricultural ownership to other policy subsystems (or silos). While environmentalism was certainly foundational to the organic movement, activists are systemically oriented.

Echoes of the unfinished business of the organic movement can be seen in state policies to address a series of issues raised by the organic movement. One of the more radical goals of early food system advocates was the decentralization of agricultural ownership. While redistribution of land is a political nonstarter in any state, Oregon encourages new entrants into farming, particularly smaller farmers, through financial and technical support. In 2013, the Oregon legislature passed HB 2700, creating the Beginning and Expanding Farmer Loan Program administered by Business Oregon, commonly known in agricultural parlance as an "aggie bonds" program. The Oregon Aggie Bonds program provides a 25 percent tax break to banks that provide funds to new farmers for land purchases, depreciation, or equipment. In this way, the program is classic distributive politics. But the eligibility requirements intend to change the landscape of agricultural ownership away from the decades-long dominance of concentration. Applicants must have a net worth less than $750,000 and must either have never previously owned a farm (for loans assisting in farm purchases) or own a farm that is less than 30 percent of the county's median farm size for loans used in constructing "depreciable farm property," such as buildings.[25]

CASE STUDY: THE DEBATE OVER GENETICALLY MODIFIED ORGANISMS

The history of the efforts to regulate GMOs in Oregon offers a clear window into issues common to Oregon food politics and policy. Regulation of GMOs can take many forms, but typical efforts in Oregon have focused on labeling at the state level to outright bans on GMOs at the local level. The state was at the forefront of efforts to further regulate GMOs beyond federal organic policy, which has interpreted "organic" produce to be that which is not genetically modified, though this is not the text of the actual legislation. Over time, activists have twice attempted to label GMOs via ballot initiative. While three counties have tried to ban GMOs, only one, Jackson County in southern Oregon, has been successful.

As with other food system issues, multiple interests converge in GMO politics. Environmentally, GMOs may be harmful because of genetic pollution, in which engineered crops may irreparably affect extant heritage varietals. Additionally, a significant portion of GMO crops are resistant to biocides, which makes their use more likely, another concern for environmentalists. Food safety issues also loom large over GMO politics. Many opponents of GMOs are concerned about the unknown health effects associated with genetically modified crops and animals. At the same time, genetic modification offers the promise of drought-resistant crops and, ultimately, cheaper and more abundant food. Social justice advocates find themselves straddling both camps.

GMO politics are active, strong, and somewhat unpredictable, given Oregon's reputation as a progressive state. In 2002, voters were asked to weigh in on Measure 27, which would have required the Oregon Department of Agriculture to develop labeling for genetically engineered products sold in or from Oregon. The initiative was overwhelmingly defeated (70.5% to 29.5%). Yet subsequent efforts twelve years later were much more competitive. What changed? Did the Oregon political landscape experience a fundamental shift in a short period of time?

As is the case in political analysis, the answer is "yes and no." The second round of the GMO debate in Oregon was much more contentious owing to issues of increased attention and some event-driven politics. Unlike the political environment of 2002, local, regional, and national attention to the issues of GMOs during 2014 was incredibly high. Well-funded, well-organized GMO-labeling initiatives were on the California (2012) and Washington (2013) ballots, with legislative action occurring in statehouses across the country. Political scientists often refer to this strategy to expand conflict as "venue shopping," where groups seek a policy foothold in a particular jurisdiction for the hope of eventually expanding policy to other locations.[26] The dominant groups that previously held a policy monopoly—in this case, large agribusiness such as Monsanto—are forced to defend the status quo in a number of different governance structures at the same time. This can be expensive and challenging, particularly for grassroots efforts such as an anti-GMO campaign.

Politically, the Oregon initiatives represented two philosophical strategies associated with regulation of harmful substances in the United States. Benton, Jackson, Josephine, and Lane Counties considered efforts to completely ban GMOs from their borders. Under this philosophy, what is known about GMOs represents fundamental threats to the food system, and the unknowns associated with GMOs are considered potentially quite harmful. The messaging of the Lane and Benton County initiatives represents the newer understanding of GMO politics as related to "food" rather than just "agriculture," each sharing the title "Local Food System Ordinance." The state initiative, Measure 92 (2014), focused on mandatory labeling of foods that contain genetically modified organisms, relying on an information-based tool to allow for consumers to make more informed decisions regarding food. The initiative's sponsor—Oregon Right to Know—relied on an assumption from similar legislation that information would ultimately lead consumers away from GMO-based products and reduce the profitability of these substances. The term "right to know" in the group's namesake appears in other successful environmental legislation, notably, the federal Emergency Planning and Community Right to Know act of 1986, which requires the disclosure of toxic releases to inform the public and emergency management plans in case of spills.

Where Measure 27 was soundly defeated, the new crop of GMO initiatives in 2014 and 2015 were fiercely competitive not only because of this heightened awareness, but also because of the discovery of non-approved wheat in eastern Oregon in late May 2013 that was resistant to the weed killer glyphosate, the active ingredient in the herbicide Roundup. This discovery of this "Roundup-ready" wheat, as it is called, was particularly shocking given that the US Food and Drug Administration had not yet approved GM soft white wheat for commercial use in the United States.[27] Monsanto, the manufacturer of Roundup, galvanized the same kinds of interests that were active during the organic movement, especially groups that feared consolidated, corporate control of food.[28] Worse, the discovery triggered a brief ban on wheat exports to the European Union, Japan, and South Korea. The battle thus created an unlikely coalition of big, eastern, rural agricultural, capitalist interests, which were concerned about the state's export business, and health-conscious urbanites.[29] The fiercely competitive new politics of the anti-GMO campaign was made possible by a traditional set of agricultural interests adopting a suspicious position toward current GMO regulations. The same interest of exporting goods, which originally encouraged harnessing the Columbia River for barge traffic nearly a century prior, continued to loom large in the battle over GMOs. Some parts of agricultural politics had not changed.

But other agricultural interests in the state—such as alfalfa, corn, and sugar beets—depend heavily on GM crops, and these interests sought to head off current and future local venue-shopping in the state legislature. Agricultural interests encouraged largely Republican lawmakers to take advantage of a three-day special session of the legislature in October 2013, originally intended to address issues related to taxation and the fiscal problems of the Public Employee Retirement System. Republicans used this policy window to pass, with limited Democratic support, Senate Bill (SB) 863, which effectively claimed state control over all GMO-related issues. One major ramification of this bill is that it prevents the introduction of local ballot initiatives to limit GMOs, though it exempted any local initiative campaigns that had already gathered sufficient signatures for the ballot prior to the effective date of the law.[30] But the bill contained a relatively rare "emergency" clause that made the effective date of the law the moment it was signed by the governor, essentially killing current attempts by Josephine and Lane Counties to put the issue on the ballot. At that time, of all the potential initiatives addressing GMOs, only Jackson County had already gathered signatures sufficient to place its GMO ban on the ballot, while other efforts were underway. Governor Kitzhaber created a "must-pass" scenario for the bill by telling the legislature that he would only sign bills if they all reached his desk by the end of the session. The GMO bill passed along with other revenue and pension bills.[31]

Senate Bill 863 created uncertainty for local ballot measures and urgency for a statewide measure to address GMOs (inadvertently, SB 863 had affirmed the right of the state to regulate GMOs). Proponents of what would eventually become Measure 92 had learned from the past policy foibles of Measure 27 and from political issues associated with similar initiatives in California (Proposition 37) and Washington (Initiative 522). Notably, Measure 92 was able to avoid opposition by the state's powerful dairy and meat sectors by exempting them from labeling requirements. The Measure 92 campaign was incredibly expensive, with over $30 million in spending and a better than 2-1 advantage for the opposition campaign. During the campaign, Jackson County voted to ban GMOs. Ultimately, Measure 92 lost by less than 900 votes out of over 1.5 million statewide votes after a recount. Benton County played chicken with the state and went ahead with a vote on a GMO ban in 2015. Benton County Measure 2-89 (another "local food system ordinance") was viewed as expansive and illegal, despite a self-conscious assertion of the right to self-governance by the county. Notably, the ordinance did not offer a formal exemption for research, which was likely a key element in its landslide defeat given the presence of Oregon State University's innovative and locally important research program in Benton County.

The politics of genetically modified organisms can be seen on the one hand as a clear break with the traditional dominance of agricultural issues in the state. The increase in anti-GMO measures shows a change in the political power of agriculture-as-food and the rise of power of food-systemic thinking. At the same time, however, the values associated with the anti-GMO movement are part of the particular kind of populist politics that historically pervades both the left and the right in Oregon.

Jackson and Josephine Counties are normally among the most conservative in the state, yet they are the epicenter of successful anti-GMO regulation. In general, these counties have shown a suspicion of scientifically engineered interventions into public health, with the highest rates of childhood vaccination exemptions in the country and some of the lowest rates of water fluoridation. Suspicions about centralized production and distribution of genetically modified crops are thus in keeping with the traditions of populist Oregon politics.

CONCLUSIONS:
THE FUTURE OF OREGON AGRICULTURE AND FOOD POLICY

Agriculture and food continue to play a prominent role in the Oregon political ethos. While the distribution of agricultural sectors has largely remained unchanged, Oregon politics has evolved to understand food through a systemic lens. Oregon food politics encompass agricultural production, distribution, environmental protection, nutrition, education, social justice, energy, and recreational drug use. A broader understanding of food systems is reflected in a policy environment in which a series of different agencies play a role in issues related to food and agriculture. The Oregon Department of Agriculture remains the single most important agency for farmers, but it also works closely with other agencies in the Oregon food web, such as the Oregon Health Authority, Department of Environmental Quality, Department of Fish and Wildlife, Department of Human Services, Department of Education, Department of Energy, and even the Oregon Liquor Control Commission (see table 16.1).

Oregon food and agriculture policy relies largely on inducements and information. These types of tools create few burdens on target populations and distribute benefits to new and existing participants. Consequently, the majority of food and agriculture politics in Oregon has relatively little conflict. Conflict that does arise in Oregon food and agricultural politics typically results from attempts to regulate industries or redistribute resources from one group to another. Regulatory tools are seldom used in Oregon in comparison to less coercive measures.

The challenge for Oregon agricultural and food politics going forward is to reconcile these related yet distinct streams of policy. When faced with what policy experts call a problem of "policy coherence," governments have a few options.[32] The first option, essentially the current status quo, is to simply provide more coordination between agencies related to specific issues. Partnerships between agencies require little new administrative structures and leverage the individual strengths of agencies. But coordination can be challenging across agencies that ultimately have different, inherently narrower, policy goals than the holistic goals for which they are partnering. A second option is to consolidate functions related to food systems under a new agency, such as a new Department of Food. A new agency would have a specific mandate, authority, budget, and autonomy to consider food issues, presumably poaching

Table 16.1. Agencies and their role in Oregon food and agriculture policy

Agency	Role in Oregon Food and Agriculture Politics	Sample Issues
Department of Agriculture	• weights and measures • technical assistance • pesticide registration and use • management of federal programs • agricultural water quality regulations • food inspection	• grants, loans, and technical assistance for new farmers and new products • Oregon crop tax credit for food donation • bee kills in Oregon • genetically modified organism labeling • marijuana edibles and other foodstuffs
Health Authority	• Women, Infants, and Children • nutrition and exercise protocols • medical marijuana • restaurant safety	• Women, Infants, and Children • genetically modified organism labeling • permitting and oversight of medical grow sites
Department of Environmental Quality	• water quality • air quality • land quality	• total maximum daily load of toxics in streams • CAFO water quality (with Ag) • open field burning (with Ag) • pesticide management (with Ag)
Department of Fish and Wildlife	• species management and protection on agricultural land	• sage-grouse protection plan • wolf depredation • salmon in the Klamath and Columbia Rivers
Department of Human Services	• food assistance	• Supplemental Nutrition Assistance Program
Department of Education	• youth nutrition • nutrition education	• national school lunch and breakfast programs • Oregon farm to school and school garden programs (in conjunction with Ag)
Department of Energy	• encourage biofuels	• tax credits for biomass
Liquor Control Commission	• recreational marijuana	• permitting and enforcement of recreational grow sites

responsibility from existing agencies. This seems highly unlikely, as it would be challenging to identify the boundaries for such an agency. Moreover, bureaucratic reorganization is extremely challenging given the interests invested in the existing system of governance. A less extreme variant might be to incorporate food into the mission of an existing agency. An example of this is California's Department of Food and Agriculture.

A third option is to create a partnership that addresses a broad range of food issues. Partnerships are used in a variety of contexts (e.g., environmental conservation, emergency food) at varying levels of government (e.g., federal critical infrastructure protection partnership, local watershed management councils). Partnerships are particularly useful in boundary-spanning issues such as food politics, but they also suffer from issues of coordination, funding, and stakeholder commitment. Food policy councils have emerged as a particular form of collaborative governance to address food issues at the local, county, regional, and state level across the United States.[33] Food policy councils can be governmental or nongovernmental. Current examples in Oregon are the Central Oregon Food Policy Council in Bend and the Treasure Valley Food Coalition, which operates in eastern Oregon and southwestern Idaho.

Future issues in agriculture and food politics in Oregon include continued debates over GMOs, a possible transition of the state's only coal-fired power plant to biomass, a rapidly changing regulatory environment for cannabis, and the looming threat of climate change. Each of these issues contains different dimensions of conflict, communities of actors, and policy subsystems that will require innovative solutions and coalition building. While Oregon state politics changes to address these new issues, barges continue to move soft white wheat down the Columbia, as they have for nearly a hundred years.

Notes

1   National Agricultural Statistics Service, *Census of Agriculture: Oregon State and County Data*, vol. 1, Geographic Area Series Part 37, USDA Publication No. AC-12-A-37 (Washington, DC: US Government Printing Office, 2012).

2   National Agricultural Statistics Service, *Oregon Agriculture: Facts and Figures* (Washington, DC: US Government Printing Office, 2014).

3   Randall K. Wilson, *America's Public Lands: From Yellowstone to Smokey Bear and Beyond* (New York: Rowman & Littlefield, 2014).

4   Virginia L. Butler and Jim E. O'Connor, "9000 Years of Salmon Fishing on the Columbia River, North America," *Quaternary Research* 62 (2004):1-8.

5   Courtland Smith, *Salmon Fishers of the Columbia* (Corvallis: Oregon State University Press, 1979); John B. Hamilton, Gary L. Curtis, Scott M. Snedaker, and David K. White, "Distribution of Anadromous Fishes in the Upper Klamath River Watershed Prior to Hydropower Dams—A Synthesis of the Historical Evidence," *Fisheries* 30 (2005):10-20.

6   Richard White, *Organic Machine: The Remaking of the Columbia River* (New York: Hill and Wang, 1995).

7   Theodore J. Lowi, "Four Systems of Policy, Politics, and Choice," *Public Administration Review* 32 (1972): 298.

8   Bill Winders, *The Politics of Food Supply* (New Haven, CT: Yale University Press, 2012).

9   Oregon Department of Agriculture, *The History of the Oregon Department of Agriculture* (Salem: Oregon Department of Agriculture, 2014).

10 Anne Schneider and Helen Ingram, "Behavioral Assumptions of Policy Tools," *Journal of Politics* 52 (1990): 510-29; Anne Schneider and Helen Ingram, "The Social Construction of Target Populations: Implications for Politics and Policy," *American Political Science Review* 87 (1993): 334-47.

11 Cassandra Profita, "About 60 to Pay Tribute to Bees Killed at Wilsonville Target Parking Lot," *Ecotrope*, Oregon Public Broadcasting, July 1, 2013.

12 Kelly House, "Oregon Bans Use of Bee-Killing Insecticides on Linden Trees," *Oregonian*, February 27, 2015.

13 The Environmental Protection Agency uses the term "concentrated animal feeding operations," or CAFO. For general purposes here, the terms are synonymous.

14 Chris Koski, "Examining State Environmental Policy Design," *Journal of Environmental Planning and Management* 50 (2007): 483-502; Chris Koski, "Regulatory Choices: Analyzing State Policy Design," *Law and Policy* 29 (2007): 409-34.

15 David Kirby, *Animal Factory: The Looming Threat of Industrial Pig, Dairy, and Poultry Farms to Humans and the Environment* (New York: St. Martin's Press, 2010).

16 Oregon Administrative Regulation 603-074, "Confined Animal Feeding Operation Program."

17 Parke Wilde, *Food Policy in the United States: An Introduction* (New York: Earthscan, 2013).

18 Center for Budget and Policy Priorities, *Policy Basics: Introduction to SNAP* (Washington, DC: Center for Budget and Policy Priorities, 2015).

19 Winders, *Politics of Food Supply.*

20 "Farmers Markets Matching SNAP," Partners for a Hunger Free Oregon, accessed April 22, 2018, oregonhunger.org/farmers-markets-snap.

21 Janet Poppendieck, *Free For All: Fixing School Food in America* (Berkeley: University of California Press, 2010).

22 In the original legislation, 12.5 percent of funds must be used for education and garden-based activities; current regulations state that "at least" 10 percent of funds ought to be used for these activities.

23 See Richard A. Clucas, Mark Henkels, and Brent S. Steel, eds., *Oregon Politics and Government: Progressives versus Conservative Populists* (Lincoln: University of Nebraska Press, 2005), esp. chapter 1.

24 Later interpretations of the OFPA would emphasize the process provisions of the act, which would legally describe genetically modified organisms as not organic.

25 Oregon Administrative Regulation 123-052, "Beginning and Expanding Farmer Loan Program ('Aggie Bonds')," accessed April 22, 2018, http://arcweb.sos.state.or.us/pages/rules/oars_100/oar_123/123_052.html.

26 Relevant readings regarding venue shopping include: Sarah B. Pralle, "Venue Shopping, Political Strategy, and Policy Change: The Internationalization of Canadian Forest Advocacy," *Journal of Public Policy* 23 (2003): 233-60; Aaron J. Ley and Edward P. Weber, "Policy Change and Venue Choices: Field Burning in Idaho and Washington," *Society and Natural Resources* 27 (2014): 645-55.

27 Eric Mortenson, "Two Weeks Into Probe of Genetically Modified Eastern Oregon Wheat, Investigators Report No More Findings," *Oregonian*, June 14, 2013.

28 Monsanto reached a settlement in 2014 with no admission of culpability.

29 Victoria Shannon, "Japan and South Korea Bar Imports of U.S. Wheat," *New York Times*, May 31, 2013.

30 A previous version of this bill, SB 633, was killed in the regular legislative session.

31 Yuxing Zheng, "Oregon Legislature 'On Track' for PERS, Taxes, GMO Bills after Chaotic Start," *Oregonian*, September 30, 2013.

32 Peter J. May, Joshua Sapotichne, and Samuel Workman, "Policy Coherence and Policy Domains," *Policy Studies Journal* 34 (2006): 381-403.

33 Saba N. Siddiki, Julia L. Carboni, Chris Koski, and Abdul-Akeem Sadiq, "How Policy Rules Shape the Structure and Performance of Collaborative Governance Arrangements," *Public Administration Review* 75 (2015): 536-47.

17

Education in Oregon

ALLISON HURST, JORDAN HENSLEY, and EDWARD P. WEBER

There is general agreement that state and local governments have a central responsibility in providing their citizens with an appropriate education that provides the knowledge and skills required to be successful contributing members to American democracy. And in almost all states, when it comes to public policies that enjoy strong, bipartisan public support, education is among the top two or three. The movement to expand the roles and authority of federal and state governments in public education policy was aided by the creation of the US Department of Education in the late 1970s and by a series of court decisions starting in the 1980s that mandated that tax revenues from local sources, primarily property taxes, be shared statewide across elementary school districts. In Oregon today, these changes, among others, have led to the kindergarten through 12th grade, or K–12, public school system taking 39 percent of the state's General Fund budget, while K–12 and public colleges together receive over half of the General Fund budget every year.

This chapter first reviews the landscape of higher education in Oregon, noting key developments and challenges for students, university leaders, and politicians alike. It then describes the state of K–12 funding, important new policies, and the many significant challenges facing the K–12 system in Oregon. Of central importance to both the higher education and K–12 policy realms is the fact that each is wrestling with how to provide an effective, appropriate education at a reasonable cost in the face of new challenges.

HIGHER EDUCATION POLICY

The US higher education landscape is a chaotic one, lacking a history of federal or state control (Hofstadter and Smith 1961; Rudolph 1962). From the beginning, when President George Washington wanted a national college, there has been a strong countervailing desire for local control, mostly in the hands of private groups (e.g., churches; Marsden 1994). A 1902 report to Congress argued against creating a national university, as higher education served elites only and therefore should be left in private powers; a federally supported university would be, variously, "godless," "elitist," and wholly unnecessary (Nemec 2006: 153). But over the course of the twentieth century, federal and state workforce development policies brought higher education increasingly into the orbit of government policy (Loss 2012).

The pattern of college attendance in the United States (and elsewhere) has often been described as a shift from elite to mass participation, to its current move toward "universal" access (Trow 2010). Policy has changed accordingly. We are currently experiencing a third major transition in higher education public policy, in which states are struggling economically and "a need for high-quality higher education to satisfy workforce needs contends with rising frustration with increasing costs" (Doyle and Kirst 2015: 194-95). In addition to raising the human capital of the workforce, higher education has been tasked with reducing inequalities among social groups. Although we have moved well past the era in which only a small elite group attends college, our current era of mass participation remains stubbornly stratified by both type of institution (e.g., elite, public, two-year, for-profit) and experience within institutions themselves. An insightful historian of higher education in the twentieth century has remarked, "The persistent tendency of intellectually elite institutions such as the universities to be also the home of the social and economic elite, is a major source of tension between the institutions of higher education and the increasingly strong egalitarian values of Western society" (Trow 2010: 92). Indeed, higher education overall has become more unequal as participation rates have increased (Calhoun 2011). Higher education policy is thus taxed with encouraging the full development of human capital for both civic and workforce ends, while also minimizing accompanying inequalities that occur when participation expands, all in a chaotic and patchwork landscape of overlapping and competing public and private institutions.

THE LANDSCAPE OF HIGHER EDUCATION IN OREGON

Oregon's higher education landscape has a distinctly western cast. The history of the western United States affected the types of institutions and the relationships between the states and higher education in ways quite distinct from other regions of the United States (Goodchild et al. 2014). Like the rest of the region, Oregon's land-grant institutions have been relatively important and well supported by its citizens and their representatives. Unlike the Northeast, where land-grant institutions came late to the scene and had to compete with much older, privately founded but state-subsidized institutions (e.g., Harvard, Princeton, Yale), the land-grant institutions were among the first postsecondary institutions in the state. Oregon has many fewer church-founded and supported colleges than other regions (particularly the South and Midwest), and fewer colleges founded on the liberal arts model (small, residential, private, often historically associated with a particular community; Goodchild et al. 2014: xiii). Thus the integration of the dominant institutions of higher education with state goals and state policy has been more complete and of longer duration than in some other states and regions.

The state of Oregon is home to seven four-year public colleges that primarily serve undergraduate students (fig. 17.1) and seventeen public two-year colleges. All together, these public institutions serve approximately one hundred eighty thousand undergraduate students. In addition, there are at least sixty-nine private institutions, most of which are relatively new for-profits. Before 2013, all seven public four-years formed part of the Oregon University System (OUS), governed by the Oregon State Board of Higher Education. This arrangement has been unraveling for the past decade and no longer exists. The state's three largest universities—University of Oregon (UO), Oregon State University (OSU), and Portland State University (PSU)—were the first to leave the system in 2013, creating their own independent governing boards, while the smaller campuses were initially governed by OUS until July 1, 2015, when the system was formally abolished by Senate Bill (SB) 80. A large reason given for the breakup was the need for universities to raise their own money and manage their own property, something felt all the more strongly in the aftermath of the Great Recession. All campuses are now loosely governed by the Higher Education Coordinating Commission, first created in 2011. The HECC answers directly to the governor and encompasses seven distinct offices, including two policy-setting departments, the Office of Student Access and Completion and the Office of Community Colleges and Workforce Development. The HECC also includes an office overseeing the private postsecondary sector. Unlike the OUS, the HECC has limited powers of governance, although the exact power balance between the independent boards and HECC is still being negotiated.

The unbundling of the OUS system occurred at a time when state appropriations for higher education had been cut drastically. According to a national study, Oregon slashed spending on higher education per student by 51 percent between 2000 and 2014, more than any other state except Michigan. This is partly attributable to rising enrollment, the

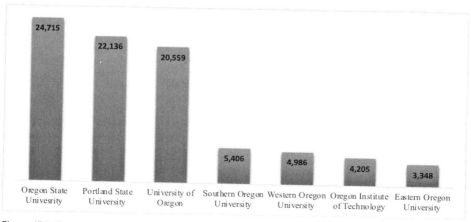

Figure 17.1. Oregon's seven public four-year colleges, ranked by size of undergraduate enrollment, 2015.

highest in the nation (Baum and Johnson 2015). This means that Oregon's colleges and universities must increasingly rely on a combination of tuition and external sources to keep afloat financially. In 2013, for example, the state shouldered less than 5 percent of UO's operating expenses. The drying up of state funding has come at the same time that the state has made increased demands on public higher education.

The second major change in structure and organization was the rise of faculty unionization. This is taking place in a national context that has seen the rise of non-tenured and adjunct labor as a way of cutting costs (DeCew 2003; Nelson 2010). In 2009, faculty at the University of Oregon affiliated with the American Federation of Teachers (AFT) and the American Association of University Professors (AAUP) began the process of forming a faculty union, called United Academics. The union was formally recognized in 2012 and reached its first collective bargaining agreement with the administration in October 2013. The union represents both tenure-track and non-tenure-track faculty. AAUP President Cary Nelson noted that "they are one of the first of two major research campuses [with the University of Illinois at Chicago] to organize for collective bargaining in decades."[1]

The Portland State University Faculty Association has represented part-time faculty and researchers since 1979. Full-time faculty are represented by the AAUP. Neither PSU nor OSU has a union representing both tenure-track and non-tenure-track faculty, but some see movement toward representing both kinds of faculty.[2] As costs increase and public funding drops, pressures mount, and faculty unionization is one way that such pressures may be confronted and managed. Graduate student organizing has been strong at all three major campuses. PSU's Graduate Employees Union began their first contract in the fall of 2016. The graduate student unions at both UO and OSU have existed for decades (1970s and 1990s, respectively), but they have also seen recent renewed activism and membership, and they have made significant gains during contract negotiations.

These changes to the structure and governance of Oregon higher education are not occurring in a vacuum. The rise of for-profit colleges and federal higher education policy affect governance and policy, as well. There are currently thirty-six private for-profit colleges in Oregon, and although many of these are traditional "professional training" centers, such as the College of Cosmetology in Klamath Falls or Le Cordon Bleu College of Culinary Arts in Portland, several are part of the national juggernaut of franchised for-profit alternatives to baccalaureate degree programs (Breneman et al. 2006). Many of these colleges have aggressively targeted returning veterans, using federal grant money to servicemembers to maintain their profitability (Mettler 2014). These schools can be quite expensive and rely on students taking on substantial debt to attend. Cohort default rates (the percentage of a graduating class whose federal loans are not in repayment) can be frighteningly high (above 65%, compared to less than 10% at comparable public institutions).

Federal grants to students have not kept up with need (St. John and Asker 2003). Although the individual amounts of Pell Grants have risen since a low point in the mid-1990s, the amounts have not kept up with either CPI changes or rising college tuition. Between 2010-11 and 2015-16, total Pell Grant expenditures declined by 28 percent in inflation-adjusted dollars. Although the maximum $5,815 award in 2016-17 is historically the largest on record, it is expected to cover less than 30 percent of the cost of college, the lowest share in more than forty years.[3] Colleges have not been making up the difference. Instead, many colleges have been shifting to merit aid instead of need-based aid to keep up with rankings (Gladieux 2004; Wilkinson 2005). One economist has called this widespread practice "buying the best" (Clotfelter 1996).

THE IMPACT OF THE GREAT RECESSION

The landscape of higher education has been changing. Partly because of the Great Recession of 2008, students, their parents, and policymakers have begun questioning the value of a college degree (Kirst and Stevens 2015). The image of a jobless graduate living in his parents' basement circulated widely in 2009 and 2010. Even before the recession hit, however, the number and percentage of young adults going to college had plateaued, putting constraints on many colleges and universities while state funding was becoming more scarce. In order to grow, or even to maintain facilities at their current state, colleges and universities are reaching out to new streams of students, particularly those who are the "first in their family" to go to college, who often require greater financial assistance. Many schools are adding or expanding the services they provide to their students in an attempt to retain a greater number. New services often add administrative costs, which in turn make it harder to attract and retain new students, especially those for whom college is not a given. So far, this problem has been resolved or managed by increasing availabilities of debt. The situation is precarious. A college degree is more expensive today than it ever has been, and yet, to survive, colleges and universities need a growing supply of students, many of whom can ill afford the rising tuition.

Access, accountability, and outcomes have become important organizing foci in this current era of precarious enrollment. Colleges and universities are trying to increase access to college among the historically underrepresented. In Oregon, this includes students from eastern Oregon (and rural areas generally), ethnic minorities (particularly Latino/a and American Indian), and students from poor and working-class families. What these groups often have in common is that many would be the first in their families to get a college degree ("first-generation college student"). Colleges and universities need to pull from these groups to remain viable, but there is also a social justice element to expanding access to underrepresented groups. This element is important in a time when rising tuition threatens to cut off access even to middle-income families and some critics accuse college of catering to the children of the elite. But expanding access is also linked to a developed workforce (Perna and Finney 2014).

In 2011, Oregon legislators passed the 40-40-20 Goal. According to this goal, at least 40 percent of adult Oregonians would have earned a bachelor's degree or higher by 2025, with another 40 percent earning some form of associate's degree or postsecondary credential, and the remaining 20 percent having at least a high school diploma or its equivalent.

This goal is ambitious, requiring almost a doubling of adults with college degrees in less than a single generation (fig. 17.2). Nationally, even today, only about one-third of young adults will earn a bachelor's degree (and only 7% a graduate degree), and *these basic figures have not changed significantly since the 1970s* (Settersten 2015: 118).

In order to reach this goal, public colleges and universities are being prodded, cajoled, and disciplined by state agencies to provide metrics that measure success. This focus on accountability is relatively new and likely to remain in effect so long as the ties between college completion and workforce development are stressed, but especially so during periods of contention over appropriate state funding of higher education. Colleges and universities are currently striving to improve student retention and timely completion. There is great variation by institution in how long it takes students to receive a degree (fig. 17.3). Many of the largest differences can be attributed to what types of students attend. For example, SOU's poor outcomes can be attributed to the fact that it admits harder-to-serve students, many of whom are more likely to take longer to earn a degree for reasons of cost and social circumstances. In the future, accountability schemes must take into account these differences if they are to be effective measures of success.

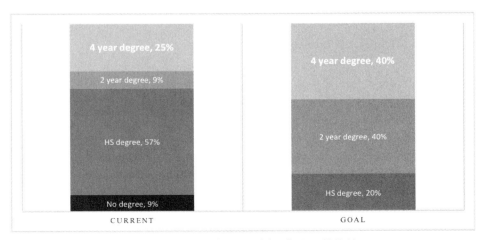

Figure 17.2. Oregon's 40-40-20 Goal compared to actual distribution, 2015-16.

Figure 17.3. Time to degree of Oregon college students, by institution.

While researchers and policymakers have been focused on addressing access, improving accountability, and measuring outcomes, the influx of new students is affecting campus life and programming. Between 2001 and 2014, the percentage of undergraduate students attending Oregon public colleges and universities who received Pell Grants (indicating a high level of financial need) more than doubled, from 16 to 34 percent (fig. 17.4). At two-year public colleges, more than half of all students are eligible to receive Pell Grants. Innovative programs have been developed to address the needs of these students. Oregon State University, for example, was a co-founder (along with Michigan State University) of the College and University Food Bank Alliance, which promotes and supports the development of campus food banks to alleviate food insecurity and hunger among its students. Western Oregon University (WOU) has a highly developed food pantry that helps the 59 percent of its students who were reportedly food insecure at some point during the previous year.[4]

Many public two-year colleges have long sought to address the needs of "first-generation" college students, but the four-year colleges and universities are beginning to include targeted programming, as well. Oregon participates in the federally funded TRiO programs, first created under Title IV of the 1965 Higher Education Act to provide competitive institutional programming for low-income and underrepresented students in higher education. Funded programs included Upward Bound (identifying potential college students in high school), Student Support Services, and McNair Scholars (providing doctoral study preparation for undergraduates). In 2008, Congress extended TRiO grants to homeless youth, those in foster care, English as Second Language learners, and students with disabilities. In 2012-13, Oregon TRiO served 11,758 students, 73 percent of whom were low-income first-generation undergraduates. WOU won the prestigious Higher Education Excellence in Diversity Award for its programming efforts in 2012. OSU began collecting information on

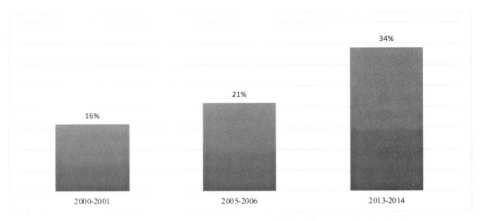

Figure 17.4. Percentage of Pell Grant recipients at Oregon public colleges and universities.

first-generation status for all incoming students in the fall of 2014. In 2016-17, 27 percent of OSU incoming students were identified as first-generation college students. It
has since begun a program—called First!—to celebrate and mentor these students.

ADDRESSING RISING COSTS

Students and their families are paying more for college today than ever before.
Although the increase in cost is linked to rising tuition, it is also a function of major
decreases in the state's ability and willingness to subsidize higher education (Mettler
2014). Figure 17.5 shows the changes in the relation of state appropriation per full-
time-equivalent (FTE) and tuition revenue since 2000; this shift in funding has contributed to the debt explosion among college graduates.[5] At the University of Oregon,
the stated annual tuition for a resident student was $3,819 in 2000-2001. By 2012-
13, tuition had jumped to $9,703. To put this in some perspective, tuition had never
exceeded $1,000 prior to 1980.

Rising costs for students have led to discussions about the economic value of a
college degree in a tight labor market. Given the ambitious 40-40-20 Goal, these concerns could not come at a worse time. How can institutions attract more students to
college, especially students who are traditionally underrepresented on college campuses, when the costs overshadow the economic benefits of a degree? Two recent programs, the Oregon Promise and the Pay It Forward plan, have been devised to address
that question.

The Oregon Promise was developed in the 2015 Oregon legislature. The state set
aside $10 million to pay for two years of community college to all qualified Oregon
high school graduates, beginning in the fall of 2016. Students are expected to offer a
"co-pay" of $50 for each term they are in college, with the state directly paying tuition
to the student's local community college. As with any program, there are trade-offs and

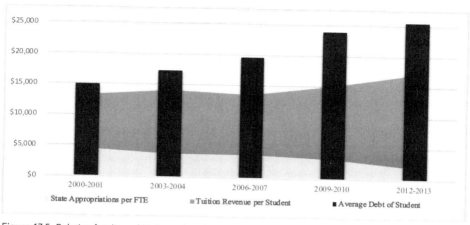

Figure 17.5. Relative funding of higher education in Oregon by state and student, 2000-2013.

policy concerns. Four-year colleges and universities have expressed concern that this program will negatively affect their ability to attract first-year students, thus reducing their revenue. Once again, however, Oregon is a vanguard in this area, and the results of this experiment will have much to offer the rest of the nation.

In 2013, a group of Portland State University college students came up with a plan they called Pay It Forward. The plan was taken up by the Oregon legislature and extensively debated and modified. But the cost of the plan (estimated between $5 and $20 million annually) has so far prevented its implementation. The basic idea is that Oregon students attending a public college or university would receive free tuition; in return, each would pledge to repay a certain percentage of their salary for twenty-four years after graduation; these repayments would be deposited in a publicly adminis-tered fund to help pay the next cohort of students. Thus the system would operate similarly to the national social security regime.

In the end, it may cost much more not do something to rein in the costs of college for students. Cohort default rates, or the percentage of a graduating class who stop making payments on their student debt, have risen substantially as the costs of college have increased and are particularly high among low-income, first-generation, working-class students and students of color. Colleges that serve those populations can have much higher default rates than the more selective universities (fig. 17.6). Rising debt may prevent colleges from reaching more students in the future, and it may also prove bad for Oregon's economy.

Ruined credit can negatively affect Oregonians' ability to buy a house, have decent transportation, and engage in the productive economy. Some studies indicate that stu-dents overwhelmed with debt are less likely to get married and to have children than their peers. The whole generation of students may not be drowning in debt, but many are swimming furiously.

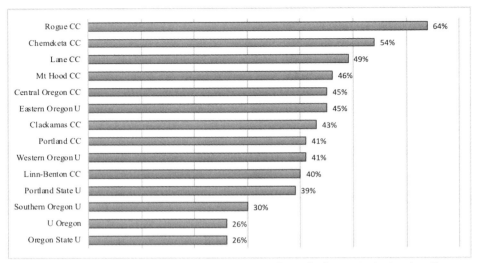

Figure 17.6. Percentage of students receiving Pell Grants at the twelve largest institutions (enrollment > 5,000), 2013–14.

MEASURING THE ECONOMIC IMPACT OF COLLEGE

Controlling rising college costs when colleges and universities are trying to attract low-income and first-generation students is difficult enough, but there is a third part of the story that makes things even more complicated. Perhaps partly attributable to rising costs, state and federal legislators have begun to criticize colleges and universities for their failures to monitor and improve the outcomes of their graduates. A focus on outcomes of college graduates is a distinct addition to the accountability regime, one that is tightly connected to the question of the value of a college degree. But no one has yet figured out how to measure outcomes effectively. More research in this area is clearly warranted.

Nationally speaking, there has been a chorus of voices criticizing "impractical" majors such as the humanities, and conflicting studies about the relative value (differently defined) of a major in STEM (science, technology, engineering, and mathematics) or one in the arts or humanities. There has also been some evidence that absolute returns to college are shrinking (Wolff 2006). One reasonable response today to the question of whether college will pay off is "it depends"—on the individual, the institution, the major, and whether one graduates in a recession year (Cappelli 2015). Students graduating in a recession year are more likely to be unemployed or underemployed than comparable peers; this situation continues or cumulates over the entire working life (Oreopoulos et al. 2006).

Oregon has not been immune to the efforts to score colleges on their ability to demonstrate good career outcomes of their graduates. The first step in this endeavor is to find ways to measure this. Senator Wyden has proposed a system that would inform prospective students how likely they are to earn with a degree from a particular program. The "Student Right to Know Before You Go Act" would lift restrictions linking information between what graduates earn and the institutions they attended (federal privacy regulations), so that students could make more informed choices about where to spend their money. Critics worry that such a narrow view of "economic value" would undermine the educational missions of many institutions. The critics have a point, but given the high cost of college and the wooing of students who are searching for a way to improve their economic prospects, such a plan seems inevitable.

Expanding access, strengthening retention, measuring outcomes, reining in costs are all issues that are tightly woven into the pattern of Oregon Higher Education in the aftermath of the Great Recession. Managing change and diversity has brought new (and old) issues to the Oregon campus.

OTHER ISSUES IN HIGHER EDUCATION

Oregon's public institutions of higher education face the same issues confronting colleges and universities across the country. Before moving to K–12 education, it is useful to briefly discuss some of the issues at the forefront of recent concern.

Black Lives Matter (BLM), a social movement coalescing around issues of systemic racism, hit the national scene in 2014 after highly publicized deaths of several unarmed black men by police in various states. At the University of Oregon, BLM protestors called for renaming several campus buildings named for historic figures in Oregon who had been associated with racist policies of the past. An academic advisor whose work focuses on student retention was quoted in the student newspaper as saying, "Oregon was founded as a white utopia so there are a lot of reasons why people wouldn't feel as though this is a place where they can move and live."[6] Oregon may have to confront its history and the perceptions surrounding its historic whiteness if it wants to continue attracting and retaining students of color, from Oregon and beyond.

In 2016, the US Departments of Education and Justice issued a "Dear Colleague" letter informing all public schools that they may not discriminate against transgender students by blocking access to bathrooms that match the students' gender identity. At the time of the letter, nineteen states had implemented or considered implementing legislation restricting access to multiuser restrooms, locker rooms, and other sex-segregated facilities on the basis of a definition of sex or gender consistent with sex assigned at birth rather than one's gender identity. Oregon was not one of these states. Oregon campuses were early adopters of nondiscrimination policies. In 2004, both UO and OSU incorporated gender identity and expression into their nondiscriminatory policies, with PSU following in 2007. By 2009, several campuses had made gender-inclusive dorms available to students, and, by 2016, most college campuses had established gender-inclusive bathrooms. In 2015, UO ranked in the top ten campuses that were most friendly to LGBTQ (lesbian, gay, bisexual, transgender, and queer) students.[7] In 2016, the Oregon Department of Education issued its own explicit recommendations for creating safe spaces for all students, including use of preferred pronouns, access to preferred attire, and gender-inclusive bathrooms. These guidelines are among the most comprehensive in the nation.

Colleges in the United States have a long and sometimes complicated relationship with student athletes. The first college football team was established in Oregon in 1893, at Oregon State University, soon followed by University of Oregon in 1894. Revenue from college sports can be substantial. High revenues call into question the traditional understanding of student athletes, who receive access to college in return for playing sports for the college. In 2014, representatives from the College Athletes Players' Association (CAPA) sought to unionize Northwestern University's football players. It is possible that discussions of exploitation of student athletes, muted in the past, will become more prominent on college campuses, especially when linked to issues of race (who gets included on college campuses and how?) and the increasingly documented long-term health effects of concussions.

Another returning issue is that of sexual assault on campus. Despite the passage of the Clery Act in 1990, reports of sexual assault are generally acknowledged to be underreported on college campuses. A recent survey conducted at UO found that more than one-third of female students (and about 15% of male students) had experienced some form of nonconsensual sexual contact or attempted assault during college.[8] Victims of sexual assault may not report crimes owing to fear of backlash. Several high-profile rape cases involving athletes at both UO and OSU shed some light on this phenomenon. In 2014, President Ray of OSU issued a public apology to a woman who had been gang-raped by four OSU football players in 1998. At the time, she stopped cooperating with prosecutors when it appeared they were not interested in continuing the prosecution. When she made her story public in 2014, Ray apologized for the way OSU had handled the rape and hired her as a consultant on sexual assault. This came at a time of renewed attention to colleges and how they handle sexual assault. In 2015, a former UO student who claimed she was gang-raped by three members of the basketball team received a settlement of $800,000 in a suit against the college for failing to take appropriate action.[9]

A relatively new set of issues confronting campuses involves guns, particularly the issue of whether a campus can or should prohibit guns on campus and the issue of responses to "active shooter" threats. As a state, Oregon is decidedly more in favor of gun rights than opposed, with its frontier history of hunting and independence. Open carry of firearms is legal statewide in accordance with the Oregon Constitution. Oregon is noted for having few restrictions on where a concealed firearm may be carried. In 2012, however, HECC banned all firearms at the seven Oregon campuses, a move that some claim is a violation of Oregon state law. On the ground, there is a great deal of confusion as to what is permitted on campus. As mass shootings continue, including one at Umpqua Community College that took the lives of ten people in the fall of 2015, pleas for both stricter gun control and more guns on campus are likely to increase.

EDUCATION POLICY

K–12 public education policy in Oregon tends to enjoy significant support from most moderate, conservative, and progressive legislators. The general public, too, gives the K–12 education system generally high marks. Public education is almost always among the "top three important issues" facing the state in any given year, and in annual surveys conducted over the past twenty-five years.[10]

Under this veneer of broad support, however, are disagreements over how best to provide the necessary resources for K–12 schools, a series of new policies designed to expand the reach and character of K–12 educational opportunities, and the growing funding challenge of these expanded programs, along with the continued growth in size of financial commitments to K–12 employee benefits, particularly the Public Employee Retirement System (PERS). This section briefly discusses these components of education policy and politics in Oregon, while also exploring the growing diversity of the K–12 student population.

K–12 SCHOOL FUNDING

The Oregon Constitution requires the legislature to establish a "uniform and general system of common schools" and created a state superintendent of public instruction to oversee and administer the system. In 1951, a state Board of Education was established to set policies for the administration and operation of public elementary and secondary schools. In 2011, Governor John Kitzhaber successfully passed a reform that transferred the superintendent role to the governor, who then appoints, with senate approval, a deputy superintendent to manage education policies along with the state Board of Education. Together, the deputy superintendent and the board are required to: (1) implement statewide standards for public schools; (2) adopt rules for the general governance of public kindergartens, public elementary and secondary schools, and public community colleges; and (3) distribute basic school support funds to districts that meet all legal requirements and maintain and operate a standard school.

Yet, until ballot Measure 5 passed in 1990, the state exercised limited control over K–12 school funds and, like many other states at the time, was heavily dependent on local sources of funding, particularly local property taxes. In fact, in 1933, the state provided only 2 percent of all school funds, while in 1990 the share provided by the state was 30 percent. Measure 5 changed Oregon K–12 funding from being predominantly reliant on local taxes to being more heavily reliant on state-level funding controlled by the governor and legislature. It did this by phasing in limits on property taxes over five years, eventually reducing property taxes by 45 percent, and limiting these taxes to no more than 1.5 percent of assessed market value, of which school districts could only

Table 17.1. Elementary-secondary public school funding by revenue source in selected western states, 2014

State	Federal Sources, %	State Sources, %	Local Sources, %
Idaho	11.2	63.3	25.5
Nevada	9.1	63.1	27.8
Washington	8.0	60.5	31.5
California	10.6	55.0	34.4
Oregon	7.9	51.6	40.4
Montana	11.8	48.0	40.2
Colorado	7.5	43.5	49.1
Arizona	13.3	38.4	48.3
Regional average	10.0	53.0	37.0
National average	8.6	46.7	44.7

Source: US Census Bureau, Percentage Distribution of Public Elementary-Secondary School System Revenue by Source and State: Fiscal Year 2014

receive 0.5 percent. Measure 5 also required state government to replace most of the lost property tax revenues for public schools, which has resulted in a significant decrease in local funding and authority for K–12 education and an increase in state funding and authority. Another consequence of this increased centralization has been more equity in funding for once poorer education districts—especially in rural areas—and a decrease in funding for once-wealthier districts such as Corvallis and Lake Oswego.

The effects of Measure 5 were profound, and by 2000 the state's share of K–12 funding had almost doubled to 56.7 percent, which was more in line with the 54.2 percent level found in other western states and the US average of 49.8 percent (Lunch and Steel 2005). This new pattern, whereby the state funds more than half of the K–12 education budget, has continued each year since 2000, including 51.6 percent of all funding for the 2015-16 school year. The 10 percent decline in state-level funding is the largest such decline since 2000 across the western states, as represented in table 17.1. But a sizable portion of the overall decline in Oregon state funding was offset by the corresponding 27 percent increase in federal funding from 6.2 to 7.9 percent of the total for K–12 schools.

Viewing Oregon's K–12 budget through the lens of per pupil expenditures also shows a decline in the aftermath of the Great Recession (see table 17.2). The Oregon system spent $10,448 per pupil in 2010, which was second highest among the eight western states in table 17.2, and at 98.6 percent of the national average expenditure. The recession, however, took a toll on K–12 funding in virtually all US states, with the per pupil funding falling in Oregon over $1,000 between 2010 and 2014, a decline of 4.8 percent. Compared to the western region, Oregon spending was again near the top, behind only Montana and Washington, but the comparison to the US average shows Oregon per pupil spending at only 90.3 percent, a drop of almost 10 percent versus year

Table 17.2. Spending per pupil in public elementary-secondary school systems in selected western states

State	FY 2010	FY 2014	2010–14 Change, %	2013–14 Change, %
Montana	$11,397	$11,017	-3.3	+2.0
Washington	$10,262	$10,202	-0.6	+3.8
Oregon	$10,448	$9,945	-4.8	+2.5
California	$10,178	$9,595	-5.7	+2.4
Colorado	$9,611	$8,985	-6.5	+2.3
Nevada	$9,210	$8,414	-8.6	-0.7
Arizona	$8,520	$7,528	-11.6	+2.8
Idaho	$7,715	$6,621	-14.2	-4.1
Regional average	$9,668	$9,038	-6.5	+2.2
National average	$10,600	$11,009	+3.9	+2.7

Note: Totals are inflation adjusted and shown in 2014 dollars. FY, fiscal year.
Source: Governing: The States and Localities (2016)

Table 17.3. US ranking by total spending per pupil in public elementary-secondary schools in selected western states

State	FY 2000	FY 2014
Montana	30	22
Washington	28	27
Oregon	19	29
California	29	34
Colorado	32	39
Nevada	40	45
Arizona	49	48
Idaho	48	49

Note: FY, fiscal year.
Source: US Census Bureau, Annual Survey of School System Finances, 2014

2010. The latest available data show a significant one-year improvement between the 2013 and 2014 school years, with an increase of 2.5 percent, suggesting that the worst of the Great Recession is behind Oregon, at least as concerns K–12 per pupil funding.

But the trends in per pupil funding also show that Oregon has lost significant ground since year 2000 in terms of how its funding levels ranks nationally. Table 17.3 displays how Oregon's former rank of 19th had slipped to 29th by 2014, following a similar trend for those western states nearest to Oregon.

MAJOR NEW POLICIES FOR K–12 EDUCATION

At the same time that Oregon has struggled to maintain or grow its per capita funding for K–12 education, the state has provided innovations likely to lessen the overall cost for the K–12 system. The state has also expanded education requirements, which has compounded the funding challenge because the expanded requirements, with one exception, have not been accompanied by new streams of revenue.

Allowing Performance-Based Knowledge Standards

In 2002, Oregon's State Board of Education approved a "Credit for Proficiency" policy, which allowed school districts to provide students with education credits through demonstrations of knowledge rather than the traditional "seat time" model, which focused on counting the amount of time students spend in class. The next step, following several pilot programs, was the establishment in 2007 of the Oregon Diploma, a key feature of which was the use of proficiency credits. In the early going, proficiency credits were generally used only for earning elective credits outside of a classroom setting. Yet in 2009, the state Board of Education broadened the program's impact by issuing a rule that allowed both school districts and charter schools to grant credit if a student could demonstrate "defined levels of proficiency or mastery of recognized [educational] standards," whether inside or outside of the classroom.[11]

Further, proficiency credits have become a key feature of what many consider to be a more rigorous Oregon Diploma for high school students, with its stated goal of ensuring that "each student demonstrates the knowledge and skills necessary to transition successfully to his or her next steps: advanced learning, work and citizenship."[12] In addition to more rigorous credit requirements in math, English, and science, as well as fewer elective credits, the revised Oregon Diploma now requires that students complete three of nine "Essential Skills" to graduate: "Read and comprehend a variety of text," "Write clearly and accurately," and "Apply mathematics in a variety of settings."[13]

All-Day Kindergarten

As with most states, Oregon's public school system has long supported the half-day model for kindergarten. But by the early 2000s, many education policy experts had concluded that the all-day model provided children with a positive, measurable educational boost, especially with regard to reading in the early grades of elementary school. The Oregon legislature acted in 2011, passing the All Day Kindergarten Bill (SB 248), with the ultimate goal of having 95 percent of Oregon third graders reading at grade level by 2019. The all-day model did not take effect, however, until the 2015-16 school year in order to give school districts and the legislature adequate time to prepare for the changes to classrooms and the state budget.

The new law does not mandate that Oregon school districts adopt the all-day model; instead, it incentivizes them to do so by providing full funding from the state budget. In response, 740 of the 750 eligible schools offered all-day kindergarten, leading to 99.7 percent enrollment in the all-day model during the 2015-16 school year, a dramatic increase over the previous year, when just over 42 percent of students were enrolled in full-day kindergarten.[14]

Ballot Initiatives: Career Technical Education and Outdoor Education

In 2016, Oregon voters said yes to two major ballot initiatives involving K–12 education: Measure 98, on Career Technical Education (CTE), and Measure 99, on Outdoor Education.

Measure 98, formally known as Oregon State Funding for Dropout Prevention and College Readiness, requires the Oregon legislature to distribute at least $800 per student (adjusted for inflation) each year to high schools for "establishing or expanding career and technical education programs, college-level educational opportunities, and dropout-prevention strategies."[15] Voters gave the initiative overwhelming support, with just under 66 percent in favor. The problem for the state Department of Education is that the measure did not provide a new source of funding, despite the fact that Measure 98 commits the state to spend a minimum of $147 million per year on career and technical education, accelerated learning, and high school graduation improvement programs.

Measure 99, supported by over 67 percent of Oregon voters, created the Oregon Outdoor School Fund. The measure allocates 4 percent of state lottery revenue in support of outdoor school programs for fifth and sixth graders across the state. Previously, there had not been statewide funding for these programs, and so students participated at varying levels depending on their district. The fund is administered by the Oregon State University Extension Service.

CHALLENGES TO K–12 SCHOOLS IN OREGON

The Oregon K–12 system faces not only the challenge of trying to successfully incorporate these new education policies into existing curriculums but also the challenges of a growing student population, entitlement spending demands, the likelihood of less federal funding from the new Trump administration, the ongoing battle against low graduation rates, and changing demographics.

The first challenge is a growing K–12 student population that, by definition, increases the cost of public education. Oregon encountered rapid student growth during the 1990s, from 472,394 students statewide in 1990 to 551,480, a 16.7 percent overall increase (see table 17.4). Student growth then slowed dramatically between 2001 and 2012, increasing by only 18,420, or 3.3 percent, to a total of 569,900. K–12 student growth continued at an anemic pace up through the latest recorded enrollment figures in 2015, increasing a mere 1.2 percent over 2012 student numbers. Future enrollment projections, however, estimate another period of strong growth going forward to 2023, when experts predict there will be 626,600 students, a 9.9 percent increase over year 2012.[16]

Table 17.4. Total percentage growth of Oregon's K–12 student population

	1990-2001	2001-12	2012-23
Total growth	16.7	3.3	9.9

A second challenge involves the rising burden of retirement, or PERS, obligations, which threaten to crowd out spending on other types of educational needs such as instructional materials, hiring more teachers, and maintaining smaller class sizes, learning (information) technologies, and so on. In the 2009–11 biennium, the basic rate to cover PERS for school districts equaled 14.4 percent of payroll. When schools' Social Security obligations are added, the effective rate in 2009–11 was over 20 percent of payroll. The combined PERS / Social Security cost rose to 25 percent in the 2011–13 biennium, to 32 percent in 2013–15, and then to 34.3 percent in 2015–17. The combined retirement burden for schools' payrolls, barring any reforms, is projected to be over 36 percent in the 2017–19 biennium. As Sharie Lewis, director of accounting and payroll in Portland Public Schools, notes, "PERS is the elephant in the room at every conference I go to."[17]

Third, the Trump administration is unlikely to be an ally of blue state Oregon, and the general expectation is that the sizable increases in federal K–12 funding during both the George W. Bush and Barack Obama years will not continue. Key to this expectation is that the US Department of Education, now led by charter school and vouchers advocate Betsy DeVos, will likely cut existing federal funding levels to the states, currently at almost 8 percent of total K–12 funding in Oregon. An opportunity might arise, however, in the expected federal push to expand funding for alternatives to traditional public schools, especially public charter schools and voucher programs that offer the government-based per pupil funding to individual students, who then get to choose where and which type of school—public or private—they wish to attend. Oregon does not have any voucher programs, but its charter school program, which currently serves 30,000 students, has struggled with making progress in reading and math, reaching minority populations, and funding restrictions imposed by the state (e.g., the state does not fund transportation costs for charter schools). New federal funds and guidelines may help in all three areas.

Fourth, Oregon businesses and communities face a major long-term challenge from the state's dismal high school graduation rate. As of the 2014-15 year, the four-year graduation rate was only 73.8 percent, compared to the US average of 83.2 percent. This ranks Oregon 48th, ahead of only Nevada and New Mexico. The graduation rates for low-income students and most minorities are even more troubling. Only 66.4 percent of low-income students graduate in four years (vs. the US average of 76.1%), and the latest available cohort data show the following graduation rates: whites, 71 percent; Hispanics, 60 percent; blacks, 53 percent; Asians / Pacific Islanders, 79 percent.[18]

The fifth challenge involves the rapidly changing demographics of the K–12 student population. In 2000, just 19.2 percent of the K–12 population were students of color. By 2010, that number had jumped to 32.5 percent and in 2015 to 36.6 percent. In addition, twenty school districts encompassing 133,700 students now have 50 percent or more students of color, with another eleven districts with at least 40 percent. The fastest-growing subgroup continues to be Hispanics, who now represent 22 percent of Oregon's overall K–12 student population. Moreover, 10 percent of K–12 students are now nonnative English speakers, with Spanish, Russian, and Vietnamese being the most common foreign languages. Given these changing demographics, State Deputy Superintendent Rob Saxton argues that a key challenge for Oregon in the future is that

> We must achieve significantly better outcomes for students of color if we want to see our achievement results increase statewide. Our state is working to address these needs with the Governor's strategic initiatives designed to help close achievement gaps, better support students, and more actively involve historically underserved communities and families.[19]

CONCLUSION

The K–12 and higher education systems in Oregon are facing new challenges from globalization; the shift to a more high-tech, digital, and service-based economy; and changing student demographics. In recent years, the K–12 system has also been asked to provide new and expanded educational programs (e.g., all-day kindergarten, outdoor education, technical education). Of central importance to both policy realms is the fact that each is wrestling with how to provide an effective, appropriate education at a reasonable cost in the face of these new challenges. Can public universities in Oregon and elsewhere keep their costs in check such that higher education is still affordable and attainable for the growing number of citizens needed to support Oregon's economy of the future? Can Oregon's K–12 system find a way to reduce its abysmally low high school graduation rates while also training students, including those not going to college, to be ready for the modern workforce? Can the state as a whole figure out how to relieve or resolve the fiscal pressure stemming from the increasing PERS costs for public schools, thereby freeing up additional funding for other K–12 educational needs? And how will K–12 and higher education in Oregon manage the needs of the growing racial and ethnic diversity of its student population?

While these questions are to be answered over time, Oregon has made strides in one area: college affordability at the two-year community college level. The Oregon Promise of 2015 program pays two years of community college tuition to all qualified Oregon high school graduates. Yet as this chapter makes clear, this small step in the direction of access and affordability is just that—a small step. The dominant picture for the higher education policy landscape is one of escalating tuition and fees, fewer grants and more loans, less affordability, and increasing student debt. In short, we are in a different world from 1862, when the US Congress passed the Morrill Act, which was designed to "ma[k]e possible the higher instruction of the children of workers and farmers and thus enabled social mobility and the equality of educational opportunity to become realities in a political democracy" (Brickman and Lehrer 1962: 11). By doing so, the individuals earning college degrees would certainly gain significant personal benefits, economically and otherwise. But of equal importance to the law's sponsors was the idea that educating more citizens would necessarily strengthen the American economy and democracy by providing a citizenry more fully capable of effective participation in civic life.

Perhaps public policy in the area of public education can find its ultimate challenge here—in how to provide an individual and collective good to all, one that develops human potential without increasing inequality through excessive cost, one that places appropriately trained workers into satisfying and necessary social positions, and one that develops the workforce while at the same time raising its citizens to participate fully in civic life.

Notes

1   Gwendolyn Bradley, "New Faculty Union at University of Oregon," *Academe* (May–June 2012): https://www.aaup.org/article/new-faculty-union-university-oregon#.V-lSpMea1PY.
2   Oregon State University successfully formed a union in June 2018.
3   "Pell Grants Help Keep College Affordable for Millions of Americans," Institute for College Access and Success, June 30, 2017, http://ticas.org/sites/default/files/pub_files/overall_pell_one-pager.pdf.
4   Lani Furbank, 2016. "Ten Organizations Fighting Food Insecurity on College Campuses," Hunter College New York City Food Policy Center, September 6, 2016, http://www.nycfoodpolicy.org/food-insecurity-on-college-campuses/.
5   No debt appears for 2000-2001 because data are not available for that year.
6   Tony Shinn and Tran Nguyen, "Black Lives Matter Has Changed UO, but Supporters Are Tired of Watching Deaths," *Daily Emerald*, July 11, 2016, https://www.dailyemerald.com/2016/07/11/black-lives-matter-has-changed-uo-but-supporters-are-tired-of-watching-deaths/.
7   "Best Colleges for LGBTQ Students," BestColleges.com, accessed May 28, 2018, http://www.bestcolleges.com/features/best-colleges-for-lgbt-students/.
8   Jennifer J. Freyd, Marina N. Rosenthal, and Carly Parnitzke Smith, *Preliminary Results from the UO Sexual Violence and Institutional Behavior Campus Survey* (Eugene: University of Oregon, 2014), http://dynamic.uoregon.edu/jjf/campus/UO-campus-results-30Sept14.pdf.
9   Diane Dietz, "UO Settles Alleged Rape Case," *Register-Guard*, August 5, 2015, http://projects.registerguard.com/rg/news/local/33366922-75/the-university-of-oregon-settles-high-profile-rape-lawsuit.html.csp.

10 Bill Lunch and Brent S. Steel, "Oregon Education Policy," in *Oregon State and Local Politics*, ed. B. Steel, M. Henkels, and R. Clucas (Lincoln: University of Nebraska Press, 2005).

11 "Oregon Diploma—Questions and Answers," Oregon Department of Education, June 2011, www.oregon.gov/ode/students-and-family/OregonDiploma/Documents/diploma-qa.pdf.

12 "Modified Diploma and Alternative Certificate," Oregon Department of Education, January 2007, www.ode.state.or.us/gradelevel/hs/transition/mdac.ppt.

13 "Essential Skills," Oregon Department of Education, accessed May 28, 2018, http://www.oregon.gov/ode/educator-resources/essentialskills/Pages/default.aspx.

14 Betsy Hammond, "Oregon's Dramatic Switch," *Oregonian*, February 4, 2016, http://www.oregonlive.com/education/index.ssf/2016/02/oregons_dramatic_switch_997_pe.html.

15 "Measure 98," Oregon Department of Education, November 23, 2016, http://www.ode.state.or.us/wma/teachlearn/cte/faq_measure_98_final_11-23-2016.pdf.

16 "Enrollment in Public Elementary and Secondary Schools, by Region, State, and Jurisdiction: Selected Years, Fall 1990 through fall 2023," National Center for Education Statistics, accessed May 28, 2018, https://nces.ed.gov/programs/digest/d13/tables/dt13_203.20.asp.

17 Betsy Hammond, "Oregon Schools' Financial Woes Aren't All Because of PERS," *Oregonian*, May 11, 2013, www.oregonlive.com/education/index.ssf/2013/05/schools_woes_arent_all_on_pers.html.

18 "High School Graduation Rates by State," *Governing: The States and Localities*, accessed May 28, 2018, http://www.governing.com/gov-data/high-school-graduation-rates-by-state.html.

19 "2014-15 Student Enrollment Report," Oregon Department of Education, February 4, 2015, www.ode.state.or.us/news/announcements/announcement.aspx?ID=10407.

Bibliography

Baum, Sandy, and Martha Johnson. 2015. *Financing Higher Education: The Evolution of State Funding.* Washington, DC: Urban Institute.

Bourdieu, Pierre, and Jean-Claude Passeron. 1990. *Reproduction in Education, Society and Culture.* Thousand Oaks, CA: Sage.

Breneman, David W., Brian Pusser, and Sarah E. Turner. 2006. *Earnings from Learning: The Rise of For-Profit Universities.* Albany: State University of New York Press.

Brickman, William, and Stanley Lehrer. 1962. *A Century of Higher Education.* New York: Society for the Advancement of Education.

Calhoun, Craig. 2011. "The Public Mission of the Research University." In *Knowledge Matters: The Public Mission of the Research University*, edited by Diana Rhoten and Craig Calhoun. New York: Columbia University Press.

Cappelli, Peter 2015. *Will College Pay Off? A Guide to the Most Important Financial Decision You Will Ever Make.* New York: Public Affairs.

Clotfelter, Charles T. 1996. *Buying the Best: Cost Escalation in Elite Higher Education.* Princeton, NJ: Princeton University Press.

DeCew, Judith Wagner. Ed. 2003. *Unionization in the Academy: Visions and Realities.* Lanham: Rowman & Littlefield.

Doyle, William R., and Michael W. Kirst. 2015. "Explaining Policy Change in K-12 and Higher Education." In *Remaking College: The Changing Ecology of Higher Education*, edited by Michael W. Kirst and Mitchell L. Stevens. Stanford, CA: Stanford University Press.

Gladieux, Lawrence E. 2004. *Low-Income Students and the Affordability of Higher Education*. New York: Century Foundation.

Goodchild, Lester F., R. Jonsen, P. Limerick, and D. Longanecker. Eds. 2014. *Higher Education in the American West: Regional History and State Contexts*. New York: Palgrave Macmillan.

Hofstadter, Richard, and Wilson Smith. 1961. *American Higher Education, A Documentary History*. 2 vols. Chicago: University of Chicago Press.

Hurst, Allison L. 2012. *College and the Working Class*. Rotterdam: Sense.

Kirst, Michael W., and Mitchell L. Stevens. Eds. 2015. *Remaking College: The Changing Ecology of Higher Education*. Stanford, CA: Stanford University Press.

Loss, Christopher. 2012. *Between Citizens and the State: The Politics of American Higher Education in the Twentieth Century*. Princeton, NJ: Princeton University Press.

Marsden, George M. 1994. *The Soul of the American University: From Protestant Establishment to Established Nonbelief*. New York: Oxford University Press.

Mettler, Suzanne. 2014. *Degrees of Inequality: How the Politics of Higher Education Sabotaged the American Dream*. New York: Basic Books.

Nelson, Cary. 2010. *No University Is an Island: Saving Academic Freedom*. New York: New York University Press.

Nemec, Mark R. 2006. *Ivory Towers and Nationalist Minds: Universities, Leadership, and the Development of the American State*. Ann Arbor: University of Michigan Press.

Oreopoulos, Philip, Till von Wachter, and Andrew Heisz. 2006. *The Short- and Long-Term Career Effects of Graduating in a Recession: Hysteresis and Heterogeneity in the Market for College Graduates*. Working Paper No. 12159. Cambridge, MA: National Bureau of Economic Research.

Perna, Laura W., and Joni E. Finney. 2014. *The Attainment Agenda: State Policy Leadership in Higher Education*. Baltimore: Johns Hopkins University Press.

Rudolph, Frederick. 1962. *The American College and University: A History*. New York: Knopf.

Settersten, Richard A., Jr. 2015. "The Radically Altered Landscape of Early Adulthood: Implications for Broad-Access Higher Education." In *Remaking College: The Changing Ecology of Higher Education*, edited by Michael W. Kirst and Mitchell L. Stevens. Stanford, CA: Stanford University Press.

St. John, Edward P., and Eric H. Asker. 2003. *Refinancing the College Dream: Access, Equal Opportunity, and Justice for Taxpayers*. Baltimore: Johns Hopkins University Press.

Trow, Martin. 2010. *Twentieth-Century Higher Education: Elite to Mass to Universal*. Edited by Michael Burrage. Baltimore: Johns Hopkins University Press.

Wilkinson, Rupert. 2005. *Aiding Students, Buying Students: Financial Aid in America*. Nashville, TN: Vanderbilt University Press.

Wolff, Edward N. 2006. *Does Education Really Help? Skill, Work, and Inequality*. New York: Oxford University Press.

18
Fiscal Policy
MARK HENKELS

As she presented the 2017-19 state budget, Governor Kate Brown expressed sentiments that have characterized Oregon budget-makers for over two decades now: "The budget I am proposing today is a short-term solution to keep Oregon on track, funding a reduced level of core state services through a combination of budget cuts and new revenue."[1] The message marked another proposed biennial budget characterized by small adaptations and statements regarding the need for bolder steps.

Change in state and local government budgets is typically characterized by incrementalism, or small alterations over time. Under normal circumstances, and especially for the national budget, the best predictor of the next budget is the current budget. But the appearance of budget stability masks how small changes can add up over time, like compound interest or inflation, and ultimately transform the structure of government budgets. Oregon's seeming stability also belies how state and local fiscal systems more often experience transformational change than the federal budget leviathan. It is more than a matter of size and inertia, however. State initiative systems can significantly alter taxes or spending commitments virtually overnight, and the need to balance their budgets periodically forces legislatures to recalibrate budget priorities. For these reasons, the Oregon state and local finance system may be better described as a "punctuated equilibrium" model than an "incremental" one.

"Punctuated equilibrium" is the label that political scientists Frank R. Baumgartner and Bryan D. Jones apply to a policy system that has long periods of stability periodically rocked by major change.[2] Baumgartner and Jones argue that most major policy areas tend to operate in relative stability until something changes in either their "policy image" (public understandings and expectations in the field) or the "policy venue" (where policies are created). The punctuated equilibrium theory seems to apply to the Oregon public finance system quite well.

The policy image dominating the Oregon's public finance debates in recent years holds that Oregonians will tolerate minor tax increases but not a broad sales tax, which they have rejected nine times, and that K–12 education gets a special claim for state general fund spending.[3] As for the policy venue, the state legislature controls the most flexible element, the General Fund, and generally follows incremental patterns in budgeting owing to the political difficulty of creating a strong majority in favor of major reforms. This pattern occasionally falls apart, however. The most recent significant major fiscal policy changes occurred when conservatives used the initiative process to strictly limit property taxes in the 1990s. One other venue is notable in this respect: the courts. The Oregon Supreme Court's recognition that existing state commitments to public employee retirement benefits are constitutionally protected reversed at least one major effort to reduce this financial risk.

This chapter has three sections: (1) a description of the basic structures and patterns of the state budget and a more generalized description of local finances, (2) a discussion of the key sources of budget change in recent decades, and (3) a brief exploration of possible forces for change in the next decade. To begin, Oregon's state budget process is basically a biennial, or two-year, one. The base budget for each two-year cycle is created in the legislature during the lengthier odd-year sessions, although adjustments can occur by necessity or choice before the next major budget is produced. Local budgets are generally annual budgets and therefore must be approved each year. This chapter focuses on operating budgets, those funding current activities, and basically ignores capital budgets, which pay for large-scale projects with borrowed money over time.

BASIC STATE AND LOCAL BUDGET STRUCTURES
The Oregon State Budget

Like all states, Oregon has multiple state budgets. The most encompassing budget is labeled as "All Funds" or "Total Funds," depending on the publication. Here, All Funds is the label for budget information that represents the total funds that flow through the state government each two-year cycle.

As figure 18.1 shows, the All Funds Budget has four components: the General Fund Budget, the Lottery Budget (which is often lumped with the General Fund, as we sometimes do here), the Federal Funds Budget, and the Other Funds Budget. Figure 18.2 shows how the flow of money through the state is dispersed to different

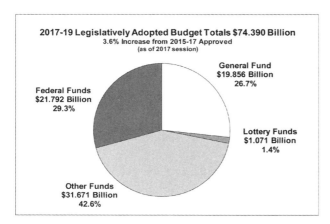

2017-19 Legislatively Adopted Budget Totals $74.390 Billion
3.6% Increase from 2015-17 Approved
(as of 2017 session)

General Fund
$19.856 Billion
26.7%

Federal Funds
$21.792 Billion
29.3%

Lottery Funds
$1.071 Billion
1.4%

Other Funds
$31.671 Billion
42.6%

Figure 18.1. Oregon State All Funds Budget, 2017-19. *Oregon Legislative Fiscal Office, Budget Highlights: Legislatively Approved 2017-2019 Budget (Salem: Oregon Legislative Fiscal Office, 2017), 1*

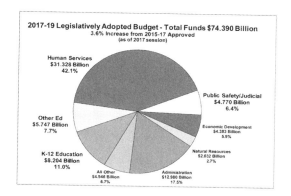

Figure 18.2. Oregon State All Funds Budget expenditures, 2017-19. *Oregon Legislative Fiscal Office,* Budget Highlights: Legislatively Approved 2017-2019 Budget *(Salem: Oregon Legislative Fiscal Office, 2017), 2*

functions of government. The significance of Human Services is notable, taking 42.1 percent of the state's total spending and mostly going to the Oregon Health Plan and other social services.

If an individual or group wants to present the biggest possible image of state spending, they use All Funds numbers. For 2017-19, All Funds spending was projected to be nearly $74.3 billion. The All Funds Budget is not created independently; it just totals the dynamics and decisions creating the four sub-budgets.

Typically, when politicians or activists, and especially legislators, refer to the "state budget," they mean the state's General Fund or General Fund and Lottery Budget, which in 2017-19 is about 27 percent of all the money flowing through state government. Unlike the other budget categories, the legislature can spend General Fund money with relatively few legal restrictions, although there are plenty of political considerations. Figure 18.3 demonstrates how Oregon's General Fund / Lottery spending has three major components: (1) education (38.8% dedicated to K–12 education and 13.8% to other education, totaling over half of the funds); (2) human services (25.4%); and (3) public safety / judiciary branch (15.4%). Battles over state

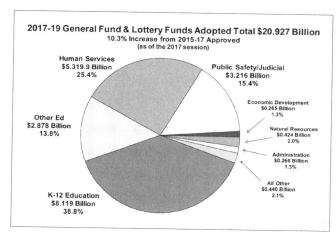

Figure 18.3. Oregon State General Fund and Lottery Fund expenditures, 2017-19. *Oregon Legislative Fiscal Office,* Budget Highlights: Legislatively Approved 2017-2019 Budget *(Salem: Oregon Legislative Fiscal Office, 2017), 5*

Table 18.1. General Fund revenue sources for selected biennial budgets, 1991-93 to 2015-17

	1991-93	1995-97	2001-3	2005-7	2011-13	2015-17
Beginning balance	392.2	496.3	363.0	308.5	0	476.6
Personal income taxes	4,561.9	6,303.4	7,699.5	11,040.3	12,284.1	15,712.4
Corporate income taxes	354.9	684.4	420.1	844.1	883.9	1,134.7
Other taxes	321.3	428.2	350.7	407.5	443.3	464.9
Other revenue	239.3	315.5	895.7	450.1	560.0	717.2
Total	5,869.6	8,227.9	9,729.0	13,050.5	14,171.3	18,505.8

Note: Values given in millions of dollars. Source: Oregon Legislative Revenue Office, 2016 Oregon Public Finance: Basic Facts (Salem: State of Oregon, 2016)

school funding, especially for K–12 programs, typically center on how the General Fund will be sliced up.

By law, the General Fund Budget cannot run a deficit. Therefore, when faced with slowing revenues, such as in a recession, the legislature must cut current or future spending commitments, or both. The General Fund's heavy dependence on the personal income tax enhances the potential for instability. As table 18.1 illustrates, personal income tax is by far the main source of the General Funds Budget, providing approximately 85 percent of the total revenue. Table 18.1 also hints at the instability of personal income tax, although it does not show how the biennial revenue from this source went from $11 billion in the 2005-7 biennium to $9.9 billion in 2007-9.

Income tax revenues are further complicated by Oregon's unique "kicker law." This law requires that if revenues of a biennium exceed the projections made by the state economist just before the budget is adopted by 2 percent or more, all revenues above the original projection go back to the taxpayers. Advocates of strong social services believe the kicker prevents the restoration of funds or the building of a reserve when the economy exceeds expectations. Fiscal conservatives think the kicker controls excessive spending commitments during unexpected good times. The largest kicker refund occurred in the 2005-7 cycle, when $1.071 billion was returned to state taxpayers, over 18 percent of the personal tax revenues collected.[4]

The Lottery Budget is the smallest distinct budget within the All Funds Budget, comprising only 1.4 percent of the total. This is still projected to be over $1.017 billion in 2017-19, too much to ignore. While the Oregon Lottery publicizes scratch-offs and big-jackpot lotteries, as well as the good things the revenue does, video gambling machines brought in over 70 percent of lottery revenues for fiscal year 2015.[5] The Oregon Constitution requires that specific percentages of lottery profits go to public education and natural resources, while specific statutes commit lottery money to gambling addiction, athletic programs at universities, county economic development, and to county fairs. In sum, 32 percent of net lottery funds were dedicated revenue in 2015, and in 2016 voters approved dedicating another 1.5 percent of the lottery's net income to veterans' services and up to $22 million for a newly established Outdoor School Fund.[6] In legislative and other public budget debates, lottery funds are often combined with the general fund. The legislature views lottery funds as fungible, meaning that legislature can trade off lottery and General Fund money when financing recipient programs.

Oregon is also the administrator and conduit for many federal spending programs, which are incorporated into the state budget as the Federal Funds Budget. Federal money amounts to just over 29 percent of the 2017-19 All Funds Budget. Figure 18.4 shows how over 85 percent of the Federal Funds Budget goes to the Oregon Health Plan (or OHP, basically what other states call Medicaid) and the Department of Human Services, which administers various social assistance programs such as Temporary Assistance for Needy Families (TANF), often referred to as "welfare."

These "gifts" from the federal government come with two major types of strings attached. First, nearly all federal grants have mandates or conditions. To get the money, states or cities must meet any attached guidelines or requirements. While Oregon has successfully obtained federal waivers (or permission) to develop a relatively unique Medicaid system, Congress and often the federal agencies can readily change the requirements. States may refuse federal grant money and the mandates that accompany them, as many states (but not Oregon) did with the Medicaid expansion program that was part of President Obama's Affordable Care Act.

The second complication with federal funds is that they typically require states to "match" the federal money. For Medicaid funds going to Oregon, the federal medical assistance percentage is 64.47, meaning that the state must spend almost 65¢ for every dollar from the federal government.[7] This may tie up money that states could spend elsewhere, and in hard times a state may lose available federal funds because it lacks the matching funds.

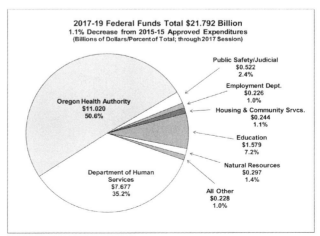

Figure 18.4. Oregon State Federal Funds expenditures, 2017-19. *Oregon Legislative Fiscal Office*, Budget Highlights: Legislatively Approved 2017-2019 Budget *(Salem: Oregon Legislative Fiscal Office, 2017), 28*

The final, and largest, portion of the All Funds Budget is Other Funds. Figure 18.5 demonstrates how the All Funds Budget is a complicated assembly of miscellaneous funds. Many funds in the Other Funds are raised through investment and transfers from other programs, such as the Public Employee Retirement System (PERS) and the Employment Department fund that covers unemployment benefits. Such trust funds have the desirable quality of earning money through the investment of their balance, but they also risk not meeting expected investment goals. Some areas in the Other Funds budget are distinctive for their independent dedicated revenue streams, such as the flows of money from highways fees and fuel taxes to transportation, and of tuition to higher education. Dedicated revenues may provide programs with alternative financial streams to counter cuts in their general fund allocations. Chapter 17 notes how higher education countered general funds cuts by raising tuition. The adequacy of these revenue sources depends on their specific design. Until the 2017 legislature passed a statewide income tax of .1% dedicated to transit, for example, the Department of Transportation faced declining revenue as cars become more fuel efficient. Because the revenues and obligations of Other Funds are typically embedded in specific legislation and isolated from the normal budget process, they are generally less subject to the constant intense fights that characterize the general funds approval process. Two exceptions to this are PERS, which draws attention for reasons discussed below, and transportation, for which, until 2017, there had been great pressure to greatly increase funding to correct the state's backlog of infrastructure problems.

Individual state agencies and programs vary in their dependency on the different state budgets. For example, the legislative branch is funded almost exclusively by the General Fund, while transportation receives most of its funds from Other Funds, and human services receives most of its money from the Federal Funds. As noted above regarding higher education, programs may be able to make up for cuts from one source

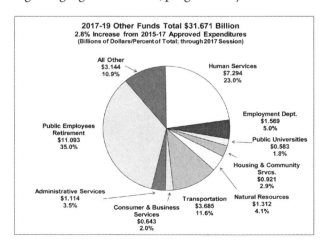

Figure 18.5. Oregon State Other Funds total, 2017-19.
Oregon Legislative Fiscal Office, Budget Highlights: Legislatively Approved 2017-2019 Budget *(Salem: Oregon Legislative Fiscal Office, 2017), 18*

by getting increases in another. This may protect a program's total funding, but the burden of payment may shift, possibly with equity implications.

Local Government Finance

Local governments are creatures of the state. They exist because the state has granted them charters or empowered them through general laws. Accordingly, all local government finances must abide by state laws and are directly affected by state grants, revenue limitations, and enabling laws. Schools districts and counties are particularly tied into state policy because they provide services that are explicitly part of state policy, such as K–12 education, planning, judicial functions, and election and voting policies. Each city, county, school district, and special district has a unique set of revenue and spending patterns.

For simplicity, this chapter looks only at the major revenue and spending patterns of cities and school districts, the latter of which is combined with educational service districts (ESDs). Although this chapter does not discuss county budgets in depth, there is one issue regarding counties that deserves specific attention: the troubles facing Oregon's timber-dependent counties.

Many of Oregon's counties have major federal landholdings and have historically benefitted from federal compensation in lieu of property taxes. Some counties in western and southern Oregon also get a direct percentage of timber sales revenues from specific US Bureau of Land Management (BLM) lands. As federal logging slowed in recent decades, in part due to environmental restrictions, these counties suffered major revenue losses despite a recently ended federal program that provided some replacement money. A 2016 audit by the secretary of state identified four of these counties (Curry, Douglas, Josephine, and Polk) as "counties to watch." Curry, Douglas, and Josephine are the three counties most dependent on BLM timber payments, which has funded more than 10 percent of their general fund. The budget futures of these timber-dependent counties are strongly tied to future federal timber policies, especially because their residents have strong anti-tax sentiments. The average permanent property tax rate for Oregon counties is $2.82, far above that of Josephine (59¢), Curry (60¢), and Douglas ($1.11).[8]

THE FINANCES OF OREGON SCHOOL DISTRICTS AND EDUCATIONAL SERVICE DISTRICTS

Funding for K–12 public education in Oregon is channeled primarily through local school districts, but some also flows through educational service districts, which provide services where the pooling of resources between multiple districts can be efficient, such as for special education programs and some technological services. Oregon's state K–12 school funding comes from three major sources: the school fund, the basic school fund, and miscellaneous other programs.

In Oregon's K–12 system overall for the 2012-13 school year, about 49 percent of funding came from the state, while local sources (primarily property taxes) provided about 43 percent. Federal funds covered roughly 8 percent of K–12 revenues.[9] Federal money comes from a wide range of diverse grants. Historically, many Oregon school districts benefitted greatly from the requirement that a share of all federal timber sales go to local schools. These federal revenues parallel those going to timber-dependent counties. This money dropped dramatically when federal timber harvests declined in the late 1980s, despite a federal program to help compensate for these losses.[10]

Spending by local school districts is concentrated on direct classroom expenses at 56 percent. Personnel costs, salaries, and benefits dominate the overall costs for education. As table 18.2 shows, overall spending continually increases in the long run, but the most recent recession reduced average total spending per student from $10,057 in 2008-9 to $9,869 in 2009-10. Oregon ranked thirty-fifth in the country for state and local revenue per student, which reflects its rankings of thirty-first in state revenue and twenty-ninth in local tax revenue going to schools.[11]

CITY BUDGETS IN OREGON

Unlike school districts, cities provide a wide and variable range of services. Many city services are at least partially funded by service fees, and because cities often administer federal and state-supported programs, their revenue and spending streams are complex and diverse. A few cities, such as Monmouth, operate their own electrical power systems, which significantly alters their budget profile. Still some basic patterns are useful to note and can be demonstrated by looking at a sample city. Hillsboro, a larger suburban city in the Portland Metro area, provides a good example of typical revenue and expenditure patterns.

Cities have many sources of revenue. Because cities provide services with major capital requirements, such as water and sewer, most carry significant reserves from

Table 18.2. Oregon K–12 operating expenditures per student

Where Dollars Were Spent	2006-7	%	2010-11	%	2014-15	%
Direct classroom	$5,047	55.3	$5,514	56	$6,063	56
Classroom support	$1,897	20.8	$2,025	20	$2,196	20
Building support	$1,752	19.2	$1,931	19	$2,077	19
Central support	$438	4.8	$462	5	$491	5
Total**	$9,134	100	$9,933	100	$10,827	100

Sources: Oregon Department of Education, Statewide Report Card, 2007-08 (Salem: Oregon Department of Education, 2008), http://www.oregon.gov/ode/schools-and-districts/reportcards/Documents/rptcard2008.pdf; Oregon Department of Education, Statewide Report Card, 2012-13 (Salem: Oregon Department of Education, 2013), http://www.oregon.gov/ode/schools-and-districts/reportcards/Documents/rptcard2013.pdf; Oregon Department of Education, Statewide Report Card, 2015-16 (Salem: Oregon Department of Education, 2016), http://www.oregon.gov/ode/schools-and-districts/reportcards/Documents/rptcard2016.pdf

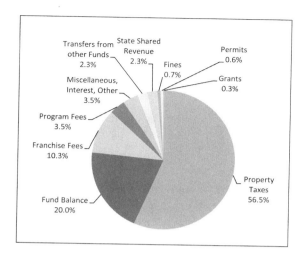

Figure 18.6. General Fund resources, City of Hillsboro, Oregon. Total dollar amount is $117,139,76. *City of Hillsboro, Oregon,* Budget in Brief: Fiscal Year 2016-17 *(Hillsboro, OR: City of Hillsboro, 2016), https://www.hillsboro-oregon.gov/home/showdocument?id=10462*

year to year to fund emergency needs and ongoing and future projects. Many city services are paid for through charges or fees, and often the cities are using these fees to pay off bonds used to borrow money to finance these facilities. In the case of Hillsboro, the total expenditures for 2016-17 were almost half a billion dollars ($499,938,230), but over $233 million was for transfers and reserves. Like most cities, Hillsboro has extensive dedicated revenues coming from utility and other service charges. In 2016-17, Hillsboro received over $60 million, or roughly 12 percent of its total budget, from utility charges.

The General Fund, which the city council has much more flexibility in spending, totaled $117,139,769.[12] Figure 18.6 demonstrates how the General Fund side of Oregon city budgets always features property taxes as a major resource, 56 percent for Hillsboro, with franchise fees generally being the second largest source of revenue. Franchise fees are charges by a local government to utilities and other users of rights of way (such as cable television) in the jurisdiction.

On the spending side, as table 18.3 shows, the largest overall expenses are associated with utilities and public safety services. Competent, experienced city workers are expensive, and cities need many police, firefighters, and operators and managers of water, sewer, park, and transportation systems. Some cities spend more on social services, public transit, senior centers, and libraries, but all must provide for their citizens' roads, safety, and basic sanitation.

KEY DRIVERS OF CHANGE IN STATE AND LOCAL FINANCE SINCE 1990

Oregon's state and local finance system changed dramatically in 1990 when voters rolled back property tax rates with the passage of Measure 5. The current state and local fiscal system follows patterns that developed as a result of that property tax rollback. Oregon's state and local governments have only two major sources of general

Table 18.3. Detailed expenditures, Hillsboro, Oregon, 2016-17 budget

Sector	Amount
Police	$31,597,380
Municipal court	$563,316
Fire	$20,370,864
Emergency management	$301,621
Total public safety	*$52,833,181*
Library	$9,541,814
Parks and recreation	$27,353,035
Total community services	*$36,894,849*
Planning	$5,234,115
Economic Development	$5,246,129
Building	$10,138,247
Water	$62,604,564
Public Works	$84,663,932
Total community development	*$167,886,987*
City manager's office	$4,156,165
Human resources/risk	$4,228,833
Information services	$8,143,666
Finance	$3,243,753
Facilities and fleet	$33,827,266
Total facility and support services	*$53,599,683*
Other*	$25,018,786
Reserves and contingency**	$163,704,794
Total	$499,983,280

*Non-department expenditures.
**Reserves for all departments.
City of Hillsboro, Oregon, Budget in Brief: Fiscal Year 2016-17 *(Hillsboro, OR: City of Hillsboro, 2016), https://www.hillsboro-oregon.gov/home/showdocument?id=10462*

revenues: income taxes and property taxes. Although the state and its local jurisdictions raise money through myriad other charges, fees, investments, and even gaming revenues, these other sources are relatively small, dedicated to specific programs, or both. Water bills must go to water systems. Tuition must go to colleges. Gasoline taxes go to transportation. As big as it seems, net revenue from the lottery was less than 8 percent of the revenues generated by personal income taxes in 2013-15.[13]

When schools, cities, counties, or the state want to fund new programs or move money from one policy area to another, the first place to go is the General Fund. For local governments, such money is primarily generated through property taxes. For the state, personal income taxes account for roughly 85 percent of the General Funds budget, making Oregon the most dependent state on personal income tax for all state and local revenues and sixth in per capita personal income tax revenues, reflecting Oregon's lower average income.[14] Since Measure 5 passed in 1990 and was reinforced in 1997 by a subsequent property assessment limit, a stable pattern of tax limits and spending obligations has powerfully constrained local and state general fund spending.

The high dependence on these two revenue sources has consequences. In the 2007 report *Principles of a High-Quality Revenue System*, the National Conference of State Legislatures (NCSL) notes that because each revenue source has distinct strengths and weakness, there is merit in having diverse revenue streams. Specifically, the NCSL report states: "There is merit in the notion that states, and local governments should balance their tax systems through reliance on the 'three-legged stool' of income, sales and property taxes in roughly equal proportions, with excise taxes, business taxes, gaming taxes, severance taxes and user charges playing an important supplemental role."[15]

Oregon is one of only five states without a general sales tax, making the state's revenue system a "two-legged stool." Before 1990, the state had high property and income taxes to compensate for the lack of a sales tax, creating constant anti-tax pressures. William Lunch and Lawrence Lipin note that Oregon history has a long stream of anti-property-tax activism, one that mixes with anti-elitism and the rise of the Republican right in the 1970s and 1980s. They note that "In 1978, 1980, 1982, 1984, and 1986, anti-tax activists placed initiatives before Oregon voters to reduce property taxes to a maximum of 1.5 percent of assessed value."[16] Led by Ray Phillips, labeled by the *Oregonian* as a "tax limitation curmudgeon," the 1982 initiative effort came within 0.5 percent of passage, but the anti-tax activists could not overcome the opposition of "virtually all state leaders and traditionally influential community organizations."[17] A former follower of Phillips, Don McIntire took up the charge, and with fellow health club owner Frank Eisenzimmer successfully convinced Oregon voters to pass Measures 5 in 1990.[18] When combined with the 1997 passage of Measure 50, Measure 5 reduced Oregon from being ranked seventh in country in per capita property taxes in 1990-91 to thirtieth in 1998-99.[19] The stool is now more like a pogo stick, as Oregon's revenue system depends so heavily on the elastic personal income taxes. In 1990-91, Oregon's total property taxes exceeded $2.5 billion, but that total would not be reached again until 1998-99 despite significant population and economic growth.

Measures 5 and 50 have a complex, interrelated impact. At its core, Measure 5 reduced property tax rates to 1.5 percent of assessed value over five years, with the exception of some limited bond measures. This rate limit was complicated by the accompanying requirement that property value assessments be updated more frequently. Despite the reduction in tax rates, updating assessments increased the property tax bills for many metropolitan-area homeowners in the early 1990s, as their property values had risen far ahead of their tax assessment value. Meanwhile, business and commercial properties generally benefitted because their assessments were closer to market value. Frustrated by the higher property taxes resulting from the revised property value assessments and rising housing prices, voters passed Measure 47 in 1996. Measure 47 rolled back assessed values by 10 percent and limited increases in assessed values to no more than 3 percent per year. Measure 47 effectively limited the impact of housing price inflation on property taxes. Errors in the text of Measure 47 that made it constitutionally suspect led the 1997 legislature to refer a legally cleaned-up version (Measure 50) to public vote, where it easily passed.

Measures 5 and 50 transformed Oregon's basic public spending patterns. Measure 5 limited local school districts to only 0.5 percent of assessed value, while other jurisdictions could get a total of 1 percent. Before Measure 5, school districts varied greatly in the revenues received from property taxes, influenced by the assessed value of the taxable property within their borders and the tax rates local voters would approve. High-spending districts like Pleasant Hill could have rates exceeding 2.8 percent, while low-taxing districts such as Brookings capped school taxes at 0.67 percent, which was still much higher than Measure 5 allowed.[20] Measure 5 also required the state government to partially compensate local school districts for the lost revenues until 1996. This requirement transformed K–12's general funds from being approximately 28 percent from state funds in 1990-91 to 66 percent in 1995-96.[21] Despite its magnitude, the replacement funding was not 100 percent because state money previously dedicated to education was part of the backfill. Measure 5 had a variable effect on local schools. School districts previously willing to tax themselves to ensure good schools were hurt greatly, but districts with lower property values or less willingness to raise taxes benefitted, since the state legislature's distribution formula equalized school funding throughout the state.[22]

The legislature's ongoing commitment to fund K–12 schools to compensate for local property tax losses meant that the state's General Fund spending pie would be greatly recut. By 2001-3, K–12 education received 42.4 percent of state General Funds versus approximately 26 percent in 1989-91.[23] Since 1990, K–12 funding has been consistently the first and foremost political consideration in General Fund spending discussions in Salem.

The initiative process has produced two other notable changes in the state General Fund since 1990: (1) an enhanced spending commitment on prisons owing to new mandatory sentencing laws and (2) some tax rate adjustments of the highest levels on income. In the area of criminal justice, Measure 11, passed by voters in 1994, created a mandatory sentencing system for personal crimes, and in 2008 voters approved Measure 57, which mandated minimal sentences for those convicted of specified drug and property crimes. These laws contributed to a doubling of those serving time in Oregon prisons in the decade ending in 2012.[24] General Fund spending on corrections went from approximately 5.6 percent in 1993-95 to roughly 8.3 percent in 2015-17.[25]

Oregon voters have, on rare occasions, supported tax increases. When revenues imploded during the Great Recession of 2008-9, the Oregon legislature raised the personal income tax rate for those earning over $125,000 ($250,000 for joint filings). Opponents successfully petitioned for the law to be placed on the ballot as Measure 66 in 2010. In the exact same pattern, the legislature increased the corporate minimum tax from $10 to $150, along with other more significant corporate tax increases, and that law was also referred to voters in 2010 as Measure 67.[26] Voters approved both bills. These bills did not fundamentally alter revenue patterns, but demonstrate that Oregonians will approve small tax increases, if only on businesses or a small wealthier minority. As of 2016, the personal income tax rates have four levels, set according to taxable personal income: 5 percent, 7 percent, 9 percent, and 9.9 percent.[27] Beginning in 2013, the top rate of corporate income tax of 7.6 percent had been scheduled to apply only to income above $10 million; however, during the 2013 special session, the legislature changed the tax bracket so that it applies to taxable income above $1 million.[28]

Health-care funding deserves note also. Voters increased the tax on tobacco products largely to support the Oregon Health Plan, so that in 2014-15, the tax going to the OHP was 86¢ per pack of cigarettes, which combined with other tobacco taxes to bring $160 million to the OHP that single fiscal year.[29] Support for health care in the 2010s was driven by the commitment of elected officials, especially Governor John Kitzhaber, and by the opportunities created by the 2010 adoption of the Affordable Care Act (aka "Obamacare"), which increased the federal funds available to support OHP. The passage of Measure 101 in January 2018, discussed in chapter 19, demonstrates that support for expanded health care continues.

POTENTIAL FORCES FOR FUTURE CHANGE

The basic revenue structure of the state and local fiscal system in the mid-2010s is clear: (1) Oregon voters accept the income tax and have tolerated small increases at times; (2) property taxes appear frozen at rates that are below the national average; (3) there is no public appetite for anything resembling a sales tax; and (4) K–12 funding has shifted to become primarily a state responsibility and takes the largest single share of the General Fund.

Currently, the Oregon state and local fiscal system appears incremental in nature, with little chance of major change. Four factors that have bent the budget in the recent past demonstrate the potential to disrupt (or "punctuate") this general equilibrium: (1) Oregon's direct democracy system, (2) economic conditions, (3) demographic shifts both predictable and less predictable, and (4) federal policy changes.

The initiative system is perhaps the most unpredictable force for change because it enables diverse groups and individuals to directly promote major revenue limitations and contradictory spending commitments, sometimes on a single ballot. In 2000, for example, Oregon voters approved Measure 1, which amended the state constitution to require the legislature to adequately fund "school quality goals," a requirement that could greatly increase state spending obligations, while on the same ballot passing Measure 88, expanding the tax deduction for federal income taxes, and Measure 86, which incorporated the kicker law into the state constitution.[30] When it comes to ballot measures, Oregon voters often to choose to have their cake and eat it too.

Although Oregon voters have favored relatively incremental tax increases, voter rejection of 2016's Measure 97, a corporate gross sales tax on sales over $25 million, by nearly 60 percent signals continued opposition to anything that can be labeled a "sales tax," although the opposition broke all spending records in their campaign.[31] Oregon's direct democracy system also constrains legislative fiscal reforms in two ways. First, in 1996, Oregon voters greatly complicated tax reform by passing Measure 25, which required all legislative tax increases to have a three-fifths majority in both houses. Second, as noted in chapter 3, the petition referendum system enables groups to place legislative actions on the ballot for public vote. The petition referendum system has cut both ways on taxes since 2000, with legislated tax increases rejected in 2004 but accepted in 2009 and 2018.

As noted above, the initiative process enables voters to create major new spending commitments for the state. This is an ongoing pattern. In 2016, voters obligated state funds by passing three initiatives: Measure 97 (dedicating lottery money to veteran's programs), Measure 99 (committing state general funds to programs that promote graduation and employment for youth), and Measure 99 (using lottery funds to support "outdoor school").

Balancing the budget is a foremost responsibility of the state legislature, and the most uncontrollable factor here is the state of the economy. Income taxes are elastic, meaning that revenues go up or down disproportionately with economic growth or decline. Because of the state's dependence on personal income taxes for over 80 percent of its revenue in recent decades, economic downturns regularly create budget crises and significant, if temporary, budget changes. For example, in the fifteen years of 2000–2014, personal income tax revenues went down three times: 2001-2 (19.0%), 2007-8 (11.2%), and 2009-10 (2.4%). On the positive side, personal income tax revenues increased by over 10 percent four times (2004-5, 2005-6, 2010-11, and 2014-15).[32]

In response to these unpredictable budget surpluses and as a diversion to early property tax initiatives, the Oregon legislature in 1979 adopted the "2 percent kicker" policy, in which all tax revenues above the original legislatively approved biennial estimates are refunded to individual and corporate taxpayers if those revenues exceed projections by 2 percent or more. Although voters in 2012 mandated through Measure 82 that excess revenues that previously went to corporations would henceforth go to General Fund education spending, the personal kicker policy still sends the positive revenue benefits of rapid economic growth back to taxpayers, not to state services. The highest proportion of tax returns returned to taxpayers for the personal income tax was 18.6 percent in 2015-17 and a whopping 50.1 percent for the business income tax in 1996-97.[33] In response to unpredicted high revenues in the 2015-17 cycle, taxpayers received credits on their 2017 taxes totaling $464 million.[34]

The volatility of income tax revenues is significantly countered by Oregon's "rainy day" funds, which accumulate extra money in good years to be used in times of revenue shortfalls. Oregon has two such funds. The legislature created Oregon Rainy Day Fund (ORDF) in 2007 to help sustain general fund programs in hard times. The ORDF was kick-started by keeping a large percentage of the corporate kicker of the 2007-9 biennium, $319 million. If revenues exceed estimates by more than 1 percent per biennium, then 1 percent is transferred into the ORDF; if less than 1 percent extra revenues occur, whatever amount more than the original estimate goes into the fund.[35]

Oregon's second rainy day fund, the Education Stability Fund (ESF), was established by voters in 2002 to convert an existing education endowment fund into a reserve fund. The ESF is built by the dedication of 18 percent of the net proceeds from the state lottery and is capped at 5 percent of the previous biennium's General Fund revenues. Once the cap is reached, 15 percent of net lottery proceeds are deposited into the ESF's school capital–matching subaccount. The legislature can spend money from the ESF "if there is an economic downturn, as defined by law, and the expenditure is approved by at least three-fifths of the members of each chamber."[36]

These funds significantly buffered some tough times in the 2000s, but they would not be adequate to match some of Oregon's historic income tax drops. As of 2016, the ORDF is estimated to have about $373 million and the ESF about $387 million, which combined with the estimated excess unallocated revenue in that budget (about $245 million) will make a total reserve for the upcoming 2017-19 budget of $1,016 million. This is roughly 7 percent of the 2015-17 General Fund / Lottery Fund, the largest reserve ever accumulated.[37] Impressive, but in 2001-2, personal income tax revenues alone declined by $871 million from 2000 to 2001.[38] When the 2017 legislature convened, Governor Kate Brown estimated General Fund / Lottery Fund revenue for 2017-19 to be $1.7 billion short of what was needed for current service levels, although economic growth and legislative actions generally filled this gap.[39]

The third factor that could erode the current fiscal system is demographics, particularly the aging of Oregon's population. One of the most direct effects of the aging of the population will likely be on the Public Employee Retirement System, which covers the retirement costs of 347,324 Oregon's state and local present and future retirees. State and local governments have made commitments to their workers for decades and now face the legal obligation to fulfill their promises. According to the Oregon Legislative Fiscal Office, systems like PERS should have a fund reserve that is at least 80 percent of the liabilities. Fearing projections that show the fund being increasingly inadequate and that state and local governments need to greatly increase payments into the system, the legislature agreed to pass major PERS reforms in 2013, including new limits on benefits. Initially this seemed like a long-term solution and briefly helped PERS reach 96 percent funding.

This favorable situation (for governments and others who dislike this spending commitment, not for PERS beneficiaries) changed dramatically when the Oregon Supreme Court rejected a key part of the reform, a reduction of the cost-of-living adjustments (COLAs) for retired beneficiaries, as an abridgement of a constitutionally protected contract. The 2015 *Moro v. the State of Oregon* decision partially contributed to PERS's unfunded liability growing from $2.6 billion in 2013 to $12.1 billion in 2014. As the Oregon Legislative Fiscal Office notes, however, the Oregon legislature's projections were also premised on the reserve fund investments earning 7.75 percent, far above what happened.[40] Debates over PERS continue, colored by the legal boundaries of reform and the uncertainties about investment returns. As of summer 2016, state and local government payments into PERS were estimated to jump from an estimated $2 billion to $2.9 billion from 2015-17 to 2017-19 budget cycles.[41] The political battle over PERS is often isolated from other budget developments, and the state legislature continues to limit taxes and to adopt new spending commitments and targeted tax reductions without regard to this legal commitment.

The aging of Oregon's population will also affect the state's Medicaid (OHP) costs. In 2015, approximately 16 percent of Oregonians were over 65 years old. Although the uncertainty of such projections must be considered, the state Office of Economic Analysis estimates that the percentage of Oregonians over age 65 will be roughly 22 percent by 2040.[42] This shift will bring a disproportionate increase in Medicaid costs. According to a 2014 Pew Trust report, elderly individuals made up only 9 percent of Medicaid enrollees in 2010, but they accounted for approximately 22 percent of payments. The average annual costs of a Medicaid recipient across the country was $6,254, while for those over age 65, the average costs were $12,958.[43] The OHP budget is hit hardest by aging because once an elder's savings have been spent, Medicaid is generally the funder of last resort for long-term care. After 2016, Medicaid spending growth is projected to average 6 percent per year through 2025, as aged and disabled beneficiaries, who typically require more expensive care, represent an increasingly larger share of the Medicaid population.[44]

The fourth easily identifiable factor that may alter Oregon's budget patterns is federal funding to the state. As noted above, federal funds constituted approximately one-third of the total money flowing through the state in 2015-17. Most of this money (about 86%) goes to human services, especially the Oregon Health Authority (over 54%).[45] With Donald Trump as the new president and Republican majorities in Congress, it is impossible to predict what might occur in federal support for state programs. Obviously, anything connected to the Affordable Care Act of 2010 is vulnerable to change. Liz Farmer, state fiscal analyst for *Governing Magazine*, notes that Trump's statements during the presidential campaign indicate that states will get less Medicaid money but more flexibility in how they spend it, but also that everything is speculative in winter 2018.[46] Changes in federal funding can have multiple forms. Not only may there be outright cuts, but also the "matching" formulas for federal grants may be altered. Oregon could receive less money, and put up more "matching funds." Similarly, congressional concern over federal deficits, intensified by tax cuts and a military buildup, threatens the continuation of matching requirements for all other federal grants. Finally, there is uncertainty of how the passage of the 2017 Tax Cut and Jobs Act by the US Congress will affect the state. Certainly, the limitation of state and local tax (also known as SALT) deductions from the federal income tax to $10,000 will mean wealthier Oregonians may pay more federal taxes over time, but it is unclear if that will increase pressure to reduce state and local taxes, or discourage wealthier people from living in Oregon.[47]

Oregon's state and local finances can also suffer collateral damage from federal policies. As noted above, federal timber policy has powerfully affected local budgets in Oregon's timber country. Other policies that could influence the local and statewide financial situation include changes in spending in specific policy areas, such as President Trump's 2017 proposed budget, which seeks to cut spending on climate change research being conducted by the National Oceanic and Atmospheric Administration (NOAA) out of Newport; alter the Bonneville Power Administration (BPA), which supplies cheaper energy to local Oregon utilities; and eliminate the National Energy Technology Laboratory in Albany.

CONCLUSION

Will Oregon's state and local fiscal system experience another punctuation in its equilibrium, as occurred in the 1990s tax revolts, or are we likely to keep "muddling through," as Charles Lindblom describes incremental policymaking? The simple ups and downs of a revenue system so heavily dependent on personal income taxes prompt periodic efforts for change. A lengthy recession could mean that the legislature enters a budget cycle with no reserves, preventing Oregon politicians from just riding things out until times get better, as seems to be the plan in 2018. But some issues may break that incremental pattern. The most visible concern for many in the state at this time is funding PERS, the contractual obligations of which local and state governments are legally bound to meet. Other forces may also alter state budgeting, such as the new Republican control of the federal government, but the impact of many of these is only speculative.

A multitude of less visible issues will also influence Oregon's fiscal world, such as the new minimum wage laws that directly affect the cost of services for the aged. Demands for more affordable higher education also illustrate the bubbling pressure for fiscal change.

According to Baumgartner and Jones, policy equilibriums change when an issue's image changes or a different venue of decision-making arises. Assuming they seek a more stable financial system to build a more progressive state, the challenge facing Oregon's current leadership is to find a way to redefine the image of the state's revenue system and to convince voters to support the creation of some sort of "third leg" to the state's revenue stool, or else the continual cycle of building up programs only to tear them down in hard times will continue. Alternatively, elected officials may find outside forces driving fiscal change.

Notes

1   Governor Kate Brown, *2017-2019 Governor's Budget* (Salem: State of Oregon, 2017), www.oregon.gov/das/Financial/Documents/2017-19_gb.pdf.

2   Frank R. Baumgartner and Bryan D. Jones, *Agendas and Instability in American Politics*, 2nd ed. (Chicago: University of Chicago Press, 2009).

3   Hillary Borrud, "Oregon's History of Rejecting Tax Reform and Spending Limits Opened Door for Measure 97," *Oregonian*, October 9, 2016.

4   Oregon Legislative Revenue Office, *2016 Oregon Public Finance: Basic Facts* (Salem: State of Oregon, 2016), 82.

5   Oregon Lottery Commission, *Comprehensive Annual Financial Report, for the Fiscal Year Ended on June 30, 2015* (Salem: Oregon Lottery Commission, 2015), 6.

6   "A City Club Report on Measure 99: Dedicated Lottery Funds for Outdoor School," *City Club of Portland Bulletin*, 99, no. 1 (2016): 6.

7   "Federal Medical Assistance Percentage (FMAP) for Medicaid and Multiplier, 2017 Table," Kaiser Family Foundation, State Health Facts, accessed April 23, 2018, kff.org/medicaid/state-indicator/federal-matching-rate-and-multiplier/.

8   Oregon Secretary of State, *Oregon's Counties: 2016 Financial Condition Review*, Audit Report No. 2016-11 (Salem: State of Oregon, June 2016), 7-10.

9   Oregon Legislative Revenue Office, *2016 Oregon Public Finance*.

10 "Struggling Counties Need More Than Temporary Lifeline," *Oregonian*, March 29, 2015.

11 Oregon Legislative Revenue Office, *2016 Oregon Public Finance*.

12 City of Hillsboro, *Budget in Brief, Fiscal Year 2016-17* (Hillsboro, OR: City of Hillsboro, 2016), 8, https://www.hillsboro-oregon.gov/home/showdocument?id=10462.

13 Calculated from Oregon Legislative Revenue Office, *2016 Oregon Public Finance*, 84.

14 Tax Foundation, *Facts and Figures: How Does Your State Compare?* (New York: Tax Foundation, March 1, 2016), tables 8 and 14, www.slideshare.net/taxfoundation/facts-figures-2016-how-does-your-state-compare-58911382.

15 National Conference of State Legislatures, *Principles of a High-Quality State Revenue System*, 4th ed. (Washington, DC: National Conference of State Legislatures, 2007), www.ncsl.org/research/fiscal-policy/principles-of-a-high-quality-state-revenue-system.aspx.

16 Lawrence M. Lipin and William Lunch, "Moralistic Direct Democracy: Political Insurgents, Religion, and the State in Twentieth Century Oregon," *Oregon Historical Quarterly* 110, no. 4 (Winter 2009): 529.

17 Lipin and Lunch, "Moralistic Direct Democracy," 529-30.

18 Lipin and Lunch, "Moralistic Direct Democracy," 532.

19 Oregon Legislative Revenue Office, *2016 Oregon Public Finance*, A5.

20 Tom Linhares, *Recent History of Oregon's Property Tax System* (Portland, OR: Multnomah County Tax Supervising and Conservation Commission, 1991), http://www.lanecounty. org/UserFiles/Servers/Server_3585797/File/Government/County%20Departments/ Assessment%20and%20Taxation/Recent%20History%20of%20Oregon's%20 Property%20Tax%20System/Recent_History_Nov_2011.pdf.

21 Linhares, *Recent History of Oregon's Property Tax System*, 18.

22 Linhares, *Recent History of Oregon's Property Tax System*, 18.

23 Oregon Legislative Fiscal Office, *Budget Highlights, Legislatively Approved 1991-1993 Budget* (Salem: Oregon Legislative Fiscal Office, 1991).

24 Chris Conrad, "The High Cost of Measure 11," *Medford Mail Tribune*, May 5, 2013.

25 Calculated from numbers found in Oregon Legislative Fiscal Office, *Budget Highlights: Legislatively Approved 1993-1995 Budget* (Salem: Oregon Legislative Fiscal Office, 1993), and idem, *Budget Highlights: Legislatively Approved 2015-2017 Budget* (Salem: Oregon Legislative Fiscal Office, 2015).

26 Oregon Secretary of State, *Voters' Pamphlet: Oregon Special Election, January 26, 2010* (Salem: State of Oregon, 2010).

27 Oregon Legislative Revenue Office, *2016 Oregon Public Finance*, C1.

28 Oregon Legislative Revenue Office, *2016 Oregon Public Finance*, C1 and C13.

29 Oregon Legislative Revenue Office, *2016 Oregon Public Finance*, J1.

30 Oregon Secretary of State, "Initiative, Referendum and Recall: 2000-2004," in *Oregon Blue Book* (Salem: State of Oregon, 2017-18), http://bluebook.state.or.us/state/ elections/elections22a.htm.

31 Betsy Hammond, "3 Big Takeaways from Oregon's Election Results—And a Few Small Ones," *Oregonian*, November 9, 2016.

32 Oregon Legislative Revenue Office, *2016 Oregon Public Finance*, A6.

33 Oregon Legislative Revenue Office, *2016 Oregon Public Finance*, B2.

34 Chris Lehman, "Here's the Kicker: Oregonians to Receive a Tax Rebate in 2018," *Oregon Public Broadcasting*, August 23, 2017, https://www.opb.org/news/article/oregon-kicker- tax-rebate-2018/.

35 Oregon Legislative Fiscal Office, *Oregon's Budget Stabilization Funds Update*, Budget Information Brief 2015-2 (Salem: Oregon Legislative Fiscal Office, November 2015), 4.

36 Oregon Legislative Fiscal Office, *Oregon's Budget Stabilization Funds Update*, 3.

37 Oregon Legislative Revenue Office, *Oregon Economic and Revenue Forecast, December 2016* (Salem: Oregon Legislative Fiscal Office, November 16, 2016), 29.

38 Oregon Legislative Revenue Office, *2016 Oregon Public Finance*, A6.

39 Gordon Friedman, "Kate Brown Releases Proposed Two-Year Budget," *Statesman Journal*, December 1, 2016.

40 Oregon Legislative Fiscal Office, *Projected Increase in PERS Unfunded Accrued Liability*, Budget Information Brief 2016-5 (Salem: Oregon Legislative Fiscal Office, April 2016).

41 Peter Wong, "Report Lays Groundwork for Higher PERS rates," *Portland Tribune*, August 1, 2016.

42 Based on calculations by author made from data in "Oregon's Long-Term County Population Forecast, 2010-2050," Oregon Office of Economic Analysis, accessed June 14, 2018, http://www.oregon.gov/das/OEA/Pages/forecastdemographic.aspx.

43 Pew Charitable Trusts and the John D. and Catherine T. MacArthur Foundation, *State Health Care Spending on Medicaid: A 50-State Study of Trends and Drivers of Cost* (Chicago: Pew Charitable Trusts and the John D. and Catherine T. MacArthur Foundation, July 2014).

44 "National Health Expenditure Projections 2015-2025," Center for Medicaid and Medicare Services, updated July 14, 2016, https://www.cms.gov/Research-Statistics-Data-and-Systems/Statistics-Trends-and-Reports/NationalHealthExpendData/Downloads/Proj2015.pdf.

45 Oregon Legislative Fiscal Office, *2015-17 Budget Highlights Update* (Salem: Oregon Legislative Fiscal Office, March 2016).

46 Liz Farmer, "What a Trump Presidency Could Mean for State and Local Finances and More," *Governing.com*, November 11, 2016.

47 Ryan Derousseau, "Three Strategies for Cutting a High State Tax Bill," *Fortune*, December 28, 2017.

IV

Conclusion

19

Change or Continuity?

RICHARD A. CLUCAS, MARK HENKELS, PRISCILLA L. SOUTHWELL, and EDWARD P. WEBER

When Oregon voters cast their ballots on Measure 101 on January 23, 2018, they were asked to vote on only one question—whether a recently enacted law, protecting health-care coverage for the poor and stabilizing health insurance premiums, should go into effect. Their response to this single question says much about the current state of Oregon politics.

In many ways, the battle lines leading up to the vote reflected the traditional conflict that has defined Oregon politics in recent decades. On one side, pushing for the adoption of the measure, were most of the liberal organizations in the states, including groups representing labor, education, women, children, minorities, and other disadvantaged groups. The opposition was the more conservative anti-tax small government wing of the state's population. These traditional battle lines were complicated by how most health professionals and organizations in the state, including doctors and hospitals, joined in support of the measure. Yet the vote ultimately got down to a traditional and fundamental question that has divided the state for many years: should the government actively address state problems, or should it be restrained and limit taxes?

The path for Measure 101 to the ballot began with the passage of House Bill (HB) 2391 during the 2017 legislative session. Among other actions, HB 2391 imposed a temporary 1.5 percent tax on the premiums provided by health insurance companies, the Public Employees' Benefit Board, and managed care organizations. It also levied a tax on the net revenue of many hospitals across the state. Supporters saw the bill as necessary to ensure that more than 350,000 low-income Oregonians, who had gained health insurance coverage under the 2010 federal Affordable Care Act, would not lose those benefits because of federal cutbacks. The bill also provided funding that kept the state's recently built psychiatric hospital from closing and helped to fill a $1.4 billion gap in the state budget. For opponents, however, the bill represented an unwanted tax, one that would ultimately reach consumers' pocketbooks.[1]

In the legislature, support for the bill largely followed party lines. Democratic legislators were unified in their support. Most Republicans opposed the bill, though one Republican in the house and three in the senate—including Senate Minority Leader

Senator Ted Ferrioli (R-John Day)—joined with the Democrats in voting for it. Even before the bill reached the desk of Democratic Governor Kate Brown on July 3, 2017, a small group of Republicans legislators, led by Representative Julie Parrish (R-West Linn), began efforts to overturn the law by forcing a statewide referendum on the legislation. By early October, the bill's opponents had gathered 70,320 valid signatures, far exceeding the required number to place the bill on the ballot.[2]

The referendum process generated controversy and partisan conflict even before signature-gathering process began. Arguing that it was important to hold the election quickly to give the legislature time to find an alternative revenue source if the voters rejected the tax increases, the bill's supporters passed Senate Bill (SB) 229 along party lines, scheduling the special election in January 2018 rather than at the next general election. Opponents denounced this action as a move to help HB 2391 survive.[3] SB 229 also gave the task of writing the ballot title, usually done by the attorney general, to a special legislative committee. Opponents were upset when the Democrat-dominated committee then wrote a ballot title calling the new charges on insurance premiums and hospital "assessments" rather than "taxes." This and other conflicts over the title eventually made their way to the Oregon Supreme Court, which ordered that changes be made to accommodate some of the Republican concerns.[4]

The partisan controversy intensified in December when Jeanne Atkins, the head of the Democratic Party of Oregon and the previous secretary of state, filed an elections complaint against Secretary of State Dennis Richardson, charging that Richardson violated state election laws by using his office's official newsletter to urge voters to turn down this new tax in January. Richardson had just released a long-awaited audit of the Oregon Health Authority (OHA), which concluded that the agency had failed to prevent or recover millions of dollars in overpayments and had also hampered auditors' attempts to access information.[5]

Not surprisingly, the partisan battles and the ballot measure attracted considerable attention in the media and on the Internet. The prominence of the debate and the significance of the issue also helped the two sides raise campaign contributions, especially the proponents. As of the end of 2017, contributions made to committees in support of this referendum had exceeded $2 million, more than twice the amount raised by those in opposition.[6]

The fine details of the partisan battle and the names of the combatants involved are less important than how voters responded to the referendum. Historically, Oregon voters have never been particularly fond of taxes despite the state's liberal reputation. Since 1933, Oregon voters have rejected a general sales tax nine times, most recently in 1993. None of the sales tax proposals received more than 29 percent of the vote.[7] In the 1990s, Oregon voters passed Measures 5 and 50, which limited property taxes and rolled back property tax assessment. In 2000, they voted to enshrine the state's kicker law into the constitution. More recently, in 2016, voters rejected Measure 97, denying the imposition of a corporate gross sales tax, with nearly 60 percent marking "no" on their ballots.

As chapter 18 explains, Oregon voters have, on rare occasions, supported tax increases. For example, voters approved two measures in 2010 that raised revenue, raised the personal income tax rate for those earning over $125,000 ($250,000 for joint filings), and raised corporate taxes, including increasing the corporate minimum tax to $150. The voters' actions in 2010 are the exception, however, and not the rule. Generally, Oregon voters have resisted tax increases.

Considering this history, it is surprising how strongly Oregon voters supported Measure 101 in the January 2018 special election. In the final tally, the "yes" side received more than 60 percent of the vote.[8] The Medicaid expansion had been preserved and additional revenue had been raised to help address the budget deficit. The outcome suggests that something has indeed changed in Oregon politics.

OREGON POLITICS IN THE NEW MILLENNIUM

The voters' willingness to support the tax increases in Measure 101 provides only a small hint at the complex changes that have reshaped Oregon politics over the past fifteen to twenty years. The changes can be seen in almost all aspects of the state's politics, from the broader socioeconomic forces shaping political action to whom is elected to public office to the policies enacted. Oregon's population has grown and become more diverse. The economy went from bust to boom to bust and back to boom again. Voters are less likely to be Republicans, finding a more comfortable home as Democrats, independents, or members of third parties. The state has become more liberal and more dominated by urban politicians. Automatic voter registration made elections more open. The prominent conservative activists, who often dominated Oregon politics in the 1990s, have all but disappeared from the scene. The initiative process no longer plays as central of a role in Oregon as it did before the *Armatta v. Kitzhaber* (1998) decision. The *Oregonian*, the state's flagship newspaper, has seen its circulation and size shrivel, and its impact decline. In its place, the public has become more dependent on online and broadcast sources.

Oregon's political institutions have also changed. The legislature is more diverse, both in membership and lobbyists, but less stifled by partisan gridlock. The governor's office became more liberal when Kate Brown replaced the more moderate Democrat John Kitzhaber. The courts are better organized and have expanded to include more specialty courts. Tribal governments have become a significant force in state politics. There have also been important changes in public policies, from an expanded reach in agricultural policies to greater support for social services, including health care.

Yet despite all these changes, some of the major characteristics that defined Oregon politics since the early 1980s continue to influence state politics. Perhaps most important of all, Oregon remains challenged by its limited revenue stream and the presence of its unique kicker law. With the state dependent almost entirely on income taxes for revenue, the story of Oregon politics is routinely a tale about the difficulties of achieving or maintaining the state's desired policy goals as revenues fluctuate with economic cycles. Every other year in the legislature's long session, and often more frequently than that, the state confronts the question of how to balance the budget while funding expanding popular programs. This situation is powerfully complicated by the need to address the current balance shortfall in the Public Employee Retirement System (PERS). Even with investment returns exceeding projections in 2018, the $22 billion in unfunded liability will demand foremost attention and increasing resources from the state and many local governments until at least 2021.[9] That perennial question seems at times to best define Oregon politics. Each time the legislature expands its efforts to address the state's problems, a major recession seems to reverse those progressive policies. And it also goes without saying that Oregonians seem resolutely opposed to a general sales tax, keeping that solution off the table.

WHERE DOES OREGON GO FROM HERE?

This book illuminates the changes and continuities in Oregon politics, and what they have meant to the state in recent years. Yet, to be honest, we cannot know whether our picture of Oregon at the end of the second decade of the millennium will be accurate for long. Change is inevitable in politics, and Oregon will undeniably see much change in coming years. This book is meant to provide a snapshot of the state of Oregon politics today, but in these final pages we reflect on some trends and forces that we believe are likely to define Oregon's future politics and policy. Besides the unresolved instability of Oregon fiscal situation described above, five forces for change deserve specific attention: the continued importance of the initiative process, the impacts of evolving federal policies and national politics, the state's ongoing commitment to environmental and natural resource values (including fighting climate change), Oregon's continuing rural-urban divide and the impact of the evolution of the Portland metropolitan area, and the growing size and changing character of the state's population.

Continued Reliance on the Initiative and Referendum Process

The initiative process remains a significant part of Oregon politics, even if less prominent than it was two decades ago. It still provides a means for groups to profoundly change state policies without going through the legislature. Although several important restrictions have been placed on the initiative and referendum process over the past decade (see chapter 3), Oregonians remain enamored of this right to direct democracy. The initiative is appealing because it ostensibly enables private citizens and groups to put legislation to a direct vote. The referendum provides a means for citizens to force a public vote on recently adopted legislation. The popularity can be seen in the many initiative petitions filed with the secretary of state. More than eighty such petitions were filed for the 2016 election, although only eight of them qualified for the ballot. As of January 2018, more than forty petitions have been filed for the 2018 general election, with six of them already approved to begin the signature-gathering process.

The passage of HB 2082 in 2007, which forbids the payment of petition signature gatherers on a per signature basis, has made it more difficult for initiative and referenda sponsors to pass those signature thresholds, but far from impossible. While the number of initiatives on the ballot dropped by almost 50 percent in the last decade, there are still routinely around five initiatives on each general election ballot.

Given the large number of initiatives filed with the secretary of state each election cycle, and the popularity of the process, it is unlikely that initiatives and referenda will disappear from Oregon politics anytime soon. Even with the smaller number on the ballot, they can still powerfully influence the direction of Oregon politics in the future.

That potential can be seen both with Measure 101 on the 2018 ballot and Measure 97 in 2016. The passage of Measure 101 meant that the legislature dodged a bullet in its efforts to protect Medicaid payments for the poor and balance the state budget. If the voters had rejected the measure, the legislature would have had to find alternative means to pay for health care and other budget items, or cut programs and services. Similarly, if 2016's Measure 97 had not failed, the financing of government programs in the state would have profoundly changed. Brought to the ballot through the initiative process, Measure 97 would have imposed a tax on corporate sales over $25 million. The state estimated that the measure would have brought in approximately $3 billion in revenue each year.[10] Considering that the state's biennial general funds budget for 2015-17 was a little over $18 billion, the influx of $3 billion more per year would have altered the state's fiscal planning. It is impossible to know what proposals will appear on future ballots, but given the state's historical and recent track record, it is safe to say that the process will have a profound effect on the direction of the state's politics in the future.

Evolving Federal Policies and National Politics

National policies and politics, most notably by the Trump administration and the Republican dominance in Congress, will also powerfully affect Oregon politics and policy. As this book is being compiled in 2018, we can only make educated guesses at what President Trump and his party's control of Congress will mean in the long run, but five areas that will certainly be affected are the state budget, health care, the immigrant community, marijuana, and environmental policies and politics. In the longer run, the increased conservatism of the federal courts will also surely alter other important policy assumptions, such as the future of same-sex marriage and even matters such as property rights and what the state can regulate. If the excellent economic conditions of 2016 and 2017 continue, Oregon should prosper regardless of specific federal policies.

The only significant legislation passed by the Republican Congress in 2017 was the Tax Cuts and Jobs Act, a major reform in the federal tax code. The key highlights of this law are a significant permanent drop in corporate tax rates (from a base level of 35 percent to 21 percent), lower personal tax rates until 2026, the ability of privately owned corporations to be taxed at the corporate rate rather than the personal income rate, and the alteration of the mix of personal and corporate tax deduction and credits. The law also ended the individual health insurance mandate, removing the penalty for individuals who do not have health insurance.[11]

For Oregonians and their state and local governments, the new tax law may create long-term pressure for revenue system change because it limits the amount of state and local taxes that can be deducted from the federal income tax to $10,000. Oregonians who pay more than that amount on their state income tax and local property taxes can no longer deduct that whole amount from their federal taxable earnings. Because of Oregon's high income taxes, its wealthier residents are hard hit by this change. This may lead to pressures for state revenue reform if people believe Oregon will lose high-income residents, who disproportionately contribute to state revenues through higher taxes and (presumably) more economic investment. Some Oregon leaders fear this could end the prosperity and low unemployment Oregon is enjoying in early 2018. Commenting on this possibility, and the already tense revenue situation, Governor Kate Brown said, "What I am concerned about is that this will impede our forward momentum . . . This tax plan will basically burst the balloon that's happening here."[12]

A second, less predictable but possibly more consequential impact of the new federal tax bill is that it may lead to major cuts in federal spending on social programs. Having facilitated a projected increase in the federal deficit by nearly $1.5 trillion over the next decade, Speaker of the House Paul Ryan (R-Wisconsin) has stated, "We're going to have to get back next year at entitlement reform . . . which is how you tackle the debt and the deficit."[13] Although Ryan will retire at the end of 2018, his words should cast a dark shadow across the future of Oregon's social service funding, as federal grants provide over 29 percent of total state spending in the 2017-19 budget, and more than 92 percent of federal funds go to health care, other social services, or education.[14] As chapter 15 notes, Oregon has been among the most active states in creatively using Medicaid funds to reduce its uninsured population, which declined to 5 percent in 2016, among the lowest in the country.[15] The Oregon legislature and governor may face the grim prospect of seeking increased taxes or reducing medical coverage for the state residents, threatening our leadership and creativity on this issue once again. Measure 101 is small change compared to the possible federal cuts.

Oregon's dominant values regarding immigration, marijuana, and environmental and natural resource policy are also greatly threatened by President Trump's statements and administrative initiatives as well as the Republican congressional agenda. Oregon has taken a strong stand against the Trump administration's immigration initiatives. Although President Obama greatly increased the deportation of illegal immigrants committing crimes, Trump's more systematic efforts to deport a wider range of illegal aliens prompted Oregon and various cities and universities to become "sanctuaries," pledging to not help facilitate the arrest and deportation of illegal immigrants unless legally required. The most notable sanctuary law was adopted by Oregon back in 1987 and prohibited the use of state and local resources to enforce federal immigration law. The legislature and governor reinforced this law in June 2017, when along straight party-line votes they authorized public bodies to decline to disclose information about a person's citizenship or immigration status unless required by state or federal law or other circumstances, such as when determining benefit eligibility. The law also directs the attorney general to create policies intended to limit immigration enforcement at public schools, public health facilities, courthouses, public shelters, and other public facilities.[16] Exactly how the federal government will respond is unclear, but US Attorney General Jeff Sessions has pledged to explore multiple possibilities, such as withholding federal grant money. One notable part of the immigration debate is the future of children who were brought across the border illegally and have grown up knowing only life in America. President Obama had used his administrative powers to give these "Dreamers" the ability to obtain temporary legal residency through the Deferred Action on Childhood Arrivals (DACA) program, and in Oregon over eleven thousand young people registered.[17] Oregon had provided Dreamers access to in-state tuition and other forms of educational support. Congress may still adopt a plan that allows Dreamers to remain, but there is less sympathy for other undocumented aliens. In the meantime, Oregon remains committed to a policy that contradicts current federal priorities.

Oregon's legalization of both medical and recreational marijuana also puts it at odds with the Trump administration. There is little doubt that the federal government can enforce drug prohibition. Marijuana is currently categorized as a Schedule I drug, meaning it is illegal for any use, production, or trade without specific federal permission. The Obama administration had adopted enforcement guidelines that said marijuana-related activities legal under state law would not be targeted for prosecution. Attorney General Jeff Sessions reversed the Obama-era guidelines, and now federal district attorneys may choose to prosecute marijuana-related activities. This policy raises great uncertainty in a business that, according to New Frontier Data, had $450 million in sales and employed more than twenty thousand people in Oregon in 2016. For the state, the new policy threatens tax revenues that have reached $70 million annually. State leaders have almost universally pledged to fight any effort to prosecute those working in this popular business.[18]

Oregon's Support for Environmental Values

The Trump administration has placed a high priority on opening public lands and resources to economic exploitation and environmental deregulation. Predictably, Oregon's Democratic leaders have taken strong stands against specific initiatives, led by US Interior Secretary Ryan Zinke, to allow offshore oil drilling and reduce the protections for the Kalmiopsis Wilderness area.[19] Beyond specific policy disputes, the current administration's public lands and resource policies may alter the dynamics of processes that promote broad-based consensus for solving resource disputes, discussed extensively in chapters 11 and 12. Zinke's push in 2017 to prevent the listing of greater sage-grouse as an endangered species, an effort developed during the Obama era, has given resource users such as ranchers and miners reason to push back on restrictions in the agreement.[20] Chapters 11 and 12 posit that the creation and encouragement of cooperative negotiated settlements may help solve difficult resource conflicts. Trump's policies, such as with the sage-grouse, place the federal government's thumb heavily in favor of economic exploitation. Resource users—including ranchers, the timber industry, and mining companies—may favor this new balance. The question here is whether various stakeholders will continue to invest in building collaborative agreements that the Trump administration and Ryan Zinke may short-circuit. Should Congress institutionalize the pro-exploitation policies in statute, such as by repealing or eviscerating the Endangered Species Act, existing collaborative efforts may collapse because resource users lose the incentive to participate.

The Trump administration's dedicated opposition to environmental regulations, particularly ones that promote the reduction of carbon emissions, seems to be stimulating states to act on their own. In areas such as immigration, health care, and notably regarding the environment, California, Oregon, and Washington are becoming known as the "blue wall" against Trump's most conservative policies.[21] This reconnects Oregon to its historical legacy as a leader among states in the fight to reduce pollution and protect the environment (see chapter 12).

Oregon's efforts to reduce carbon emissions began with the Business Energy Tax Credit in 1979. Since then, the state has spent almost $1 billion to promote renewable energy and energy efficiency. In 2007, the state passed the Renewable Portfolio Standard (RPS), requiring that 25 percent of all electricity sold by the state's investor-owned utilities be from renewable resources by 2025. In recent years, these efforts have accelerated. Driven by the Democratic Party's stronger control of the legislature and Trump's policies, liberal Democrat Governor Kate Brown pushed the adoption of stronger climate change policies, including 2016's landmark SB 1547, which made Oregon the first state to ban coal-fired, carbon-intensive electricity starting in 2030. President Trump's withdrawal of the United States from the international Paris Climate Agreement in June 2017 has further motivated state leaders to respond.[22] In November 2017, and with strong support from Democrat legislators and environmental advocacy groups, Governor Brown signed two executive orders designed to promote the use of electric vehicles and the construction of more "green" buildings that meet higher energy efficiency standards.[23]

Oregon has emerged as a leader in battling climate change. In a 2017 ranking of states' commitment to clean energy, the Union of Concerned Scientists employed twelve metrics, including pollution reduction from power plants, renewable energy in the electricity generation mix, and policies to advance clean energy such as electric vehicle. This study rated Oregon sixth among all fifty states.[24] Given the global significance of climate change, and the emergent liberal dominance of Oregon politics, it is likely the state will continue to lead the way in this policy area.

Oregon's activism on the issue will not make it immune from the effects of climate change, however. Climate change is projected to alter the state's weather patterns, reshape the environment, harm its ecosystem, and reduce mountain snowpack. Agriculture, timber, ranching, and fisheries in the state may suffer. The state is also likely to see more natural disasters, including more forest fires, more severe flooding, more frequent summer water shortages, and worsening public health. Climate change will also bring some benefits. Warmer winters and longer seasons may boost some crops. Overall, however, climate change is projected to cause severe problems for the state, harming the state's economy, businesses, local communities, and individual citizens.[25] In addition, it is possible that Oregon may become a destination for climate refugees in the future. The effects of climate change in Oregon are projected to be less severe than in many regions of the nation and world, possibly promoting major in-migration and altering the state's demographics.[26] Should these changes occur, state and local governments will have to adopt new policies and redirect scarce tax dollars to curtail or manage new environmental challenges and address new social demands.

THE URBAN-RURAL DIVIDE

Trump's environmental policy initiatives are generally greeted with strong opposition by the state's Democratic leaders, but US Congressman Greg Walden, a Republican representing eastern and southern Oregon, often takes a different if not opposite perspective.[27] Walden is on safe ground politically. Trump's opponent in the 2016 presidential election, Hillary Clinton, took just eight of Oregon's thirty-six counties. Salem's consistently anti-Trump policies mask the state's ongoing urban-rural divide. The Democratic Party's unified control over state government is built on political support heavily concentrated in the more urban and suburban areas of Oregon. The rural parts of the states, as well as the smaller cities, remain conservative and Republican.

The partisan and ideological differences reflect Oregon's strong economic divide, with the urban areas thriving and the rural ones facing greater challenges. The pro-development, anti-regulatory, and socially conservative rhetoric and policies currently flowing from Washington, DC, may reinvigorate traditional agricultural and forest-based industries, and their associated social values. Rural areas are less likely to move toward the knowledge-based economy and postindustrial society of the Portland Metro area. As chapter 2 concludes, these trends may mean ongoing conflict over associated social values. For the near future, the urban-rural split seems unlikely to diminish unless growth in areas such as the thriving region around Bend brings in immigrants and alters the dominant cultural values.[28]

Oregon's population is anticipated to grow over the next few decades. But this growth will not occur evenly throughout the state. Rather, the urban areas, especially in the industrial corridor from Portland to Salem, are projected to have strong growth, while many rural areas will experience only small population increases or possibly even declines. A study by the State Office of Economic Analysis, released in 2013, projected that the population growth in the tri-county region (Clackamas, Multnomah, and Washington) between 2015 and 2025 would be only slightly less than the rest of the state combined. At the other extreme, Grant, Harney, Wheeler, Wallowa, and Sherman Counties are projected to see population losses.[29] These patterns indicate how unlikely it is that rural Oregon will move toward the postindustrial nature of the Portland Metro area. Overall, the concentration of power in the state will remain in the more urban areas, further exacerbating the rural-urban divide. This trend may lead to new political frustrations for rural Oregon, but the non-metropolitan regions will likely remain an important political force and cause Oregon's political parties to adjust strategies over time.

The socioeconomic, demographic, and geographical differences between the urban and rural parts of the state not only affect political attitudes, but also lead to different policy needs. The Portland Metro area may have avoided the worst problems confronting other cities in the nation as it has tried to create a livable environment, but it still faces problems that are not as common, or as severe, in rural areas and small towns. These problems include a lack of affordable housing, worsening traffic congestion, higher crime, and more frequent conflicts between different cultures. Homelessness is a good example of the particular problems of urban areas. While homelessness exists across Oregon, the state's largest homeless population is, by far, in Multnomah County. In its 2017 count of homelessness, Oregon Housing and Community Services found that 30 percent of Oregon's homeless population was concentrated in Multnomah County.[30] The problem will likely worsen with the Portland area's rising housing costs. Air pollution is another issue that is particularly severe in urban areas. The greater use of automobiles, the continued use of wood-burning stoves, and the presence of concentrated industry intensify urban pollution. As the state's biggest city, Portland not surprisingly has the worst air quality in Oregon. The air quality in the metropolitan area is so poor, in fact, that the risk of cancer in Multnomah County is twice the state's average.[31]

While a few non-metro areas, such as the Rogue River Valley, have pollution challenges related to their geography and extensive wood-burning, rural Oregon's concerns generally center on the weaker, less diverse local economies and the difficulty of providing key public services such as health care. The overall economy of rural Oregon has improved since 2012, but still lags the Portland Metro and the Willamette Valley's larger cities in the pace of recovery. Unemployment remains higher and wages are growing much slower in rural areas.[32] The great exception to this pattern is the Bend area, which was second in growth among 350 US urban areas in 2016.[33] Changes in the rural economic base have affected who lives there, particularly as young people leave to find better work. Grant County, where John Day is located, has experienced a 42 percent decrease in wage and salary employment since 1970.[34]

Rural Oregon also faces great uncertainty about future availability and quality of health care, which is intensified by the higher proportion of older people living in those areas. On the positive side, the broadening of health insurance coverage under the Affordable Care Act put the hospital in Burns, Oregon, into the black for the first time in years. As Charlie Tviet, chief executive officer of Lake Health District, which runs a hospital in remote Lakeview, asserts, "I'm in hardcore Republican territory, but there's no question the expansion of coverage for people who didn't have coverage before is a marvelous thing." These communities will face a potential crisis should the "repeal and replace" health-care policy of congressional Republicans reduce the insurance coverage or subsidies for these providers, although there is the possibility that the pro–resource development policies of the Trump administration could mitigate this threat.[35]

Growing Population and Diversity

Oregon's population will continue to change over the next few decades. As described in chapter 2, Oregon emerged from the Great Recession as one of the most rapidly growing states in the nation. From 2010 to 2016, the state gained more than 310,000 new residents. By July 2017, the state's population was estimated to have reached 4,142,776.[36] That number is expected to grow. The Oregon Office of Economic Analysis projection from December 2017 estimates that the state's population is going to reach over 4.6 million in 2026.[37]

What may be more important than the general growth in population are underlying changes in the state's demographics. The state's population is becoming older, more diverse, and more urbanized. As of July 2017, almost 17 percent of the state's population was over 65 years of age, compared with almost 14 percent in 2010.[38] This figure is anticipated to rise as the baby boom generation ages and more out-of-state residents consider Oregon as a retirement option. Deschutes County has experienced the largest percentage of growth in those over age 65, increasing by 31 percent between 2010 and 2014. Washington and Clackamas Counties came in second and third with gains of 24 and 23 percent, respectively. While these increases in the metropolitan counties are substantial, the rural counties tend to have among the oldest populations in Oregon. More than 35 percent of Wheeler County's population, for example, is over 65, compared with 12.6 percent in Multnomah County. All counties in Oregon, however, have experienced a growth in residents in this older age group.[39]

Along with the graying of the population, Oregon is becoming more ethnically diverse, as the minority population growth outpaces that of the white population. The greatest gain has been among Latino residents. Between 2000 and 2016, the Latino population increased by 72 percent, which is a rate higher than the national average. By the 2016, Latinos represented 12 percent of the state's population. There are sizable Latino communities throughout Oregon. In fact, Hood River, Malheur, and Morrow Counties have the largest Latino populations of any counties, with more than 30 percent of their residents identifying as Latinos. Growth in the Latino population is projected to exceed that of other ethnic groups in the state. Overall, about 24 percent of state residents identified themselves as having some ethnic minority heritage as of July 2016.[40]

Another important demographic trend has been the increased urbanization of the state. Not only is the Portland Metro area reaching outward, but previously smaller cities such as Salem, Eugene, and especially Bend are becoming centers of larger urbanized areas.[41]

All these demographic trends will affect politics and policy in Oregon in the future. The aging of the population will place increased demand for community and social services, including adequate health care, for an older retired population. The increased diversification will require government organizations to be more attentive to the needs and perspectives of different cultural groups. Oregon's governments may confront more intercultural conflicts and greater demands to address discriminatory practices in the workplace and the community. The impact of greater diversity can already be seen in public education. As discussed in chapter 17, nearly 37 percent of K–12 students were minorities as of 2015; nearly 23 percent were Latino, and some 10 percent were non-native English speakers. The continued growth in these populations will force schools to adopt policies that recognize cultural differences and better serve students and families whose native language is not English. Increased urbanization will likely exacerbate the urban-rural divide, further strengthen the political power of the urban and suburban areas, reinforce the growing influence of liberal Democrats, and generate greater demands for programs that serve the urban communities.

CONCLUSION

Oregon politics has gone through a significant transformation since the start of the new millennium. Important changes are evident throughout the state's political system and in public policy. In each chapter in this book, the authors identify and explain the different ways in which the state's political context has evolved. A variety of forces are likely to bring additional changes in the near future, some further intensifying current characteristics of the state's politics and others taking the state down unknown paths. Yet, as much as the state has changed over the past several years and will likely change again in the near future, much remains the same. Oregon has gone through a significant transformation, but many aspects of the state's political system remain unchanged and continue to shape state politics and policy. Thus the best way to describe the political landscape in Oregon at the end of the second decade of the new millennium is as one whose historical continuities structure its future change.

Notes

1   Hillary Borrud, "Oregon House Passes $550 Million Tax Bill to Fund Medicaid," *Oregonian*, June 15, 2017; Diane Dietz, "Senate Approves Tax to Preserve the Oregon Health Plan," *Statesman Journal*, June 21, 2017; Kristena Hansen, "Health Care Tax Passes Oregon Legislature, Heads to Governor," *Associated Press*, June 21, 2017; Claire Withycombe, "Provider Tax Referral Puts $333 Million in Play," *East Oregonian*, July 12, 2017.

2   Nigel Jaquiss, "Oregon Secretary of State Dennis Richardson Greenlights January Special Election on Tax Repeal," *Willamette Week*, October 16, 2017; Connor Radnovich, "Signatures Submitted for Hospital Tax Referendum, Could Be on January Ballot," *Statesman Journal*, October 5, 2017.

3   Claire Withycombe, "GOP Cries Foul over Attempt to Push Special Election," *Portland Tribune*, June 29, 2017.

4   Withycombe, "GOP Cries Foul"; Chris Gay, "Supreme Court Orders Cleaner Ballot Title for Measure 101 Healthcare Tax," *Lund Report*, October 25, 2017; Connor Radnovich, "Oregon Health Care Tax Referendum Ballot Title Completed, Legal Appeal Threatened," *Statesman Journal*, September 20, 2017.

5   Gordon R. Friedman, "Democrats File Election Complaint against Dennis Richardson," *Oregonian*, December 2, 2017.

6   ORESTAR website, accessed April 22, 2018, https://secure.sos.state.or.us/orestar/CommitteeSearchThirdPage.do.

7   Hillary Borrud, "Oregon's History of Rejecting Tax Reform and Spending Limits Opened Door For Measure 97," *Oregonian*, October 9, 2016.

8   Connor Radnovich, "Oregon Voters Pass Health Care Tax Measure by Wide Margin," *Statesman Journal*, January 23, 2018.

9   Ted Sickinger, "Public Pension System Exceeds Return Expectation," *Corvallis Gazette-Times*, February 2, 2018.

10 Oregon Secretary of State, *Voters' Pamphlet: Oregon General Election, November 8, 2016* (Salem: State of Oregon, 2010), 66.

11 Heather Long, "The Final GOP Tax Bill Is Complete. Here's What Is in It," *Washington Post*, December 16, 2017.

12 Alan Rappeport, "States Warn of Budget Crunch under Republican Tax Plan," *New York Times*, November 22, 2017.

13 Julian Zelizer, "Blowing Up the Deficit Is Part of the Plan," *The Atlantic*, December 19, 2017, https://www.theatlantic.com/politics/archive/2017/12/blowing-up-the-deficit-is-part-of-the-plan/548720/.

14 Oregon Legislative Fiscal Office, *2017-19 Budget Highlights* (Salem: Oregon Legislative Fiscal Office: September 2017), https://www.oregonlegislature.gov/lfo/Documents/2017-19%20Budget%20Highlights.pdf.

15 "Health Insurance Coverage of the Total Population, 2016," Kaiser Family Foundation, accessed April 23, 2018, https://www.kff.org/other/state-indicator/total-population/?c urrentTimeframe=0&sortModel=%7B%22colId%22:%22Location%22,%22sort%22:%2 2asc%22%7D.

16 Ericka Cruz Guevarra, "Bill Expanding Oregon Sanctuary State Law Clears Legislature," *Oregon Public Broadcasting*, July 7, 2017, www.opb.org/news/article/oregon-sanctuary-state-law-expand-pass-legislature/.

17 Lauren Hernandez, "Oregon Officials, DREAMers Praise, Blast DACA 'Wind Down,'" *Statesman Journal*, September 5, 2017.

18 Shane D. Kavanaugh, "Oregon Leaders Vow: We Will Protect State's Marijuana Industry," *Oregonian*, January 4, 2018.

19 Christine Pitawanich, "Oregon Officials Blast Trump Proposal to Open Up Oil Drilling Off Coast," *KGW*, January 5, 2018, http://www.kgw.com/section/news/politics; Andrew Theen, "Cascade-Siskiyou National Monument Would Shrink under Trump Administration Proposal," *Oregonian*, September 19, 2017.

20 "Walden Cheers, Senators Slam BLM's Sage Grouse Moves," *Associated Press*, October 5, 2017, http://www.ktvz.com/news/feds-pull-protection-from-10m-acres-of-sage-grouse-habitat/632309592.

21 David Sarasohn, "Trump Batters against West Coast Blue Wall," *Oregonian*, December 3, 2017.

22 Leigha Threlkeld, "Oregon Delegation Reacts to U.S. Pulling out of Paris Agreement," , *Source Weekly*, June 1, 2017, https://www.bendsource.com/Bent/archives/2017/06/01/united-states-pulling-out-of-paris-agreement.

23 Hillary Borrud, "Kate Brown Adopts Broad Green Building Mandates and Electric Vehicle Goals," *Oregonian*, November 7, 2017.

24 Union of Concerned Scientists, *Clean Energy Momentum: Ranking State Progress* (Cambridge, MA: Union of Concerned Scientists, 2017), https://www.ucsusa.org/sites/default/files/attach/2017/04/Clean-Energy-Momentum-full-report.pdf.

25 US Environmental Protection Agency, *What Climate Change Means for Oregon* (Washington, DC: US Environmental Protection Agency, August 2016), https://19january2017snapshot.epa.gov/sites/production/files/2016-09/documents/climate-change-or.pdf; See also Kathy Dello, *Climate Change in Oregon: Report to the Oregon Legislature* (Corvallis: Oregon Climate Change Research Institute, 2017), occri.net.

26 Meghan M. Dalton et al., *The Third Oregon Climate Assessment Report* (Corvallis: Oregon Climate Change Research Institute, 2017); Lara Whitely Binder and Jason Jurjevich, *The Winds of Change? Exploring Climate Change-Driven Migration and Related Impacts in the Pacific Northwest: Symposium Summary, June 24, 2016* (Portland, OR: Population Research Center, Portland State University; Seattle: University of Washington Climate Impacts Group, 2016).

27 "Walden Cheers."

28 Elliot Njus, "New Population Estimates Put Bend among Nation's Fastest-Growing Cities," *Oregonian*, May 27, 2017.

29 "Forecasts of Oregon's County Populations and Components of Change, 2010–2050," Office of Economic Analysis, Department of Administrative Services, State of Oregon, March 28, 2013, http://www.oregon.gov/das/OEA/Pages/forecastdemographic.aspx.

30 Oregon Housing and Community Services, *2017 Point-in-Time Estimates of Homelessness in Oregon* (Salem: Oregon Housing and Community Services, 2017).

31 Alice Callahan, "The Air We Breathe," *pdxparent,* January 2018, 24.

32 Office of Economic Analysis, *Oregon Economic and Revenue Forecast December 2017*, vol. 37, no. 4 (Salem: Oregon Office of Economic Analysis, 2017), http://www.oregon.gov/das/OEA/Documents/forecast1217.pdf.

33 Kathleen McLaughlin, "Central Oregon Economic Growth Slows," *Bend Bulletin*, November 1, 2017.

34 Alana Semuels, "The Graying of Rural America," *Atlantic*, June 2, 2016.

35 Jeff Manning, "Rural Oregon Doctors, Hospitals Fear Republican Plan," *Oregonian*, March 11, 2017.

36 US Census Bureau, "Quick Facts, Oregon"; Population Research Center, *Oregon's Road to 4 Million* (Portland, OR: Portland State University, n.d.).

37 Josh Lehner, *Oregon Population Outlook* (Salem: Oregon Office of Economic Analysis, December 8, 2017).

38 US Census Bureau, "Quick Facts, Oregon."

39 US Census Bureau, "Quick Facts, Oregon"; Semuels, "Graying of Rural America"; Richard A. Clucas, Mark Henkels, and Brent S. Steel, "The Problems of One Oregon," in *Toward One Oregon: Rural-Urban Interdependence and the Evolution of a State*, ed. Michael Hibbard, Ethan Seltzer, Bruce Weber, and Beth Emshoff (Corvallis: Oregon State University Press, 2011), 113-42.

40 Oregon Employment Department, *Population Growth Faster among Minority Groups* (Salem: Oregon Employment Department, March 16, 2015); US Census Bureau, "Quick Facts, Oregon"; Oregon Community Foundation, *Latinos in Oregon: Trends and Opportunities* (Portland, OR: Oregon Community Foundation, August 2016).

41 Kyle Spurr, "Census: Deschutes, Crook County Growth among the Nation's Fastest," *Central Oregon Bulletin*, March 23, 2017.

Contributors

Editors

RICHARD A. CLUCAS is a professor of political science in the Political Science Department at Portland State University (PSU) and the executive director of the Western Political Science Association (WPSA). The WPSA is the nation's second-largest regional political science association, with more than thirteen hundred members. Professor Clucas has written extensively on legislative politics, state government, and Oregon politics. Among other works, he is coauthor of *The Character of Democracy*, editor of *Readings and Cases in State and Local Politics*, and co-editor of *Oregon Politics and Government*. He also oversees the Political Science Internship Program at PSU.

MARK HENKELS is a professor of politics, policy, and administration at Western Oregon University. His research and publications center on state budgeting and Oregon politics. He teaches in a wide range of areas, including "policy dimensions of the aging society," administrative law, and political and administrative internships. He currently serves as the chair of the Division of Social Sciences at Western Oregon University.

PRISCILLA L. SOUTHWELL is a professor of political science at the University of Oregon. She has published widely on political parties, political behavior, and electoral reform. She received a National Science Foundation grant in 1996 to examine the effects of vote-by-mail elections in Oregon.

EDWARD P. WEBER is the Ulysses G. Dubach Professor of Political Science in the School of Public Policy at Oregon State University. He has published widely on natural resource/environmental policymaking, policy implementation, democratic accountability, and the design and operation of alternative decision-making and governance institutions, particularly collaborative governance arrangements. He also is the chair of the Committee for Family Forestlands for the Oregon Department of Forestry and the former leader of the Thomas Foley Public Policy Institute at Washington State University.

Authors

WARDA AJAZ is a PhD candidate in the School of Public Policy at Oregon State University. Her research focuses on the role of community microgrids in enhancing the reliability of the electric power grid and supporting community resilience. In the past, she has worked on the feasibility of renewable energy microfinancing. Her work "Demand Assessment of Solar Electrification in Off-Grid Rural Communities of Pakistan through Microfinancing of Solar Home Systems" was published in *Springer Proceedings in Energy*.

JEANINE BEATRICE is chief of staff with the Oregon Department of Human Services (DHS). Her career has spanned public policy administration; enterprise project management; and a variety of programs for adolescents and children with DHS, the Oregon Department of Administrative Services, the Oregon Youth Authority, and the Oregon Health Authority. Jeannine holds a bachelor of science in health education from San Francisco State University and a master of public administration degree from Portland State University.

DAVID BERNELL is an associate professor of political science in the School of Public Policy at Oregon State University. His research and teaching focus on US energy policy and energy security, international security, and international political economy. He is the author of *The Energy Security Dilemma: US Policy and Practice* and *Constructing US Foreign Policy: The Curious Case of Cuba*. He formerly served with the US Office of Management and Budget in the Natural Resources, Energy, Science and Water Divisions and with the US Department of the Interior as an advisor on trade and the environment.

JOE BOWERSOX is the Dempsey Endowed Chair of Environmental Policy and Politics in the Department of Environmental and Earth Science at Willamette University. His research and teaching focus on the nexus of human communities and complex ecosystems, and his publications include work on federal forest policy, western water policy, and environmental values. Professor Bowersox has also worked as a congressional fellow in the US Senate on forestry and energy issues, and continues to consult on state and federal forest policy. He also helps manage his family's forest and farm in the Oregon coast range.

ALEXANDRA BUYLOVA is a PhD candidate in the School of Public Policy at Oregon State University. Her dissertation research focuses on investigating the influence of risk perception and personal social networks on behavioral intentions in natural disasters.

PAUL J. DE MUNIZ served on the appellate bench for more than twenty-two years, including as chief justice of the Oregon Supreme Court. He retired from the Oregon Supreme Court in 2012. In addition to the many law-related articles he published over his legal career, De Muniz is also the author of *A Practical Guide to Oregon Criminal Procedure and Practice* and coauthor of *American Judicial Power: The State Court Perspective*, a legal treatise emphasizing the importance of America's state courts. De Muniz currently teaches at Willamette University College of Law as a distinguished jurist in residence.

MARK EDWARDS is a professor of sociology in the School of Public Policy at Oregon State University. His publications focus on public policy related to American social safety net programs, food insecurity, inequality, and poverty.

LEANNE GIORDONO is a PhD candidate at Oregon State University' School of Public Policy and a National Science Foundation graduate research fellow. Her research interests include social policy decision-making processes and governance, especially those in employment-related services and supports. She received her MPA from the Woodrow Wilson School at Princeton University in 2000, and has almost fifteen years of experience conducting program evaluation for government agencies and nonprofit organizations.

DANIEL GRAY is a master of public policy student in the School of Public Policy at Oregon State University. His primary policy focus is on renewable energy, and his master's thesis examines the passage of the Oregon law that bans the use of coal to produce electricity for utility customers in the state. An interest in state government led him to intern both at the Oregon Department of Environmental Quality and the Oregon State Legislature's policy and research office.

SAJJAD HAIDER is a PhD student at the School of Management at Lanzhou University in China and a visiting research scholar at the Mark O. Hatfield School of Government at Portland State University. His primary research areas are public service motivation, performance-based governance, and human resource management. He was formerly on the faculty of business management at Karakoram International University in Pakistan.

JORDAN HENSLEY earned a master of public policy degree in 2017 from the School of Public Policy at Oregon State University. His main area of research is education policy, specifically the relationship between scholarships and student success.

ALLISON HURST is an associate professor of sociology in the School of Public Policy at Oregon State University, where she teaches courses on the sociology of education and theory. She has written two books, *The Burden of Academic Success: Loyalists, Renegades, and Double Agents* (2010) and *College and the Working Class* (2012). Her current research focuses on the outcomes of college graduates, specifically the role of class and the impact of student debt. She was one of the founders of the Association of Working-Class Academics, an organization composed of college faculty and staff who were the first in their families to graduate from college, for which she also served as president from 2008 to 2014. She is currently serving as chairperson of the Working-Class Academics Section of the Working-Class Studies Association.

ABDULLAH HUSAIN earned his PhD in environmental sciences at Oregon State University and is currently an assistant professor at the University of Kuwait. His research focuses on the narrative of sustainable development and how it fits into Kuwait's social context that was shaped by the war in 1991. In the past, he was elected for four terms as a board member of the National Union of Kuwait Students. His experience with messaging and dealing with government institutions propelled him to focus on the nexus between environmental policy and the concepts of stewardship and sustainability in his home country of Kuwait.

PHIL KEISLING is director of the Center for Public Service at Portland State University's Mark O. Hatfield School of Government. He served as Oregon secretary of state from 1991 to 1999 and as a member of the Oregon House of Representatives from 1989 to 1991. His journalism career includes a stint as a reporter for Portland's *Willamette Week* and as an editor of *Washington Monthly* magazine in Washington, DC, from 1982 to 1984. He continues to write about a variety of subjects, including election reform and public administration, for *Washington Monthly*, *Governing* magazine, and other publications.

CHRIS KOSKI is an associate professor of environmental studies and chair of the Political Science Department at Reed College. He publishes research in policy process theory, environmental policy, food politics governance, climate change, and public budgeting.

JUSTIN MARTIN has over twenty years of experience in government working at the federal, state, local, and tribal levels. Justin owns and operates Perseverance Strategies, Inc., a government relations and public affairs firm. His clients include the Confederated Tribes of Grand Ronde, where he is also a tribal member. Justin received his master's degree in public administration from the Harvard University John F. Kennedy School of Government and his bachelor of arts degree in public policy and public administration from Western Oregon University. Prior to working in government, Justin played baseball in the California Angels minor league system between 1988 and 1992.

MELISSA BUIS MICHAUX is an associate professor of politics at Willamette University and contributes to the Women's and Gender Studies Program. Her research and teaching focus on welfare and health-care policy, issues of gender in the American family, and the politics of criminal justice reform.

DOUGLAS MORGAN is a professor emeritus of public administration and director of the Executive MPA Program in the Mark O. Hatfield School of Government at

Portland State University. He has held a variety of public positions, both elected and appointed. His research interests focus on the role that career public administrators play in ensuring effective and responsive systems of local democratic governance. His work has appeared in leading academic journals, and he is the lead author for several monographs, including *Foundations of Public Service* (2013), *Budgeting for Local Governments and Communities* (2014), and *New Public Governance* (2015).

SANNE A. M. RIJKHOFF is a postdoctoral associate at the political science department of the University of Calgary. Previously, she was an adjunct assistant professor of political science at Portland State University. She holds a PhD in political science from Washington State University and a master's degrees in social and organizational psychology and political science from Leiden University, the Netherlands. Her dissertation research on political cynicism won the Best Dissertation Award from the Western Political Science Association in 2017. Dr. Rijkhoff's research interests include political psychology, public opinion, media and rhetoric, and political behavior. Her work has been published in numerous journals and she is also a contributor to the 2018 book *Governing the Evergreen State, Political Life in Washington.*

ETHAN SELTZER is an emeritus professor in the Toulan School of Urban Studies and Planning at Portland State University. He has actively contributed to research and practice in the areas of regional planning and governance, regional development, and public engagement. His work has also addressed metropolitan and statewide land-use planning, particularly in Oregon and Cascadia.

BRENT S. STEEL is a professor and the director of the Graduate Program in the School of Public Policy at Oregon State University. He has published numerous journal articles, book chapters, and books concerning public policy in areas such as forestry, rangelands, endangered species, coastal and marine issues, environmental issues, sustainable development, and the politicization of science.

CASEY TAYLOR is a postdoctoral research associate in the Department of Political Science at Idaho State University. She holds a PhD in public policy from Oregon State University. Her research focuses on the role of science and technical expertise, collaborative learning, and voluntary action in natural resource management.

REBECCA L. WARNER is a professor of sociology in the School of Public Policy at Oregon State University. She serves as the principal investigator for Oregon State Advance, a $3.5 million National Science Foundation grant for institutional transformation focused on recruiting and retaining women and other underrepresented faculty in academic science, technology, engineering, and mathematics careers.

Acknowledgments

Publishing a book is always a collective endeavor, even for single-authored works. Beyond just the authors, there are others behind the scenes who are essential for taking an idea or proposal and turning it into a published work. In our case, we could not have succeeded without the valuable support provided by Oregon State University Press. We particularly want to thank Mary Elizabeth Braun, the acquisitions editor, for her support of this project from start to finish. Micki Reaman, the editorial, design, and production manager for the Press, was continuously helpful in overseeing the project. It has been a pleasure to work with Tom Booth, the associate director, and Marty Brown, the marketing manager. Ashleigh McKown did an outstanding job in copyediting the manuscript. We are very pleased with the cover designed by Jeff Puda. Thanks also have to go to the anonymous reviewers whose suggestions were perceptive and invaluable.

This book, however, was not a single-authored work. Rather, it was a collective effort of scholars from six different Oregon universities and colleges, along with several others who are deeply engaged in Oregon politics, including both current and former government officials. What particularly pleased us was the large number of experts on Oregon politics who were willing to work collaboratively to produce this work. Moreover, this crew did an extraordinary job in providing thoughtful analysis, meeting deadlines, and addressing concerns raised by the editors. Our thanks go out to all of them.

There are also a few other individuals we would like to thank who contributed in one fashion or another, including in tracking down details, compiling data, and checking facts. These include Nichoel Holmes of Perseverance Inc., and two students: Melissa Bates and Michael Trujillo.

The book is dedicated to Beth Blenz-Clucas, Marcella Dupler Henkels, and to Nick, Cody, and Alexis Weber (the best children a father could ever ask for). Priscilla Southwell would like to thank her husband, Kerry Ahearn, and their children, Karen Keiter, Tom Spettel, Mark Spettel, Sara Spettel, and Christopher Ahearn; her colleague and friend, Jerry Medler; and her parents, Priscilla and Eugene Richardson, for their support over the years.

Index